Midnight Riders

Midnight

Scott Freeman

 Little, Brown and Company

Riders

The Story
of the
Allman
Brothers
Band

Boston   New York   Toronto   London

First Edition

Library of Congress Cataloging-in-Publication Data

Freeman, Scott.
    Midnight riders : the story of the Allman Brothers Band /
Scott Freeman. — 1st ed.
        p.   cm.
    Includes index.
    ISBN 0-316-29288-5
    1. Allman Brothers Band.   2. Rock musicians — United States —
Biography.   I. Title.
ML421.A43F74   1995
782.42166'092'2 — dc20
    [B]   94-29301

10 9 8 7 6 5 4 3 2 1

MV-NY

Published simultaneously in Canada by
Little, Brown & Company (Canada) Limited

Printed in the United States of America

This one's for Bryant Steele and J.,
and in memory of John G. Williams, "Papa-san,"
who knew about this book even before I did

Contents

Part IV: Purgatory

Part V: Resurrection

Part I
_____

Beginnings

Blond bombshell . . . travels in a Triumph . . . speed demon.

— Description of Gregg Allman under
his senior picture in the 1965
Seabreeze High School yearbook

One

The Saddest Christmas

GREGG ALLMAN called it "the fever," and he caught it in the summer of 1959 when he was eleven years old. He and Duane, his big brother, were staying with their grandmother in Nashville. Gregg walked outside one afternoon and saw a neighbor named Jimmy Banes sitting on his front porch picking country songs on a Sears Silvertone guitar. Gregg was drawn to the music and he shyly walked over and spent the afternoon listening to the man playing songs like "Wildwood Flower" and "Long Black Veil." Jimmy Banes took a liking to the kid. He had blond hair the color of sand, a face of angelic innocence, and he seemed to worship the cheap guitar. Banes let Gregg hold the instrument and soon wound up teaching him everything he knew — about three chords.

When Gregg's mother came to take Duane and Gregg back home to Daytona Beach, Florida, at the end of the summer, Gregg was already certain: he had to have a guitar. But Geraldine Allman had been through this once before. A couple of years earlier, Gregg had decided he had to have a trumpet. It became known around the house as Geraldine's two-hundred-dollar folly after she bought one and Gregg promptly lost interest. This time, his mother was smarter: if Gregg wanted a guitar, he could get a job and buy it himself. He soon had himself a paper route, and by the end of the school year he had saved $21.00. Gregg rode his bicycle down to the Sears, Roebuck store and learned to his dismay that the guitar cost $21.95; the store wasn't about to bend, even for a kid with eyes full of disappointment. But Geraldine was sympathetic and she gave her son the extra money. The next day, Gregg was the proud owner of his own Sears Silvertone guitar. After taking a few lessons, he got a Mel Bay instruction book and taught himself to play. "I wouldn't eat or sleep or drink or anything," Gregg said. "Just played that damn guitar."

Gregg had "the fever"; it wouldn't be long before his big brother would catch it too.

MUSIC was a tradition in the Allman family. They came from the hill country in Tennessee's Dickson County, about forty miles west of Nashville. Duane and Gregg's paternal grandparents, John Alfred Allman and Myrtle Beatrice Allman, lived on a small farm, where Alfred raised row crops and worked odd jobs, mainly in the lumber business. Willis Turner Allman, the boys' father, was the oldest of the siblings, born in 1918. Willis's baby brother, Howard Samuel Allman, was born nineteen months later. A third brother, David Allman, came in 1935.

Like most of the southern country folk who barely scratched out a living, the Allman family spent their weekends listening to WSM and its live radio broadcasts from the Grand Ole Opry. Several of the family members sang and played traditional instruments, performing gospel music along with the songs of Bill Monroe and the Carter Family. "My daddy sang in a barbershop quartet, and his brothers were musicians," said Howard Allman. "My Uncle Walton played several different instruments — mandolin, guitar, banjo — and he sang bass in a quartet."

For someone like Willis or Howard Allman growing up in the rural South at the beginning of the Roosevelt era, there were few choices. A kid coming of age could work on the farm, try to get a factory job in the city, or join the army. For Willis, the army had always held an allure. He studied military history with a deep fascination, and he thought being a soldier would be a way to see worlds that he could never experience if he stayed on the farm. But he had a tough time joining up. First, Willis was turned down for military service because the army doctors discovered he had a hernia. When Alfred heard what had happened, he sold a few acres of land to pay for an operation for his son. Willis went back to the induction center a few months later and learned to his chagrin that he didn't weigh enough to get into the army. He went back home and ate bushels of bananas and starchy foods until he finally put on enough weight to qualify. "He was sworn in on the seventeenth of December, nineteen thirty-seven," Howard recalled. "He really wanted in as much as anybody I ever heard of."

After Willis made it into the army, Howard began laboring in a sawmill. It was backbreaking work, and it didn't take much effort for Willis to convince his little brother to join up too. Eventually, the two brothers were reunited when they were assigned to the same outfit. Willis was assigned to recruiting duty and began traveling all over the Southeast. One of those trips took him to Rocky Mount, North Carolina, where he met a pretty blond secretary named Geraldine Alice Robbins. After a long-distance romance, they married just before World War II broke out. Both Willis and Howard were sent overseas, and they stormed Normandy on D day. After the war, the brothers moved to Nashville and worked together as recruiters. Willis bought a house on Westbrook Avenue — a sedate, tree-lined street in a middle-class neighborhood west of downtown — and Howard moved in too.

Geraldine soon became pregnant, and Willis named his first son after his baby brother: Howard Duane Allman was born in Nashville on November 20, 1946. The second son, Gregory Lenoir (it rhymes with "Renoir" and was taken from an elderly couple friendly with his parents) was born thirteen months later on December 8, 1947. Willis accepted a commission as a lieutenant and the family moved to Fort Story, just outside Norfolk, Virginia, in 1949. Willis used to call his brother from the base and chuckle when he talked about Duane. The little three-year-old was precocious and eager to explore. Duane would tug on Willis's pants. "Daddy," he'd say. "Let's go to the Officers Club." And Willis would take him.

Willis received an early Christmas leave in 1949. The family went back to Nashville to visit friends and relatives and returned to the base before the holiday because Willis had drawn the Christmas Day assignment. While her husband worked, Geraldine took the two boys to Rocky Mount to spend the day with her family. The day after Christmas, a Monday, Willis rode into Norfolk with Second Lieutenant Robert Buchanan, Fort Story's athletic officer and Willis's best friend on the base. They visited a bar called the Oriental Gardens, watched a shuffleboard game, then challenged the winners. One of the players was Michael Robert Green, a twenty-six-year-old combat vet and unemployed plumber's helper. They had a couple of drinks with Green, and the three of them went to another bar before the two officers decided to head back to the base. Green asked them for a lift to another tavern and Buchanan, who was driving, agreed.

Nobody knows why Green shot and killed Willis Allman; he said later in court that he didn't even remember pulling the trigger. But soon after he climbed into the backseat of Buchanan's car, he pulled out a .32-caliber automatic pistol, put it against Willis's back and forced them to drive to a muddy cornfield off Route 168 in an area called East Ocean View. Green took all the money the two men had — $4.85 — and marched them up the furrows of the plowed field. As they neared the woods, Willis whispered to Buchanan, "You go left, and I'll go right." Green overheard them and ordered the two soldiers to lie down on the ground.

Willis turned and lunged for the gun. Buchanan heard it go off, then saw Willis running. Buchanan ran in the opposite direction and heard a couple of more shots. He phoned for help, then went back to search for his friend. He found Willis lying in the field, dead from a slug that had entered his chest near his right armpit at point-blank range.

Geraldine learned about the murder of her husband a few hours later, and she and the two boys returned to Fort Story that night. Howard was in California, received an emergency leave to fly to Fort Story, and spent the next night sleeping in Gregg's room. The little two-year-old was fast asleep in his crib, too young to understand that his father was gone forever.

Michael Robert Green was convicted of murder in 1951 and sentenced to die. On January 22, 1952, one day before his electrocution, Virginia governor John S. Battle commuted the sentence to life imprisonment, saying Green's combat experience had left him mentally unbalanced.

Every Christmas after that, Howard Allman religiously sent a letter to Virginia's Bureau of Prisons to ask if Green was still in jail; every January for twenty-three years, they wrote back. The last letter, in 1975, carried the news that Green was again a free man. "Life has to go on, and the more time passes, the easier it gets," Howard said. "But Christmas is still a sad time for us. I never really enjoy it. It always reminds you."

GERALDINE ALLMAN was a young widow with two young sons in an era when opportunities for women were limited. At first the family moved in with Willis's parents and Geraldine found work as a secretary at an automobile parts place in Nashville. But that was no way to raise a family, and she soon decided to go to college in order to become a certified public accountant. The problem was what to do with the kids. "Somebody suggested that she put us in an orphanage," Gregg said. "She politely told them to fuck off." Instead, Geraldine decided military school would be best for her boys. Geraldine could go to college using Willis's military benefits and get a break in the tuition at the military academy because her husband had died while in the army.

The day that Geraldine packed the boys up and drove them to the Castle Heights Military Academy in Lebanon, Tennessee, is one that Gregg never forgot. As an adult he could still recall the sinking feeling deep in his stomach and the body-shaking fear that made him weep uncontrollably. He was too young to understand; all Gregg knew was that he had no daddy and now his mama was leaving him, too. As his mother pulled away, Gregg sprinted after her until the car was out of sight. Duane bravely stood his ground and stoically watched his little brother. Gregg slowly walked back to Duane, tears streaming down his cheeks. Duane said nothing. Instead, he reached out, put his arm around Gregg's shoulder. And he squeezed as tightly as he could.

DUANE and Gregg hated military school. Life was regimented: up at the crack of dawn, classes all day, uniforms and marches. "It was rough," Gregg said. "I was in the third grade and the first day I was there, I think I learned every cuss word. I thought, 'Lord, what have I done to get thrown in this place?' Get to go home three times a year. Days seemed like weeks and there were fights nearly every morning when you woke up. They turned out warmongers, fags and scholars. I couldn't get it on in school worth a shit."

The nightmare ended in 1957 when Geraldine finished college and moved the family south to Daytona Beach. Duane was eleven, Gregg a year younger. After military school, Florida was like paradise to the two brothers. Geraldine bought a ranch-style house shaded by palm trees on Van Avenue, just a few hundred yards from the Atlantic Ocean. Duane and Gregg would spend hours on the beach, swimming and sunning and watching the tourists walk by. One day, they were lying on the sand, and Duane rolled over on his stomach and went to sleep. When he woke up, the bottoms of his feet were so sunburned that Gregg had to carry him home.

It was one of the few times that Duane ever had to lean on his little brother. Duane had a forceful personality and he basked in the freedoms of Daytona Beach. Geraldine Allman raised her children with a loose hand, and Duane wasn't afraid to be brazen. A lot of people who met Duane thought he was crazy. He was cocky and aggressive, hungry for adventure. He could be brutally honest, and if he didn't like something, he wasn't hesitant about speaking his mind. Gregg, on the other hand, was shy and reserved, his identity almost submerged by Duane's personality. Gregg idolized Duane and, mostly, he did what his big brother wanted them to do.

Yet it was Gregg who found the key to the universe — the guitar. The two brothers had flirted with music for much of their lives. There was the brief interest in the trumpet, and both Gregg and Duane had taken piano lessons. Duane's piano teacher noticed that he had a natural talent for music. "My teacher, man, she was always telling me, 'What beautiful hands you have,' " Duane said. "She kept telling me I oughta study, and the last thing I said to her, I said, 'The reason I don't want to do this is because I'm never gonna need it for the rest of my life. I'll never need this music.' I always regretted that."

Daytona Beach was a bikers' town, and Duane's first love was motorcycles. He got a Harley-Davidson 165 when he turned thirteen, the same year that Gregg got his Sears guitar. Duane flew all over Daytona Beach on that bike, his reddish-blond hair slicked back like James Dean. "That thing had a big buddy seat, would do fifty miles an hour," Duane said. "Boy, I had a great time with it." But Gregg's new hobby was beginning to fascinate Duane too. He would skip school and while Gregg was in class, he'd pick up the Silvertone and try to copy what his little brother had been playing. At first there were fights; Gregg told Duane to leave his goddamn guitar alone. Then he began teaching Duane what he knew. Both brothers were naturally left-handed, but they learned to play right-handed. When Duane wrecked his motorcycle, he traded it for his own Silvertone. Gregg had graduated to a Fender Music Master, and Geraldine eventually bought Duane a purple Les Paul, Jr.

For a few weeks every summer, Duane and Gregg would go to Nashville to stay with their grandparents, and it was there that they began to receive a musical education. Their grandmother would take them to the Ryman Auditorium to hear the Grand Ole Opry, and the summer after they took up the guitar, she let them go see a rhythm-and-blues show. Jackie Wilson was the headliner, and Otis Redding, Patti LaBelle, and B. B. King were the opening acts. It was like catching "the fever" all over again. During the show, Duane leaned forward and turned to Gregg. "Man, Gregory, what have we got here?" Duane said with awe. "We got to get into this."

Gregg was just as enchanted. "B. B. King had this organ player with big, red processed hair," he said. "He was playing this Hammond B-3 [organ] like Jimmy Smith. And Jackie Wilson. Oh, god, I had goose bumps I thought were permanent."

Duane entered Seabreeze High School in 1960, and Gregg became a freshman the following year. It was a perfect time to be a teenager in Daytona Beach. With a beach that stretched for twenty-three miles, Daytona was becoming a getaway for people from all over the East Coast looking for a cheap vacation in the sun. The influx of tourists meant lots of teenage boys on the prowl for girls wearing daring swimwear and looking for summer romances. Surf music by the Ventures was the rage, and the Daytona natives were learning that knowing a few chords on the guitar could be extremely helpful in getting a date. "Everybody in my neighborhood seemed to surf and play guitar," said Michael Babic, who attended Seabreeze with Gregg. "A bunch of us would hang out around the motels during the evenings and meet the tourist girls."

Duane and Gregg were soon bored by the beach music; instead they were developing a passion for the exotic-sounding black music they had heard in Nashville, and they soon discovered a radio station called WLAC. Based in Nashville, WLAC was a rhythm-and-blues counterpart to WSM, the station that had spread the gospel of country music throughout the South. On a clear night, you could pick up the 50,000-watt WLAC on AM radios for hundreds of miles and hear the latest blues and r&b hits — songs by Ray Charles and Howlin' Wolf and Roosevelt Sykes and Sonny Boy Williamson and Little Milton, Gregg's favorite along with Bobby "Blue" Bland.

The station served as a beginning point for a whole generation of Southerners who turned the dials late at night and found themselves enraptured by the soul-stirring rhythms of black music. "The first stuff you hear is so important, man," Duane said. "Like Hank Williams. I love it. It's good ol' foot-stompin' stuff. When I got a little older, the Dick Clark stuff started coming on, and I realized that that wasn't for me. Then I started listening to WLAC. They were just a bunch of crazy old drunk guys playing rhythm-and-blues records, and it was just great."

Each brother had a best friend who fanned the interest WLAC had created. Duane had been eleven when he met Jim Shepley in a pool hall; Shepley was three years older than Duane, a hot guitarist who could play Jimmy Reed blues licks and was soon teaching Duane what he knew. "Ol' Lightning Fingers," Duane called him. "If you wanted to learn to play something right, anything, you'd go to him. He was the baddest cat, a very influential cat in my life. I can't even talk about him; he's so hip, he glows in the dark." Shepley taught Duane the songs of B. B. King and Muddy Waters and John Lee Hooker.

Meanwhile, Gregg had done something unthinkable for a white kid living in the Deep South in 1960 — he had become best friends with a black kid, Floyd Miles. Shepley played guitar in a band called The Untils and the Houserockers, and Miles was one of the singers. The two brothers went to hear the group at a Daytona Beach club called the Ocean Pier, and Gregg and Floyd became instant friends. "The Untils were the singers, four black guys, and the Houserockers were all white," said Floyd. "Eventually, Gregg and Duane started sitting in with the band."

Racial tensions in the South had been heating up ever since a young Baptist preacher named Martin Luther King, Jr., had led a successful boycott to end segregation on the public buses in Montgomery, Alabama, and blacks in other cities also began making demands for equality. And here were the Allman brothers in the middle of all the turmoil — two white kids playing in a black band and going to black clubs to party. The white audiences took a liberal enough attitude about being entertained by an integrated band, but when the music stopped, the Untils had to head back to their side of town. Duane and Gregg would go with them and hang out with Floyd Miles at black clubs like George's Place or the PI, the Paradise Inn. "Everybody got to know Duane and Gregg, so they were just like one of the guys," Floyd said. "They were known as 'those white boys who can play that funky music.' Duane could just play it all. Even if you called a jazz tune, he'd jump right on it."

Duane and Gregg were color-blind, especially when it came to music. "Gregg was a long-haired musician, so back then he was a freak," Floyd said. "And I'm black. So we both knew what it was like to be discriminated against, which is probably why we got along so well. We had each other and we had the music."

Geraldine Allman, however, wasn't quite as liberal about race relations as her sons. "Going to play with them niggers again?" she would chide them, although she never actually forbade them to go. "We had to turn my mother on to the blacks," Gregg said. "Took a while, but now she's totally liberated."

Gregg credits Floyd Miles with becoming his mentor when it came to r&b music. "I met him when everybody else was listening to Surfer Joe," said Gregg. "He caught a lot of hell from his friends for hanging out with this white boy. He took me across the tracks, liter-ally. In Daytona Beach, black people live west of the beach, over across the railroad tracks. He took me over there to this little old combination barbershop, pawnshop, record shop. They had these records that were obscure. They were in these bins, like a truck had just dumped all these forty-fives in there. You were lucky if they weren't scratched and half of them didn't have any covers. But I found some incredible records in there."

It wasn't long before Duane and Gregg were starting up their own groups. Gregg had begun playing with two friends in a garage band not long after he took up the guitar. All three played guitar; none of them wanted to play a bass because it had only four strings. The trio was recruited to play at a school assembly, and about two hours before they were to go onstage the other two guys disappeared. Gregg was forced to perform alone. It was his first public gig; he was terrified and thought he was terrible. He says he avoids class reunions to this day because he fears someone will remember it.

By the ninth grade, Duane had lost all interest in school — "the fever" was becoming all that mattered. He dropped out the next year, and, in a last-ditch effort to make sure that Gregg didn't follow in his big brother's footsteps, Geraldine sent Gregg back to Tennessee to Castle Heights for his sophomore year in 1962. "My mother decided to send me back there because we were running wild and playing music and our grades were biting the dust," Gregg said.

But the ploy didn't work. When Gregg returned the following summer, the brothers formally joined the Houserockers backing up the Untils; Gregg would play one night and Duane the next. "We were a smokin' band," Duane said. "Boy, I mean we would set fire to a building in a second. We were just up there blowing as funky as we pleased. Sixteen years old, forty-one dollars a week. Big time."

THE house on Van Avenue became a hangout for teenage musicians in Daytona Beach. Geraldine Allman seldom seemed to be around, and it was cool to drink beer at Duane and Gregg's place while you were working on guitar licks. When their mother was there, the beer stayed out of sight, but she was known to fix up some sandwiches or dinner for the boys to eat when they took a break from the music. All the loud guitars made the Allman house the subject of disdain from some of their neighbors. "Oh, they were a pain in the neck," one said. "They used to practice at home with their electric guitars up full blast.

The noises that used to come out of that house, it sounded like they were killing a couple of cats in there."

One of the most frequent guests was a kid named Sylvan Wells, who had known Duane at Seabreeze High but didn't become close with him until after Duane had dropped out of school. "I decided I wanted to take up the guitar and I started going down to their house a lot," Sylvan said. "We'd sit around and play. Well, most of the time, it would be sit around and listen to Gregg and Duane play. At the time, it was no big deal. We were all growing up and none of us were thinking, Hey, you're going to be a legend and I'd better pay attention. Besides, I knew three guitar players in Daytona Beach who could blow Duane away."

Duane and Gregg taught Sylvan the rudiments of the guitar, and, once he graduated from high school in 1964, Sylvan started up a band called the Nightcrawlers that made the Daytona Beach music scene explode. All five members were enrolled at the local junior college and none of them was exactly an accomplished musician; they wrote their own material because they weren't good enough to learn songs off the radio. "We formed the band to make money while we went to junior college, and the plan was to quit when we all graduated," Sylvan said. "And that's exactly what we did."

Not long after the Nightcrawlers formed, Sylvan met up with a Daytona Beach musician and electronics wizard named Lee Hazen who had set up a recording studio in his kitchen, and the band began practicing there and taping some of their songs. The first gigs were in front of mostly friends and family at the Seabreeze Recreation Center. The group finally decided that releasing a record and having it played on the local radio station might drum up some business. One of Lee's friends, Mike Stone, arranged to get a 45 pressed, and the plan worked. When Mike went to the next gig and saw that the room was packed with teenagers, he signed on as the Nightcrawlers' manager.

One afternoon in Lee Hazen's kitchen, there was some tape left at the end of the reel, and the Nightcrawlers decided to record a weird song written by guitarist Charlie Conlan called "The Little Black Egg." The drums were so loud that Lee had the singers stand out in the backyard and sing into a microphone that was hanging from a tree limb. Mike Stone took the tape down to the radio station and received a call the next day from the disc jockey. "The egg thing, man, it's a fucking smash record," the deejay said. The band was dubious, but had 250 singles pressed anyway. It sold out within days. "It was a monster," Mike said. "A record shop in Orlando called; it was being played over there and they wanted five hundred copies. And then Jacksonville calls." The song was picked up on a national label, became a hit, and sold over a million copies.

Duane and Gregg had started a band called the Escorts, which they thought was the hottest group in Daytona Beach. And when the Nightcrawlers, led by a guy *they* had taught to play the guitar, hit it big, they were a little pissed off. "It used to drive them crazy because we were getting all the jobs and all the recognition, and they were so much better musicians that it was ridiculous," said Sylvan. "I mean, I hadn't been playing guitar for two months and we had a record out. It was that quick. They'd been playing for years and most everything I'd learned, I'd learned from Duane and Gregg. But we were playing original material. That was the difference."

Sylvan told them about Lee Hazen's place, and the Escorts began going there to rehearse and record. "An awful lot of musical talent happened at that apartment," Sylvan said. "We spent countless hours there and I know the Allmans spent as much time as we did. Lee's got probably five or six hours' worth of tapes of the Escorts."

By that time, Lee had decided he needed a vocal booth, something to shield the singer's microphone from the roar of the drums so that he wouldn't have to send the vocalist outside. Mike Stone solved the problem: there were some empty coffin crates lying around at the funeral home where he worked, so he picked one up, put it in a hearse, and took it over to Lee's cottage. It was almost seven feet tall and Duane and Gregg leaned into it as they put their voices on tape for the first time.

THE songs Lee Hazen caught on tape include covers of "She's a Woman" by the Beatles and "Last Time" by the Rolling Stones. The Escorts also cut Roy Orbison's "Candy Man" and "Oh, Pretty Woman," along with "Hi-Heel Sneakers." Duane sang most of the songs, and Gregg played rhythm guitar. The bassist was Van Harrison and Maynard Portwood played drums. "To my knowledge, these are the earliest recordings of Duane and Gregg Allman," Lee said. "We made what we called presentation tapes so they'd have something to play for club owners to get gigs. They're just rehearsal tapes, but they're damned good. I've got a couple of recordings of 'You've Lost That Lovin' Feeling' that'll put goose bumps on your arms."

At that formative stage, the Allman brothers sound remarkably similar to the Beatles back in the days of the Star Club in Hamburg, or the Rolling Stones on their early records. Duane's guitar work is compact, in the style of early Keith Richards and George Harrison. Many of the songs have no lead guitar and on those that do, the breaks are brief. But already Duane was a very accomplished guitarist, playing sophisticated rhythm patterns and concise leads. "They were a garage band," Mike Stone said. "But when you listened you said, 'All right, somebody's playing guitar here.' "

Gregg had only begun to sing and, at that stage, Duane was without doubt the better singer of the two. Gregg's first attempts at singing are sometimes painful to hear; it could have been any seventeen-year-old kid trying to sing. Before gigs, Gregg often ate at a barbecue joint; he said eating good soul food gave his voice an extra edge. "Gregg loved the raspy voice, the whiskey voice of a lot of the black singers, and even then he was trying to modify his voice to make it sound like those guys," Escorts bassist Van Harrison recalled. "Gregg could carry some tunes, but his voice was a little thin." Only one song, Bobby "Blue" Bland's "Turn On Your Love Light," gives a glimpse of what would come. Gregg manages to make his voice sound gravelly, and he shows hints of the mannerisms that would later become his trademark; soulfully slurring and growling the lyrics. "It is just purely awful noise," Gregg said when asked about some of his early recordings. "I sound like a cross between Hank Williams with the croup and James Brown with no lips."

The first big break for the Escorts was an Easter weekend show in 1965 with the Nightcrawlers; the two local bands opened for the Beach Boys at what is now the Jackie Robinson Ballpark. The equipment of all three bands was set up onstage at once; for the opening set, the Nightcrawlers were to the left of the Beach Boys, and the Escorts were to the right. The two bands were onstage simultaneously, alternating songs. Duane always insisted that the band members dress well when they played, and on the night of this, their biggest gig, they wore matching dark suits and ties; from a distance, the Escorts resembled the Beatles. Gregg played a Fender Stratocaster and stood with Van Harrison at one mike. Maynard Portwood was on the drum kit behind them. And Duane stood a few feet away, alone at a second microphone and holding his Gibson semi-hollowbody guitar.

Lee Hazen caught the concert on tape. "Thank you very much," a very confident-sounding Duane told the crowd when the bands took the stage. "We're the Escorts combo from here in town. We'd like to start the show for you with a song made popular by Marvin Gaye."

The band kicked into "Hitchhike" with Duane singing, and then he sang James Brown's "Good Lovin'." Gregg sang the final two Escorts songs, "Game of Love" and "Turn On Your Love Light," in a struggling, youthful voice. The grand finale was a hair-raising six-minute-and-thirty-second version of Ray Charles's "What'd I Say?" The two bands alternated verses: the Escorts, with Gregg singing, would play a stanza; then the Nightcrawlers would sing and play the next.

Musically, there was no comparison between the two groups. Duane was picking crisp guitar phrases while the Nightcrawlers could barely play the song. But Gregg couldn't keep up with Robbie Rouse, lead singer for the Nightcrawlers. "It's quite amazing because you hear Gregg just beginning to learn how to do that kind of music," said Sylvan Wells. "And you hear the guy with us who already knew how to sing, and he made Gregg look bad."

With the success of the Nightcrawlers, Daytona Beach began bursting with teen clubs looking for bands that played rock 'n' roll. Everyone knew that Duane and Gregg, who had begun calling themselves the Allman Joys, had the hottest group in town. The best club was a little joint called the Martinique, where the Allman Joys played regularly. "It was just like a nightclub," said Mary Ann Babic, an Illinois native who used to go to the club when her parents vacationed in Daytona Beach. "Kids would be dancing. It was great. I thought the Allman Joys were fantastic. Gregg was like the wild rocker, outrageous. He's the one you looked at. Duane just stood there and played music with his eyes closed. You could tell he loved what he was doing. Onstage, with the lights on, their hair was just glowing. I thought Duane was just the end."

Girls flocked to the two brothers in the clubs, turned on by the power of the music and their handsome features. Duane was adventurous and had numerous girlfriends, but Gregg was shy around girls. Friends say he didn't become sexually active until 1965, and then he almost immediately impregnated a girlfriend, although he wouldn't acknowledge paternity for another twenty years.

IN high school, Gregg was full of mischief and ready to use charm and good looks to get by. In his "senior will," he bequeathed his "ability to talk Coach Simmons out of suspension to any poor soul who might need it." He struggled with his grades because the music was interfering with his class work, and Duane would often do Gregg's homework for him. Not many people remember much about Gregg from

Seabreeze High; his life was unlike theirs, defined by his friendships with black musicians and not by the usual high-school adolescent dramas. He was different, so he was left alone and seemed to prefer it that way. "Gregg was pretty quiet in the classes I was in," Michael Babic said. "But when he was a senior, he let his hair grow out real long. That was just about the time the Beatles were coming out, but the Beatles hairdo wasn't nearly as long as he had his hair."

The boys were independent, and friends said Geraldine Allman gave them wide latitude. "I always thought their mother was doing the best she could with the situation as it was," Van Harrison said. "There was another guy from Tennessee they had there from time to time who stepped in as kind of a surrogate stepfather, but Duane and Gregg didn't talk about that too much."

When Sylvan Wells came around to play the guitar, he seldom saw their mother. "All I knew was we could go down there and drink all the beer we wanted and nobody ever got excited," he said. "Their mother was never there. I don't know how else to say it. I only saw her four or five times and I went down there hundreds of times. I don't think I would recognize her today if I saw her. I think that they pretty much raised themselves."

Taking on the responsibility of being "the man of the house" at such a young age was a heavy burden for Duane. He had a troubled adolescence, and his friends learned to live with his bursts of energy and sullen periods of depression. "I think he was suffering from all these conflicts," Van Harrison said. "Some days he was really high on doing music and then some days he'd get so damned depressed, he'd disappear for a while and you wouldn't know where the hell he was. Duane was real aggressive. If he wanted something a certain way, he'd push it. He was more the leader and Gregg the follower. Gregg was more laid-back, easygoing. I saw him get upset only a couple of times — once when Duane went on one of his binges and didn't show up for a while. We were playing at the Safari Hotel and there's the three of us playing, doing the best we could. We hadn't seen Duane and he was supposed to be there. And here comes Duane with two girls, and he says, 'Hey, you guys sound great.' And Gregg goes, 'Where the hell have you been?' And Duane says, 'I found these girls up in Georgia and I've been staying with 'em for a while.' "

It seemed as though Duane was always trying to squeeze three days of living into each day. Any thrill, any high, Duane would seek it out. Then he would push it to the absolute edge. Once, Jim Shepley and Duane climbed to the top of the Towers Apartments building in

Daytona. The building was new; it was December and the owners had put a huge Christmas tree up on top for good luck. Duane decided they should get up on the roof of the twenty-story structure and hang off the tree. They made it inside the building, and Duane was soon scaling the cedar, which caused it to hang over the edge of the roof. And there was Duane, dangling hundreds of feet up in the air and loving it.

Duane was one of the first white kids in town to discover drugs. He would get high by sniffing Testors airplane glue, drinking beer, or sipping some Jack Daniels. Later, Duane and Shepley would slip over to the black side of town to cop some pot from a guy named Available Jones. One day, they bought four joints for four dollars and they each smoked two of them. Shepley was out on his ass, but Duane was bitching: "Ah, this shit's no good. This stuff doesn't work."

The guitar had become Duane's way of defining himself. And it was something he was damned good at. Van Harrison played the bass in the Allman Joys and the Escorts, but he also played guitar. One week, Van spent hours learning a tough Chet Atkins song, then proudly went over to Duane's house to show it to him. Duane listened and declared, "Aw, man, that's easier than hell." It took him about fifteen or twenty minutes to figure it out. "That's when I decided I'd better stick to bass," Van said.

In the band situation, Duane pushed constantly to make the music better. "He was always trying to learn new music and trying to figure out a way to do something different, invent something new in the way of sound or a technique," said Van. "His energy level was extremely high, and if things weren't going right, he was easy to frustrate. But he was never happier than when we'd figure out something new, put it in the show, and it went right. We'd go out to eat sometimes at two or three in the morning after a gig and talk about it. He'd say, 'Man, that was great. That was as good as it gets. If we just do that good tomorrow, I'll be happy.'"

Duane's friends seemed to admire him and fear for his future at the same time. Some of them never expected Duane to reach the age of thirty. "He was absolutely on a self-destructive path, and I don't mean that in a malicious way," Sylvan Wells said. "If you had a bike, a motorcycle, you wouldn't let Duane drive it. It's gone. Probably come back wrecked. Duane was on a destruction trip. The only question was how much life before he killed himself."

TWO

Crossroads

AFTER Gregg graduated from high school in 1965, he and Duane came to a crossroads. Duane wanted the band to turn professional; Gregg wasn't so sure. He wanted to go to college to become a dentist, but he decided he'd stay with the band at least through the summer and see what happened. Drummer Maynard Portwood was also in, but Van Harrison decided to enroll in college and Bob Keller replaced him on bass. The Allman Joys traveled all over the Southeast, from Alabama to Florida to Tennessee, playing at clubs and fraternities. "We had our own sound system, amps, and a station wagon — big time," Gregg said. "Our first gig was in Mobile at a place called the Stork Club. Boy, it was a nasty, fucking place. I was homesick, and the band had broken up about fourteen times before we got there."

Gregg hung with the Allman Joys, but he had another problem: the draft. Willis and Howard may have viewed the military as a way to escape the poverty of middle Tennessee, but for Duane and Gregg's generation the army meant being sent to a death trap called Vietnam. Duane was exempt from the draft because his father was dead and he was the oldest son in the family. Gregg, however, had the misfortune of turning eighteen just as the United States became serious about a land war in Vietnam. Duane decided there was no way his little brother was going and he came up with a surefire scheme: Gregg would shoot himself in the foot and get a medical exemption. Duane even threw a "foot-shootin' party" the night before Gregg's physical and invited over a bunch of girls. Sylvan Wells and a few other friends were there as well.

"We had a box outside with a bunch of sawdust and I had on these moccasins and I painted a target on my foot; I didn't want to hurt myself," Gregg said. "The long bones in your foot come to a V, and I wanted to hit it right there so it would crack two of them but not really upset anything permanently. So the girls are all crying and we're drinking all this whiskey. It comes foot-shooting time. I go out there and sit down and I've got this Saturday-night special. I took aim and I thought: 'Wait a minute, what am I doing here? I'm getting ready to shoot myself.' So I went back in and said, 'Look, I gotta have a couple more drinks before I do this.' "

Duane refused to let his little brother back down. The drunker Duane got, the more he egged Gregg on. "Come on, you can do it," he kept saying. When that didn't work, Duane began berating Gregg, trying to push his buttons. "Well, you're just a chicken," Duane announced. "I invited these nice ladies over here to see a foot shootin', and you're going to let them down?" Finally, Gregg could take no more. He slugged down a couple more shots of whiskey, made a quick telephone call, grabbed the pistol, and went outside.

Minutes later, Sylvan began to hear a faint siren. "The next thing I know is *bang!*" he said. "Then the ambulance was there; he'd called the ambulance before he shot himself. I'll never forget that: you heard the ambulance before you heard the gunshot."

Gregg was taken to the hospital, and in all the rush he and Duane forgot there was a target painted on his moccasin. The bull's-eye did not escape the notice of the emergency room doctor, who sensed a scam and seemed to jerk the sticky shoe off Gregg's injured foot with particular relish. The doctor slapped a Band-Aid on the flesh wound and told Gregg to go home. The next day they wrapped up his foot in a big bandage, and Gregg limped into the induction center on crutches. The ruse worked, and Gregg successfully dodged Vietnam.

IF you could beat the draft, the mid-sixties were a wonderful time to be a young white kid with a guitar. Rock 'n' roll had grown sanitized after Elvis went into the army; its blues roots were perceived as too raw-edged, too sexual, for white teenagers. The irony is that young musicians across the ocean in Britain were the next to lock in on the music that had been born in the Mississippi Delta. While kids in

America were being fed white-bread music by singers with whole-some names like Frankie Avalon and Bobby Rydell and Pat Boone, hip English kids were digging the dark music of men with wonder-fully mysterious names like Howlin' Wolf and Muddy Waters and T-Bone Walker. Soon, there were groups like the Rolling Stones and the Yardbirds doing rock versions of songs like Wolf's "Little Red Rooster" and John Lee Hooker's "Boom Boom." A whole generation of American kids grew up listening to the British mimicking music from their own backyard.

Because of the influence of Jim Shepley and Floyd Miles, along with the late-night music on WLAC, Duane and Gregg had a firm foundation in blues and r&b, and hearing groups like the Yardbirds play wild, electric versions of the songs they loved was liberating. "When we first started, Gregg and me were playing rhythm and blues," Duane said. "We always had blues roots, and the only way we could break into the scene was to try to play black music in white clubs. The best thing that happened was that the British intervention on the scene made it possible to play what you wanted to play, and do what you wanted to do without having to be relegated to the funky places. We didn't have to be restricted. Everyone began to dig the blues and everyone was getting into it."

The brothers started incorporating the music of English bands into their set list. Gregg even switched from the guitar to a Vox stand-up organ because it was favored by the British groups. The Allman Joys spent much of the summer of 1966 in Nashville after catching the ear of John D. Loudermilk, one of Nashville's best writers and the author of songs like "Tobacco Road," "Abilene," and "The Language of Love." Duane and Gregg were playing in a little club called the Briar Patch one night when Loudermilk heard them and told them they had potential.

Loudermilk began teaching Gregg how to write songs and con-vinced Buddy Killen, a seasoned producer and music publisher who was president of a small record label, to catch the Allman Joys at the Briar Patch. Killen, who had discovered Joe Tex, was impressed enough to book them into a studio called Bradley's Barn. Housed in a rustic red barn about twenty miles east of Nashville, the studio was owned by Owen Bradley, the legendary producer famed for his work with Patsy Cline. It had just opened in 1966, and the Allman Joys were one of the first rock bands to record there. The sessions showed a marked maturity in their abilities, especially in Gregg's voice. But they were still basically just a hot-sounding cover band, recording songs already done by British groups. Killen was less than impressed with the few, amateurish originals Gregg had penned. "He listened to the tapes and said, 'No, man. You cats better look for a day gig. You're the worst I ever heard,' " Duane said.

It was a crushing response for a band that thought it was on the verge of its big break. The Allman Joys went back on the road and even managed to land a gig in New York City at a Greenwich Village club, but Duane was virtually the only one who still believed, and the grind was even beginning to get to him. "There's a garbage circuit of the South, man," Duane said. "You make about a hundred and fifty dollars a week and eat pills and drink. It's a bad trip. It was killing us."

Duane and Gregg performed frequently in Tallahassee, often with pickup bands. Sylvan Wells had broken up the Nightcrawlers and he was going to Florida State University, and the brothers would stay with him whenever they played in town. Gregg spent many late nights in Sylvan's living room mulling over his future. "I can remember clearly Gregg telling my wife that he was only doing this temporarily to get money to go to college," Sylvan said. "He still wanted to be a dentist." By the end of 1966, the Allman Joys sputtered to a halt and broke up.

The closest rival Duane and Gregg had on the club circuit was a group from Alabama called the Men-its; the two groups were friendly and even shared the same management. The Men-its' drummer, Johnny Sandlin, met the Allman brothers at a little club in Pensacola, Florida. "They were the first people I'd ever seen with long hair," he recalled. "This was a navy town and it wasn't safe to have even fairly long hair and theirs was shoulder-length blond hair. I thought that was the strangest thing I'd ever seen. I'd heard about them, about how good they were, and after hearing them I was blown away. Duane and Gregg were just amazing."

When the Men-its broke up at just about the same time as the Allman Joys, it seemed only natural for those still committed to the dream to band together. The new group included Duane and Gregg, Johnny Sandlin, keyboardist and guitarist Paul Hornsby, and bassist Mabron McKinley. It was obvious to everyone from the Men-its that they had come across something unique. Gregg had learned to sing and was beginning to sound like a white Bobby Bland. And Duane was an incredible guitar player who seemed to come up with a new riff every day. He was maturing — no more missed gigs — and he had learned to channel his boundless energy and curiosity. His resolve inspired them to have the faith to follow him wherever he went. "Duane had this purpose, and the purpose was music," Johnny Sandlin said. "And he didn't let other stuff get in the way. If there was something bothering you, he'd tell you to get it out of the way. It was almost as though he knew he had a limited amount of time to do what he was going to do, and he didn't have the time to bullshit and put up with things that would slow him down or get in his way."

"He had this presence," Paul Hornsby observed. "You might not know who he was, but if he came into a room you noticed him. What he was saying might not be important but you would listen. There was something special about him. I've never come across anyone else like that."

The band went through a couple of names — the Allman Joys, Almanac — before settling on Hour Glass. The new group rehearsed for a couple of weeks, then played at a club called Peppys A Go Go in St. Louis in March 1967. It seemed like fate was with them. The bass player had gone to the airport to pick up his wife, and ran into a group of longhairs who turned out to be the Nitty Gritty Dirt Band. "At that time, if you saw another person with long hair you felt an instant kinship," Johnny said. Mabron invited them to come hear us play." The Nitty Gritty Dirt Band had established a solid reputation but was still three years away from its huge hit single, the cover of Jerry Jeff Walker's "Mr. Bojangles." Bill McEuen managed the band and was knocked out by what he heard when he went to Peppys to hear Hour Glass. "He calls Liberty Records in Los Angeles and tells them that he's found the next Rolling Stones," Paul said.

When McEuen urged the group to move to Los Angeles, Gregg didn't want to go. He had never been west of the Mississippi River. "Los Angeles just seemed like it was forever away," he said. But Duane was the leader and Duane said they were going; everybody packed up and moved west to become stars.

IT turned out to be one time when Gregg's instincts were sharper than Duane's. For a bunch of unsophisticated kids from the South, Los Angeles was frightening and they all felt completely lost. "It was the largest city I'd ever been to," Johnny said. "We didn't know how to act there, what to do. We were used to playing a lot, four or five nights a week, and we went out there and it was like once every two or three weeks."

When the band first got to California, everyone crashed at the Nitty Gritty Dirt Band's house. That lasted only a couple of weeks before they moved into the Mikado Motel, near the Hollywood Bowl. "A real garbage motel, and all of us in one room," Gregg said. "The manager caught us and we moved down to an even worse joint on Lash Lane. This place had no name at all. I got up the first morning we lived there, thinking I'd go swimming. As I'm walking down the hall, there was this door open. I happened to look in and there's this guy lying on the floor, covered with a blanket. Cop standing there. The cat had left a note and downed ninety-five Seconals. It was the first dead person I'd ever seen."

Hour Glass made its LA concert debut as the opening act for the Doors at the Hullabaloo Club. "Man, that scared me to death," Gregg said. "I could barely sing. There must have been two thousand people in that place and my knees were knocking together." Hour Glass closed with a finale straight out of the Who. As the final song ended, Duane made his Telecaster go into a feedback frenzy. Then he walked to the front of the stage, reached under the body of the guitar and just flipped it straight up in the air and kept on walking without looking back.

The band signed a management contract with McEuen and a recording contract with Liberty Records. No one realized until it was too late that Liberty was primarily interested in Gregg as a singer. "It took us a fair amount of time to understand that," Johnny said. "They could care less, in my case, who plays drums as long as they don't get in the way of Gregg singing. I can understand them not appreciating the rest of us. But Duane, I can't understand how anyone could overlook his playing."

The liner notes on the first album, called *Hour Glass*, promised r&b music "reeking in soul." But it was obvious the label had a rather loose definition of those terms. "Our producer [Dallas Smith], his claim to fame had been he had done the Jan and Dean records," Paul Hornsby said. "He knew nothing about Southern r&b; to him it was like a foreign language. He'd ask us if we were going to do some Motown, which is just a little off geographically."

The label was determined to keep tight reins on the group. Instead of allowing Hour Glass to do the kind of music that it performed onstage, Liberty chose songs for the band to record. "They'd send in a box of demos and say, 'Okay, pick out your next LP,' " Duane said. "We tried it, figured maybe we could squeeze an ounce or two of good out of this crap. We squeezed and squeezed, but we were squeezing rock. Those albums are very depressing for me to listen to. It's cats tryin' to get off on things that cannot be gotten off on."

Part of the blame was the band's; they couldn't fight back by arguing they had better original songs than the ones they were being given to record. Even the few good songs that Liberty gave them, "Nothing but Tears" and Jackson Browne's "Cast Off All My Fears," were buried under horns and overwrought production. There's very little evidence on the record that Duane Allman is even a member of Hour Glass. The guitar is completely buried until a song called "Heartbeat," and it's as though Duane decided he had been shackled on the entire record and was going to throw every riff he knew on this one short lead break. One flash of brilliance and it's over. It was an era of budding guitar heroes, and Liberty had one of the absolute very best buried so far in the mix that he couldn't be heard. "A good damn band of misled cats was what it was," Duane later lamented.

Onstage, the band performed few of the songs from the album and reverted to its roots, playing hard-edged r&b music. Duane stepped out and played sharp solos on a hybrid Fender guitar that had a Telecaster body and Stratocaster neck. "We did a lot of r&b stuff, a lot of Gregg's stuff that he was writing, some Otis Redding tunes and Yardbirds stuff," Johnny said. "The longer we were in LA, the more we started doing original songs."

Hour Glass became known as one of the hottest live bands in Los Angeles, and its gigs at the Whiskey A Go Go drew packed houses. The band brought an old jazz-and-blues tradition to its concerts by inviting other players to come up and sit in. "Back then, nobody in LA knew what the word 'jam' meant and we kind of started that," Paul Hornsby said. "I remember one night we had Buddy Miles, Paul Butterfield, Stephen Stills, Neil Young, Eric Burden, and Janis Joplin all sitting in with us at once. We didn't stop playing and used up the other band's time and, man, they were pissed off. But how could you quit with that group of people up onstage?"

Liberty wouldn't allow Hour Glass to play many gigs in Los Angeles for fear of overexposure, and with the record bombing no one outside of Southern California had heard of the band. Money was short and the group had to survive by borrowing from its management and record company. Everyone was growing frustrated and eventually, Mabron McKinley disappeared. Pete Carr, another Daytona Beach guitar player who had been in the Men-its, happened to be in California visiting Johnny and Paul. "We were playing the Whiskey A Go Go and we were all getting ready — it was an hour or two before gig time — and our bass player had disappeared," Paul remembered. "It later turned out that he'd caught a plane to Florida and failed to notify us that he had quit the band. So we had to have a bass player real quick and Pete Carr, who had never played bass guitar in his life, was standing handy and we said, 'Come on, you're our bass player tonight.' He played with us for the rest of Hour Glass."

Mabron wasn't the only one longing to go back home. "Things got real difficult as far as money and not playing enough," Johnny said. "That was the main thing that bothered me; we never got to play enough. If you're a musician and you're playing, all the other stuff you can get out of the way. We used to get so lonesome for the South. I didn't realize I loved the South until I lived out there. We'd call information in Nashville or Alabama just to hear a southern voice."

The boredom was driving Duane crazy. He was intense, thriving on action, and all he seemed to be doing was sitting around, waiting for something to happen. The band members passed the time drinking cheap wine, trying to score dope and pick up women, and even came up with silly nicknames for themselves. Gregg was "Wile E. Coyote," because of the way he howled when he sang and for his sly mischief. They thought Johnny favored a duck, and that became his nickname. And Duane was called "Dog" because with his long hair he looked like an Afghan hound.

When Hour Glass went back into the studio in January of 1968, Gregg had a batch of new songs, and the band was determined to get its sound on tape. Since the first record bombed and Liberty's formula hadn't worked, the band was in a better bargaining position. The second Hour Glass album, *Power of Love*, was a vast improvement over the debut. For the first time, Gregg's voice was recorded in a sympathetic setting. It had matured into an evocative and expressive instrument, especially on the bluesy "Home for the Summer," a song appropriately about longing to go home to the South.

And this time, Duane was in the forefront. He played electric sitar on one of the record's most interesting tracks, a jazzy version of Lennon and McCartney's "Norwegian Wood (This Bird Has Flown)." He played soulful licks on a cover of Solomon Burke's "I'm Hanging Up My Heart for You" and on "Down in Texas." The latter song was cowritten by Eddie Hinton, the old lead singer of the Men-its who had stayed in Alabama to be a session guitarist for a hot new studio in Muscle Shoals, Alabama. The Muscle Shoals team of Dan Penn and Spooner Oldham, who would write and play on several of Aretha Franklin's hits, wrote the title track, which was eventually released as a single. The label probably thought "Power of Love" would appeal to hippies celebrating peace and love, but the single bombed. "Down in

Texas," perhaps the best song on the album, has the sound of a hit
single but it was never released. Like the debut album, *Power of Love*
was a flop.

Even though Hour Glass had been given more freedom in the
studio, the band members were still disappointed with the record. In
April of 1968, a month after *Power of Love* was released, Johnny convinced everyone the band should go to Muscle Shoals and record at
Fame studio. The idea was to get away from the influence of the pop
producers in Los Angeles, and do what came naturally. The result was
revelatory, especially three old blues songs strung together and called
"B. B. King Medley." It was the first evidence on tape of the full
power of Duane Allman. The song begins with a count-off, and then
Duane's guitar comes out screaming with succinct blues licks that
quiver with emotion. Gregg's voice swings with the blues, and the
rhythm section is solid and concise. "The Muscle Shoals stuff was the
only stuff the band as a whole felt good about," Johnny said. "Liberty
thought it was garbage. That was kind of the ultimate blow. We said,
'Well, this is us. This is how we think we sound and it's a good performance of what we do and what we want to be.' And they hated it. So
what future was there for us with Liberty?"

The band bolted from Los Angeles and returned home, but finding themselves back on the same old circuit was depressing. "We'd
been filling these big clubs back in LA, and we got back east and that
didn't matter to anyone," Paul Hornsby recalled. "They wanted to
hear 'Mustang Sally' and all those other songs. It was quite a come-
down."

Hour Glass split up weeks later. Duane and Gregg drifted back
to Florida and wound up cutting demos and playing gigs with a band
called the 31st of February — an old buddy named Butch Trucks
played drums — that had released a folk-rock album on Vanguard
Records. The recordings with the 31st of February, later released on
Bold Records, are essentially practice tapes of poor quality, although
there are some interesting moments. One track, "Nobody Knows You
When You're Down and Out," sounds like it was recorded in somebody's basement on very primitive equipment. But it is significant for
two reasons: Duane's lead guitar and the arrangement, which would
turn up a few years later on a version Duane would record with Eric
Clapton. The sessions also included the first recording of "Melissa," a
song Gregg wrote with Sandy Alaimo, who was running the studio the
band was using.

Gregg's heart wasn't in the 31st of February. He longed for the carefree lifestyle of the hippies out in California, and he was ready for a taste of life on his own without the influence of Duane. Even though it was no longer a functioning band, Hour Glass owed money to Liberty Records and to its management. Liberty was threatening to sue, but said it would forgive the debt if Gregg returned to California to record as a solo artist. Gregg jumped at the chance. He could have beaten it; record companies routinely invest thousands in new bands that never become successful and then write off the losses. Even if Liberty had sued, Gregg had no money to pay off a judgment. Whether Gregg was fooled or not, he wanted to go back to California and he used Liberty's pressure as his excuse. He went west, vowing to return within weeks. "He knew all along he wouldn't come back, but he never told us," Butch Trucks said. "We were in Daytona, and he called to say he wouldn't be back." It effectively broke up the 31st of February and prompted a grudge that Butch would carry for years.

The two brothers were separated and the dream was foundering. Then Duane got a phone call from Fame studio owner Rick Hall. He had been impressed by the lead guitar on the Hour Glass songs recorded in his studio. Would Duane be interested in coming to Muscle Shoals to cut some songs with Wilson Pickett?

Three

Hey Jude

THERE couldn't be a more improbable place for a world-renowned recording studio than Muscle Shoals, a little town in the middle of rural Alabama. But in 1959 someone opened a tiny studio and just like Lee Hazen's kitchen in Daytona Beach, it began to attract local musicians — people like Rick Hall, Donnie Fritts, Spooner Oldham, and Dan Penn. After a couple of songs recorded there became hits, Hall opened Fame studio in a cinder-block building on the edge of town and took most of the musicians with him.

Muscle Shoals remained an obscure musical outpost until 1966, when a local hospital orderly and aspiring singer named Percy Sledge recorded a song there called "When a Man Loves a Woman." Atlantic Records released it, and it became the first southern r&b record to top the pop charts.

That record began a brief but memorable association between Muscle Shoals and Atlantic Records, the rhythm-and-blues giant. Atlantic vice-president Jerry Wexler was impressed enough by the studio band backing up Percy Sledge to bring down Wilson Pickett, one of the hottest r&b singers around thanks to the classic "In the Midnight Hour." His first sessions produced three more recordings for the ages — "Mustang Sally," "Funky Broadway," and "Land of 1,000 Dances." Later, Wexler brought down a black female singer. No one knew who she was, but when she sat down at the piano and began singing "I Never Loved a Man (the Way I Love You)," they listened with their mouths agape. Aretha Franklin was soon to become the Queen of Soul, and Muscle Shoals had solidified its place as Atlantic's new studio of choice.

"The Muscle Shoals Rhythm Section was a unit without a lead guitar," said Jerry Wexler. "And then came Duane Allman. He brought something new into the game." Duane arrived in Muscle Shoals in November 1968 with his Stratocaster guitar and Fender Twin amplifier. It was a heady experience for the twenty-one-year-old guitarist: months earlier he had been covering "Mustang Sally" in clubs and here he was, about to back up Wilson Pickett in the studio. If Duane was intimidated, he certainly didn't show it. One of the first things Duane did was suggest that Pickett cut a version of "Hey Jude." The soul star, who had a reputation for a fast temper, balked — he wasn't about to record a song about "no Jew."

Duane didn't back down. Here he was, his first session in Muscle Shoals and already locked in a battle of wills with Wilson Pickett. Duane started playing the song, the band fell into a funky groove behind him, and Pickett began to warm to the idea. But Duane didn't stop there. On the song's long fade-out, he cranked up his Stratocaster and began playing lead guitar behind Pickett's soulful wails. Pickett loved it and began calling Duane "Skyman" because the guitarist was always up, always riding high. Since Duane's other nickname was "Dog," the two eventually evolved into "Skydog."

The musicians in the studio band knew instantly that they had come across a major talent. "Most people have to work their way in," said Jimmy Johnson, the Muscle Shoals rhythm guitarist who had produced the Hour Glass session. "When Duane did that date with Pickett, he was in. Overnight. That's never happened before or since."

Once the session ended, Rick Hall did two things — he told Duane to go get his things and move to Muscle Shoals, and he gave Jerry Wexler a call and played "Hey Jude" over the telephone. "He had done that only one other time, after he recorded 'When a Man Loves a Woman,' which was a pretty good song, you know?" Wexler said. "My feeling when I heard 'Hey Jude'? Euphoria. You had to get excited when you heard that guitar."

Duane went back to Florida, packed up his gear, and moved to Alabama. "I wasn't doing much in Jacksonville, just drinking and jiving around, so I went up," Duane said. "I rented a cabin and lived alone on this lake. I just sat and played and got used to living without a bunch of jive Hollywood crap in my head. It's like I brought myself back to earth and came to life again through that and the sessions with good r&b players."

DUANE ALLMAN was quite a sight in rural Alabama. He had long hair, wore crazy clothes, and drove around in an old milk truck. "I was just totally amazed by this strange creature," said David Hood, who played bass in the studio band. "Compared to everybody else, Duane seemed like he was from Mars." Duane soon proved the Wilson Pickett session was no fluke. He added blistering solos to Clarence Carter's "The Road of Love" and Aretha Franklin's version of "The Weight," and he played a funky-sounding sitar behind the scorching saxophone of King Curtis on a version of "Games People Play." The latter record won a Grammy in 1969 for the best r&b instrumental.

Duane was an anomaly in r&b music. Traditionally, saxophones were used for solos and to play the fill-in notes that echo the vocalist. In Muscle Shoals, it was Duane Allman's guitar taking that role, and many of the arrangements seemed to revolve around what he was playing. "He had a good sense of what went into recording and if you had good sense, you listened to him because he gave very good advice," Jerry Wexler said. "And people did listen to him because he never lorded over them."

When Duane Allman played on a session, the studio band knew it was going to be special. He energized them, inspired them to play at their best. Duane was so deep into the music and took his playing to such heights that the other musicians always picked up in intensity; they wanted to soar up there with him. White blues singer John Hammond, Jr., saw it firsthand when he went to Fame. "I expected it to be a bunch of heavy-duty black players who really knew the blues," said Hammond. "And they expected me to be black. So they looked at me really weird when I showed up. I spent three days down there and it wasn't going well."

A day or two later, all the musicians walked in, excited. "All right, man, Duane's here," they kept saying. Hammond was bewildered. Then he looked up and saw this skinny guy stroll into the studio. He had reddish blond hair tied up in a ponytail, and he was wearing a T-shirt that said "City Slicker." "Where's John Hammond?" he said loudly. "I've got to meet this guy." Hammond walked over and introduced himself, a little embarrassed because he had no idea who this person was. When he asked to sit in, Hammond said, "Sure." He figured the sessions couldn't possibly get any worse.

Duane strapped on his Stratocaster and Hammond felt like he was playing with a different band. "All of a sudden," he said, "those guys really understood what I was doing." Duane dug the guy, and in the eyes of the Muscle Shoals band, that gave John Hammond instant credibility. Hammond was enthralled by Duane's guitar playing. One time he asked Duane how he got so good. Duane just laughed. "Man, I took speed every night for three years and practiced."

As he had done on "The Road of Love" and "The Weight," Duane pulled out an empty Coricidin cold medicine bottle, put it on his left ring finger, and played slide guitar during the John Hammond session. Bottleneck, or slide, guitar has been a blues tradition from the turn of the century. People called it "bottleneck" because musicians would use the neck from a broken wine bottle and slide it up and down the frets rather than using their fingers. The beauty of bottleneck guitar is that a player can slide the bottle over the point of natural intonation and create a sound like the vibrato of a singing voice. The secret is in finding that "sweet spot" of perfect pitch, and then it is a long and arduous process to learn to hit it with consistent precision.

Duane had begun playing the bottleneck about two years earlier, when Hour Glass was in St. Louis. Paul Hornsby had put the new Jeff Beck album on a record player, and Duane listened to the brief slide solo on a song called "Beck's Bolero." Duane thought it was the hottest thing he'd ever heard. "He loved that slide part and told me he was going to learn to play it," Paul said.

After Hour Glass went to Los Angeles, Duane saw a concert by Taj Mahal, who did an up-tempo version of an old country blues song called "Statesboro Blues" that was propelled by the slide work of his lead guitarist, Jesse Ed Davis. Because Hour Glass performed so rarely, Duane spent hours learning the Jesse Ed Davis bottleneck solo from "Statesboro Blues." It drove the rest of the guys in Hour Glass crazy. "Have you ever heard somebody trying to learn slide?" Paul Hornsby said. "There's nothing worse. Unless it's a fiddle player."

Duane's first recorded slide had been a halting yet lovely bottleneck on the version of "Melissa" recorded by the 31st of February. And he had used a slide in Muscle Shoals. But he had yet to unlock the final secret of bottleneck guitar. Blues players have traditionally used what is known as "open" tunings when they played slide. Strum the strings of a guitar that is in standard tuning and the sound is non-sensical; you have to put your fingers on the strings to create musical chords. Do the same thing with a guitar in open tuning and you get a pretty, harmonic sound. In open tuning, the guitar is tuned to a chord, usually a G or D.

It is possible to play functional, even inspired, slide guitar in standard tuning. But most of the masters — Robert Johnson, Muddy Waters, Tampa Red, Elmore James — played in open tuning; it allows for a richness of sound that is otherwise impossible. Many slide players never attempt to learn open tunings because it essentially means mastering a new instrument. Duane was playing slide in standard tuning until John Hammond taught him about open tunings. Hammond, a master of acoustic bottleneck, remembered showing Duane some of the basics when they jammed on country blues during breaks in the Muscle Shoals sessions. "Back then he played everything in a straight tuning," Hammond said. "We jammed and I was using open tunings and he asked me, 'How the fuck do you do that?' That felt special, as much of a hotshot as he was, for him to ask *me* something about the guitar."

Duane used Fame as a sort of laboratory to hone his skills. He knew that playing lead guitar for the Muscle Shoals Rhythm Section was not his career destination. When Aretha Franklin summoned the Muscle Shoals players to New York City for recording sessions in early January of 1969, Duane and Jimmy Johnson went to the Fillmore East theater for a B. B. King concert. Guitarist Johnny Winter was the opening act. "Johnny is really good, but I can cut him," Duane told Jimmy during the concert. "Do you see that stage down there? Next year by this time, man, I'm going to be down there."

RICK HALL and Jerry Wexler weren't the only ones amazed by the guitar player on "Hey Jude." Phil Walden, who had managed Otis Redding until the singer's death in 1967, thought it was one of the wildest things he'd ever heard. He called in one of his assistants, Twiggs Lyndon, to listen. Twiggs had worked as a road manager for Little Richard and Percy Sledge, and he'd spent a year listening to Jimi Hendrix playing guitar for Little Richard. After that Twiggs wasn't easily impressed. He had little patience for white guitar players; for his tastes, you had to be black to make a guitar cry.

"What do you think of that guitar player?" Phil asked him when the song finished.

Twiggs was sitting there with a huge grin. "Man, he is great."
There was a pregnant pause. "He's white," Walden said.

"No!" an astonished Twiggs replied. "He *can't* be."

Phil and Twiggs were soon on their way to Muscle Shoals
to meet Duane Allman. Phil signed up as Duane's manager while
Rick Hall signed him as a recording artist. But Hall was unsure of
what to do with Duane as a solo act, and he called Jerry Wexler at
Atlantic.

"Nothing positive was happening, so I bought Duane's contract
from Rick Hall, even though Duane had no apparent prospects," Wexler said. "What I bought was the contract of a sideman who couldn't
sing or write songs. So, ostensibly, it wasn't too good of a move. Except
that I had Phil Walden in the picture. I knew Phil from Otis Redding,
of course. It was with Phil's encouragement that I did this, because
Phil was going to build a band around him. I didn't know what would
become of it, but the more I worked with Duane and heard him play,
the more I realized that we had a tremendous talent."

The first thing Duane had to do was put together a band. Phil
had been gathering musicians in Macon, Georgia, for a studio he
hoped would duplicate the success of Fame; he told Duane about
someone who might work out. "We got a drummer over here in
Macon, and nobody knows if he's any good or not because he plays so
weird," Walden told him. Duane told his new manager to bring the cat
over to Muscle Shoals so he could check him out.

A couple of days later a tall black kid with a short, thick Afro
showed up at Fame. "Is Duane Allman around?" he said. "I'm supposed to play in his band." A couple of guys knew him; he had played
in the road bands of Otis Redding and Percy Sledge. His name was Jai
Johanny Johanson, although most people called him by his nickname:
Jaimoe.

Almost from the time he first picked up a set of drumsticks in
1959, jazz had been Jaimoe's first love. He was born Johnny Lee Johnson on July 8, 1944, in Ocean Springs, Mississippi, and grew up in
nearby Gulfport. He dreamed of being an athlete when he was young,
but a stray ball that hit him in the face left him unable to control his
right eye. After that, drums became his passion. Jaimoe cleared out an
area in his mother's wash house, put a record player out there, and
began practicing for hours, playing along with his beloved jazz albums.
His best friend, a kid named Lamar Williams, took up the bass and
often joined him.

Jaimoe's first experience on the road came in 1965 with r&b

singer Ted Taylor. Along the way he met Otis Redding and, a year later, joined his road band. By then, Otis was the king of the soul charts and was on the cusp of superstardom. The backup band played behind all the acts that went on tour with him — Sam and Dave, Percy Sledge, Patti LaBelle and the Bluebells, James Carr. Each concert was so strenuous that Otis carried two drummers with him; one played while the other rested. Jaimoe cut a deal with the other drummer so that he could play primarily behind the warm-up groups.

"Otis was into that rock 'n' roll type thing," Jaimoe said. "I'm talking about energy. I didn't have the experience playing like that. And I wanted to play behind all the other artists because it gave me the chance for variety. I'd rather play for three hours behind them rather than play for an hour behind Otis." Jaimoe stayed with the band for six months. He left when Otis set up a tour of Europe; Jaimoe had lost his wallet and had no identification for a passport.

He landed a gig with Percy Sledge in late 1967, and then played with Joe Tex's band until June 22, 1968; he left with a new nickname that someone in the band had given him, "Jaimoe." It had Caribbean origins, but the young drummer never did find out what the name meant. It was melodic and exotic; he liked it and kept it. For much the same reasons, he inserted an "a" into his first and last name. After he left Joe Tex, Jaimoe went back home to Gulfport. Twiggs Lyndon, Percy Sledge's former road manager, called him and said that Phil Walden wanted to start a studio in Macon. Jaimoe packed up his gear and headed to Georgia.

Jaimoe soon learned that the studio was a long way from getting started up. He met Bob O'Dea, a Macon r&b fixture, and they formed a duo — O'Dea on the Hammond organ and Jaimoe on drums. "Bob and I used to work out at this place called the Barrel House," Jaimoe said. "We called ourselves 'Bob and Jai.' Man, we used to have wall-to-wall people. A lot of the stuff I'd been practicing at home — Tony Williams, Elvin Jones, Max Roach, Buddy Rich — I was finally getting a chance to play. So I got a lot together there." It was with Bob O'Dea that Jaimoe learned the art of drum solos. They'd be playing a song and O'Dea would whisper, "Jai, you got it; I'm goin' to get a Coke." The organist would disappear into the crowd and leave Jaimoe with no alternative but to perform alone.

Phil Walden didn't forget about Jaimoe, and tried to keep him busy. There was a Macon guitarist named Johnny Jenkins who Phil thought could be marketed as another Jimi Hendrix, and Phil enlisted

Jaimoe to drum for the group. That deal soon fell apart and Jaimoe was upset because Ray Charles had called to offer him a job, and he couldn't take it because he was contractually bound to Johnny Jenkins. It was just the latest in what seemed to be a string of disappointments. "I'd made up my mind that I was going to New York and pursue what I'd always wanted to pursue, jazz," Jaimoe said. "If I was going to starve to death, I decided I might as well starve to death doing something I love."

Then Phil Walden began courting him again, this time to play in a band with some white guitar player in Muscle Shoals. Jackie Avery, a singer and songwriter, called Jaimoe from Alabama to rave about the guy. "Jai, you gotta hear this white boy," Avery told him. "Man, this motherfucker can play." One night about two in the morning, Jaimoe was listening to the radio when Pickett's version of "Hey Jude" began playing. He heard that screaming lead guitar challenging Pickett for the spotlight and knew: it had to be that white guy.

A few days later, about the third week in January 1969, Avery called again. Jaimoe already felt burned once by Phil with the Johnny Jenkins experience. But Avery persisted: Rick Hall was behind the project and, more important, so was Jerry Wexler. "I decided I had nothing to lose," Jaimoe said. "I figured the guy will probably be a star overnight, make a bunch of money. I was tired of not getting paid to work with all these fabulous rhythm-and-blues artists that I worked with. So I packed up my stuff, got on a Trailways bus, and zipped right on up there. I walk into this room, Studio A, and see this guy standing there with a Twin [amplifier] sitting up on a table. I think he was doing a King Curtis session. He looked like he was about as big as a bean pole. So I walk over to him and I said, 'You're Skyman Allman?' He looks at me and goes, 'You're Jaimoe Johnson.' And that's where we started."

Jaimoe may have gone to Muscle Shoals with the intention of making a mint off a white rock star, but he quickly realized he had found what all true musicians seek — magic. "After we started rehearsing things just sounded so good and loud — Duane played loud and, man, I mean *loud* — that I forgot all about the star trip," Jaimoe said.

Duane's enthusiasm was infectious. He kept telling Jaimoe, "Man, wait till you hear this bass player. Shit, this cat's bad, man. We're gonna have a helluva band." Two days later, Jaimoe walked into Studio B and found a guy who looked as skinny as Duane setting up his bass amp. It was Berry Oakley.

*   *   *

RAYMOND BERRY OAKLEY III was born in Chicago on April 4, 1948, the oldest child of Raymond Berry Oakley II and Margaret Sweeney Oakley; a younger sister, Candace, was born twenty-two months later. Berry's father worked for a real estate company, and his mother was a schoolteacher. Not long after his birth, Berry's family moved to a Chicago suburb, Park Forest, where he grew up. Berry was an altar boy, attended parochial schools, and was a devout Catholic. At one point, he even decided to go to the seminary.

When he was fourteen Berry bought an acoustic guitar. He took three lessons from a local jazz guitarist and then began soaking up the natural influences in Chicago, where many of the masters of the electric blues lived. "By the time he was seventeen, he was playing guitar on Rush Street," Candace Oakley said. "It was the beginning of his senior year in high school, and he was playing in the city at night and getting home at the crack of dawn."

Berry dropped out of high school that fall, his eyes set on playing rock 'n' roll. Not long after that, Tommy Roe was in Chicago and word spread that he needed a bass player. Berry had never played bass and Roe's brand of bubblegum pop certainly wasn't his preferred style of music. But Roe was a star, first hitting number one on the pop charts in 1962 with "Sheila" and eventually following it up with "Dizzy." Berry borrowed a bass, auditioned, and got the gig.

Berry moved to New Port Richey, Florida, where Roe was based, and stayed for about a year before moving to Jacksonville to join a band called the Second Coming. Duane Allman had just come back from California, and he sometimes jammed with the group. Even then, Duane knew he had never come across such an adventuresome bass player. Berry pushed him as no one else ever had, with a style powerful and melodic. And when Duane began putting together his new band in Muscle Shoals, he called Berry and convinced him to come to Fame studio.

In January of 1969 the initial three members of the Allman Brothers Band played together for the first time while members of the Muscle Shoals Rhythm Section stood by the door and listened. "We played, and none of those guys would pick up an instrument," Jaimoe said. "They'd just come in, sit around the wall and look at us. You'd try to get them to jam and they'd say, 'No, not with you.' Man, the three of us used to play and we scared the hell out of people. Some of that shit used to scare me."

Jerry Wexler and Rick Hall envisioned Duane leading a power trio, sort of like Jimi Hendrix or Cream. But Duane wasn't sure. James Brown used two drummers onstage, and Duane thought that kind of power could really propel a rock band. When Hall invited Duane to start cutting tracks for an album, he brought in his old Hour Glass buddies Paul Hornsby and Johnny Sandlin to flesh things out. "Duane told me he wanted two drummers and we tried it," Jaimoe said. "Johnny was more experienced at working in a studio than I. Prior to that, I had only did some things around town with a local guy trying to get a record deal." Jaimoe sat out the sessions; he didn't feel confident enough in the studio.

Duane recorded several songs: "Goin' Down Slow," "Down Along the Cove," "Dimples," "Happily Married Man," "No Money Down." The tracks were okay, but it was obvious that Duane was no singer. He excelled on the slow blues "Goin' Down Slow," an old Champion Jack Dupree song about dying young, but his voice leapt in and out of key on up-tempo numbers. Duane knew he wasn't the right vocalist for this band and began calling his little brother, trying to talk him into leaving California and coming back south to round out his new group.

But Gregg wouldn't budge, and neither Paul Hornsby nor Johnny Sandlin wanted to join Duane's new band. After the breakup of Hour Glass, Paul had gone back to his hometown of Tuscaloosa and put together another group, Southcamp. "We'd just been through this with Duane before and it hadn't worked out," said Paul. "I was making a good living teaching guitar and playing with my band, and I was married."

Johnny Sandlin felt the same way. "I don't think there had ever been a rock band that had broken out of the South," he said. "Anybody from the South that made it had to go to LA or New York, and I definitely didn't want to go that route. We'd just been through it, and I was just burned out from it. I wanted to produce records."

Jaimoe was the only one who would make a commitment. Even Berry Oakley was wavering. He had recently married, and his first child was due in the spring. He also felt loyalty to Second Coming and especially to the band's guitarist — a guy named Dickey Betts. But Duane decided to wait him out: he was confident that the music they were making was too good for Berry to walk away. "We stayed in Muscle Shoals for about ten weeks," Jaimoe said. "They'd be doing a recording session in Studio A and I'd be in Studio B with this record player that Rick Hall let me use. I'd sit there and practice eight, ten hours a day. And when Duane would get a break, he'd unhook his Twin and roll it over. Duane and I must have sounded like three people and when Berry was there, shit, man, we sounded like five people."

Finally, Duane grew impatient and he walked in one day and told Jaimoe to pack up. "What's the matter, man?" Jaimoe asked. "Man, I'm tired of doing this shit in the studio," Duane said. "Let's go. I'm ready to play." Duane decided that if Berry Oakley wouldn't come to him, he would go to Berry Oakley. Duane and Jaimoe went to Jacksonville, determined to steal Berry away for their band.

Four

The Jacksonville Jam

DUANE ALLMAN and Jaimoe showed up on Butch Trucks's doorstep in Jacksonville in early March of 1969 looking for a place to crash. Duane was like a hero to Butch and he was glad to let him stay at his place; besides, he had crashed on Duane's floor many a night. But he had never dealt much with black folks, and Jaimoe scared him to death. "Duane stopped by my place and introduced me, his old drummer, to his new drummer," Butch said. "Jaimoe came in and sat down. He had on this tank top, this bear claw necklace, muscles bulging out. And I thought, 'Oh, hell, a militant nigger; he's going to come in and kill me.' He came in and sat down on the couch with his head down. I figured he was trying to figure out a way to tear up the place. They wound up staying two weeks. And immediately, I mean as soon as Jaimoe started talking, we were best friends."

Claude Hudson Trucks, Jr., was born in Jacksonville, Florida, on May 11, 1947, the first son of an optician and the oldest of three children. Butch was classically trained, beginning with piano at the age of nine and then voice lessons. "I had a very good boy soprano voice and our church's minister of music took me under his wing," Butch said. He eventually became the youth director of music at North Jacksonville Baptist Church, and he was a member of the National Honor Society when he graduated from Englewood Senior High School in

1965. Butch was named to the All-State High School Orchestra, and played tympani for the Jacksonville Symphonette.

But Butch was also listening to the radio, and he wanted to play the kind of music he heard from Bob Dylan and the Byrds. To do that, he had to have his own drum kit. "My parents were devout Southern Baptists and didn't want me to have a set of drums," Butch said. "They felt like that was the Primrose Path to damnation." He finally convinced them and joined a couple of teenage bands — the Vikings and the Echoes — before moving to Tallahassee to attend Florida State University. "My major was staying out of Vietnam," Butch said.

He formed a band with two other FSU students, Scott Boyer and David Brown, who shared Butch's love for folk-rock music. They called themselves the Bitter Ind (for "individual") and went to Daytona Beach in 1966 because the city was hopping with clubs. "We auditioned at every damned bar and they loved it, thought it was great, but said, 'You can't dance to it.' And so we couldn't get a damned job," Butch said.

The last place they tried was a bar called the Martinique — the same teenage hangout that had served as a headquarters for the Allman Joys and the Nightcrawlers. During the audition, Butch noticed two guys with long blond hair standing in the audience. It was Duane and Gregg Allman. "We didn't get the job and we just sat there; no money and no place to stay," Butch said. "We wound up spending the night on Duane and Gregg's living-room floor."

Butch took a job at a Daytona Beach warehouse and a few weeks later he filled in when the Allman Joys needed a drummer for a gig at a bar in Jacksonville. Butch parlayed that into a steady job for the Bitter Ind. "The manager just happened to love the Byrds and Dylan," Butch said. "The navy guys would come in and pick up chicks, so it didn't matter if they could dance to it or not."

The Bitter Ind eventually signed a contract with the prestigious folk label Vanguard Records, but the band had to change its name to the 31st of February because the New York nightclub Bitter End wouldn't allow the group to use the name. The first album flopped and the band lost its record contract. By then, Duane and Gregg were back from Los Angeles and they joined the 31st of February long enough to cut some demos to try to get a new record deal.

After Gregg left for California, Butch stayed in Jacksonville but had not hooked up with a new band; his playing consisted mainly of going to a park to jam with a bunch of hippie musicians who played for free on Sunday afternoons. Berry Oakley had organized the jam and his group, the Second Coming, was usually there. "We'd get all the equipment in town and set up a mountain of amplifiers," Butch said. "And we'd jam until the acid wore off."

DUANE'S immediate task was to pry Berry Oakley away from the Second Coming. The band had been together for a couple of years and had some of Florida's finest players — guitarist Larry Reinhardt, who would later go on to Iron Butterfly, and organist Reese Wynans, who would later play with Stevie Ray Vaughan and Double Trouble. Rounding out the group was guitarist Dickey Betts and his wife Dale, who sang and played piano. Berry and Dickey had developed a strong kinship, two opposites who complemented each other. Berry was gentle, the quintessential hippie; Dickey was strong, and didn't take shit from anyone. Berry's loyalty to Dickey became Duane's major stumbling block to putting together his band. Finally, Duane came up with the solution. He threw the idea of a trio out the window and told Berry: "If you're worried about Dickey, hell, he can just play in the band with us."

Forrest Richard Betts had been a musician longer than any of them. The oldest at twenty-five, Dickey had begun playing music when he was so young that a ukulele was virtually the only instrument small enough for him to hold. "I was a little weirdo because I started playing when I was about five years old," Dickey said. "I was playing 'Davy Crockett' and those kinds of songs on a ukulele. Then I got a mandolin and a banjo when I was about ten years old, and I liked to play country music."

He was born on December 12, 1943, in West Palm Beach, Florida, one of three children. Dickey's grandparents had been homesteaders in Florida, and his father, Harold Clemon Betts, was a carpenter. Music was the common bond between father and son. Harold Betts was an amateur fiddle player, and Dickey's uncles played guitar. Dickey and his brother would join in when the family gathered on Sunday afternoons to play bluegrass tunes and traditional Irish folk songs.

"I liked playing with my family but when I got up around sixteen, I realized I wanted to do something a little faster," Dickey said. "So I got my first real guitar. It was a Stella acoustic and I put a pickup on it and got a Gibson amp." Dickey also took up the drums, and they became his main instrument before his friends convinced him that he

was a much better guitarist than drummer. It wasn't long before
Dickey got himself a real electric guitar, a red Gretsch hollow body
like Duane Eddy played. Eddy, the king of twang, was one of
Dickey's first heroes. Then he discovered Chuck Berry and that led
him to the blues — B. B. King, Freddie King, and Albert King.

Dickey had played in several garage bands, and when he was
seventeen he went on the road with a rock band that traveled in a
carnival up the East Coast on the state-fair circuit. He returned to
Sarasota with a wealth of experience and eventually put together a
band called the Jokers. It was a cover band, but Dickey infused it with
blues songs like "Stormy Monday." One night, a kid named Rick Der-
ringer heard the band and was so impressed that, years later, he im-
mortalized "the group with the funky sound" in his hit song "Rock
and Roll Hoochie Koo."

Like seemingly every other rock musician who played the Florida circuit, Dickey had met the Allman brothers. "I was going with a
girl who used to go with Gregg," Dickey said. "She kept telling me
about this band from Daytona Beach. They were called the Allman
Joys back then, and they were something. I really didn't know either
of them, but we would run into each other in clubs and they'd come
by to say hello and sit in with my bands."

By the time he met Berry Oakley, Dickey was into his second
marriage and had an infant daughter, Elena Christine Betts. The two
men formed Second Coming; the name was supposedly selected because, with his long, flowing hair and full beard, Berry looked messi-
anic. "Back then, we were all playing Top-Forty stuff and would throw
in an original song here and there," Dickey said. "You could make
three hundred dollars a week and that was a lot of money. But you
weren't getting anywhere. Then I met Berry and he convinced me to
leave the club circuit and go for broke. Berry said, 'Man, we've got to
break out of these clubs and start doing strictly concerts.' So we joined
together and were trying to do some original songs. We did that for
about a year and, man, it was tough."

Dickey may have felt betrayed that Berry would even consider
abandoning him to play with Duane Allman after they had made their
pact and spent months just barely scraping by. Or maybe he thought it
would be crazy to throw away the base of fans they'd worked hard to
build, just to start over again in another unknown band. But Dickey
resisted his overtures to join Duane's band. "Berry talked to him and
talked to him about playing with us," Jaimoe said. "But it wasn't until
we played together — it really knocked everybody out, you know?"

Dickey first jammed with Duane at the park on Sundays. "Duane was coming to Jacksonville to jam with us, kind of getting used to playing with Berry," Dickey said. "And hell, you know, during that process everybody started noticing some extra things happening that nobody was really planning on. And that was those two guitars like that, building the harmonies."

One Sunday afternoon, March 23, 1969, a group of musicians gathered to play at the Second Coming's house rather than the park. Duane and Jaimoe were there. So were Berry and Dickey. So was Butch. Rounding out things was Second Coming organist Reese Wynans. "We started a little shuffle, and about three hours later we quit," Butch said. "And in that three hours we went through everything. We'd go from a shuffle into a funk into a slow blues. Everything just flowed. One minute I got chill bumps up and down my neck. The next minute I was crying, and the next minute laughing. I just went through all of the emotions. I finished and just sat there stunned. I'd never felt anything like that."

Neither had Duane. He knew he had found his band. "When we finally quit, man, everybody was speechless," Duane said. "Nobody'd ever done anything like that before. It really frightened the shit out of everybody. Right then, I knew. I said, 'Man, here it is, here it *is*.'"

He immediately walked over to the doorway and blocked it. "Okay," Duane announced in a dramatic voice. "Anybody in this room who's not going to play in my band, you've got to fight your way out."

Nobody moved a muscle.

Five

Macon

EVEN back in Muscle Shoals, Duane had been telling Jaimoe about his little brother. "Man, my brother's always fucking up and going on doing this and doing that," Duane said. "And we don't get along too good sometimes. But, man, he's the only motherfucker who can sing in this band. My brother is the blues-singingest white boy in the world. If there's another, I ain't heard him."

Duane had been trying to get his little brother to leave Los Angeles for months, but Gregg balked. He recorded numerous songs for Liberty, and spent much of his time trying to get high and enjoying the bohemian lifestyle of Southern California. Gregg met a struggling songwriter named Jackson Browne, who wrote "Cast Off All My Fears" on the first Hour Glass album, and they lived together for a while. Gregg's best friend was Kim Payne, a biker from Montgomery, Alabama, who had gone to Los Angeles to work as a roadie with a band called the Rock of Gibraltar. He met Gregg just after Hour Glass broke up. "Times were pretty hard," Kim said. "Gregg was selling songs for about two hundred bucks a pop to a studio down there so we could go buy us a bunch of pills and some wine and get loaded. Duane was constantly calling, trying to get Gregg to come join up with his new band."

In late March, Gregg decided he'd had enough of California. Duane called to tell him about the Jacksonville jam ("We got it shaking down here and all we need is you"), and Gregg figured it was time to go home.

Before leaving, he told Kim Payne to hang tight. "Look here, man, if this thing works out good, we're gonna need a roadie. Several of them probably. I'll call you." Kim drove him to the airport and never expected to see Gregg Allman again.

Gregg reached Jacksonville on March 26, 1969, and when he walked through the door of Berry Oakley's house the band was playing the old Muddy Waters song "Trouble No More." Gregg's first reaction was to throw up his hands like a gunslinger who has been disarmed. He listened to them do another song that Muddy Waters made famous, "Hoochie-Coochie Man," with Berry singing. "Man, that's the finest singing I have ever heard and what *I* am doing here, I don't know," he told Duane. "There's nothing I could do to possibly make that any better. I just cannot cut this gig."

Duane already had a Hammond B-3 organ waiting for Gregg, with four joints sitting on top, and he didn't appreciate Gregg's reluctance. Duane did what he would always do when Gregg balked at one of his ideas: he began berating him, pushing Gregg's buttons. "You can snivel on out of here but *I* know you can cut it and *you* know you can cut it," Duane told his little brother. "If you don't try, don't call yourself my brother. I've bragged to these people, bragged about *you.*" It pissed Gregg off, and he grabbed a piece of paper with the lyrics to "Trouble No More" and told the band to kick it off. Gregg gathered up his courage and sang the song with everything he had. It was, Gregg said, "like getting born again, brother."

Three days later there was a concert in Jacksonville's Beach Coliseum. The group was billed as "Duane and Gregg Allman, Berry Oakley, Dickey and all the rest formally [*sic*] of the Second Coming." And those who plopped down the $2.50 admission can say they witnessed the debut of the Allman Brothers Band.

EVERYONE in the band was impressed that Duane had hooked up with the manager of Otis Redding. There was just one catch: Phil Walden wanted them with him in Macon. They were all Florida boys, except for Jaimoe and Berry, and they weren't keen on the notion of leaving, especially to go to some place in the middle of redneck country. "We were a little apprehensive about going to a real small southern town," Dickey said. "I mean, we were some pretty off-the-wall characters."

But there was no other way: Phil was their manager and they all had to be together to make the thing work. Phil had to know they weren't lying around, using the money he was fronting them to get high, and they had to know that he was actually doing something about getting them a recording contract. Phil was rooted in Macon; it was there or nowhere. The final kicker was a little problem with the Jacksonville police over some suspicious plant stems found in the group's living quarters. In April of 1969, they all packed up their instruments and went to Georgia.

Macon is a city of 120,000 people situated about eighty miles south of Atlanta. It sits in the heart of Georgia, near absolutely nothing except scores of towns often too small to be included on a Rand McNally road map. The city is picturesque, full of antebellum houses that were spared during Sherman's March to the Sea. Macon was long a cotton and farming center, and when factories began springing up during the New Deal, blacks streamed into the city from all over middle Georgia looking for jobs and a better life. Rhythm and blues was starting to kick up its heels, and Macon became a nurturing ground. "Little Richard" Penniman washed dishes at the Greyhound bus station by day, and learned his craft by night at the Douglass Theatre and in little clubs like Miss Ann's Tick Tock. Riding the r&b crest was deejay Hamp Swain, who hosted the popular "Night Ride" show on WIBB and drew musicians to Macon to perform live on his radio program. Hamp helped introduce Little Richard to the world and also put a young kid just out of reform school on his show one night, launching the career of the Godfather of Soul, James Brown. Hamp's final discovery was Otis Redding.

Hamp had devoted white listeners, and one of them was a brash kid named Phil Walden, who had grown up in Macon. "I was just fascinated by that music," Phil said. "I had never been exposed to something that *raw* in my life. When I heard 'Wop bop a lubop a lop bam boom,' I knew I didn't want to sell insurance or used cars. I wanted to be in the music business." He opened up a management and booking agency when he was still in college and one of his first clients, a local group called Johnny Jenkins and the Pinetoppers, included Otis Redding as a part-time member. Phil and Otis became fast friends, and when Otis went out on his own in the early sixties, Phil became his manager. By 1967, everything was going right for Phil Walden and Otis Redding. Otis was on the cusp of superstardom and Phil had the largest agency in the business, representing r&b stars like Sam and Dave, Percy Sledge, Joe Simon, Joe Tex, and Clarence Carter.

And just like that, it was over.

Late that year, Otis wrote and recorded an odd-sounding song called "Dock of the Bay" that he thought was going to be his breakthrough on the pop charts. The people at Stax Records weren't as sure and some even argued against releasing it. Two days after finishing that record, on December 9, 1967, Otis was scheduled to appear at a club in Madison, Wisconsin. The weather was bad and commercial flights in the area had been grounded. Otis insisted on making the gig, and he and his backup band climbed into a small plane. As it approached Madison, the plane plunged into the icy waters of Lake Monona. The King of Soul was found the next day, strapped into the copilot's seat and still wearing a headset plugged into the control panel.

Redding's death was much more than a professional loss for Phil Walden; a part of him died with Otis Redding in that airplane. "I swore I'd never get so involved with another artist," he said. "And then Duane Allman came along."

THE Chamber of Commerce likes to brag that Macon boasts more churches per capita than any other city in America. The town is conservative and God-fearing and, after having to coexist with the outrageousness of people like Little Richard and James Brown for twenty years, most of the locals were ready for the music industry to get out of town so the city could slip back into its natural sleepy anonymity. Then Phil Walden brought the Allman Brothers Band to town.

"Those people thought we were from another planet," Gregg said. "It was a real culture shock." Dickey was expecting the worst, a place where long hair could get you shot. "We'd go to places like the Waffle House and you'd think, 'Oh, man, we've only been in town for a week, what's going to happen?' " he said. "But people realized we were there for the music and not for any underground kind of reason."

The band set up housekeeping in a two-room apartment in the bottom floor of a three-story tenement at 309 College Street. The house was the mongrel on a row of worn-down houses in what had once been one of Macon's most exclusive neighborhoods. The band called the place the Hippie Crash Pad. It was small and cramped, and the only furniture was five or six mattresses thrown on the floor and a Coke machine full of beer.

The band was soon joined by Kim Payne and another roadie, Mike Callahan, both rough-and-tumble bikers. Callahan liked to regale them with mysterious tales of the drug trade in Florida, where he had grown up and then worked as a roadie for Second Coming. Later, they would be joined by Joseph "Red Dog" Campbell. "He'd been selling little matchboxes full of marijuana out at the park in Jacksonville," said Kim. "When he came around, we had to change his name. It was just 'Dog' and everybody was calling Duane 'the Dog.' " Campbell had flaming red hair, so he became "Red Dog."

It didn't take long for trouble to develop with the neighbors, especially over the late-night indoor corkball games. "We'd be in there, sliding into third base — that was the Coke machine — and just yelling and a-hollering," Butch said. "Goodness gracious, how we stayed out of jail, I'll never know. I mean, this was four in the morning and this is an apartment building full of people. Instead of calling the cops, everybody moved out. Within a month, we had emptied that apartment building. I mean, there was nobody left."

One afternoon three or four of the guys strolled into a little soul food joint called the H&H Restaurant. The guys sat down at a table, huddled over the menu, and then ordered one plate of food. The co-owner of the H&H, a matronly looking black woman named Louise Hudson, known by everyone as Mama Louise, took the order out to their table and they sat there eyeing it, obviously embarrassed and determined not to make a move until she left. Mama Louise turned the corner back into the kitchen but peeked back out. When she saw they were all eating off that one plate, she shook her head, walked into the kitchen, and emerged with a plate of food for each one of them.

Mama Louise took a liking to Duane and the rest of them, and she would turn her head if the fellows were too broke to pay the tab. That was an all-too-common occurrence, since the only steady income was the government checks received by Red Dog and Twiggs Lyndon, the Phil Walden assistant put in charge of the band. The job situation was rather unconventional: the employees paid their bosses a salary rather than the other way around. "Twiggs and Red Dog would get in their VA checks and we would take three dollars a day apiece," Butch said. "We learned how to buy cigarettes and wine and food for three dollars a day. And that's how we lived for about two years."

Life was uncomplicated; the days were spent making music, trying to get high, and trying to get laid. Every afternoon, their stomachs often full on soul food from Mama Louise, the band would gather in an old warehouse complex that Phil owned and play music for hours.

Phil had set up a rehearsal hall in a big room that had once been a sheet metal shop. The warehouse also had a barbershop, and just behind that, an old upholstery shop that Phil was turning into his recording studio.

The band relied heavily on old blues songs and worked up arrangements of songs like "Hey Joe," "Born in Chicago," "Crossroads," and "Born Under a Bad Sign." They were depending on Gregg for original material, but of the twenty-two songs he brought back from California they liked only three. One of them, "Whipping Post," initially received a lukewarm reaction from the others. Only Berry was interested. "He heard something in the song that none of the rest of us heard, this frightening kind of thing," Dickey said. "He sat up all night messing around and came back in the next day with a new opening in 11/4 time and after that ideas started flying from every direction." The band rehearsed it over and over until they had transformed the song into something that was menacing, almost dangerous.

"Our rehearsals consisted of a lot of sitting around and playing, improvising," Dickey said. "Gregg would have a song with chords. We'd forget about the song and just play off two or three chords, and just let things kind of happen. Berry would start a riff, and everybody would go to that and try to build on it. And if it didn't happen, we'd go on to something else. As vague as it sounds, I think that's why it sounded so natural; that whole thing was a real natural process."

The new band took the best parts of Hour Glass and Second Coming and fused them into a unique new sound. "Hour Glass was really heavily influenced by the urban blues, whereas Oakley and I were cosmic travelers," Dickey said. "We were taking psychedelics and we were really putting that into what we were doing musically. When those things collided, sparks flew."

While drugs were used as a critical component of the band's creative process, dope was scarce. "We were dirt broke and we didn't have anything in the way of recreational drugs really, except for scrounging or bumming," Kim Payne said. Then came a godsend; a friend of Mike Callahan's dropped by and left behind a big paper sack full of psilocybin tabs — psychedelic mushrooms.

"Every day we'd go down to the barbershop and practice all day, and then come back and take some psilocybin and raise hell all night," Butch said. Psilocybin was so essential to those early days that the band adopted mushrooms as its symbol, and every member had a tiny mushroom tattooed on his upper calf.

For companionship, they soon picked up on the presence of

Wesleyan College, a conservative all-female school and, before long, the band had its first groupies. "We had these two fine little girls from Wesleyan that just loved to come to orgies there at the Hippie Crash Pad," Butch said.

The school had a curfew for its students, and they couldn't leave unless someone came to sign them out. "We used to go over there and check these girls out for the weekend," Kim said. "I remember me and Duane went over there one time. We were tripping our brains out on psilocybin. We were just wired up, man. That stuff did that to you. It was real electriclike. It'd make your hair stand up. Duane had on this fringe jacket and that red hair was just standing straight out. We went in to sign them out and you'd just make up a name. So he signed it, 'Electric Duane.' I mean, it's supposed to be somebody like their parents, or aunts or uncles. Electric Duane. That just blew me away."

Late at night, the band members would often walk a couple of blocks down College Street to Rose Hill Cemetery, a quaint and rambling graveyard that dates back to 1840. They had a favorite spot far away from the main entrance, a grassy area near the railroad tracks. They would sit in a semicircle, passing around joints and a bottle of Ripple. Then they would pull out acoustic guitars and play music until the wee hours. There, in the shadow of moonlit tombstones, the Allman Brothers Band wrote and rehearsed the songs that would make them famous. It was a ritual no less eerie than the legend of Robert Johnson going to the crossroads in the black of a Mississippi midnight, trading his soul to the devil for the ability to play the blues on the guitar.

DUANE often brought in some extra cash by going back to Muscle Shoals to play studio sessions. In early May of 1969, he lent his lead guitar to the debut album of Boz Scaggs, a singer who had grown up performing with Steve Miller and had hooked up with Phil Walden. Jann Wenner, publisher of *Rolling Stone*, was there coproducing the record. Duane played lovely bottleneck on a National Dobro on two cuts, "Look What I Got" and an old Jimmie Rodgers song, "Waiting for a Train." Playing electric slide on the fade-out of a song called "Finding Her," Duane introduced a lick that would later become famed — the sound of a crying bird.

Out of those sessions came a blues called "Loan Me a Dime," written by Fenton Robinson, that was transformed from a simple four-minute song to twelve minutes of scorching emotion in the hands of

Duane, Boz Scaggs, and the Muscle Shoals studio band. It begins with a sad, sorrowful intro; Duane's guitar seemingly crying over the soft backing. Duane sets the mood, then Boz comes in to tell the story: "Somebody, loan me a dime," he sings mournfully. "I need to call my old time, used-to-be." The band is barely present, only the funeral-toned organ of Barry Beckett and the laid-back drums of Roger Hawkins can be heard distinctly as the singer recalls the woman he loved, lost, and now longs to find again.

At the end of the second verse, the music stops. The silence is a desperate, musical plea. Duane's lead guitar comes in over a bass line by David Hood that sounds like a thumping heart. Moments later, the whole band jumps in and Duane begins spitting out notes, carefully measured, yet unabashedly passionate. From then on, his guitar is locked behind the vocals, accenting each line. With Boz's final plea for the woman he has lost, the tempo slowly creeps faster and faster. Duane launches a five-minute solo that begins controlled and restrained, and then explodes with pure, wild abandon. It was one of the best white blues ever recorded, an instant classic.

Six days later, the Allman Brothers traveled to Atlanta to continue a tradition that had started in Jacksonville — performing for free in a public park on Sunday afternoons. "Playing the park is a good thing because people don't even expect you to be there and about the nicest way you can play is just for nothing," Duane said. "And it's not really for nothing, it's for your own personal satisfaction and other people's, rather than for any kind of financial thing."

Atlanta's growing hippie population was centered in the area of Tenth Street, near the large and rambling Piedmont Park, and an underground paper called *The Great Speckled Bird* had begun sponsoring weekend "be-ins." On May 11, 1969, a band from Macon that no one had heard of showed up to play. The jam kicked off with "Trouble No More" and the hundreds of hippies who sauntered over to the ball field were mesmerized. The following week, Duane's picture was on the cover of *The Great Speckled Bird*, and a story inside raved about the music. "The general opinion going through the crowd was that these guys could stand up against the best — Hendrix, Cream, etc.," wrote Miller Francis. "I am not alone in the opinion that they may be one of the great pop music discoveries of 1969."

The Allman Brothers Band may have been building a reputation with the hippies in Atlanta but it was still, for all practical purposes, a garage band out in the middle of nowhere with a hotshot manager and little else. Despite Jerry Wexler's involvement, Atlantic Records wasn't eager to sign the group to a recording contract. So Wexler came up with a rather novel idea: Phil Walden should launch his own record label and record the Allman Brothers Band, and then Atlantic would distribute the album. That way, Atlantic would have no financial risk and nothing to lose; it just had to put the album out there. Since the two men shared Capricorn as their astrological sign, Wexler came up with a perfect name: Capricorn Records.

Before Wexler sprang his idea, Phil Walden had moments when he doubted the wisdom of his faith in the Allman Brothers Band; the group was running through money like a sieve, and nobody other than Wexler seemed remotely interested. Phil's decision to stake his future on Duane Allman, and spend $18,000 to get Duane out of his contracts, must have struck many as the ultimate in foolishness. "It doesn't sound like much now, but it was a lot of money for a guitar player who did not sing particularly well, and people in the business thought his particular tour de force existed as a session player," Walden said. "There was not a long line of record companies outside my door when I signed Duane Allman and his group."

Like Phil Walden, Jerry Wexler had also thrown away his customary caution. "It's not my style to get a producer, give him a lot of money, and tell him to go do something," Jerry said. "I made an exception in the case of Capricorn because of my trust in Phil Walden and Duane Allman. Although nothing had been proven yet, I had a feeling that something good would come out of it."

In July of 1969, Phil Walden presented the band a three-page contract. "I have carefully considered the advisability of obtaining your assistance and guidance in the furtherance of my career in the entertainment field, and have made independent inquiry concerning your ability and reputation," the agreement begins. "I have determined that your services would be of great value in the furtherance of my said career by virtue of your wide knowledge of and reputation in the entertainment field. I have determined that I wish you to act as my exclusive, personal manager in the entertainment field." The five-year deal gave Walden a 25 percent cut of the band's income and included a clause in capital letters that Walden must have put in his standard management contract sometime during his r&b career: "YOU ARE NOT AN EMPLOYMENT AGENCY. YOU HAVE NO OBLIGATION TO SECURE ANY EMPLOYMENT FOR ME."

No one read the contract, and no one hired a lawyer to explain it. They were all kids — Dickey was the oldest at twenty-five, Jaimoe was twenty-four, Duane and Butch were twenty-two, and Gregg and

Berry were twenty-one. All they cared about was the incredible music they were creating. "Phil came in and laid it down on an amplifier during a break. And I signed it on top of a Sunn speaker cabinet," Butch said. "In fact, you can probably look at the paper and see the 'Sunn' indentation from the amp. Our only thought at the time was making music. We had found something new and hot and that's about all we cared about. Once I signed the contract, he took it. I didn't worry about it. None of us did."

Jaimoe was the only one who didn't sign, although Phil worked as his de facto manager for the next five years. "Jaimoe had been involved with Phil before and didn't like the way he did business," Butch said. "Jaimoe had been a sideman with people like Sam and Dave, and Joe Tex, and Phil's approach was to take care of the star and to hell with everybody else."

One month later, Capricorn Records was set up under the umbrella of Phil Walden's No Exit Music corporation and the band inked its recording contract using the tentative name of "The Allman Band." The contract stipulated a modest 5 percent royalty rate and gave Phil veto power over any personnel changes. It also entitled Phil to recoup the $18,000 he had spent to free Duane of his old contracts; that money would be deducted from the band's future royalties.

In retrospect, many of the terms of the five-year pact were hardly favorable to the band; there was no provision for an accounting of expenses deducted from royalties, the contract didn't stipulate an advance, and there was no annual audit to track the income the band was generating. But at the time, they were happy just to have a recording contract. Besides, they trusted Phil and that was enough. Duane knew *this* was *the* band, and he was glad to have a record company that would stick with the group if their first, or even second, album didn't sell. He wanted no more Allman Joys or Hour Glass experiences. Phil was willing to take that chance.

"The main thing was, he believed in us," Dickey said. "All those big record executives from New York and Los Angeles would come hear the band and say, 'It's never gonna work; all the songs sound the same and it's too different.' And Walden would say, 'I hear it.' And I have to give him credit for that. He heard it and he stood behind it."

Part II

The Rise

My, my, my, right before my very eyes
Satan came with fire to burn me . . .

— Gregg Allman, "Stand Back"

Six

Dreams

THE band's first gig outside of the South was a showcase that Phil set up in Boston at a club called the Boston Tea Party before an audience primarily made up of booking agents, music executives, and rock critics. "There was a lot of pressure on them that night and things really didn't go all that well," said Jon Landau, the *Rolling Stone* writer who is now Bruce Springsteen's manager. "The group really hadn't found its identity yet. I remember a couple of music business people came over to me and said they didn't really think the band had it. You knew there was something going on, but it really hadn't taken its shape yet."

The club's owner was among the minority who liked the band, and he offered to book them again in a couple of weeks. They couldn't afford to drive all the way to Macon, then come back to Boston in a few days, so they took up residence in a condemned building in Boston. The place had no electricity and was full of huge rats; to get power, they talked a neighbor into letting them run an extension cord. "We think that's where Dickey caught the hep," said Kim Payne. "Right after that, he had a bad case of hepatitis. He was just dark yellow and looked like he was dead. He was flat on his back for weeks."

True to tradition, they played free in a park the next Sunday, and the second Tea Party gig was better than the first. But the failure at the showcase had serious ramifications — the band had performed in front of the industry heavyweights and failed to impress them. "Atlantic Records is telling us we don't have a chance, you know, a white band from the South just standing there," Butch said. "They wanted us to get Gregg out from behind the organ, put velvet pants on him and stick a salami down his pants and get him to jump around like an English sissy boy. But we wouldn't do it, said to hell with it."

Duane Allman had a vision for his band, and they all held to it steadfastly. When the band went to New York in mid-August of 1969 to cut its first album, they were determined never to repeat the experience of having a record company dictate their music. "Before we went into the studio, we had a very clear idea of what we were all trying to do musically and that it was unique, totally different from anything else that anyone was playing," Dickey said. "From the earliest rehearsals, we all had the same mind-set."

Commercial success wasn't a real priority; they were all seduced by the music they were playing and they knew that, sooner or later, it would find an audience. "All of us had been in bands where you'd get some jack-leg producer who gives you five or six songs and says, 'Record these just like this, and in six months you'll be farting through silk,' " Butch said. "And we'd all do it and we'd hate the stuff. But the producer would say, 'It's great, it's a hit.' Well, it didn't sell nothing. So when we got together playing this stuff, it felt so good that we just had a tacit agreement that that's what we were going to do. We never expected to make a lot of money. We felt like we'd get a good solid following, but not a big one, and be strong enough to make three or four thousand dollars a night. That was fine; that's really what we were after."

THE Allman Brothers Band came along just as a fundamental change in the way rock bands were presented to the public was taking shape. For much of the rock era, bands playing original music had traveled primarily as part of package tours. The theory was that no single act could draw enough fans on its own to fill a hall, so a concert would feature four or five stars and each group would have a thirty-minute time slot, with the headliner playing for maybe an hour, even less. The only place to play lengthy shows was in teen clubs like the Martinique in Daytona Beach or small venues like the Whiskey A Go Go in Los Angeles. There was no money in that, and people tended to want to hear some Top 40 hit they could dance to.

All that started to change when Bill Graham opened the 2,200-seat Fillmore West in San Francisco, followed by the Fillmore East in New York City. Graham had a creative instinct for bookings and he brought an eclectic array of rock and blues and jazz groups to his venues. One night, Albert King might open for Jimi Hendrix. Then Led Zeppelin would be on a bill with jazz great Woody Herman.

Graham fast became one of the most powerful people in the rock industry and was one of the first people Phil Walden contacted once he signed Duane Allman's band. Hour Glass had played at the Fillmore West, so the promoter knew Duane and Gregg. But he knew Phil even better because of Graham's intense love for the music of Otis Redding. Because he had managed Otis Redding, Phil Walden had instant credibility with Bill Graham, who booked the Allman Brothers Band into the Fillmore East before he had even heard them perform.

In late November of 1969, the band returned to New York to play its first gig at the Fillmore East. No one had ever heard of them, and the crew around the Fillmore expected a bunch of redneck yokels — an image that was reinforced when the band drove up in a beat-up, old Ford Econoline van and began setting up a bunch of ragged Marshall amps. Then the sound check began. The band launched into an old blues song called "You Don't Love Me," and everyone in the building stopped working; they just stood there and listened.

The Allmans opened for Blood, Sweat and Tears that night, and suffered the humiliation of getting booed. But the band picked up a strong ally in Bill Graham. He recognized the potential of the Allman Brothers Band, and knew that Blood, Sweat and Tears didn't attract the kind of fans that would be into blues-based rock. He began booking the Allman Brothers regularly in his two halls when the group was hard-pressed to find gigs anywhere else. There was just one problem: one of his theaters was on the West Coast and the other was on the East Coast.

The band's debut album, called *The Allman Brothers Band*, was released in November of 1969. The first few moments offered a strong statement of purpose, especially for a band that seemed suddenly to appear out of nowhere. The two guitars were locked in unison on a five-note melody, behind them was a driving bass, and the drums — it sounded like there were two sets of those as well — pulsated with powerful precision. There was the hint of an organ. Then the beat shifted. One drummer concentrated on his hi-hat as if playing jazz, and the organist played a solo right out of the Jimmy Smith songbook. The tempo shifted again and settled into a lazy blues shuffle.

The first guitar solo was elegant, almost hypnotic. The second guitar came in behind the first one for a darting buildup that sounded like something taken from Brahms. It ended quickly as the second guitar took over for a solo; the tone was fatter, the vibrato more pronounced. Then the buildup came again, this time taking the melody higher and higher until it stopped, to be picked up by the first guitar, this time with a sharp and nasty tone. The tempo was guided into a slow blues while someone with gravel in his voice cried out in an unintelligible wail. It was impossible to categorize, but whatever it was, it was a stunning introduction to the Allman Brothers Band.

That opening instrumental, an old Spencer Davis tune called "Don't Want You No More," had been on the Second Coming song list and it segues into a traditional blues sound on a song Gregg had written in Los Angeles for an old girlfriend, "Not My Cross to Bear." Another song Gregg penned about the same lady, "Blackhearted Woman," follows, and the guitars are still locked together, creating three different recurring themes in the first forty-five seconds.

The album shifts back to the blues for a searing version of "Trouble No More," and it marks Duane's debut on the bottleneck guitar. Again, the guitars create a trademark riff, then Gregg comes in with snarling vocals while Duane plays brief countermelodies in the pauses between lyrics. "Trouble No More" is the first example of how the Allman Brothers could significantly alter a traditional blues arrangement, staying within the song's structure yet also expanding it.

"Dreams," another song Gregg wrote in Los Angeles, is a brooding and melancholy masterpiece. It begins with intricate, subdued drums playing under a soft organ with only the hint of guitars before Gregg begins singing about disillusionment and broken dreams. Duane takes a long solo; his guitar is achingly sad, and the first notes bend out of his Les Paul like a muted cry. Halfway through, he slips the Coricidin bottle onto his left ring finger. The emotions simmer, rising and falling, then climb to a crescendo as he glides the bottle up the neck of his guitar with a dramatic flourish that builds and builds until it gently touches down with the crash of a cymbal.

If "Dreams" is haunting and sad, then "Whipping Post" is threatening and ominous. Gregg had written the song in Jacksonville just after his return from Los Angeles. The house was dark, and he was about to go to sleep when the song came to him. Gregg knew he had to write it down before he forgot it, but there was a child in the room and he couldn't turn on the lights to find a pencil and a piece of paper. He improvised. There was an ironing board next to the bed, and Gregg decided it would do fine as a paper substitute. He struck two kitchen matches; he used one for light and blew out the other, using the burnt charcoal as a pencil. Striking match after match, he began writing down the words on the cover of the ironing board. "The next morning I caught hell for it, too," Gregg said.

The song begins with Berry's bass rumbling hot and angry; then Duane joins in followed by Dickey, all playing the same notes at different places on the scale, until Gregg comes in to sing the tale of betrayal. Duane and Dickey take quick solos before the song builds to an anguished climax. When the band stops, Gregg's voice is alone, stripped bare and chilling: "Good Lord, I feel like I'm dyin'." The band comes back with soft strains of sorrowful guitars that finally fade away into nothingness, closing the album.

IN early January of 1970, the band climbed into its old van to drive out to San Francisco for a gig at the Fillmore West. "We went all the way to California, got as far as the Golden Gate Bridge, and didn't have the fare to pay the toll to get across," Butch said. "So Oakley's out going from booth to booth looking for young ladies to get the money to get across the bridge."

Berry finally found two women who gave him the toll in exchange for backstage passes to the Fillmore. From there, the band headed down the coast to Los Angeles to play the Whiskey A Go Go, the old stomping ground of Hour Glass. Then they had to drive straight through to New York. It was about as miserable as miserable gets; the heater kept quitting and it got so cold that they could see ice starting to form inside the cab. Everyone was grumpy, buzzing on downers and cough syrup with codeine.

"We only had a couple of days to make it," said Butch. "We had two mattresses laid in the back of the van, and we'd picked up about five hundred Mexican reds and Jaimoe got about two gallons of Robitussin A-C. So we got in that van and everybody's taking four or five reds, and drinking three or four ounces of A-C. If you had the misfortune of waking up, you'd just take some more reds and drink some more A-C. After about a day of that, you talk about attitudes. If somebody rolled into your space, you'd have to pull the van over to duke it out."

They pulled over for a bathroom break at a truck stop near

Chicago, and by then, it was going to be a minor miracle if someone didn't get murdered inside the van on the way. "It was snowing and there was ice and slush everywhere," Butch said. "So we got back in the van. Oakley had just had his little girl and he comes in with this damned life-size stuffed Saint Bernard. He had a hard time getting that thing in the van. I mean, everybody's got this good barbiturate hangover and is pissed off already. And there's no space as it was. Before he got in, he had to promise that that damned Saint Bernard wouldn't touch anybody."

The snow finally grounded them, and they stopped for the night. These were kids from the South and the snow intrigued them — they had to go outside and play. "We'd been drinking Ripple all night, we had enough money to get a case of Ripple," Butch said. "So we walk outside the motel and it's all farmland. We've got a bottle of Ripple with us and come up on this horse that's out there. And the poor horse has got an inch of ice all over him. We felt sorry for him. We went up, petted him for a minute, and gave him some Ripple. He drank about a half a bottle and turned around and kicked at us. We're way out in the middle of this field and there's three or four feet of snow out there and we'd never seen snow. So somebody says, 'I wonder what it'd be like to run around in this shit naked?' Me and Gregg pulled our clothes off, and I'd give anything for a film of that, the two of us gallivanting around in the snow. And we almost died because we got so cold that we couldn't get our clothes back on; my hands were so numb, I couldn't feel anything. We were lucky we didn't freeze to death. I guess the Ripple was the antifreeze that kept us alive."

The Fillmore gigs were crucial; reputations could be made or forever tarnished at Graham's two concert halls. New York was the media center of the world, and Fillmore East shows always attracted industry heavyweights. In San Francisco, the stakes were just as high because *Rolling Stone*, which had quickly grown into the most influential music magazine in the country, was based there. Phil lobbied hard with the magazine's editors for a write-up of the first album, but he couldn't have anticipated the response of critic Lester Bangs when a review finally surfaced in early 1970. "For all the white blooz bands proliferating today, it's still inspiring when the real article comes along, a white group who've transcended their schooling to produce a volatile blues-rock sound of pure energy, inspiration and love," Bangs wrote. "The Allmans know what they're doing, and feel it deeply, and they communicate immediately."

With Bill Graham's seal of approval and the impressive *Rolling*

Stone review, bookings began picking up considerably. The band was on the road five days of the week and would perform about five hundred shows over the next two years. The Allman Brothers used those early concerts to hone the band's sound. They rarely performed a song the way it had been released on the album. Instead, the studio versions served as a road map for the audience, a frame of reference. Songs that clocked in at four minutes in the studio were often doubled or even tripled in length during concerts.

"The first year or two on the road, we'd get up and play, and in most places the audience was sitting out there drugged and they didn't really know how to react to it," Butch said. "They knew something was going on but they really didn't know what. And half the time, we'd get very little response. So we'd just kind of drop a wall between us and the crowd and just play for ourselves. That music's what kept us going."

The band was always experimenting with arrangements and kept adding influences to its blues-rock base. Elements of jazz, already present in Jaimoe's drumming, were beginning to turn up in other ways. "Duane and Berry was very much into rhythm and blues, and I kind of turned them on to a lot of jazz things," Jaimoe said. "John Coltrane and Miles Davis were Duane's favorite jazz people. 'My Favorite Things,' by Coltrane, he loved. And that Miles Davis thing, *Kind of Blue*. Duane's favorite song was 'All Blues' from that record."

In the beginning, the jams had been built from songs like "Hey Joe" and old blues tunes. But with Jaimoe's influence, the band began stretching out. "Jaimoe turned us on to Miles Davis and Coltrane and that's about all we listened to for a long time," Butch said. "We didn't listen to any rock 'n' roll at all. We started getting a little more complex and experimenting with rhythms and melodies."

Several jazz groups, most notably Miles Davis and the Mahavishnu Orchestra, were incorporating rock beats into their music, but the Allman Brothers Band was the first to approach that synthesis from the opposite direction. It was a rock group with a jazz sensibility and the skill to pull it off. The influence was most apparent on a song Dickey had written, a complex and melodic instrumental called "In Memory of Elizabeth Reed," which used "All Blues" as a blueprint with its dominant and secondary themes and long improvised solos.

The two guitarists played off one another like Miles and Coltrane, often both going at the same time and always pushing the other to take the music further and further. "One thing that made the music unique is the fact the two guitar players weren't clones of each other," said Jaimoe. "And it was the same thing with the drums."

The two drummers had an instinctive ability to communicate musically. Butch laid down the solid beat and Jaimoe added intricate jazz flourishes; Butch drove the band and Jaimoe gave it grace. "The fun thing I discovered early on with me and Jaimoe was that you could do anything you wanted to," Butch said. "I mean, half the time I'd just go for it. I'd get so goddamned lost that I wouldn't have any idea where the 'one' [in the four-bar beat] was. But I'd act like I knew what I was doing, you know, keep going and stay in the meter and start looking over at Jaimoe until I found out where that 'one' was. And then I'd jump right back in. And everybody'd go, 'Goddamn, did you hear that? That's jazz, man.' And I had no idea what I'd just did. But it worked. It always worked."

Seven

A Brotherhood of Enlightened Rogues

DUANE was not only the father figure for Gregg but the one everyone in the band looked to when a decision had to be made. "Duane was the force," Butch said. "We all had talent, but Duane is the one that put the fire in us. He's the strongest person I've ever known. He's the type, you'd be sitting in a room with about two or three hundred people talking and he walks in and everybody looks. Something just came through, charisma, whatever you want to call it."

Backing up that aura was a talent for knowing how to read the members of his band. He knew when to cuss and when to cajole, when to soothe and when to shout. Butch had come from a folk-rock background and he had periods when he would totally lose his confidence — if the band started a jam and things didn't seem to be coming together, Butch would think it was his fault. "I'd get nervous about my playing and get shy and start apologizing," he said. "One day, we were playing this shuffle, that started happening, and I started backing off. Duane whipped around and stared me in the eye and got way up high on his guitar and hit this lick and just looked at me like, 'Come on, you son of a bitch.' I went, 'Oh, shit,' and really backed off. He did it again and after about the third or fourth time, I started getting mad and started bearing down and saying, 'Motherfucker' under my breath. After about thirty seconds or so, he just backs up and smiles and says, 'There you go.' And it just sunk home that there ain't no reason to back off. I could play and I knew it and I never did that again. He did that with just about everybody in the band. Dickey used to be real sensitive."

Dickey's strength was his talent for coming up with unique melodies; many of the dual guitar riffs were sparked by his ideas. But he was still in the process of developing a distinctive voice on lead guitar, and it was both a blessing and a curse for him to be in a band with Duane Allman. Every solo Dickey played either preceded or followed that of a master, and it was hard for him not to get brushed aside in the excitement over Duane's genius. Dickey could brood and he had a fierce temper; one day he was the friendliest person in the world and the next he could strike fear with his glaring, cold eyes.

Duane understood that Dickey's insecurities had to be soothed and always made sure that Dickey understood he was a vital component of the band. Even more, Duane went out of his way to play up his partner's abilities to the public. When they performed one of Dickey's songs onstage, Duane nearly always mentioned to the crowd that Dickey had written the tune. He seldom did that with his little brother. Once, during a radio interview, a listener called in and asked if Duane was going to continue playing twin guitar leads. "That's Dickey Betts playing that other guitar, that's not me," Duane responded. "He is just as bad as there is, man. He can smoke the guitar, man. See, I'm the famous one, man; he's the good player."

For Gregg, Duane remained the protector. He gave Gregg direction and would lay into him if he saw that Gregg was screwing up. When Kim Payne first came to Macon, he had been wary of seeing them together; back in Los Angeles Gregg had told him he fought with his big brother constantly. "I didn't see it; I saw a lot of love there, especially from Duane," Kim said. "It was 'Baby brother this' and 'Baby brother that' and 'Baby brother can't do no wrong.' Now when he talked *to* baby brother, it was a little different. Then it was: 'Get your fucking act together and quit acting like a fool.' And Gregg would always cower and say, 'Okay.' "

AS their reputation grew, it was as if the Allman Brothers Band and Phil Walden had turned on a soft flicker of light; white musicians from all over the South saw it and then sought it out. Long-haired kids toting guitars began migrating to Macon, checking out the scene and hoping Phil Walden would make them stars.

Duane kept telling Johnny Sandlin to move to Macon, and finally he agreed. "Phil called me several times," said Johnny. "I told him that I wanted to produce and he said he'd give me a shot. A lot of my friends were in Macon. And Phil, the fact he had managed Otis Redding, that was about enough right there for me." Duane and Johnny then went to work on Paul Hornsby. "Where the hell is Macon?" had been his initial response, but he eventually agreed to join them. Then came Scott Boyer and David Brown from Butch's old band, the 31st of February. They would all, in turn, convince musician friends to come to Macon. It grew into a close-knit community, the beginnings of a vibrant rock scene. Phil Walden would give it direction but Duane Allman was the figurehead.

The members of the Allman Brothers began settling in and putting down roots in Macon. First, they had brought their wives, girlfriends, and children to town and moved into apartments near the Hippie Crash Pad. Duane was living with a tall, model-thin blond named Donna Rooseman, who had been with him off and on since Muscle Shoals and came to Macon pregnant with his child. Galadriel Allman, born on August 25, 1969, was named after the wise and beautiful Queen of the Elves in Tolkien's *Lord of the Rings* trilogy; Duane was a voracious reader and the series was one of his favorites. Galadriel was three months premature and at birth weighed only three pounds, ten ounces. She spent the first five weeks of her life in an incubator.

For a while, Dickey lived with his wife, Dale, and their daughter, Christi, who was just over a year old, in a flat on College Street. But ever the lone wolf, Dickey soon moved his family out to an old lakefront cabin on a farm west of Macon called Idlewild South, where the band often rehearsed. Berry's wife, Linda Oakley, had given birth to Brittany Annie Oakley the previous April, and the family moved to an apartment with his sister Candace. Butch and Linda Trucks moved into the same building. Since there were two Lindas in the extended family, they started calling Linda Oakley "Big Linda" because she was about six feet tall, a few inches taller than Berry.

By the spring of 1970, Linda Oakley had rented a fourteen-room, Grand Tudor–styled house in a historic neighborhood on Vineville Avenue about a mile from downtown Macon. The $235 monthly rent was split three ways: Berry and Linda; Duane, Donna, and Galadriel; and Gregg and Candace, who were in a short-lived relationship. It became known as the Big House and served as the center of the extended family. One of Berry's first purchases was a huge dining-room table. "It was important to him to maintain some semblance of normal family life when they were not on the road," Candace said. "He took great pleasure in supervising all the meals, including the planning and preparation. Berry was like the self-appointed master of ceremonies to everyone."

In many ways, the household was very traditional — the men worked, and the women raised the children and kept house. But it had its hippie touches. Miles Davis played on the stereo. Berry kept two big jars of tea in the kitchen; regular tea was in one and in the other, marked with silver duct tape, was the "electric tea," laced with acid or some other psychedelic. Duane put baffling up on the walls of a front parlor and they used it for rehearsals and jams.

As the band settled into Macon, it began reaching out to the community. In early 1970 the Macon Jaycees were trying to raise $2,500 to help build a high school for mentally retarded children, and it shocked a lot of people when Twiggs Lyndon called up the president of the organization and offered to have the band perform a benefit concert. Many of the Jaycees were fresh out of college and into the music of the Allman Brothers Band, so they were pleased. But when the organization wanted to do the show at the staid Grand Opera House, Macon's blue bloods were afraid it would be destroyed if longhairs were allowed inside.

The Jaycees prevailed and the show went off without a hitch. Berry told the local paper it was the band's way of giving something back to Macon. "We've had a lot of success professionally, and we're now in a position to do something for the good of the community," he said. "We live here, together as one big family with children of our own, and we realize how precious it is to be able to enjoy the harmony and good health of a happy home."

There was a definite communal spirit within the band and its extended family, a togetherness and warmth that translated into the music. "We were out there, it was just us," Kim Payne said. "A lot of the places we were doing gigs in, there were not any long-haired people. A lot of the towns we had to pass through to get to those places didn't approve of long-haired people. They had signs out that said, 'Hippies and dogs keep out.' We all stuck together. We depended on each other and we became real close. We were a brotherhood."

That obvious bond and the band's southern sense of place were becoming a part of the band's aura. The Allman Brothers went against the stereotype, beginning with the fact that it was one of the few integrated rock bands around, and gave many people their first insight into what was grand and distinctive about the South.

"Macon was not the hub of the music world, and they were working against some kind of odds," writer Jon Landau said. "Ultimately, it was one of the things people found so attractive about them. They conveyed a sense of roots, a sense of stability, a sense of realism. And that became very, very important. They were authentic. As someone who came from the North, Duane Allman represented something that was going on in the South that most people where I lived didn't know anything about. I saw young people asserting themselves in the South in the same way young people had in Boston and San Francisco and New York, which came as quite a surprise to people with too many preconceptions about the South. Duane Allman was in the vanguard of the New South."

ENLIGHTENED rogues. That's how Duane used to describe his band. And there was an intriguing duality. They were a group of guys from the South playing brilliant, sophisticated music who projected the image of peaceful hippies totally devoted to their art. And yet they also were throwbacks to the outlaw days of the Old West, like Butch Cassidy's Hole-in-the-Wall Gang — lovable yet dangerous as they roamed from town to town, playing rock 'n' roll rather than robbing banks. "One thing I can say about the people in our band is that they're straight with themselves," Duane said. "If you've got something good to lay on them, you can enlighten them. And if you've got something bad to lay on them, you can get your teeth knocked clean down your throat, man. Dangerous people. Lovely people."

It was a grueling lifestyle: driving hundreds of miles every day and playing for two or three hours, and then getting up to do it all over again. In early 1970 the band junked the old van and bought a Winnebago. It was a big improvement, but it was still a lot like picking up the Hippie Crash Pad and setting it on wheels. The drugs numbed them to the endless monotony of strange faces, darkened stages, and indistinguishable roadsides. In the beginning, there were the psychedelics that they used to pull the music from inside themselves. Then came pills and cocaine and heroin.

One rule of the road was that when the band was traveling, the "old ladies" stayed at home. Berry was devoted to Big Linda and Jaimoe was painfully shy around women, but most of the guys freely indulged in the women who hung around backstage looking to bed a rock star. "Back in the early days, we'd all take speed, man, and just

have a damn fuckathon," Gregg said. "It was like three of us [and] six
or eight groupies, just laughing like hell, crazed."

It was inevitable that someone would pick up something, and
Butch caught a case of the clap that proved hard to cure. "It ate penicillin for breakfast," he said. When the standard treatment didn't
work, the doctor tried something else. "It was this syrupy stuff that
forms a knot in your ass and it takes about a week to dissolve. For two
or three days, I couldn't even walk. We were out on the road, bouncing
around in that Winnebago. I'm out there thinking that I'm going to be
the first guy in rock 'n' roll history to die of the clap." His doctor
finally figured out that the infection was resistant to penicillin.

Then somebody came down with the crabs. "Living like that
and one person gets it, well, it spreads," Butch said. "Everybody
wound up getting them but me. I was laying in the bunk one night
and saw this little dot walking towards me. I looked down and it
got right up next to me, then turned around and went the other way.
So I figure I'm immune to them. We're heading out west and everybody was just scratching themselves raw. We got about as far as
Amarillo, Texas, and we stopped and got one motel room. Twiggs
goes down to this drugstore, walks up to this pharmacist, and, as loud
as you please, says, 'I want a case of Pyronade A-two hundred.' The
guy says, 'A case?' So he comes back to the motel room; all of us
proceed to shuck down and start to line up. You ever used that stuff?
It burns like the dickens, and in a minute or two, you've got all
these guys, buck naked, lathered up, and jumping all over the place.
But nobody wanted to be the first to break for the shower because
you're supposed to keep it on you for a while. Finally, one of the
roadies broke and then everybody broke for the showers. I wasn't
quick enough; last in line. By the time I got in there, all my skin was
burned off. Christ, I guess we left about ten million dead crabs in that
motel room."

There wasn't much Twiggs couldn't fix. He was wily, resource-
ful, and absolutely devoted to Duane Allman. "His role was anything
from conducting the daily business affairs to baby-sitting," Phil Walden said. "Checking in and out of hotels, collecting money, making
sure the equipment worked — just about every function that could be
assumed with a traveling band." So when it seemed that the band was
getting jerked around by a club owner at a little dive in Buffalo called
Aliotta's Lounge, Twiggs went to take care of it. The gig was on April
29, 1970, and the band had driven all night across New York State to
get there. It was yet another long trip that had them all teetering

on the edge; the road was like a monster that had a never-ending appetite.

When they arrived, the club owner, Angelo Aliotta, told them they were to do two shows that night. The band was tired but agreed. They left the equipment overnight at the club and when Kim Payne and Mike Callahan went back the next afternoon to pack up, Aliotta said they had breached their contract because they had shown up fifteen minutes late the previous evening. He refused to pay them unless they agreed to play one more night.

Kim called Twiggs. A few minutes later, he showed up at the club and Kim spied the scabbard tip of Twiggs's ten-inch fishing knife underneath his coat. Twiggs went behind the bar and demanded to be paid. He and Aliotta began arguing and they were soon on the floor. Kim and Mike Callahan figured Twiggs was beating up the guy. They thought he was an asshole who deserved a little roughing up, so they deliberately walked slowly over to the bar to pull Twiggs off the fifty-five-year-old club owner.

Twiggs stood up when they got there. Kim looked down and saw that Twiggs was holding the fishing knife. It was drenched in blood. Then Aliotta pulled his shirt off and Kim saw the stab marks. Twiggs went to a table and Kim followed him. "What'd you do to him?" he asked.

"I stuck him," Twiggs said.

"Man, you better fucking haul ass," Kim told him. "The cops are gonna be here."

Twiggs shook his head and sat there. "I ain't running," he said. "I ain't going nowhere."

Aliotta had been stabbed three times — once in the arm and twice in the abdomen. He died about an hour later and Twiggs, twenty-seven at the time, was arrested for first-degree murder. "We'd been pushing it real hard, hitting a lot of speed and all that shit," Kim said. "He was trying to put the squeeze on us. And Twiggs just snapped."

There was nothing the band could do; Twiggs was being held without bail. They made sure he got a good lawyer, then hit the road for the next gig. The monster had to be fed.

THE making of the album that would be called *Idlewild South* stretched over seven months in 1970. The band would go out on the road, then zip down to Miami to Criteria Studios for a few days of recording before heading back out. Named after the farm where Dickey lived, *Idlewild South* stands alone among Allman Brothers albums. Tom Dowd, the legendary Atlantic Records producer, was brought in to supervise the sessions, and the record's overall sound is gentle and reflective, layered with acoustic guitars. Jaimoe plays congas almost exclusively, as though someone feared that two drummers would overwhelm the record, and Dickey plays a subservient role to Duane.

The first song, "Revival," states the intentions. Instead of two wailing guitars, the tune begins with a lone acoustic that is soon joined by the twin Les Pauls playing a relaxed melody that soars to the upper reaches of the fret boards until it comes gliding down. Then Gregg comes in. "People, can you feel it? Love is everywhere," he sings. "Revival" marked Dickey's emergence as a songwriter and meant the band now had two people who could come up with tunes. It was a perfect opening number for the album, highlighting the image the band was projecting of a group of carefree hippies from the South in love with their music and their families.

A song Gregg wrote, "Don't Keep Me Wonderin'," follows. Duane plays slide and the recording includes harmonica player Thom Douchette, who was an old friend of Berry's from Florida. Butch propels the song; Jaimoe does little more than tap the side of his drums or a cowbell. Duane is aggressive during his solo and, at the end of the song, his bottleneck guitar and Douchette's harmonica lock in together as the song builds to a powerful finale.

"Midnight Rider" is the song most associated with Gregg. Co-written with Kim Payne, it was very nearly lost before the band had a chance to hear it. Gregg came up with it one night after they had come off the road and were resting up in Macon. All the amplifiers and guitars were stacked up in the old rehearsal hall on Broadway; it wasn't the best neighborhood, so Kim was spending the night with the equipment to protect it from burglars. "Gregg came down to the warehouse," Kim said. "He was playing and we were doing a bunch of speed and he kept going on about this midnight-rider thing. He was having a time with the words and it was actually getting irritating."

Gregg was stuck on the second verse and Kim kept trying to get him to shut up. "Well, I'm trying to get this thing," Gregg snapped back.

Kim shouted out: "Look, the road goes on forever. Use that."

Gregg grinned. "Yeah, yeah; that's great, man."

They quickly finished the words. Gregg knew the song was good and he was afraid he would forget it before he could get it on tape. "Well, I ain't got no fucking tape recorder on me, man," said Kim.

Gregg looked over at the wall that separated the warehouse from Phil's recording studio. "Well, there's a whole fucking studio next door, man," he said in a conspiratorial tone. Kim was there to protect the studio and warehouse from burglars; now, he found himself busting out a window and breaking in so Gregg could get the song on tape.

Dowd's production on the final version is brilliant. The low-key performance has the feel of everyone sitting on a front porch and jamming on a nice April evening. Jaimoe's congas are prominent and help set the song's mood, as does the inventive riff Berry uses for his bass part. Duane's solo is right out of the style of James Burton, the renowned rockabilly guitarist who can make his Telecaster sound like a pedal-steel guitar. Then Dickey joins him and plays long, sustained notes while Duane answers each time with quick flourishes.

Dickey's other masterpiece on the album is the band's first instrumental, "In Memory of Elizabeth Reed," the band's homage to Miles Davis. The droning organ behind the lovely melody is haunting, and the song evokes emotions that shift with the tempos — gentle memories, bitterness, loss. Then comes Dickey's lead guitar, full of hot passion, with Butch's drums accenting every note. It is Dickey's first real solo on the record and he plays with fury, alternating quick bursts of notes with slow, bending ones.

Gregg follows on the organ before Duane begins a long solo that showcases his near-perfect sense of drama and resolution. Duane takes the song to a screaming climax, and then the band falls out. All that's left is Butch alone on drums gently bringing the song back down with Jaimoe soon following on congas. The full band comes back and, like a resigned farewell, repeats one of the themes. There is one final cry of emotion and it's over.

"In Memory of Elizabeth Reed" is stunning in its originality and imagination, a sophisticated blend of intricate melodies and furious jamming. Dickey has always been mysterious about the origins of the song. "I've never told the truth on that," he said. "About half the truth is, there used to be this place I'd go that runs along the river in the old graveyard in Macon. And I'd sit there and write a lot. It was just a good place. And the part that I really can't tell the truth about is who the song is written for. It was a girl of Italian descent and that's why the song has that Latin feel to it. I didn't know what to name it because I couldn't name it after this particular person. So there was this gravestone that said 'In Memory of Elizabeth Reed Napier,' and I used it."

Elizabeth Reed, who was born on November 9, 1845, was a popular belle who moved to Macon to study art and music at Wesleyan College and married into the prominent Napier family. She died in 1935 at the age of eighty-nine on Rogers Avenue, only a couple of hundred feet away from the Big House. The woman who actually inspired the song was the girlfriend of Boz Scaggs, who was living in Macon and being managed by Phil Walden. "Some writer once asked me how I wrote the song and Duane said, 'Aw, he fucked some girl across the tombstone and that's what it's about,' and don't you think that got printed in an instant," Dickey complained. "You can imagine how the girl I wrote it for felt after that."

The first real blues on the album is "Hoochie-Coochie Man" with Berry on lead vocals. It begins with his ominous-sounding bass and then builds to a crashing crescendo. Dickey takes the first solo and then Duane comes in, playing low bass notes before he jumps up high on the guitar neck and ends with a flourish. "Please Call Home" is Gregg's best vocals on the record; his voice is tender and pleading, and Duane adds soulful fill-in notes.

Idlewild South may be the best studio album the band would ever record. The music is warm and inviting, and it was a big step in boosting the band's popularity. The first record had sold a scant 34,000 copies but the second would crack the *Billboard* charts. With their fame growing, the members had not forgotten Mama Louise and her soul food at the H&H Restaurant. The album cover included the simple credit "Vittles: Louise."

The reputation of the Allman Brothers was spreading by word of mouth, and it seemed as though every time the band played a venue there would be more people in the crowd than the time before. Already, there were whispers that they were the most exciting live band around; maybe even the best, period. "The Allman Brothers' live dates were great, greater, greatest," Phil Walden said. "You were not disappointed. They were always very, very good. Some nights, they were absolutely unbelievable."

THE Second Annual Atlanta Pop Festival was held on Fourth of July weekend in 1970, though it was in Atlanta by name only. The festival grounds were actually at a stock car racetrack in a small farming community called Byron about fifteen miles below Macon. Much of Georgia braced for the worst, and Governor Lester Maddox called the festival "one of the worst blights that has ever struck our state." To the kids, it was no such thing; this was Woodstock, man, *southern-style.*

Considering that 100,000 people crashed the gate and at least 300,000 eventually showed up, things went amazingly well. The temperature hovered around 100 degrees and water was scarce, but the kids shucked their clothes and swam in a nearby lake. The sound system was excellent and drugs were plentiful — dozens of hippies set up roadside concession stands of pot, pills, and LSD while agents from the Georgia Bureau of Investigation walked by filming the scene with movie cameras.

The Atlanta Pop Festival would later be described as the first great rock event of the seventies; Jimi Hendrix was there, and so were Richie Havens and B. B. King and Spirit and Johnny Winter and Bob Seger. But they were all outsiders, coming from places that most of the kids in the Deep South had only read about. The Allmans were different. This was their home and it was as though the band had invited the rest of the rock world to come to Middle Georgia and check out the neat stuff going down in Macon.

The Allmans played on a Friday night, and Duane and Berry rode down on motorcycles with Roger Cowles, who had come to Macon from England to do public relations for Capricorn Records. "About seven o'clock in the evening, the sun was pretty low in the sky, and someone was standing up on stage in Indian attire talking about peace and harmony," Cowles said. "He gave a simple mantra and it went out over this whole place and it was amazing to feel the energy going around as the sun was going down." Minutes later, a woman in the crowd gave birth. Then the Allman Brothers Band took the stage.

The thousands of kids greeted them like heroes. Duane plugged in his guitar and turned his back to the crowd to tune up. When he finished, he played a little hot lick. He turned back around and faced his first standing ovation of the night, just for that one throwaway riff. In front of the biggest crowd they had ever seen, the guys played over two hours as a light, cool rain fell. At one point, the parachute roof over the stage partially collapsed. Instead of stopping the music while it was repaired, Butch and Jaimoe just kicked into a drum solo.

It had started out as a sort of homecoming; it ended as a coming of age for the Allman Brothers Band.

Eight

Layla

TOM DOWD had been in the midst of recording *Idlewild South* when Eric Clapton's manager called to ask if he would produce Clapton's next album. When he hung up the phone, Dowd turned to Duane: "Boy, a guitar player you're going to love is coming here — Eric Clapton." Dowd didn't know that Clapton had been one of Duane's heroes. "Oh, man," Duane responded in an excited voice. "I'd love to meet that guy." And he picked up his guitar and played a series of Clapton licks for the producer.

The Clapton sessions kicked off a few weeks later, and Duane called down to Criteria Studios and told Dowd that the Allman Brothers would be playing in Miami; he wondered if he could stop by the studio and meet Eric Clapton. When Dowd hung up the phone, he turned to Eric and said, "There's a chap I've been working with named Duane Allman who's coming to town." The Allman Brothers Band had made virtually no impact in England, but Clapton immediately recognized the name. "The guy that plays all those licks on 'Hey Jude'?" he asked. And Clapton began playing some of Duane's riffs for Dowd. The orbits of Duane Allman and Eric Clapton, the two best white guitarists in rock, had just come together.

One thing they already shared were stints with Delaney and Bonnie Bramlett, a husband and wife team from the South who had become popular in England. After leaving the spotlight of Cream,

Clapton had sought anonymity by playing lead guitar for the couple. And when Clapton recorded his first solo album in 1969, Delaney produced it and his band backed up the guitarist. Not long after that, the band staged a mutiny over low pay and left Delaney and Bonnie to play with Clapton full time.

The move left the couple without a back-up group as they were going into the studio in mid-1970 to record *From Delaney to Bonnie.* They used Atlantic studio musicians, and Delaney told Jerry Wexler that he wanted a slide player for the sessions. Delaney requested Ry Cooder, but he was unavailable. When Wexler suggested a substitute, Delaney was dubious. He'd been in England for the better part of two years, and had never heard of Duane Allman. "I don't think you'll be disappointed," Wexler smugly promised.

Once they met and played together, Duane and Delaney became immediate friends. They used to drive out to Jerry Wexler's house on Long Island and jam until the wee hours. "The best I ever heard Duane play wasn't on a record, it was with Delaney," Wexler said. "The two of them would play acoustic guitars at night. They'd be outdoors on my deck, singing Jimmie Rodgers and Robert Johnson songs." Duane often stayed over, usually going to bed only when he was at the brink of exhaustion. "He used to sleep so hard," Wexler said. "Once, he had a gig and I couldn't get him up. My kid played the trumpet, and he got his trumpet and played it in Duane's ear. And he finally woke up."

As Delaney and Bonnie were finishing their album, the core of their old back-up band — pianist Bobby Whitlock, bassist Carl Radle, and drummer Jim Gordon — was in London with Clapton putting down tracks for *All Things Must Pass*, George Harrison's first solo record. After that was finished, Clapton kept the group together and they began performing incognito in clubs, using the moniker "Derek and the Dominos." The audiences quickly recognized Eric Clapton, but they didn't recognize a lot of the music. Instead of his hits with Cream, Clapton was playing blues tunes and songs of obsessive love that he had written about Patti Boyd Harrison, George Harrison's wife, and the inspiration for his most famous song, "Something."

Clapton had grown close to George and moved to a place not far from the Harrison household. He visited often and soon realized that he was going to see Patti as much as George. "I remember feeling a dreadful emptiness because I was certain I was never going to meet a woman quite that beautiful for myself," Clapton said. "I knew I was in love. I fell in love with her at first sight."

A friend had given Clapton a book by the Persian poet Nizami called *The Story of Layla and Majnun,* the tale of a man whose love for a woman drives him to madness. Her beauty was so intoxicating, the first spark of connection so intense and magical, that Majnun had "already given his heart to Layla before he understood what he was giving away." Eric immediately identified with the characters and "Layla," the song and the album, became Eric Clapton's cry of love for Patti Boyd Harrison and his plea for her love in return.

THE Allman Brothers concert in Miami was August 26, 1970, a Wednesday night. Duane had planned on stopping by Criteria after the show to meet Clapton, and he was hoping to be invited to sit in on a song. But Clapton insisted on shutting down the sessions and going to the gig; he wanted to hear the Allman Brothers Band. The only place for Clapton to sit was at the audience barricade in front of the stage, and he had to crawl on all fours to get there. Duane was in the middle of a solo, and when he looked down and saw one of his heroes sitting a few feet away, he froze. Dickey was puzzled when Duane stopped playing; he figured Duane had broken a string, decided he'd better cover for him and came in on lead. Then Dickey looked down and saw Clapton. And he turned his back, or else he would have frozen, too.

The guys from both bands hung out together after the show, and they spent the entire next day and evening in the studio jamming on old blues songs. Dowd recorded some of the jam sessions, and he caught on tape an intimate moment when Eric and Duane were alone and quietly playing their electric guitars on a couple of Elmore James songs, "It Hurts Me Too" and "Dust My Broom." Clapton plays a soft rhythm while Duane plays bottleneck on the first one. Duane then shifts into the famous riffs that open "Dust My Broom" and Eric quickly falls in behind him. Duane was nervous; the jam falls apart when Eric comes in on lead and Duane begins playing rhythm to the wrong song.

"It turns out they were both afraid of each other," said Criteria engineer Karl Richardson. "Duane was obviously in awe of Clapton and Clapton had been listening to Duane and he was in awe of Duane. So the two of them, when they finally met, they looked at each other and it was like, 'Oh, I'm scared of you' and 'Yeah, I'm scared of you, too.' "

For most of the night, Duane and Eric sat in the studio showing each other guitar licks and playing blues standards. "It was four-way conversation; the guitars were talking to each other, and the heads were talking to each other," Dowd said later. "They went on like that until four-thirty or five in the morning."

Duane got his wish: Clapton asked him to play on a track or two of his album. The following day, Duane helped cut a tune Clapton and Bobby Whitlock had written called "Tell the Truth." Even on that first song, there was an instant kinship and immediate interplay between Duane Allman and Eric Clapton. The song kicks off with a concise Clapton guitar riff, then the band comes in. Duane glides up the fret board with his bottleneck and plays fill-in notes in the pauses between the lyrics. Clapton also played slide on the song: when he and Bobby Whitlock join together to sing "Can you feel it," Clapton plays the guitar chords using a bottleneck. He also plays slide on the rising melody after the second verse while Duane plays a secondary lead behind him.

Nothing was recorded Saturday. But the next day, Dowd was able to catch a moment of inspired spontaneity. The band had kicked into a medium-tempo blues, and Dowd was so taken by it that it took him a couple of minutes to notice that the tape recorder wasn't rolling. He whipped around to the engineer and yelled, "Hit the goddamn machine!" The tape comes on at the conclusion of a bottleneck lead by Duane, and Eric comes in with a solo that is relaxed, brassy, and superbly confident. He plays two bars, then lays back for Duane to take over. But it's as though Duane wants to hear Clapton play some more; he hits only a couple of brief riffs before Eric comes back in to fill the empty spaces. Then Clapton begins singing Big Bill Broonzy's "Key to the Highway."

When Duane comes in on bottleneck, Jim Gordon suddenly picks up the beat on his drums and they all fall in behind him. There is a moment during Duane's solo when he has slowed the tempo to a crawl, then picks it back up with an old Chuck Berry phrase. The two guitarists are so in sync that Clapton had begun to play the very same lick; he hits one note of it, realizes Duane is already there, and stops cold. Duane and Eric play on for nearly ten minutes, pushing the song through ebbs and flows, trading lead licks and obviously getting off on hearing the other play.

It must have been at about this point that Clapton started getting serious about using Duane Allman on the entire record. Until then, there hadn't been a whole lot on tape worth keeping. Everyone in the band was indulging in prodigious amounts of hard dope and the sessions lacked focus. "We didn't have little bits of anything; there were no grams around, let's put it like that," Bobby Whitlock said. "Tom couldn't believe it, the way we had these big bags laying out everywhere. Cocaine and heroin, and Johnnie Walker." When writer Robert Palmer went to Miami to do a story on Clapton, he walked into the studio and found everyone on the floor, nodded out. With Duane's arrival, things began to fall into place. Right away they had nailed "Tell the Truth," a song they had struggled with even back in England. "All of a sudden the catalyst was there," Dowd said. "It was just a matter of putting things into shape."

Clapton absolutely loved to listen to Duane play, and having him there kept the pressure off; Eric was very content to sit back, play a lot of rhythm guitar and let Duane Allman run free. "I was just going to play on one or two [songs] and then as we kept on going, it kept developing," Duane said. "And Eric said, 'Okay, man, we're going to make us a record here and we're going to have two guitar players instead of one.' We worked our butts off on it. Everybody got behind it, with no ego trips or anything. It's just good music all the way through."

If the first two songs hadn't cemented things in Clapton's mind, then the next two, recorded the day after "Key to the Highway," did. First, they cut "Nobody Loves You When You're Down and Out," the old Bessie Smith classic. Duane came up with the arrangement — the same one he had used two years earlier with the 31st of February. Then he laid down wonderful bottleneck notes underneath Clapton's vocals, which Clapton followed with one of his best solos on the album.

The second song recorded that day was one that Clapton and Bobby Whitlock had written in England, "Why Does Love Have to Be So Sad?" It was the first of the songs written for Patti Boyd Harrison that Duane would be involved with, as though he had passed the gauntlet and they now trusted him to share in their secret stash of magnificent songs of love and despair.

The intensity level on the session picked up considerably beginning with "Why Does Love Have to Be So Sad?" Eric plays a two-chord riff to start it off, Whitlock's organ swells and rises up, and Duane's lead guitar comes in at the apex. From that point on, Duane is locked in behind Clapton's vocals in one of the most emotionally charged performances of his career. He hurls out notes that echo every word Eric sings, lyrics that are like one continuous primal scream from the depths of Clapton's love. It is the first time that Duane has played straight guitar on the session, and he takes the lead break. Clapton soon jumps in and they are both playing at the same time, each of them pouring out notes with such intensity that it often seems to border on going out of control until they ever so slightly rein it back in. As Duane Allman and Eric Clapton over-dubbed the lead breaks, everyone in the studio stood in awe, mesmerized by the electricity flying between them, the complete concentration and instinctive anticipation, as these two masters focused in and combined the power of their music into one singular statement.

Duane left Miami after recording that song, but the group carried on and recorded "Keep On Growin'," followed by "I Looked Away" and one of the record's masterpieces, "Bell Bottom Blues." Duane was back Wednesday for "Have You Ever Loved a Woman?," a slow blues that had been popularized by guitarist Freddie King. Clapton and his band had been trying to get the song on tape ever since they got to Miami, but two early versions failed to capture the burning intensity that would ultimately show up on the version recorded with Duane.

The track begins on a Clapton riff and he plays a passionate Freddie King–inspired lead before he begins singing. The tempo shifts into a heavy beat when Duane comes in for a bottleneck lead that pushes the song's emotions higher and higher. Clapton then takes over on his Stratocaster, beginning at the crest where Duane left off and then taking it even further. It wasn't a case of one-upsmanship — they were bringing out the best in each other and daring one another to take it up an extra level. There are blues solos as good as the ones Duane and Eric play on this song but very few that are better.

Thursday was a full day in the studio. They recorded "I Am Yours," a ballad Clapton had written after reading *The Story of Layla and Majnun*, and he pulled enough of the lyrics directly from the book to give Nizami co-writing credit. It is a simple yet beautiful song, one of the album's tenderest moments; he tells her that he will love her forever, no matter how much distance comes between them. "Any Day" was another Clapton and Whitlock song, and Duane decided the introduction needed punching up. "Hey, let's make it like a Roman chariot race," he said, playing a riff that started on the bass notes and then slid high up the scale. The song begins with Duane playing at the bottom end while Clapton uses a slide for the high parts and then for a quick lick during the interlude before he comes in on vocals. Both guitarists use bottlenecks on the chorus; Clapton plays full chords while Duane echoes the melody playing single notes. Duane takes the solo, playing the first half of it with his fingers, and then slipping on his Coricidin bottle at the end for a three-note progression that seems to scream, "Believe in me!" over and over and over. The third song from that Thursday session was "It's Too Late," written by r&b star Chuck Willis and propelled by Duane's bottleneck solo.

Duane had skipped a couple of Allman Brothers Band gigs to play with Clapton, but he tore himself away from Miami for the next six days and nothing else was cut until he returned. Despite the haze of heroin and cocaine, the band had been recording at a furious pace. Duane Allman had met Eric Clapton on August 26 and had gone into the studio with Derek and the Dominos two days later. The band had recorded eleven songs over the next seven days, some of them among the greatest in rock history. Everyone present in the studio was keenly aware they were witnessing something magical. "We knew it was phenomenal," engineer Karl Richardson said. "Absolutely. You couldn't *not* know that the music flying out of Studio B was phenomenal. You'd have to be deaf."

The songwriting was the heart of the record. The music was all firmly based in the blues, full of odd turns and twists that come unexpectedly yet instantly feel right. And in the lyrics, Clapton was laying bare a very private part of his being — he was a romantic Don Quixote, tilting at windmills and making poetry out of the seeming futility of his eternal hope. The final crucial ingredient was Duane Allman, who always rose above the level of the material he had to work with. If it was good, he could make it great; if it was great, he could make it brilliant.

Duane was back in Miami on September 9, and the band cut "Little Wing," a beautifully winsome song written by Jimi Hendrix. Duane's guitar is heavily echoed as he sweeps up the fret board on the introduction. On the lead break, his bottleneck creates swirling menages of sound that have a haunting, heartbreaking undertone. "Little Wing" was intended as a tribute, from two members of the triumvirate of guitar greats of that era to the third. But Jimi Hendrix never heard the loving version of "Little Wing" that Eric and Duane crafted in his honor. Nine days after the song was recorded, Hendrix was found dead in his London apartment from a drug overdose.

The other track they recorded that day was a song that Eric had written back in England after he'd first read *The Story of Layla and Majnun*, a ballad called "Layla" that he described as "just a little ditty." Then Duane encouraged him to speed it up and make it a driving, rock 'n' roll song. Butch Trucks happened to be hanging out in the studio control room the day they recorded it. "Eric and Duane were playing the song back for us and all of a sudden Duane said, 'Let me try something,' " Butch recalled. "And he put on his guitar and came up with that signature phrase that just kind of set that song on fire."

Those seven heart-stopping notes that open "Layla" comprise the most exciting introduction in rock since Chuck Berry's "Johnny B. Goode." This is the song where all the emotion and all the desire burst loose in one furious blaze of impassioned lyrics and driving music. There is an army of overdubbed guitars — no fewer than seven guitar tracks are used on the song — and a brilliant shift of key between opening notes and the verses that adds drama to the music before Clapton comes in to sing the desperate opening lines: "What will you do when you get lonely, when nobody's waiting by your side?"

Duane is mixed underneath the vocals, playing nonstop lead guitar while Clapton sings in a tone that is angry and biting, chiding Layla for hiding behind her foolish pride. Yet the chorus is a plea: *Please, come back to me.* The song rides a delicate balance between his anger and his need to believe there is still hope, and the final lines quote Robert Johnson as Clapton begs her not to tell him that his love is in vain. From there, the song soars on the energy of the screaming slide guitars of Eric and Duane, with Duane breaking free to play an otherworldly counter-melody.

Three minutes later, the song gently touches down and it is Jim Gordon, the drummer, who sits down at the piano and begins playing a sweet and tender melody. That final section of the song was recorded a couple of weeks after the first part and, in an inspired moment, was put at the end of "Layla" with a nifty tape-splicing job by Tom Dowd. "Jim Gordon wrote that and had been secretly going back into the studio and recording his own album without any of us knowing it," said Clapton, who played only the acoustic guitar on the coda. "We caught him playing this one day and said, 'Come on, man. Can we have that?' And we made the two pieces into one song." The piano coda becomes the personification of the vulnerability and sadness of his love for Layla. The one theme is played over and over, rising and falling in intensity and always colored by the gliding bottleneck symphony crafted by Duane. It fades with Duane making his guitar sound like a crying bird.

Everyone sat in a circle in the studio with acoustic instruments when the final song, "Thorn Tree in the Garden," was recorded. Eric fingerpicks the rhythm guitar and Duane plays chiming notes and soft slide on the chorus. "Maybe some day soon," Bobby Whitlock sings at the song's conclusion. "Some way." Somehow, the hope remains. Beyond everything else, still, he *believes*.

MIXING the album — balancing all the instruments and the vocals and deciding which parts of the music to emphasize and which instruments to downplay — was difficult. Often, three or four or more guitars were going full throttle at once, and Dowd had to find the right blend among them. Dowd had captured a huge guitar sound, and most people assumed that Duane and Eric were playing through powerful Marshall and Fender amplifiers.

In truth, both guitarists used tiny amps, primarily two Fender Champs about a foot tall. "We closed the top of the piano and set the amps up on it so that the Champs were at ear level," said engineer Ron Albert. "It was the only way that Eric and Duane could hear themselves. You'd turn them up to ten, stick a microphone on them and go."

Dowd faced a tight deadline of two days to do the mix, and the final night was even more rushed because Clapton was about to return to England. "Eric had the last flight out," Karl Richardson said. "Tommy was in there mixing with him, and I was sitting in another room putting the album together. It was in the middle of the night, around five in the morning, and Eric had a six o'clock flight. I remember it was scrambled eggs there at the last."

They also faced technical problems. One night a couple of women were hanging out in the control room, and one of them spilled coffee on the master tapes. "I remember Tommy Dowd and I standing at the tape machine with what they call Chem-Wipes, which are very absorbent, non-chemical–treated tissue," Karl said. "And we passed the master tape back and forth through the reels getting all the coffee out of it."

In addition, a quirky tape player caused most of the songs to turn out either faster or slower than their natural tempo. "Layla" came out so fast that it was nearly a half music step up, and many thought the variations were deliberate. "There's no reason for it except the mixdown machine was an old Ampex three-fifty-one," Karl said. "At the beginning of the reel, you'd record a little slow, and at the end you'd record a little quickly."

When the album was finished, Clapton took it to Patti and played it for her. "She didn't give a damn," he would cynically say later. Following a brief Derek and the Dominos tour after the album was released, Clapton would spend the next two and a half years holed up in his house feeding his heroin habit, longing for Patti and barely touching his guitar.

Clapton was eventually saved by Pete Townsend, himself a former junkie who had managed to wrangle free of the powerful tentacles of heroin. As Clapton came out of his fog, Patti was growing apart from George Harrison and Clapton decided to make his move. He drove over to the Harrison house one evening with Pete Townsend and, while Pete and George chatted in one room, Eric was in another talking Patti into leaving her husband. "He did two remarkable things," Townsend said. "He actually straightened himself out from being a junkie, and then he went out and made his fantasy happen."

Eric and Patti began living together in 1974 and married five years later. The always fragile union would end in divorce in 1988.

Nine

Live at Fillmore East

FOUR weeks after finishing the *Layla* album, Duane was obviously buzzing when he showed up at a New York radio station for a live interview. The words raced out of his mouth. "Hello, everybody out there in radio land; take off your underwear, relax, and let ol' Duane tell you just how it is," he said following his introduction. The disc jockey asked how he was doing. "I'm drunk, man," Duane responded. "I feel good, man. Let's talk. Man, I've been doing bunches of D-O-P-E and acting C-R-A-Z-Y and all the other stuff you can't talk about on the air."

Duane had never been shy about doing drugs, from the Testors glue back in Daytona Beach to "Vitamin C," the band's nickname for cocaine. He had a high tolerance level and if he didn't think he was getting off enough, he'd just go do some more. A couple of weeks later, in late October 1970, the band made a stop in Nashville, Duane and Gregg's hometown. There was a jam session that night and someone showed up with a bunch of "tar," the slang for opium. Everybody ate a chunk of it and no one thought twice when Duane asked for a second helping.

The band seldom traveled at night, preferring to sleep and then leave during daylight. But early that morning, everyone except Duane was wide awake and they decided they might as well get a head start to the next gig. Duane was asleep in another room and someone went to wake him up. They couldn't rouse him, but he was a hard sleeper anyway. Then they turned on the lights. Duane's lips and fingertips were the strangest tint of blue, and he seemed to be having trouble breathing.

An ambulance was called, and they drove the Winnebago to the hospital and anxiously waited outside. When a doctor finally came out, he was somber. "We'll do what we can but there's not much hope," he told them. "He's pretty far gone." They listened in stunned silence. Tears began streaming down Berry's face and he looked up to the sky. "Please, just give him one more year," Berry pleaded. "Whatever there is up there, please, just one more year."

About an hour later, the doctor returned: Duane had come around. He was going to be okay.

ROLLING STONE gave *Layla and Other Assorted Love Songs* only a lukewarm welcome. While Ed Leimacher called it "one hell of an album," he also accused *Layla* of being full of filler material like "Bell Bottom Blues" and "Have You Ever Loved a Woman?" It was indicative of the public reception the record received. Tom Dowd had walked out of Criteria thinking *Layla* was the best record he had made in ten years. To his dismay, it was hardly noticed after its release. "The pity of it was that it took a year for the thing to hit," Dowd said. "When it didn't hit in the first six months, I just thought, 'The public is just a bunch of assholes. They don't know what the hell is good or bad anymore.' Then six months later, it was like the national anthem."

Rolling Stone did pose the question that music fans would ask for years: Who plays what? When is it Eric Clapton and when is it Duane Allman? The album's sound was so dense that it was often next to impossible to tell the two apart. No one realized just how much room Clapton had given Duane on the record, and the final consensus was that Duane must have played the bottleneck parts and Eric must have played the straight leads.

Duane beamed with pride when he talked about his role on the album, especially when he played "Layla" for friends. "He brought a rough tape of the album back after he'd been working on it," Johnny Sandlin said. When the tape reached "Layla," Duane jammed his thumb against his chest and said, "That's my lick." But in public, Duane went out of his way not to hype himself. To Duane, it was a team effort. "For anybody who don't know and cares enough about it to know that, I play the Gibson, Eric plays the Fender," Duane said.

"If you can tell between a Gibson and a Fender, then you'll know who played what."

It wasn't much help, but Duane knew what he had done and that was enough. *Layla* was Duane Allman's personal validation as a guitar player. He had stood on equal ground with one of his heroes and, for perhaps the first time, he began to realize just how good he was.

Rolling Stone was kinder to *Idlewild South*, calling it a "big step forward" for the Allman Brothers Band and describing "In Memory of Elizabeth Reed" as "stupendous." The *New York Times* also reviewed *Idlewild South*, calling it "exciting and bold." Sales exceeded expectations and it rose to number thirty-eight on the *Billboard* charts. Still, the guys grew less and less satisfied with it as time passed. There was a huge gulf between the Allman Brothers Band onstage and the Allman Brothers Band in the studio, almost as if it were two different groups. "The stage is really our natural element and we haven't got a lot of experience in making records," said Duane. "We get kind of frustrated doing the records and I think our next album will be a live recording to get some of that natural fire on it."

The logical place to do the live album was the Fillmore East. Bill Graham had supported them early on when no one else thought they would amount to anything, and besides, they loved playing there; the New York crowd was hip and the building had a great sound onstage. "I played the Fillmore with Otis Redding when it wasn't the Fillmore. It was the Village East Theatre," Jaimoe said. "That stage was smoking, believe me. You could walk on that stage, man, and you could hit your instrument and the presence of it was *there;* it had echo off the back of the room. The acoustics were just great."

The band was booked at the Fillmore on March 12 and 13, 1971, a Friday and Saturday, two shows each night. From the moment Duane's bottleneck rang out on "Statesboro Blues" until they called it a night with the majestic ending of a long instrumental called "Mountain Jam," the band gave definitive performances. "That's all for tonight, thank you," a weary-sounding Duane told the audience after the last song. When they protested and continued to yell for more, Duane went back to the microphone. "Hey, listen, it's six o'clock, y'all," he said in a gently scolding tone. "Look here; we recorded all this. This is gonna be our third album and thank you for your support. You're all on it. We ain't gonna send you no check, but thanks for your help." Duane giggled and walked off the stage.

Tom Dowd was there to record all four concerts, and each night after the shows he and the band members would ride up to the Atlantic Studios and listen to the tapes. When the stand was finished, they were flush with the knowledge that they had pulled it off. It was there. On tape. Finally.

The *Fillmore East* album would be a glorious testimonial to a truly great rock band at the height of its power. It had been a weekend when the musical decisions were all in perfect sync. The melody lines screaming out of the guitars seemed almost mystical. And for the first time on record, the magic of the Allman Brothers finally came into the sharpest focus.

The songs they selected to kick off the album were four blues that progressively grow more sophisticated and act as a homage to the band's roots. "Statesboro Blues," the Blind Willie McTell song that had inspired Duane to play the bottleneck guitar, quickly kicks the album into high gear. The arrangement is basically the same one Duane and Gregg had used in Hour Glass, true to the Taj Mahal version. But the Allman Brothers play it with a strength and grace that Taj Mahal hadn't imagined. Jaimoe and Butch propel the band with the authority of a churning, revved-up '57 Chevy, and Duane plays the bottleneck with pure confidence, using compact licks to accent Gregg's growling vocals. Duane takes the first solo, and on the second half, when he reaches for the high notes, the band lifts up behind him with such subtle grace that it almost goes unnoticed.

The second song is a version of the Elmore James classic "Done Somebody Wrong." Duane is again on the slide, and Gregg sings in a voice that, in the finest blues tradition, is remorseful on one verse and boastful on the next. Harp player Thom Douchette sits in with the band and takes the first solo, followed by a bluesy lead break by Dickey. After another verse the traditional arrangement is thrown away. The band plays a fast buildup of notes that Duane somehow performs on slide. Then he guides the bottleneck high on the fret board, playing in a way that Elmore James could not have ever imagined. Few slide guitarists even try playing that high — the space between notes on the guitar string has narrowed to virtually nil and it demands instant precision. Yet with Duane it seemed natural, effortless.

Duane Allman was taking the bottleneck guitar to places it had never been. He had an inherent talent to play exciting combinations of notes, but his style also developed because he learned to play in a vacuum. His only reference point was old blues records, and because he had no one to show him the traditional styles, he veered off into directions that no one had ever considered before. Duane was the next link in a bridge that stretched back to Elmore James and then on to Robert Johnson. Even more, he also was a master of standard guitar playing and developed a style every bit as unique as his slide work. The bottleneck masters seldom played standard guitar; Duane was a true rarity, a dazzling voice in both.

"Done Somebody Wrong" is followed by another song that echoes the band's roots, T-Bone Walker's "Stormy Monday." The best-known recording of "Stormy Monday" had been cut by Bobby "Blue" Bland in the early sixties. That was the one that Duane and Gregg first heard, and many of the guitar parts played by Duane and Dickey come directly from the Bobby Bland version. The Allman Brothers Band's version is another unique arrangement of a traditional blues. Duane takes the first solo; he starts out slowly, then builds to a scintillating crescendo of notes that leap back and forth between two musical scales. As the song segues into Gregg's organ solo, the tempo shifts into a swinging beat, a daring touch that the group also used on an old Ray Charles blues, "I'm Gonna Move to the Outskirts of Town." Then Dickey comes in with a solo that also starts out laconically before building to a rousing finale that shimmers with emotion and clarity. Gregg sings the final verse in his world-weary voice, and when the song concludes, Duane hustles to the microphone and says with pride, "Brother Gregg Allman singing the blues" as the crowd roars its approval.

"You Don't Love Me" is the bridge between the blues songs that have preceded it and the long jazz-influenced jams to follow. Duane kicks it off and Butch falls in behind him, tapping the side of his snare drum. Then Jaimoe begins playing a funky beat that gets even funkier once the whole band comes in. After the vocals, Duane and Dickey each take solos, followed by Gregg and Thom Douchette.

By then the song is already six minutes long but the band is far from finished. Duane begins a second solo, and everything comes to a sudden halt, leaving him playing all alone. The room is silent, the crowd transfixed. Duane finishes up with a snarling bass line and the audience springs to life with applause. Dickey immediately comes in and Butch joins him with a steady rhythm on his hi-hat. Jaimoe begins throwing in little accent beats and before long both drummers are going full tilt while Dickey's guitar rings out over them. When the whole band comes in again, Duane steps out and plays fat-sounding, two-string riffs. The song touches down yet again and, once more, the band falls out and leaves Duane and his Les Paul all alone. Someone in the crowd yells out "Play all night," and it sounds like he might just do that. The band eventually comes back, and by now the song bears no resemblance to how it sounded when it began nearly twenty minutes earlier. The Allman Brothers Band has just taken an old, simple blues and twisted it inside out. The song doesn't conclude until Duane plays a spattering of the Christmas song "Joy to the World," which also had shown up at the conclusion of "Why Does Love Have to Be So Sad?"

"Hot 'lanta" is a driving instrumental that evolved out of a chord change Gregg had come up with during a jam session; they played it for about thirty minutes, then Dickey set down his guitar and went outside. "I started humming this melody, and I ran back in and started singing it into Gregg's ear," Dickey said. The song is a showcase for Berry Oakley, who powers the band with a bass that walks up and down the scales when most bassists would have been satisfied with finding a simple two- or three-note progression and sticking to it. Berry was developing into perhaps the best bass player in rock. He had a jazz musician's sense of melody and timing, and possessed an incredible anticipation; whenever Duane reached for the high notes, Berry would be right there behind him. It was always said that Berry's style was defined by the fact he had started out on guitar, but that disregards the enormity of his talent; probably half the bass players out there started out on the guitar, and they don't play like *this*.

After Duane and Dickey take solos, the song comes to a halt, and Butch and Jaimoe join for a brief drum solo. Then the band comes back to repeat the opening melody, and the song glides down until the instruments softly fade out, leaving things to simmer with only the drone of Gregg's organ, and Jaimoe's quiet cymbals and occasional rolls on the snare. Then comes a rumble like distant thunder — Butch playing the tympani. Jaimoe hits a brief roll on his snare, and Gregg's organ begins swirling. Jaimoe pounces on a cymbal, and the instruments come together like a rising storm that shoots out of the speakers, then immediately dissipates. The crowd sat stunned at the beauty of the moment, then rose in acclamation.

By now, the band had considerably expanded "In Memory of Elizabeth Reed." The *Fillmore East* version begins with a long, laconic intro by Dickey using volume swells, a rock equivalent of the dreamy trumpet Miles Davis used to play to open many of the songs on *Kind of Blue*. Jaimoe had played congas on the studio version, but here he throws in little jazz flourishes on the drums that counter what Butch is playing. Dickey takes the first solo, playing fluid and lonesome notes that are pushed by Berry's aggressive bass. Gregg's organ solo is evocative and, behind him, Duane is playing a driving rhythm guitar.

Duane's solo on this version of "Elizabeth Reed" is John Coltrane on the guitar; he plays notes that seem as though they shouldn't exist, like he's creating a new musical language as he goes along. The solo has several ebbs and flows before he takes the song to a peak and his Les Paul flails out with raw emotion. Duane then guides the tempo back to a crawl and changes the tone on his guitar. Now the notes are gorgeous, measured and controlled. It all boils up again and he takes everything even higher than he did before, reaching up to end the solo on a wailing two-note riff. It is brilliant guitar playing, perhaps the pinnacle of Duane's career.

Other than the opening bass lines and the lyrics, the live version of "Whipping Post" bears little resemblance to the one from the first album. The studio recording had been just over five minutes long; this one goes on for over twenty-two. "We got a little number from our first album we're gonna do for you," Duane says with clear understatement. "Berry starts her off." Someone in the back cries out "Whipping Post" and then someone up front yells it as well. "You guessed it," Duane answers, barely able to get the phrase out before Berry starts playing the dangerous-sounding introduction and the whole band falls in behind him.

Gregg's vocals are transformed on the live recording. Everything that needs to be said is evident in the tenor of his voice and the way he seizes the mood of the lyrics. Duane takes the first solo, eventually building up to the same riff that he used to close out "Elizabeth Reed." Dickey takes the second solo and this is his moment in the sun. His playing is unrestrained and travels rapidly through an array of emotions until he leads the band to the wonderful buildup that marked the ending on the studio cut. But onstage, the finale stretches on and on as Duane and Dickey play a half dozen little melodies. Butch again goes to the kettledrum as Duane plays long, sustained notes that wind the song down. Then Butch picks up the beat of "Mountain Jam." Duane is playing the opening lines as the music fades out and the album is over.

SHADOWING the euphoria of the Fillmore concerts was a string of bad luck that seemed to latch on to the brotherhood. Three days after the Fillmore gig, Kim Payne was shot by an off-duty Macon police officer on Vineville Avenue, a few blocks away from the Big House.

The police version was that Kim had been placed under arrest for refusing to accept a speeding ticket, then tried to break away as he was being handcuffed.

Kim said the cop was riding a motorcycle with no police markings, so he refused to stop. He ignored the officer for nearly a mile, stopping at traffic signals and stop signs, until he pulled out a .357 Magnum and leveled it at Kim's head. That move convinced Kim to pull over. "I'm gonna stop you goddamned hippies and dopers," the angry cop vowed. He tried to put Kim into handcuffs, but couldn't get them over his leather gloves and jacket. "By that time, something about the whole thing just tickled me and I busted out laughing," Kim said. "And that's what I was doing when he popped the cap. The bullet went through my right thigh and just missed the bone. That hurts like nothing you've ever had happen to you. I fucking screamed. I cried like a baby."

He was charged with speeding, disorderly conduct, and resisting arrest. Kim passed out and nearly bled to death in the parking lot before he was taken to the emergency room. When he woke up, Duane was leaning over his bed. "Look, man, it's going to be okay," Duane said gently. "Don't worry about it. No vitals hurt. No bones. You're okay."

A couple of days later, the band and the roadies met down at Capricorn Studios to load up for a March 19 gig at the Warehouse in New Orleans, and for a photo session for the cover of the live album. All the equipment was stacked up in a narrow lane across the street from the studio, and the band gathered in front of it for the photo. Phil Walden had hired noted rock photographer Jim Marshall to get a shot of the band, along with one of the road crew for the back cover. But Marshall was having a hard time — the band members hated posing, and the roadies refused to cooperate unless he bought them a six-pack of beer. "He went and got us that damned Pabst Blue Ribbon shit," Kim said. "Nobody drank that stuff; it's like horse piss."

The band members sat down in front of the equipment, and Marshall tried to get them to change their expressions from the dour, slightly pissed-off look that was on everybody's faces. Suddenly Duane jumped up and ran off. Marshall went ballistic. "Where the hell did he go?" he kept yelling. Duane skipped over to the other side of the alley; he had spied a friend who had a little bag of "Vitamin C" for him. Duane came scooting back and sat down with the cocaine in his hands, and Marshall snapped the photo that would be used for the cover. Duane is sitting there, a smug grin on his face, a bag of coke safely hidden in his hands, while everyone around him collapses with laughter.

It was typical of the Allman Brothers Band to immortalize their roadies by putting their photo on the back cover of the album. The road crew had suffered through the lean times; three of them had been there every step of the way, and this was the band's way of showing its appreciation. Legends were already growing about their antics, like the night in Rochester, New York, when Duane had burst out laughing in the middle of a solo. He kept jerking his head to his left and the spotlight moved over in that direction and found Red Dog, who was standing near Duane's amp getting a blow job from a groupie kneeling in front of him.

The work was backbreaking for all of them — long hours, short pay, and miles upon miles of travel. "When I got to Macon I was twenty-five and I was older than most everybody else," Kim said. "Man, I felt old by the time I was through with it all. Real old. In 'seventy-one, we did two hundred and seventy-seven dates. You'd get the equipment tore down and loaded up and then you'd get to the next gig just in time to set it all up again. I've slept soundly lying down behind a line of amplifiers, and them sumbitches would be booming."

For the photo, Jim Marshall lined up Red Dog and Kim and Mike Callahan along with two new guys, Joe Dan Petty and Willie Perkins. Twiggs was still in jail up in Buffalo, and the band had replaced him with Perkins, a twenty-nine-year-old with a degree in business administration. Willie had heard the band perform in Piedmont Park, become a fan, and told them he'd love to work for them. They called him a couple of weeks after Twiggs landed in jail, and Willie came on board as the road manager. One of the first things he did was go over the books and discover the band's finances were a mess. The band wasn't generating much income to begin with — Gregg had made all of $13,923 in 1970, and $5,590 of that was in songwriting royalties — and there was heavy debt. As Perkins organized the books, he soon realized that he was making more money each week than anyone in the band. "Things were somewhat in disarray when I took over, as far as finances," Willie said. "I had to start a record-keeping system from scratch. All of their expenses, living expenses and personal expenses, had been advanced by the management company and they had very little, if any, income to offset it."

The other newcomer, Joe Dan Petty, had played bass in Dickey's old group the Jokers. "We were down at Criteria Studios doing the second album and we were looking to hire another roadie," Kim Payne said. "We'd tried out several people and they didn't last long. And then, here's Joe Dan, and he don't weigh ninety pounds. He was real skinny. I went to Dickey and I said, 'This ain't gonna work. That B-3 organ weighs four hundred and fifty pounds and I gotta have somebody on the other end who can handle it because we're going up and down stairs all the time.' Dickey said that Joe Dan was tough, to give him a chance. And it worked out great."

Kim was still laid up, but the others went and checked him out of the hospital for the photo shoot. "I wasn't physically ready to get out," Kim said. "If you look at that picture, you can see that. I was sitting on Joe Dan's lap. Actually, I fell there. I was standing on my crutches and the guy said, 'The crutches need to go.' So I threw the crutches down, fell on Joe Dan, and my leg busted open and started bleeding." The grainy black-and-white photo makes them look gritty, tough, and scowling. It was exactly the outlaw image they liked to project. The band didn't forget Twiggs; they had the record company superimpose a photo of him up on the wall.

Right after the photo shoot for the *Fillmore East* album, the band took off for New Orleans. On the swing back they had gigs set up in Montevallo, Alabama, and then in Tuscaloosa. They stopped at a truck stop in Jackson, Alabama, on March 22. A cop sitting inside saw the bunch of hippies walk in and quickly surmised that they had to be under the influence of something illegal. There had already been a few close calls with drugs over the months; one time they were driving around in New York City carrying heroin and someone spotted a cop. They dropped the bag out the window and, after the cop went on his way, drove back around the block, picked it up off the street, and went on.

This time it was rural Alabama, where cops routinely hassled hippies. His instincts were good; the guys were a walking drugstore. They were charged with possession of heroin, marijuana, and phencyclidine, the animal tranquilizer better known as PCP. Duane, Gregg, Jaimoe, Dickey, Butch, Berry, Willie, Joe Dan, and David "Tuffy" Phillips, who drove the equipment truck, were all arrested and charged with possession of narcotics and spent the night in jail. Gregg had a paranoid fear of jail cells and he went crazy, climbing the bars and screaming, before Duane made him shut up. They each posted bonds of two thousand dollars, and were released the following morning. The arrests were serious; in Alabama, a narcotics conviction could mean years in a state prison. The charges hung over their heads for months. Finally, a plea bargain was arranged. The cases against Willie Perkins and Joe Dan Petty were dropped; everyone else pleaded guilty to disturbing the peace and they paid a total of $4,350 in fines and court costs.

Kim Payne had his day in court in late March. Found guilty of speeding and resisting arrest, he was fined $200 and hobbled out on his bum leg. "I could have sued, but Phil Walden was dead set against it," Kim said. "He wanted everything quieted down. We were a struggling young hippie band in a kind of hostile little southern town that didn't really care too much for our presence. And if we were going to continue to live there, which was the general plan, it helped to keep things quiet."

Ten

Soul Serenade

NOT long after the Allman Brothers Band recorded their shows at the Fillmore East, Bill Graham called up and told them that he was closing both his theaters. The grind of flying coast-to-coast two or three times a month to operate the two theaters was beginning to get to him, and he felt betrayed when bands that had begged him for a gig two years earlier were now pricing themselves out of his buildings. Graham was getting together some of his favorite groups for the final Fillmore East concerts on the weekend of June 26: would the Allman Brothers headline?

Those lucky enough to catch the Saturday-night show witnessed the greatest performance the Allman Brothers Band ever gave. "We weren't onstage until about two in the morning," Butch said. "The audience was into the set and it was just one of those nights where everything was perfect. On every song, any time I started playing something, two or three other guys in the band were already doing it. The communication was just incredible. We came back for the encore, I guess around four-thirty, and we quit at seven o'clock that morning. We finished and . . . just total silence. No applause, nothing. They opened the doors and the sun came pouring in and everybody just got up and quietly walked out. Nobody even talked, just smiles from ear to ear. I remember Duane walking by me dragging his guitar behind him, saying, 'Goddamn, it's like being in church.'

"We got outside, the sun's out. And this is New York people, they're usually tearing up their cars and stuff, and they're walking by with a smile saying, 'That was nice, thank you.' That was, musically, the high point of my life. That is the spot you try to get to every night and, if you're lucky, you'll do it once in a lifetime. I still keep running into people who were there that night. It's something they'll never forget and we'll never forget. It was religious."

IT wasn't unusual for the band members to fly girlfriends to their gigs but the date Gregg had flown in for the final Fillmore shows was growing in significance. Gregg had met Shelley Kay Winters that summer at a concert in San Antonio, Texas. She was pretty and petite, a flower child from Corpus Christi who left home at seventeen and wound up living with some friends in Mexico. When she returned to the States she went to work for her boyfriend at his concert promotions company, and met Gregg when she was sent to chaperon the band to a gig. Gregg struck up a conversation and talked her into coming up to his room after the show, as he did with most of the women he picked up. But Shelley was different; rather than having sex, they stayed up all night talking. For Gregg, it was an intriguing change of pace.

He had always found it almost too easy to seduce women; they would hear the lonely blues rolling out of his voice and want to soothe his pain. They virtually threw themselves at him at concerts, and after the shows it was like a beauty pageant backstage. "By the time we finished playing, the roadies had done picked out a lot of the prime ones," Butch said. "Most of them [the groupies] thought we had our old ladies with us anyhow, so they figured they might as well get with the roadies. And then Gregg would get the rest. Even if you did happen to pick one up, he'd get them anyhow. Gregg was the worst. I've seen him have as many as six in one night, and all of them in different rooms. One night, I'd picked up this fine young thing and I was sitting in there talking to her and here comes this knock on the door. It's Gregg. He comes in and wants a bump [of cocaine]. I went back to get it and by the time I get back, him and the chick's walking out the door. It was me and Rosie that night."

The guys down at Criteria loved it when the Allman Brothers Band were in town. "The lobby was the place to be," said Karl Richardson. "The girls who used to hang out with the Allman Brothers were the prettiest groupies in the business. They used to get the best-looking women to come by, and they'd be wearing shorts up to their neck." Engineer Ron Albert said that often it was just a matter of walking out to the lobby and taking your pick. "You didn't need a date," he said. "You could just walk into the studio with the group, and you had a date. There was a lot to choose from. It was unbelievable. These sucky old hillbilly, shit-kicking, tobacco-spitting, plaque-toothed fools, they had the women. God, they had beautiful ladies. It's true. Every word of it is true."

Gregg usually took care of as many as he could handle; it often seemed as if his hotel rooms had revolving doors. But Shelley didn't follow the pattern. She was a challenge, a woman who didn't throw herself at him. And she didn't seem to have stars in her eyes; when they met, she was only vaguely aware of the Allman Brothers Band. She seemed to be a woman who was attracted to Gregg for who he was, not what he was. After meeting her in San Antonio, Gregg invited her to come to Macon for a few days, and then he flew her to New York City for the final Fillmore shows.

"I was backstage and they were passing around liebfraumilch," said Shelley. "I said it was delicious and somebody else said, 'Yeah, and it's laced with liquid acid.' I'd already gone through my LSD days and I was into a downer, more mellow phase of my life. I didn't even smoke pot. It was too psychedelic. I was more into barbiturates and that kind of thing. So I freaked out because the last trip I was on, I was high for three days and I never wanted to take another one. I got a couple of yellow jackets, Nembutal, took those, and got a taxi and went back to the hotel and crashed out. Gregg thought that was really cool, that I would just decide to leave the Fillmore East and go back to the hotel."

A few weeks later, Gregg convinced Shelley to come back to Macon and move in with him. And they began to fall in love.

AFTER the Fillmore East gig, Duane stayed in New York to do something he'd always wanted to do: play on a jazz session. Flutist Herbie Mann was recording his *Push Push* album and asked Duane to add some lead guitar. Ten days later, Duane and the rest of the band drove up to Rhode Island to perform at the Newport Jazz Festival, the most prestigious music festival in the country. Each summer beginning in 1954, the greatest musicians in the world had gathered in the resort town of Newport playing shows that had become part of jazz lore. The Allman Brothers Band was to be the only white band on a

Sunday-night blues program that also featured Ray Charles, B. B. King, T-Bone Walker, Joe Turner, and Eddie "Cleanhead" Vinson. For a bunch of kids who grew up admiring blues artists and were now striving to have their jazz leanings taken seriously, being asked to play the Newport Jazz Festival was a high honor, and a chance to mingle with their heroes.

On July 4, the night before the Allman Brothers were to perform, about twenty thousand fans gathered on the festival grounds and at least as many hung around the outside gates. Among the musicians scheduled that night were Freddie Hubbard, Eubie Blake, Gerry Mulligan, Dave Brubeck, and Jimmy Smith. A headline in the *Providence Journal* had confidently forecast fair weather, good music, and no trouble, and that held up until just after 10:00 PM. As Dionne Warwick was singing "What the World Needs Now Is Love," a large group of kids crashed the fences and stormed the grounds, causing a riot. Police used tear gas to restore order, and three hundred people were treated for injuries. The blues night scheduled for the following evening was canceled, along with the rest of the festival. The following year, the Newport Jazz Festival would move to New York City.

Later that month the string of bad luck seemed over when *The Allman Brothers Band at Fillmore East* was released. Everyone in Macon had been convinced all along that the new live album was going to be the breakthrough, but Phil Walden had a tough time convincing the record executives in New York City. They could see the logic of putting out a concert album, but they were against making it a two-record set. Three of the songs the band wanted to use, "Elizabeth Reed" and "You Don't Love Me" and "Whipping Post," were so long that they almost took up an entire side of a record each, a strict taboo in the industry.

Their resolve strengthened when Walden wanted to price the set at just above the cost of a single album. "That was a very innovative thing at the time," Phil said. "The Allman Brothers had this 'people's band' image that we were trying to develop. We were concerned about concert prices and the prices of records. We felt we couldn't do a single album because of the nature of their playing and the structure of their tunes. And it was a small battle between us and Atlantic. They finally conceded; we made some publishing concessions to accommodate them."

The album shot up to number thirteen on the *Billboard* charts and went gold, selling 500,000 copies by the end of the summer. *Rolling Stone* proclaimed: "The fact of the matter is [the Allman Brothers] comprise the best damn rock and roll band this country has produced in the past five years."

The whispers had turned into exclamations.

MACON had become a kind of refuge for the band, the perfect place to escape the craziness of the road. One radio interviewer made the mistake of mentioning to Duane that Macon seemed to be turning into a musical center. "No, man, Macon's real quiet," Duane shot back, as if the guy were revealing a deep secret. "It's not going to be the center of anything. That's why we stay there, it's just good and quiet and there's no trouble. Well, there's no *nothing*, especially not trouble."

When they went home the band members kept to themselves and their small circle of friends. There were dinners and rehearsals at the Big House, jam sessions in clubs downtown, and midnight runs on their motorcycles over to Rose Hill to smoke a joint. Even the relationships tended to be inbred. Donna's sister, Joanie Rooseman, moved to Macon and dated Kim Payne, then married Mike Callahan. Kim was now living at the Big House with Candace Oakley, who had split up with Gregg.

Dickey was headed for a divorce; he had met a tall, beautiful Ojibway named Sandy "Bluesky" Wabegijig and fallen in love with her. By then, Duane and Donna had split up and Donna had returned to St. Louis with Galadriel. Duane and Donna had never formally married, but in Georgia if a couple live together and tell people they're married, it is considered a common-law marriage. The couple had separated in November of 1970 and the divorce was finalized four months later. Duane was now seeing a woman from Mississippi named Dixie Lee [Wilbourne] Meadows, who was part of a group of women the band called the "Hot 'lanta groupies"; they lived together in Atlanta and welcomed the guys in the band and road crew to visit them.

Duane and Dixie eventually moved into a small house in a middle-class neighborhood in west Macon, a couple of miles away from the Big House. Duane seemed to be head-over-heels in love with Dixie. "I think if he had ever gotten married again, she would have been the one," said one friend. "She was so sweet, man, pretty as could be with these dimples." One afternoon, he called Duane, who picked up the phone and the first thing out of his mouth was: "I don't know who this is, but you're interrupting a beautiful moment."

But Duane made no move toward the altar. He had decided that marriage and music didn't mix, for him or for his little brother. He treated Shelley as if she didn't exist. "Duane was real funny about me," she said. "He made me real uncomfortable." Duane could see that a wedding was in the offing, and tried to talk his little brother out of it. When that didn't work, he encouraged Gregg's friends to begin a campaign against the marriage. All it seemed to do was make Gregg even more resolved.

The band enjoyed its restful retreats in Macon but spent most of the time on the road. The Allman Brothers Band was on its way to Boston in mid-August of 1971 when the news broke that one of Duane's best friends, legendary saxophonist Curtis Ousley, had been stabbed to death in New York City. Ousley, known as "King Curtis," had played the rippling sax on the Coasters' hit "Yakety-Yak" and had backed dozens of r&b stars — Aretha Franklin, Sam Cooke, Wilson Pickett, Ray Charles — and even John Lennon and Bobby Darin. Duane met King Curtis at a session in Muscle Shoals and they became very close. Duane called him "one of the finest cats there ever was, an incredible human being," and spoke with admiration of the power and emotion that King Curtis cajoled from his tenor saxophone.

The funeral was August 17 in New York City at Saint Peter's Lutheran Church. Days before, the band had played an open-field concert in Boston and Duane performed a tribute to his friend. "Everyone gradually stopped playing and Duane was just standing in front of the stage," writer Jon Landau remembered. "Without saying anything, he worked the jam into King's greatest song, 'Soul Serenade.' It was just him playing on the guitar. That was a stunning moment, just stunning. He was trying to communicate through the song and it was one of the most beautiful things I ever heard Duane play."

At the funeral, Duane was badly shaken and openly wept. Death seemed to be all around. Janis Joplin had overdosed on heroin just two weeks after Jimi Hendrix died. Jim Morrison had died under mysterious circumstances in Paris. Brian Jones of the Rolling Stones had drowned, and a fan had been stabbed to death at a Stones gig at the Altamont Raceway outside San Francisco. "If anything ever happens to me, you guys better keep it going," Duane told Butch. "Put me in a pine box, throw me in the river, and jam for two or three days."

GREGG and Shelley decided to marry, one of the few times that Gregg would go against his big brother. Still, to allay the fears that his friends had stirred up, Gregg tested her. With the success of the *Fill-*

more East album, the band was now collecting about $7,500 per gig and people warned Gregg that Shelley was only after his money. One time when the band went on the road for a few days, Shelley stayed in Macon and Gregg gave her $20 for spending money. "He wanted me to write down every single thing I spent the money on," she said. "I never could figure that out. I didn't know whether he was testing me, if it was a result of his celebrity, his childhood, or what. I could have cared less whether he was worth a million dollars or not; it didn't matter. The money was rolling in pretty good by then. It wasn't unusual for him to say, 'Here, take the limo and go shopping,' and he'd give me a wad of bills. I considered that just the fun part of it. It didn't make any difference as far as the relationship went, because I was just totally in love with him."

Gregg had Shelley sign a prenuptial agreement and then they were married September 15, 1971, by Bibb County State Court Judge J. Taylor Phillips. Gregg was twenty-three, Shelley twenty-one. "We flew to New Orleans the very next day for a gig," Shelley said. That night, someone snapped several photos of the new bride and groom and, in one of them, Gregg is sitting at a table, slumped forward with his eyes half-closed. "He had just snorted, I think it was heroin. In one of these pictures you can see it. He had just put it back in his wallet. And he was getting ready to go perform."

For all his passive hostility, Duane warmed up to Shelley as soon as she was a member of the family. The newlyweds flew up to New York for a honeymoon and met Duane and Dixie at the apartment of Deering Howe, an heir to the Deering family's International Harvester fortune who lived off a trust fund. "Deering had the whole penthouse of One Fifth Avenue, and he lived up there with some princess from the Middle East," Shelley said. "Duane and Dixie were up there and Duane had this book on colors, interpreting colors and auras. He didn't understand something that was in the book and he asked me about it, probably the first time he'd ever asked me anything. And we sat there and talked. From that point on, we were friends. He was still always a little stand-offish; he always seemed very preoccupied."

For a wedding present, Gregg and Shelley were given a big block of cocaine, so pure it looked like a cake of soap. "It was in this huge brass platter and we spent our honeymoon doing coke," Shelley said. "Gregg was getting into heavy drug use back then. So was I. So was everybody."

The same week that Gregg and Shelley married, the band's

lifestyle was the focal point at Twiggs Lyndon's murder trial in Buffalo. Twiggs had pleaded not guilty by reason of insanity to stabbing Angelo Aliotta to death and had been in jail since his arrest over eighteen months earlier. Twiggs was charged with first-degree murder, which meant it was considered premeditated, and he faced life in prison. He offered one basic defense: being on the road with the Allman Brothers Band was so grueling that any reasonable person would have snapped from the experience. Berry and Kim Payne flew up to Buffalo to testify for Twiggs. "We were pretty strung out and Berry talked to this lawyer, the one that picked us up at the airport, about getting us some methadone," Kim said. When the lawyer balked, Berry said, "Fuck it, I ain't testifying unless you get me some goddamned dope."

Finally, the lawyer relented; Berry was, after all, his key witness. "That sumbitch took us around to different places until we came to this drugstore. I guess the pharmacist was a friend of his," Kim said. "It was the wee hours of the morning. He tells him that we need some methadone and the guy said he couldn't give that without a doctor's permission."

The lawyer persisted. Finally, the pharmacist turned to Berry and said, "If you tell me it's for pain, I'll give it to you."

Berry shook his head. "Nope, it ain't for Payne," he deadpanned. "He can get his own dope. It's for me."

The nonjury trial must have been one of the more bizarre ever held in a Buffalo courtroom. Twiggs's lawyer wanted to prove that the road had driven his client crazy, and Berry and Kim put on a method-acting performance to make sure the point wasn't lost. One of the side effects of methadone is vomiting, and a wave of nausea hit Berry on the witness stand. "He kept having to say 'Excuse me,' then get up holding his mouth and run into the bathroom to puke," Kim said. "He hadn't taken that methadone to take the edge off, he'd taken a handful to get a buzz. The cross-examiner was really pushing him hard: 'Did you take any dope in the last month?' And Berry said, 'Mm, huh.' 'Have you had any drugs in the last week?' 'Oh, yeah.' Then he asked, 'What about in the last hour?' And Berry said, 'You bet.' "

The strategy worked. Twiggs was found not guilty by reason of insanity. "He got in a mental hospital for six months, and then hit the road," Kim said. "The first time I saw Twiggs after that, he was riding a BSA motorcycle down Riverside Drive in Macon, free as a bird, with a shotgun strapped to his back. He wasn't going to let none of those

Aliottas get him." Twiggs would soon be back on the road with the Brothers.

The defense lawyer's depiction of life with the Allman Brothers was closer to the truth than he probably realized. Phil Walden had nurtured an image of a band that thrived on the road, but it was an illusion. Someone once said that the drugs in rock 'n' roll weren't for the times you were onstage because those were the times you enjoyed; rather, the drugs were to help you survive what it took to get you there. And it was all beginning to get to them. Drugs seemed only natural for someone like Duane, who wanted everything in life magnified, every sensation heightened. But they were taking it to the extreme, especially the "Vitamin C," cocaine. Worse, they had discovered heroin.

An extremely addictive derivative of morphine, heroin is clinically a painkiller. It produces sensations of warmth, calmness, and a loss of concern for outside events. It is a musician's drug, a traditional favorite of jazz players because it made them feel "at one" with their instruments. They believed that by getting high on heroin they could unlock the door to a delicate tunnel of communication that reached into a fertile, virgin place deep inside their soul, and then coax out those deep emotions and translate them into music. Heroin also is one of the most effective means of deadening feelings, and many addicts use it when they have run out of internal defenses against emotional pain. Gregg would become hooked on heroin nearly as soon as he discovered it. "Me and Gregg both had some insatiable appetites for that shit," Kim Payne said. "We'd go riding around to some really sleazy black neighborhoods to try to procure it."

Some heroin users drew a line between recreational use and hard-core addiction by eschewing needles. Many, like Eric Clapton, snorted it because it gave the illusion that they weren't really hooked: only junkies mainlined the stuff. Duane talked about finding a needle in the shaving kit of one of the roadies and threatening to fire him if he saw one again. "I ain't putting up with none of that shit," Duane said. "I'm not gonna sit back and watch this whole thing go down the tubes. I don't hold drugs against anyone; I just ain't having no one shooting up in this band." There was even a $500 fine instituted for track marks.

There is a substantial difference between snorting heroin and injecting it. When you shoot it, you can literally feel the drug traveling through the veins on the way to your heart. Then it is pumped throughout the body and you feel sudden, total relaxation. Snorting it doesn't give that same rush. As soon as he discovered the needle, Duane's little brother started shooting up, and eventually Duane and others in the band were as well.

AFTER Twiggs's trial, the band was back on the road for a brief, grueling tour of ten cities crammed into a fifteen-day period. Everyone was exhausted and on edge. It was a bad time to have a *Rolling Stone* reporter and photographer on the road with them, and the band was about to receive a hard lesson in gonzo journalism. No one liked the reporter, *Rolling Stone* associate editor Grover Lewis, and Duane and the others seemed to ignore him. Lewis wound up spending much of his time talking to Willie Perkins.

Things came to a head when photographer Annie Leibovitz showed up a few days into the trip. First Duane and Gregg stood her up for a photo session, and when it was rescheduled they refused to have their photos taken apart from the band. "Fuck, man, we ain't on no fuckin' star trip," Duane snarled.

Gregg nodded his head. "Naw, man, we ain't on no fuckin' star trip," he said.

A third session was not the charm; again Duane stood Leibovitz up. At the fourth session, Duane finally showed. She asked everyone to pull up his pant leg so she could get a picture that showed the band members' tattooed mushrooms. Everyone grumbled, but complied until Duane pulled another scene. "This is jive bullshit, man," he said, refusing to participate. "It's silly."

Gregg nodded his head. "Jive bullshit," he said.

Grover Lewis offered that it seemed no sillier to shoot a picture of the tattoos than it was to have them in the first place. Duane, in return, offered to punch him out.

They all piled into rented cars, and on the way to a concert in Los Angeles Duane agreed to stop along the road for a fifth attempt to get a group photo. Leibovitz tried to arrange the band so that everyone's face would show up in the photo. "Fuck it," Duane screamed at her. "Either take the fuckin' picture or don't take the fuckin' picture. I'm not gonna do any of that phony posin' shit for you or nobody else."

Leibovitz climbed into a station wagon with them to go to a gig at the Whiskey A Go Go. During the trip, Leibovitz snapped her famed photo of Duane and Gregg sleeping in the backseat. At the gig, she tried to take some candid shots backstage. By then, it was a lost cause. She asked someone to replace a few burned-out bulbs in the dressing room so she would have better light. Gregg walked over and told them to leave the lights as they were. "Don't screw in that bulb, my man," Gregg said. "I like it in here the way it is." Finally, Annie Leibovitz gave up, said, "Oh, screw it," and left.

Lewis's story would portray the band as a group of southern hicks, running from gig to gig and snorting up piles of cocaine with rolled-up hundred-dollar bills. There would be four references to band members reading comic books and Lewis went out of his way to make fun of everyone's southern drawl. Duane was described as resembling a skinny orange walrus who looked bowlegged even when he was sitting down. With Gregg, there was the "principal revelation that [he] is not, after all, a stone catatonic, as he appears to be everywhere except in front of a microphone."

Lewis told the story of a band out of control and ready to hit the wall. One night, after a concert that never really seemed to take off, the guys huddled in the dressing room over a pile of coke. "I couldn't hear *shit*," Gregg complained between snorts of cocaine.

"Coulda been a dynamite gig, too, man," Berry said.

Duane slumped down on a wooden bench. "I think maybe it was the audience," Duane said. "But then again, it coulda just been too much fuckin' coke. You know what I mean?" He sniffled and reached for the vial of coke. "Goddamn," he sighed. "I'm sopped, brother."

THE two years of nearly nonstop travel had built up a large, devoted audience, but it also had extracted a heavy toll from the members of the band. They had been feeding the monster until there was nothing left; they had been run into the ground. "You didn't have time to take care of your family life," Jaimoe said. "You didn't have time to go to the record company and see how your business was. You didn't have time to do anything because as soon as you were home, you'd sleep for three days and then you'd be back out there on the road. You cannot produce under those conditions. The management and the record company, which were both the same, should have taken into consideration that a wheel can only spin for so long and then you're going to have to retread it or change the tire."

The band came off the road in mid-October of 1971. They went down to Criteria to finish up two songs they'd put down earlier and to record a sweet-sounding acoustic instrumental Duane had written for Dixie called "Little Martha." The session was short-lived. It had become obvious from the last road trip that things were getting out of hand, that the drug use was getting serious. Phil Walden set up a visit to a heroin detox center in a New York hospital. Duane, Gregg, and a couple of others flew up and checked in. But the trip seemed useless; they all left thinking the program had been a joke.

Duane spent about a week in New York City and called up an old friend, blues guitarist John Hammond, Jr., before he left. They hung out for a while at Deering Howe's penthouse apartment; then they went over to Hammond's loft and spent the night listening to old blues records and jamming on acoustic guitars. Hammond thought that Duane looked good, refreshed; his stay in the hospital seemed to have been good for him, if only for the rest. They talked about doing another album together, this time a record of acoustic blues. "I had to fly out early to go to Nova Scotia the next day," Hammond said. "And he flew down to Macon."

Big Linda's birthday was October 29, and Duane wanted to be back in town for a party at the Big House. He reached Macon the night before, and Gregg and Shelley picked him up at the airport. Duane slept late the next morning, while Dixie and Candace were in his kitchen making a cake. That afternoon, the three of them went over to the Big House to take flowers to Linda and sing "Happy Birthday" to her. The backyard had been turned into a garden and they sat out back in the warm sunshine for an hour or so, playing with little Brittany.

Just after five-thirty, Duane climbed onto his Harley-Davidson Sportster to head back over to his house. Candace and Dixie followed in one car, and Berry tagged along behind them in his car to pick up the cake and presents stashed at Duane's place.

Candace followed Duane down Pio Nono Avenue until they turned right onto Hillcrest Avenue, the shortcut to west Macon. Berry was a horrible driver and, typically, he missed the turn and had to take a longer route over to Duane's house. Duane guided the big Harley chopper down Hillcrest, a flat stretch of road with big trees hanging over the street. The speed limit was thirty-five but Duane ignored it. When he came up behind a slow car, he simply shot around it.

It was a perfect day to be on a bike, Indian summer. Duane loved the big Harley chopper; he'd been looking for one and finally came across a kid in Macon who had one for sale. The bike was modified with fork legs, which gave it the Easy Rider look but also made it hard to handle. It needed new tires, and the day before, Duane had called a Harley dealer in Macon from New York City to ask about getting a new set.

Duane eased the bike on a little faster when the street began to crawl down a sharp hill. He zipped under the flashing yellow light at the intersection of Inverness Avenue. There was a bump in the road — a sudden dip like a roller coaster — and with a little speed, it gave the illusion of free-falling. He must have been doing forty-five, maybe fifty. Duane was in a hurry; always a hurry.

Candace was probably four or five car lengths behind him by now. From the hill, she could see Duane approach the intersection of Bartlett Avenue. A Chevy flatbed truck that was coming toward them slowed down and began crawling into a left turn in front of Duane. It had a yellow crane boom on the back for unloading lumber. Duane gently pushed the bike to his left, toward the centerline, so he could swing around the truck. Then the truck did the unexpected: halfway through the turn it stopped dead in the road, blocking Duane's entire lane. Duane pushed the bike farther toward the middle of the street. He was only a few feet away from the truck now, and it was still stopped in front of him. Duane had two options: he could lay the bike down, or he could try to veer around the truck. He had an instant to make the decision.

For a moment, it looked as if Duane was going to be able to finesse his way through. Then Candace and Dixie watched in horror as he came off the bike. He had hit something, the cable hanging from the crane or a big weight ball dangling on the cable or maybe the rear corner of the truck. His helmet flew off and the bike bounced up in the air, landing on top of him and driving him hard into the pavement. The bike skidded ninety feet, leaving three gouge marks in the pavement, then slammed into the curb. It slid along the edge of the street a few more feet and came to rest between the curb and the right tire of an oncoming car. The bike's engine was revved up at full blast. It was screaming. The truck driver climbed out of the cab. He checked the boy lying in the road. Then he walked over to the motorcycle and shut it off. It was 5:44 in the afternoon.

Duane was unconscious when Dixie and Candace reached him. His shirt was gathered up around his chest; there were some scratches on his stomach and forehead, but he was breathing and there were no other visible injuries. "In my mind, I see Duane laying on the pavement and I'm looking at him with relief because nothing was torn open," Candace said. "He looked to be in one piece other than a few scratches."

She pulled the seat covers from her car and put them over him. A crowd was gathering and she kept screaming for somebody to call an ambulance. Nobody moved. "I started running around to houses," said Candace. "I'd knock at the door. I guess I must have been acting pretty crazy because they wouldn't let me in, they'd say they didn't have a phone. I went to three houses. I guess they thought I was some kind of hippie lunatic. Finally an ambulance got there. It seemed like we waited forever."

Dixie climbed into the ambulance with Duane and he was taken to the Medical Center of Central Georgia, the downtown hospital where Galadriel had been born just over two years earlier. Duane stopped breathing twice during the trip, but was revived each time by mouth-to-mouth resuscitation. Candace raced over to Duane's house, where Berry was waiting. She told him what had happened and made a few quick calls before they took off for the hospital.

Gregg and Shelley were at their apartment when Candace called. Gregg hung up the phone and sprinted down to the Medical Center. "I remember we were sitting at the kitchen table and the hospital was right down the hill," Shelley said. "Somebody said Duane had broken his arm and everybody was freaked out that he couldn't play. It's really strange when you try to get back into a memory like that. I remember the kitchen table and the horrible chairs; they were like white wrought-iron and the table was like mesh metal. It was nighttime and I remember running down to the hospital. And then, that's it. I have no idea what happened after that. Everybody was so screwed up; I think Duane was the only one who was straight that night."

Johnny Sandlin happened to be over at the Capricorn offices on Cotton Avenue, a few hundred yards away from the Medical Center. "Somebody called and said that Duane had been in an accident," Johnny said. "When we first heard, we decided to go up and see how he was doing. We never thought it was anything critical. Everybody around there was getting hurt; we'd have a Sunday-afternoon softball game and everybody would end up in the emergency room with sprains and stuff. We had no idea it was serious until we got up to the hospital." Phil Walden was vacationing in Bimini and his secretary, Carolyn Brown, began trying to reach him.

People started gathering at the hospital, and Berry and Candace kept going outside in the hallway to talk to the doctors and get updates on Duane's condition. Dr. Charles Burton examined him and decided to take him into emergency surgery. "We saw Duane being wheeled into surgery and we stood with him for a minute," Candace said. "I don't even remember what the doctors were saying. I just remember listening and standing there with Berry, trying to comfort Berry and praying. Berry was real shook up. He took it real hard."

Gregg was out of it, so messed up that he was almost falling down. They told him Duane was okay and sent him home. But what Burton discovered in the operating room was not encouraging. The patient had not regained consciousness; there were probably head injuries. His chest had collapsed and there were massive internal injuries, including a ruptured coronary artery and a severely damaged liver. Any one of the injuries alone could be fatal. Burton worked feverishly to stabilize the damage. His patient clung to life for three hours until he could fight no more.

At 8:40 PM, Howard Duane Allman, twenty-four, was pronounced dead.

Eleven

The Broken Circle

GREGG was back at his apartment with a couple of friends. He'd taken some more painkillers to take the edge off, and he was passed out on the bed when there was a knock on the front door. It was Red Dog. He looked stunned, vacant. No one said a word. To see Red Dog was to know. "Don't tell him now," somebody finally said, unaware that Gregg was walking into the room.

"Don't tell him what?" Gregg asked.

Red Dog looked at him. There was a silence. "They lost him, man," Red Dog said. "Duane's gone." Gregg looked back at him like a deer trapped in car headlights.

For two days stunned visitors passed by Duane's casket at Snow's Memorial Chapel. The funeral was held at the chapel the following Monday, November 1, 1971. Nobody wanted a circus and the service was private, with about three hundred friends crowded inside. Delaney and Bonnie Bramlett were there. Dr. John had flown down from New York with Jerry Wexler. Everyone from the Muscle Shoals Rhythm Section came. Duane's guitar stood in front of the floral-wreathed casket and the band's equipment was set up behind it.

At three o'clock, Gregg and Dickey and Berry and Butch and Jaimoe grimly walked into the room along with Thom Douchette. They took their places at their instruments and began playing a slow blues, an old Elmore James song. "The sky is crying," Gregg sang.

"Look at the tears roll down the street." They played "Key to the Highway" and "Stormy Monday" and "In Memory of Elizabeth Reed." Some of the people began hesitantly applauding and Red Dog encouraged it. Duane would have wanted people to celebrate the music and, even more, to celebrate the courage of his band to get up and play for him this one last time.

They were joined by Dr. John and Delaney Bramlett. Delaney made his way to the center of the stage, and they all joined hands and began singing "Will the Circle Be Unbroken?" The three hundred mourners inside the room joined in, clapping in time. Gregg sang two songs by himself, including an old song of his that Duane had liked, "Melissa." Then the band came back and played "Statesboro Blues," with Dickey using Duane's Les Paul. When the song was finished, Dickey took the guitar and stood it up in front of the casket and walked off.

The eulogy was given by Jerry Wexler. He read from a hastily written statement and had to stop often to collect himself. He talked about the last time he had seen Duane, in tears at the funeral of King Curtis two months earlier. "They were both gifted natural musicians with an unlimited ability for truly melodic improvisation," Wexler said. "They were both utterly dedicated to their music and they would never permit the incorporation of the commercial compromise to their music — not for love or money."

Wexler recalled the nights he sat on his back deck in Long Island and listened to Duane and Delaney Bramlett jamming, playing the songs of Robert Johnson, Blind Willie Johnson, Jimmy Rodgers. "Those of us who were privileged to know Duane will remember him from all the studios, backstage dressing rooms, the Downtowners, the Holiday Inns, the Sheratons, the late nights, relaxing after the sessions, the whiskey and the music talk, playing back cassettes until night gave way to dawn, fishing in Miami and Long Island, this young beautiful man who we love so dearly but who is not lost to us because we have his music, and the music is imperishable."

THE death of Duane Allman left everyone in the brotherhood shattered. Duane had been such a forceful personality, such a catalyst, that they had put their complete faith in his vision and tied their destinies to his. "The leader of our little community, our friend and everything else, was gone," said Johnny Sandlin.

It was the first close experience with death and its finality for just about everyone in the band. Both Butch and Dickey began having strangely similar recurring dreams about Duane. "Have you ever lost somebody your own age, that close to you?" Dickey said. "It's a real funny thing; I mean, it was such a damned surprise that my mind never really accepted it. It was so tough that it's hard to try to explain to somebody. I'd have these dreams that he was playing with Bonnie and Delaney. Eric Clapton was playing in the band, and there Duane was. And everybody was saying, 'Man, you've been playing with them? So that's where you've been.' And then you gradually begin to realize that Duane Allman is not playing with Bonnie and Delaney. He's gone."

The same dreams haunted Butch. "I had that dream many times," he said. "We were out on the road, and there was Duane up there playing with Delaney and Bonnie. That's where he'd been all this time, and he just didn't tell anybody. It probably took months before it really sank in. You just couldn't believe it."

But it was Berry and Gregg who had the most difficult time coping. "Berry, I think, took it the hardest," Kim Payne said. "He was just devastated. Berry and Big Linda were the original flower children. Especially Big Linda. Earth mother; that was her, man. Just mellow and never a harsh word about anybody. Berry was real mellow too, and he just became totally disoriented when this thing with Duane happened. His situation deteriorated terribly. He went from being a perfect family man — he just loved his wife and little girl — to being a person who didn't care about nothing. He said, 'I want to *get* high, *be* high, and *stay* high.' He was dead serious about it."

Gregg had suddenly lost the big brother he had depended on for all his life. When he lost his father, he'd had Duane to take care of him. Now, Duane was gone too. "You never know how much you lean on somebody until they die," Gregg said. "And I was pissed. I was pissed off at him for dying. I was pissed off at me for leaning on him. I was afraid. Man, I was every emotion you could be. You immediately have to muster up all the strength that you can possibly have in your being at a time like that. It's a real test. One I hope I don't ever have to go through again."

From the moment Duane died, everything took on a surreal quality. Berry totaled his car that night on his way home from the hospital, and walked away from it. Then, two days later, Shelley totaled her car; she had gone to a pharmacy to pick up a prescription for Gregg, another car hit her, and her Opal GT wound up lying upside down on the pavement. *Rolling Stone* printed a long, poignant obituary by Jon Landau, but the article by Grover Lewis was published in the same issue and the timing could not have been worse. It was taken as the ultimate sign of disrespect, slamming a man who didn't deserve it, and doing it the week after his death. It left the band with a long-standing resentment of the magazine and helped fuel a suspicion of journalists in general.

Then Gregg disappeared. Shelley had no idea where her husband was; she thought he had run off to Montego Bay. But Gregg never left Macon. He hid out at a friend's house, numbing the pain with drugs. Shelley went back to Texas and ended up in the hospital from injuries she had suffered in the wreck. "I figured it was the end of the marriage; he'd gone crazy and left and everybody was nuts," she said. "And then he called and said to get my butt back to Macon. He wouldn't pay for the airplane ticket because he was furious I'd left."

She scrounged up the money and flew to Atlanta. There, she got on another plane to return to Macon. Before takeoff a stewardess came back to her seat. "Are you Shelley Allman?" she asked. "You need to come up front." Shelley protested that she didn't have a first-class ticket. The stewardess ignored her and again told Shelley to follow her to the front of the plane. "So I went up there," Shelley said. "Gregg had bought the whole first-class section and he was sitting there with a bottle of champagne and flowers. And that's how we got back to-gether."

When Shelley returned to Macon everything was different. It was like a house that had lost its foundation and crumbled; everyone was scrambling to put the pieces back together and Duane was no longer there to tell them how to do it. Because the Opal was totaled, they had no car. Shelley's old Mustang was back in San Antonio, so Gregg told her to go get it. She asked him to come with her. And with as strong a voice as she'd ever heard from him, Gregg turned and said, "No, I can't do that. I've got a band to put back together."

Most people at the funeral thought they had witnessed the fare-well performance of the Allman Brothers Band. "My impression was that was it," Shelley said. "But when he made that comment about having a band to put back together, I realized that they were going to keep going. That's where his energies were going to go and he was very, very focused about it."

The group was scheduled to perform two shows at Carnegie Hall on November 25, and to the surprise of many, they went back on the road as a five-piece band and the date was honored. The music became everyone's therapy. There was never any discussion of breaking up; that would have been emotional suicide. "We were going to take about six months off," Butch said. "But we were all just about going crazy. I mean, grief was starting to sink in and there was just no way to deal with that at home. So we hit the road. That's the only way to get it out of your system. It was very, very difficult. The hole was there. We'd be playing, I'd keep looking over and expecting Duane to come in. And he's not there. It was hard."

Once it was established that the band would go forward, rumors began flying. Eric Clapton was going to join the Allman Brothers Band. Or maybe Jimmy Page. But it was quickly decided to keep the group as it was; how could you replace Duane Allman? It would have been morbid, cheapening the brotherhood, to bring in someone and teach him Duane's licks. "I think they did everything right from the standpoint of not trying to replace Duane Allman," Phil Walden said. "That would've been very foolish and I don't think their fans would have accepted it. The band felt confident enough to continue with the remaining lineup and it was a very, very smart decision."

It also became a cross to bear for Dickey. He was suddenly thrust into the glare of the spotlight and put in the uncomfortable position of having to play guitar parts that Duane Allman had made famous. "I actually started thinking, man, you know, you must have really acted like it didn't bother you too much because you all got out and played a month after it happened," Dickey said. "A lot of it was he would have wanted it to carry on. That gives you the strength to go out there and try to play his parts and not be bothered by it. It was really hard to stand there and look at everybody's faces and play those parts."

They were all struggling to make sense of it, to put their world back together. Gregg didn't have the strength to face it. He buried his pain by sedating himself with the hardest drugs he could find. "Everybody was so completely stoned all the time that it was submerged," Shelley said. "It was hidden. There was no talking about it."

Geraldine Allman, whom everyone called "Mama A," stayed in Macon after the funeral to be with her remaining son, and she was into alcohol the way Gregg was into drugs. Mama A kept a glass by the kitchen sink. She'd finish a glass of whiskey, rinse out the glass, and put it upside down on a paper towel by the sink, ready for her next drink. Everybody knew to leave Mama A's glass right where it was. "Geraldine was an awfully strong presence in his life," Shelley said. "She was pretty heavy into alcohol when I knew her. She was into Canadian Mist and she could put that stuff away. I mean, she could drink Gregg under the table by noon."

*   *   *

A CORONER'S jury would judge Duane Allman's death "an unfortunate accident." A test turned up no traces of alcohol in Duane's blood,
and no charges were filed against the driver of the truck, Charles
Wertz. The bluecoats at the scene told reporters that Duane had
avoided the truck and just lost control of his bike. But two
eyewitnesses — Candace Oakley and Mike Kovar, who was driving a
car that had been directly behind the truck — said later that Duane
had collided with it.

Charles Wertz told investigators that he hadn't seen the motorcycle coming when he'd started to make the left onto Bartlett Avenue.
Bartlett was a dirt street and, as Wertz turned, the pavement stopped
and there were huge potholes in front of him. Because of that, Wertz
had made a complete stop halfway through his turn. He said he
looked up, saw the motorcycle coming and thought there was time for
the bike to slow down. By the time he tried to pull up and get out of
the way, it was too late.

Mike Kovar had been about three-quarters of a block behind the
truck when it began the left turn. He told police that the motorcycle
was driving near the curb as it came down the hill and when the driver
saw the truck, he began guiding the bike toward the centerline. Kovar
sensed the danger, and had stopped his car about eighty feet behind
the truck to give the motorcycle room to get by. "I think the boy on
the cycle thought the truck would clear the intersection by the time
he reached the end of the hill, and it didn't," Kovar said.

It took only two weeks for a legal fight to break out over Duane's
estate. Duane's affairs were typical of someone who is twenty-four
years old and without a lot of money. He'd never drawn up a will and
owned very little. His estate included the Harley-Davidson, a 1971
Volvo, a checking account with $116, a savings account with $2,023,
and $857 in cash that was found in his pocket at the hospital. The
Volvo would later be sold at public auction for $2,400 and, at the same
auction, Berry would pay $100 to buy all of Duane's furniture and
household furnishings. The local Harley dealer, the one Duane had
called from New York to check on new tires, bought his wrecked
Sportster for $500.

Donna Allman and Galadriel had been on a camping trip outside
St. Louis when Duane was killed. Most of the twenty or so campers
were big fans of the Allman Brothers, and word quickly spread that

Donna had been married to Duane Allman and that Galadriel was his daughter. The day after the accident, unaware that Duane's widow was among the campers and knew nothing of the incident, a second group had joined the others and mentioned they'd heard on the radio that Duane Allman had died. Donna returned to Macon for the funeral and quickly appointed Robert Steele, one of Macon's most skilled and liberal lawyers, to administrate Duane's estate on behalf of his lone heir, Galadriel.

Then, just fourteen days after the accident, Dixie Meadows filed a $6-million lawsuit in Bibb County State Court against Charles Wertz and Sam Hall & Sons, the company that owned the truck. She used the name "Dixie Allman" in the suit, claiming to be the "surviving widow of Duane Allman," and she said the amount of money she was demanding was equal to the full value of the life of Duane Allman. Then, days later, Dixie filed papers in Probate Court asking for money from Duane's estate for support.

Donna was determined not to lose a penny of Galadriel's inheritance. She protested Dixie's request for money from the estate, and filed a motion to block Dixie's lawsuit. She said Dixie's claim that she was Duane's wife was bogus, and filed a countersuit demanding $300,000 in damages for Galadriel from the driver and his employer. Dixie's lawsuit and her plea for support in Probate Court were dismissed in December when Donna's lawyers learned that Dixie was legally married in Mississippi and had been the entire time she was living with Duane. Donna's lawsuit on behalf of Galadriel against the driver remained active, and the defendants countered that Duane had lost control of his motorcycle due to his own negligence. The lawsuit would eventually go to nonjury trial and the same judge who had married Gregg and Shelley would award Galadriel $22,500 in damages; of that, $7,500 went for attorney fees.

IT was a hard Christmas for Gregg in 1971, another anniversary of his father's murder and his first Christmas without his big brother, and Gregg and Shelley invited friends over for dinner. "I made a big meal and Mama A made the eggnog," Shelley said. "It had so much brandy, or whatever it is you put into it, that everybody passed out. Our apartment was like, all these bodies. Everybody called it 'Mama A's Egg Nod.' "

It was one of the last happy times for the couple. Shelley had just learned she was pregnant, but she and Gregg were fighting constantly and he would disappear for days without letting her know where he was. "The drugs were heavy duty, I was pregnant, and that was it; the marriage was over," Shelley said.

Dickey was getting a divorce as well. Sandy Bluesky was pregnant with Dickey's child, and he made the split with Dale as cut-and-dried as possible. An agreement between them was already in the works, with Dickey promising to pay $20 a week in child support until their daughter, Elena Christine, was twenty-one. Dale also received a $3,000 cash settlement. Dickey's divorce may have been quick and quiet, but Gregg's was public and prolonged. Shelley said she originally went home to Texas with nothing. "I had told him to get screwed because I didn't want the money, and then I realized what I'd done," she said. Shelley had a child due in August, so she returned to Macon to hire an attorney.

Shelley and a friend checked into a hotel using her maiden name and hadn't been there very long before there was a knock at the door. "It was Gregg and Red Dog," Shelley said. "To this day, I don't know how they knew I was there. Somebody must have seen me. And he walked in and Red Dog looked at me. Of course, I was straight then and Red Dog goes, 'Aw, man, you're in trouble now. She's got her shit together and she's back to get you.' Gregg turned around and looked at me and said, 'How much do you want for this kid?' He was horrible. He was stoned. And I said, 'How much is your son worth to you, Gregg?' That did it. He stormed out of the room."

Then Phil Walden called her and asked her to stop by his office. "He wrote me a check for two thousand dollars. And he said, 'You need to go get on with your life.' And I said, 'Screw you' and gave him the check back. That was supposed to be it. He knew I was pregnant and the prenuptials, of course, weren't worth shit."

Shelley's lawyer, Kice Stone, began playing hardball. Within days of the separation, Jenny Arness — the daughter of "Gunsmoke" star James Arness — moved to Macon to live with Gregg. Stone filed a brief in court charging Gregg with "living in a meretricious relationship with the daughter of Jim Arness, alias Matt Dillon." It was designed for flashy headlines and got them, Gregg's first brush with tabloid journalism. A few days later, Gregg reached a settlement with Shelley. She was given $50 a month in alimony until she died or remarried, and $150 a month in child support until her unborn child reached the age of twenty-one.

Jenny Arness was in love with Gregg, but their relationship was short-lived. Jenny had a history of emotional problems and would commit suicide in 1975, overdosing on drugs and leaving behind a note that said she was despondent over the loss of a man she loved, Gregg Allman. One of her final requests would be for Gregg to sing "their song" at her wake. Gregg didn't make it.

THE first post-Duane album, *Eat a Peach,* came out in February of 1972. It was the band's second double album in a row, and nearly three sides were culled from leftover material recorded at the Fillmore East. There had been three new songs in the can at the time of the accident, and the band recorded three others afterward. The myth was that the band used the title because Duane had crashed into a peach truck when he died; in truth, it came from one of Duane's throwaway lines in an interview. "How are you helping the revolution?" Ellen Mandel of *Good Times Magazine* had asked him. "I'm hitting a lick for peace," Duane responded. "And every time I'm in Georgia, I eat a peach for peace."

Eat a Peach was a pivotal album. Before Duane died, the band was beginning to ride a wave of stardom that was still in its early stages but showing no signs of weakening. Interest in the record was keen; it would contain Duane's final performances and, even more, it would determine whether there was a future for the Allman Brothers Band without the most important brother.

Typically, when the guiding force behind a band quits or dies, it is over; no one knew what to expect from the new Allman Brothers Band, but Duane had been so central to the band's essence that no one expected very much. In order to succeed, the band had to draw from a hidden reservoir of talent that had been overshadowed by the sheer magnitude of Duane's presence. "When Duane was killed, there was a definite empty space there," Dickey said. "So somebody had to move forward in a hurry and fill that up with whatever they had. So Gregg moved forward and I moved forward and that changed it. It wasn't so different from the Allman Brothers Band; it was like playing up another part of the Allman Brothers Band."

Eat a Peach — "Dedicated to a Brother" — begins with the three new songs recorded without Duane. The band wanted to make an immediate statement that the surviving members could carry on the tradition. The album kicks off with a song Gregg had written in the weeks following the accident, "Ain't Wastin' Time No More." In the first four lines, Gregg lays himself as emotionally bare as he ever had in a song, writing poignantly about his struggle to come to terms with the death of his big brother. There's a sadly revealing look at Gregg's

Phil Walden, wearing a Jimmy Carter button on his lapel and holding a Capricorn cup, making a point in front of the offices at 535 Cotton Avenue. (*William Berry*)

Gregg and Cher on their first date in Macon at Le Bistro. (*William Berry*)

Scooter Herring after his conviction. "There are no hard feelings," Scooter said. "Gregg was a junkie. He would have testified to anything to get away and get a fix." (*William Berry / Courtesy Macon Telegraph and News*)

Backstage during the Win, Lose or Draw tour as everything was falling apart. (*Courtesy Macon Telegraph and News*)

Dickey playing his prized gold-top Les Paul with BHLT at the Moonshadow in Atlanta. (*Scott Freeman*)

Back in Macon at the City Auditorium, March 5, 1983. (*William Berry*)

Dickey plays it sweet and low in his den in Bradenton, Florida, in 1984. (*William Berry*)

Jaimoe behind his drums in 1984 in the practice room at his home in Macon. (*William Berry*)

Elise Trucks with Butch and Melinda in 1984 at their home in Talla-hassee; behind them is a mural painted by Melinda. (*William Berry*)

Duane, Jessica, Paulette, and Dickey on the dock behind their house. (*William Berry*)

Phil Walden and Zelma Redding, the widow of Otis Redding, at a U.S. Postal Service ceremony in Macon in 1993 honoring the late singer with a stamp. (*James Borchuck / Courtesy Macon Telegraph and News*)

Shelley Allman Jefts and Devon Lane Allman. (*Scott Freeman*)

Warren Haynes is a key element in the band's great comeback. (*Danny Gilleland / Courtesy Macon Telegraph and News*)

Gregg at the City Auditorium in Macon during the Dreams reunion tour. (*Danny Gilleland / Courtesy Macon Telegraph and News*)

The surviving original four in Florida for the 1989 reunion tour. (*William Berry*)

way of dealing with his loss; if you look inside yourself and don't like what you see, he sings, then leave your mind alone and just get high.

The biggest surprise is Dickey's transformation into an electric bottleneck guitarist. It was a revelation; no one in the band even knew he played it. Dickey uses simple licks, but it is immediately apparent that slide isn't something he had picked up a couple of weeks earlier. In fact, Dickey had been listening to records by people like Kokomo Arnold and Robert Johnson since his teens, and he was an accomplished acoustic bottleneck player even though he had never been recorded on the instrument. Dickey sounds comfortable and confident on electric slide, and he had obviously learned a lot from Duane.

Dickey wrote a new instrumental that he called "Les Brers in A Minor" — Cajun-French for "The Brothers in A Minor" — and it was the most sophisticated and challenging piece of music the band had tackled. Berry is dominant throughout; his bass is almost a second lead guitar. The introduction is dreamy, often dissonant, and there is layer upon layer of percussion. Butch plays drums, tympani, and a gong. Jaimoe is on congas and drums. Even Dickey gets into the act by playing monkey skulls. The opening movement lasts nearly four minutes and then Berry comes barreling through with a supercharged bass line.

The third track is a lovely version of "Melissa," the song that Gregg had originally recorded for the 31st of February with Duane playing bottleneck guitar. When Gregg and Sandy Alaimo wrote it in 1967, "Melissa" had seemed like a nice love song; now, five years later, it seemed like a downright spooky premonition about his brother's death. Gregg sings it in the third person, talking about a man on the road, the gypsy, whose mind stays locked on thoughts of his sweet Melissa waiting for him back home. The tempo is slow and mournful. Gregg's tender vocals, along with Dickey's haunting guitar lines, set the mood. The gypsy dies in the final verse, and there is an eerie reference to the Robert Johnson myth when Gregg asks if the crossroads will ever let go of the dead man's ghost.

Two of the songs that came from the Fillmore East shows are next. Sonny Boy Williamson's "One Way Out" begins with Dickey playing a funky opening riff and Butch riding his cymbal behind him. Jaimoe comes in and, with a little drum roll, the whole band falls in. The Allman Brothers Band completely remake "One Way Out," from Dickey's opening guitar lines to two new verses — the only real similarity to the original is in the title and opening lines. Gregg's voice is perfect, bragging and boastful and cocky, and Dickey follows the opening verses with one of his finest solos from the Fillmore shows. His guitar lines, fluid and sinewy, offer traces of the loping style that would become his trademark. Duane's bottleneck solo is short and, as in "Done Somebody Wrong," he wails from high up on the fret board.

There is a live version of "Trouble No More," followed by the last tracks the band cut in the studio with Duane. "Stand Back," co-written by Berry and Gregg, sounds as if it was left over from the *Idlewild South* sessions. Duane said in one of his final interviews that he didn't begin to feel comfortable with the bottleneck until he recorded this song, and he does something here that he had never done before. Rather than playing his trademark fill-in riffs, he makes his guitar sound like a full-blown horn section with a two-note riff that could have been the Memphis Horns backing up Otis Redding.

"Blue Sky" is a striking departure, an outright country-and-western tune. It is Dickey's love song to Sandy Bluesky, a projection of contentment against a backdrop of southern images like church bells ringing on a Sunday morning and birds singing on a backwoods dirt road. The song marks Dickey's first appearance as a vocalist on an Allman Brothers album; his voice was so earnest and sincere that they couldn't imagine him *not* singing it. Though far from the band's traditional sound, it was still unmistakably the Allman Brothers. There are a half dozen beautiful guitar runs, intricate, difficult lines that Duane and Dickey play effortlessly.

Duane again uses pedal-steel guitar effects, as he had on "Midnight Rider," and his solo has some of the sweetest licks of his career. The notes are warm, soaked with feelings of love and springing to heights of joy, and his control of the bending notes is spectacular. Dickey comes in to play a solo filled with wonderful flurries of notes that are tied together by interlocking melody lines. Berry asserts himself underneath Dickey, and together they push the song to its climax.

Just as "Blue Sky" was Dickey's ode to Sandy, Duane considered "Little Martha" his song for Dixie. The acoustic instrumental is the only song that Duane wrote by himself, and it came to him in a dream — he was in a room at some Holiday Inn with Jimi Hendrix, who was telling Duane about his new song; he walked over to a sink and, using the faucet as a guitar fret board, he began playing it for Duane. When Duane woke up, he picked up his acoustic guitar, tuned to open D for bottleneck, and recaptured the music that Jimi Hendrix had shown him in the dream.

The title came from Rose Hill. Just off one of the main passageways in the cemetery is a four-foot-tall statue of a sad-eyed little girl standing over her grave. She has a single rose in her left hand, and is forlornly looking off to the distance. Her name was Martha Ellis, and she died in 1896 at the age of twelve. "Our baby," reads the inscription on her grave. "She was love personified and her memory is a sweet solace by day, and pleasant dreams by night to Momma, Papa, brothers and sisters. We will meet again in the sweet bye and bye."

"MOUNTAIN Jam" was also recorded at the Fillmore. Taking up two entire album sides, it is the Allman Brothers Band at its most ambitious. The jam, tracking in at over thirty-three minutes, grew out of a short and simple folk song by Donovan called "There Is a Mountain." Duane had first played it sitting in one night with the Grateful Dead at the Fillmore East in early 1970. The Brothers had opened for the Dead and everyone was flying on LSD. Fleetwood Mac showed up that night, and Mick Fleetwood sat in on drums while Duane and Peter Green and Jerry Garcia jammed on "Dark Star" and then the Donovan song. The Allman Brothers soon added the "Mountain Jam" to its song list and, in a year's time, it had gone from a meandering, seemingly directionless jam into a focused and often majestic song that was divided up into several separate and distinct movements.

The *Fillmore* album had faded out to the opening strains of "Mountain Jam" at the close of "Whipping Post," and that's where the song begins on *Eat a Peach*. Butch pounds the tympani and Duane comes in to state the theme while Dickey plays counternotes during the pauses. Jaimoe comes in and Berry begins rambling on his bass. Duane and Dickey and Berry play over and under one another, then Butch sits down behind his traps and the band locks in together for the primary melody. They play a second verse and Berry asserts himself, pushing his bass and momentarily challenging for the spotlight. Then the tempo shifts into a swinging shuffle as Duane begins a solo that starts off almost hesitantly, until he digs in for a series of gritty guitar riffs.

It's over quickly and Gregg plays a solo filled with interesting little melodies before it leads to Dickey's guitar. Dickey's lead is packed with inventive flourishes; he creates a riff, then repeats it over and over, playing it just a little differently each time. Then he goes to another one and, again, sticks with it until he's played nearly a half dozen different combinations of the notes. Berry always stoked Dickey, and here he plays wonderful rising melodies on the bass behind the lead. Dickey takes his solo higher and higher until Duane and Berry join him, and all three lock in on the same riff way up on the necks of their guitars. Then the song gently glides down and settles back into the main theme. The tempo begins to slow to a crawl, and Duane gets out his Coricidin bottle and re-creates the crying bird from "Layla" just before the band falls out, leaving Butch and Jaimoe on-stage alone.

Until the Allman Brothers Band, drum solos came primarily from jazz players. D. J. Fontana never performed a solo behind Elvis. Ringo Starr hated drum solos to the point he had to be practically forced to do a brief one on *Abbey Road,* the only solo he ever performed on record. And the few rock bands that tried it usually put the audience to sleep.

The Allman Brothers Band was different. There were *two* drummers, two very good drummers, each with distinct styles and the ability to merge them into something musically dynamic. "I'd have to look real hard to find two drummers that could play like we do together," Butch said. "That's probably not possible. I've played with a lot of other drummers and you just can't do it. The Grateful Dead tried it but it doesn't work, it was very contrived. They'd work out patterns and each one does a certain type thing. Their whole approach is very structured. And with Jaimoe and I, it is just totally free, totally spontaneous, do what you feel like doing. And it works. Somehow our styles just mesh perfectly. It probably has to do with our backgrounds. We both started in marching bands, have a good background in rudimental drumming and in technical approaches. Then I went into very patterned drumming, and Jaimoe went into jazz and rhythm and blues. So they meshed. They meshed beautifully."

The drum solo on "Mountain Jam" starts off with Butch playing like Buddy Rich on speed, pounding his toms and snare while Jaimoe keeps the rhythm. To hear them, you'd think they were using two huge drum sets to get their wall of sound. But each plays small kits — a kick drum, snare, one tom, and a floor drum. Jaimoe even uses a small, jazz-sized kick drum. Butch settles into a rhythm beat and Jaimoe comes in, emphasizing his floor drum and cymbals before going into jazz rolls while Butch keeps time. Butch does a roll and soon they are both flailing away together.

Berry comes in for a bass solo that goes through several funky beats before he settles into a run that is frightening, like the intro to "Whipping Post" magnified and extended. He goes back to the main theme, and Duane counts off "One, two, three" for the whole band to join in. Butch is late and, for a few seconds, everything's off-kilter, stumbling. Then Butch plays a short, angry-sounding drumroll, and he and Jaimoe are back in perfect sync, as is everyone else.

What follows is Duane Allman at the pinnacle of his powers. He begins his solo on bottleneck — one of only three times he would play slide in standard tuning on an Allman Brothers song — with notes that are gentle and caressing. Then he slides the bottle up high, and the band pushes him with a series of descending notes played in unison. Duane brings it back down, and the music comes to a near halt. Duane takes off the Coricidin bottle and guides the song into "Will the Circle Be Unbroken?" The notes bend upward as though it's music escaping from the very core of his soul, and every so often he'll suddenly jump high on the scale. The sounds coming from his Les Paul are filled with sadness and finality — as if he knows he is playing his own eulogy.

The song drifts back into the main theme and, for one final moment, the Allman Brothers Band is in full glory. Butch hustles back to the tympani and the ending rumbles up in a wave of sound. Dickey plays screaming notes over the finale while Duane uncharacteristically lays back and is hardly noticeable, as though he is making a symbolic passing of the torch.

"Thank you," a breathless Duane yells into the mike when the song is finished. "Berry Oakley, Dickey Betts, Butch Trucks, Jai Johnny Johnson, Gregg Allman, and I'm Duane Allman. Thank you." It is as if he is closing the book on this magnificent group of musicians, waving to the crowd and walking off the stage. For the very last time.

Part III

The Fall

Duane put that fire and that confidence into everybody.
And after he was gone, that was the one thing that stayed,
that kept us vital and kept us strong. He kind of started
the religion and left us as the apostles.

— Butch Trucks

Twelve

Blues for B.O.

EAT a Peach acted as both a benediction and a promising bridge to the future, and the decision to keep the band together had the opposite effect that many had predicted. People didn't tune out the Allman Brothers because the guiding force was no longer there; instead, their admiration grew because of the band's determination to carry on. In a review that helped give the new lineup important credibility, *Rolling Stone* lauded the album. "The Allman Brothers are still the best god-damned band in the land," wrote reviewer Tony Glover. "I hope the band keeps playing forever — how many groups can you think of who really make you believe they're playing for the joy of it?"

The Allman Brothers had been on the brink of superstardom and *Eat a Peach* shifted the momentum into fifth gear. They hit the road in the spring of 1972 for a tour that would last until the fall. For a group in dire need of good news, it came in droves. *Eat a Peach* zipped up the charts and landed in the Top 5. The band was playing bigger and bigger halls, and headlined the Mar Y Sol Festival in Puerto Rico. Dickey and Sandy Bluesky had a little girl, Jessica Leigh Betts, who was born May 14. Butch and Linda Trucks also had a little girl, Melody Louise Trucks, who was born on June 28. And Devon Lane Allman was born in Corpus Christi to Shelley on August 10.

But beneath the tranquil veneer, the Allman Brothers Band was already showing signs of meandering like a rudderless ship. Because Gregg was now the sole Allman in the band, the public naturally assumed he had picked up the leadership mantle. But Gregg was incapable. "Gregg depended on Duane to kind of get him in gear and point him in the right direction," said Johnny Sandlin. "Once he was pointed, Gregg was a great musician and singer. After Duane died, he didn't have that sense of direction and no one was there to make sure he had direction. It was so sad. I know how it affected me, and me and Duane were real close friends. I can't imagine how it affected his brother, especially his little brother. I can't even imagine a loss like that."

With Duane no longer there to show his baby brother the way, it was as if Gregg had lost his voice of reason. "Duane was more like Gregg's father than his brother," Butch said. "And when he went down, you know, Gregg just got uncontrollable. You just couldn't count on him for anything."

No one in the band really looked to Gregg to step into Duane's shoes; they probably wouldn't have let him had he even tried. But they were waiting for *somebody* to step up, and much of the burden fell onto Berry Oakley's shoulders. He became the band's new father figure. More than anyone else, Berry had bought into Duane's dream and loved him like the brother he never had. Duane may have led them, but Berry had been his first lieutenant.

It soon became apparent that the leadership role was too heavy a weight for Berry to carry alone — and no one was volunteering to help him. He was too sweet-tempered to prod them the way Duane had, and he was having a difficult time pulling out of his mourning. Berry and Duane had been soul mates, and without him Berry felt lost. He was drinking heavily, doing far too many drugs. The band played one gig in Chicago, Berry's hometown. His friends and family were seated at banquet tables in front of the stage; Berry was so out of it that he fell off the stage and crashed into one of the tables. Joe Dan Petty, who had played with Dickey's band back in Florida, picked up Berry's bass and the band finished the gig with the roadie sitting in with them.

"I'm not saying anything derogatory about Berry because I love him to death," said Kim Payne. "But if Berry had been a stronger person, with the leadership capabilities to pull everything together, it all might have turned out differently. He was just too into his own grief. He'd gotten on a real downhill spiral, and everybody was just hoping he'd pull out of it."

People began whispering that Berry had a death wish. He started listening to Robert Johnson, especially "Hellhound on My Trail," Johnson's song about the mortal consequences of having been to the crossroads. It was one of the last songs Robert Johnson ever recorded, and he sang it as though he was out of breath and had stumbled into a temporary sanctuary just long enough to tell the tormented tale. Berry seemed to talk incessantly about the hellhound, that it was on his trail and closing in. Then he developed a motorcycle fetish. He was not a motorcycle person and was known as a terrible rider, but there he was, embracing the very thing that, in his mind, had destroyed his world.

Candace Oakley still gets defensive when she hears people talking about her brother's problems. "Yes, he was drinking too much," she said. "Yes, he was doing a lot of cocaine. Berry wasn't doing anything that everyone else wasn't doing and there were several that were doing it a lot worse." She said Berry was trying to do his best to hold the band together and to look after the business end. He kept a little black book of every place the band played, including head counts and money totals, and he wasn't happy with what he was seeing. Berry didn't think things were adding up, and he even spoke to his father about hiring someone to audit Capricorn Records. "He knew the band was losing money it was due," Candace said. "He tried to get each one in the band to go in with him. They didn't want to hear about it."

By then, many of the others in the band had stopped looking to Berry for leadership; he was having a tough enough time just keeping himself together. They ignored his call for a financial review and, instead, held a secret meeting and went to Linda and tried to convince her to commit Berry to get him off alcohol and hard drugs. The intentions were good but, considering the lifestyles of the others, it was a move that some viewed as dripping in hypocrisy.

With the success of *Eat a Peach*, the money was beginning to roll in. The band members got their take after everything else was deducted — expenses, the salaries of the road crew, and Phil Walden's 25 percent. They had made less than $15,000 each in 1970. But Gregg alone had earned $62,734 in 1971 and that figure would jump to $103,526 by the end of 1972, incredible money in that era. With Dickey as the catalyst, the band bought a 440-acre farm in Juliette, a whistlestop town a few miles from Macon. The band laid out $160,000 for the spread, more than three times what the owner had paid just two years earlier. The farm had open pasture and it was good horseback-riding country. Eventually, the band had about twenty quarter horses and built a stable to house them. The farm quickly became Dickey's domain. "It was like squatter's rights," Candace said. "At one point, Berry was going to build a house on the land; well, Dickey had just started building. Nobody ever sat down to figure out how to divide up the land. That farm was running the band ninety-two thousand dollars a year."

The property was bordered by a game reserve on one side and a hunting club on the other. "It was pretty dangerous going in and out of there," said Kim. "You had to roll your windows up during bow season because those arrows would come flying by from the hunting club. One of those sons of bitches shot my horse with a high-powered rifle; my horse was an Appaloosa and don't look nothing like a deer. She turned out okay, we got a vet out there. We all started taking turns riding fence after that. Armed. Well armed. Keeping them hunters out of there. We posted it."

The fence around the spread ran nearly five miles and they often rode out to guard it; Dickey usually carried a .30-.30-caliber bolt-action rifle that he kept on his hip. One day he caught someone hunting on the property, a guy Dickey described as looking as if he'd just gotten outfitted at Kmart. The ground was wet, and the intruder didn't hear Dickey and Joe Dan Petty ride up until Dickey popped a cartridge into his rifle chamber. The hunter claimed he was lost, but he had climbed over the fence within five feet of a No Trespassing sign. Dickey marched him back to the cabin at gunpoint — over a mile through woods and swamps — then called the Sheriff's Office and had him arrested.

"Which surprised me, Dickey usually didn't want to have nothing to do with the law," Kim said. "He was a serious outlaw to start with. That's how he got into music, so he could make money to buy parts for his motorcycle. He used to ride all over southern Florida with a denim jacket on that had 'Eat Shit' written across the back. Is that ballsy or what? It's there for the whole world to see: 'It don't matter who you are, kiss my ass and eat shit; I'm not interested in striking up a relationship or nothing, just eat shit.' He got busted by the cops down there for cattle rustling and they threw his ass in jail. He'd gotten hungry, stopped along the road and jumped a fence and knocked a cow in the head and killed it. And he was butchering that damned cow when they came up on him. That's a true story. It happened before the Allman Brothers. He got some jail time about that. He was kind of like an independent loner biker. He was rough and rowdy. You could say he had a bad attitude. Dickey had to work on his attitude."

*   *   *

WHILE the Allman Brothers Band was struggling to regain its balance, Capricorn Records was beginning to gather some real momentum and fulfill Phil Walden's dream of a recording empire in his
hometown in the backwoods of Georgia. When Duane died, Phil was
on the verge of breaking Capricorn's ties to Atlantic for a multimillion-
dollar distribution deal with Warner Brothers Records. Phil's three-
year contract with Atlantic was up, and he thought the label was less
than appreciative of what he had going down in Macon. Warners was
an industry powerhouse; it even owned Atlantic Records.

Duane's death had threatened to throw the whole deal into
limbo; at the time, the Allman Brothers Band *was* Capricorn Records,
and Phil had to scramble to convince Warner Brothers that the band
could go forward. "We convinced Warners we could not only continue,
but rise to new heights," Phil said. "The deal was concluded about six
days after Duane's death, before the Allman Brothers had even gone
back on the road, before another concert, and before another record
came out."

Phil Walden didn't set out to make Capricorn Records the label
of choice for southern rockers, it just naturally veered that way. Capricorn soon became the destination point for dozens of talented southern bands that saw no hope at all in trying to interest Yankee record
companies in their style of music. "There are hundreds of these little
bands in the South," Frank Fenter, Capricorn's executive vice-
president, said. "These southern groups could never afford to get into
a truck and go to LA, go to San Francisco, or go to New York and get
an audition with a big company. Nobody has ever bothered to look
down here, and that's basically why southern bands didn't happen."

Phil had kept his word about giving Johnny Sandlin a chance to
produce records, and Johnny was in charge of most of the albums
recorded at Capricorn Studios. Tom Dowd was tied to Atlantic and
after Phil made the switch to Warner Brothers, Johnny was the natural
choice to become the band's producer when work began in the fall of
1972 on the album that would become *Brothers and Sisters*. In addition,
Gregg simultaneously decided to start work on a solo album with a
batch of songs that he didn't think fit the style of the Allman Brothers,
and Johnny was put in charge of that project as well. One of the musicians he called to play on Gregg's record was pianist Chuck Leavell,
an old friend from Alabama who had settled in Macon. "I'd known
Chuck since he was fourteen; he was a great singer who played piano,

and we always wanted to get him over to Macon as a singer," Johnny said. "It turned out that he had stopped singing and started really playing piano."

Chuck was only nineteen years old, but already he was the best piano player in town. Johnny had a hidden agenda: the Allman Brothers Band could never replace Duane Allman, but what if they added a pianist? "I wanted Chuck to play on *Brothers and Sisters*. I talked to Gregg about it and Gregg, I guess, convinced the rest of them to try him out." By then bringing in new blood was looking like a good idea. The band had found it difficult to perform many of its old songs onstage because they depended on twin melody lines. Without another lead instrument to reinforce Dickey, those songs often lost a lot of texture. And Dickey welcomed someone to take the pressure away from him. "Chuck gave a different color to the band," Johnny said. "It gave them somebody who could play some of the twin stuff that Duane had played but it wasn't like somebody taking Duane's place as a guitar player. I was definitely hoping they would add Chuck."

CHARLES ALFRED LEAVELL was born on April 28, 1952, the son of William Alfred Leavell and Frances Earle Harrison Leavell. The youngest of three children, Chuck grew up in Tuscaloosa and was barely out of diapers when he began playing the piano. "My mother played and I would listen to her and imitate her," he said. Chuck played tuba in junior high and also learned to play the guitar. "Then something really big happened," he said. "I couldn't have been any more than twelve or thirteen years old, and my sister took me to a Ray Charles concert. And that changed my entire life. I'd never seen anything like that. It just totally blew me away, what he did with music and with his voice and with the piano and with the arrangements with the big band. It all of a sudden opened up a totally different world."

Chuck started a band called the Misfits that became popular around Tuscaloosa and soon had its own television show, "Tuscaloosa Bandstand." It was just like "American Bandstand," only there was a live band instead of records. "It was just so much fun, having a band back then," said Chuck. "You were popular and all the girls liked you because you were in a band, all the guys looked up to you because you were up there on a stage, and I decided that was what I wanted to do. There was no doubt in my mind."

After that, Chuck joined Southcamp, the group Paul Hornsby

had put together following the demise of Hour Glass. Paul, who played organ and guitar in the band and left the piano work to Chuck, was a tremendous influence. He had the patience to teach Chuck many of his licks, especially stuff he had copied from Ray Charles records. The band broke up when Paul decided to go to Macon. Then, halfway through his senior year of high school, Chuck got a phone call from Paul, who was getting ready to produce an album by a Capricorn band called Sundown. "Hey, I don't know what you're up to, but if you're interested, there's a band looking for a keyboard player over here," Paul told him.

The offer intrigued Chuck. He had friends in Macon and with the legendary Barry Beckett entrenched at Muscle Shoals, he knew his future was limited as a studio pianist in Alabama. But at Capricorn, the horizons could be endless. By then, Chuck was in trouble in school. He was playing so many gigs that he was piling up absences. The principal had called him in and told him state law mandated so many days of attendance; even though Chuck was maintaining a B average, he couldn't afford to miss any more classes if he wanted to graduate. "There was no way I could attend every day," Chuck said. "I was just too involved in music." The call from Paul Hornsby felt like fate knocking. Chuck decided to quit high school and told Paul he was on his way to Macon.

The Sundown album flopped but Chuck went on the road backing up Alex Taylor, one of James Taylor's brothers. "That was my first real road gig," Chuck said. "We went all over the country at least five times." Many of Alex Taylor's gigs came as the opening act for the Allman Brothers Band. Chuck had just turned eighteen and, like nearly every other young white musician from the South, he revered the Allmans. People thought it was kind of cute the way Chuck would roll his upright piano to the back of the stage when the Allman Brothers were performing and then, like a kid playing along with records at home, sit down behind the curtains and spend two or three hours blissfully accompanying them.

When Alex Taylor had a falling out with Phil Walden and left the label, Chuck and the entire backup band went to work with Dr. John, the New Orleans piano master who also was managed by Phil. "That was a real, real education for me," said Chuck, who primarily played organ for Dr. John. "He is such a wonderful cat. The most enjoyable times would be sitting in a dressing room. There'd be an old upright piano sitting there and that guy would sit down and play and play and play."

The gig with Dr. John lasted only five months and Chuck found himself unemployed again. He didn't know whether to go back to Alabama and regroup or stay in Macon and hope he landed another job. Then came a call from Johnny Sandlin. "What are you doing?" Johnny asked him.

"Well, I'm looking," Chuck replied.

"How'd you like to play on Gregg Allman's solo record?" Johnny asked.

After a couple of rehearsals, Chuck was told to come back to Capricorn Studio to begin the actual recording. He got there early and sat down behind the piano to warm up and to make sure everything was in working order. Butch Trucks walked in. And Jaimoe. Then came Berry Oakley and Dickey Betts. And Gregg. No one said much to him and Chuck was puzzled. This was supposed to be a session for Gregg's solo album, yet here was everybody in the Allman Brothers Band kicking into a blues. Chuck didn't know whether to get up and leave or stay and join in. Since no one had told him to get out, he began playing along with them. By then, Chuck was very confused: what was he doing playing with the Allman Brothers Band?

A few days later, Gregg sauntered over to him in the studio. "How would you like to be in the band?" Gregg asked.

Chuck was puzzled. He thought he was already in Gregg's band, for the solo album. "What band?" he replied.

"Our band," Gregg said.

The implication began sinking in. "Let's get this straight," said Chuck. "What band are we talking about? You mean the Allman Brothers Band?"

There was a meeting at Phil's office to make it official. After some chitchat, Phil dramatically leaned over his desk. "Chuck, are you interested in being a member of the Allman Brothers Band?"

Chuck grinned. "Hell, yes," he said.

For such a major move, Chuck's emergence as a member of the band seemed almost casual. He was taking over the musical chair of one of rock's all-time greatest guitarists. He also was stepping into one of the most popular bands in the country; everyone was expecting the next album to put the group over the top. It was a highly charged situation, but Chuck was so innocent that it rolled off his back. "I was just happy to have some work," he said. "I never really felt pressure all that much. Music is music, and it's not meant to be felt as pressure. The attitude was: take your time, everybody's here to enjoy the music and let's play. I was excited more than anything else to be playing with the guys. I felt for the first time, you know, man, I got a break. I'd sort of climbed the ladder a little bit and, all of a sudden, I was hurled into one of the top groups of the day. And, hey, man, I was nineteen years old."

The recording sessions for *Brothers and Sisters* went at a relaxed pace once they commenced in October of 1972. "We were just taking our time and they were feeling me out and I was feeling them out," Chuck said. "We'd come in every night and just play. It was largely just jams, not really songs. Every now and then somebody'd say, 'Let's learn a song,' and we'd learn one and then we'd put it down on tape."

Outside the sessions, there was tension building over the band's recording contract. With the success of *Eat a Peach*, their 5 percent royalty rate was beginning to seem measly and they went to Phil to try to renegotiate. "We had achieved a great deal of success and cruised through just thinking everything was fine," Butch said. "Little by little, we started talking to other people — specifically, Charlie Daniels, who had very little success at that time and had just signed a fourteen-percent record deal with Epic. It got us to thinking. We went to Phil and said we wanted another contract. He said no. We went back to him and he eventually came up with an eight-percent offer. This was a verbal agreement and the next statement we received didn't reflect the eight percent. So Dickey took it upon himself to go in and try to force Phil to give us a new contract. He went back and said, 'Hey, we get a deal up around twelve percent or I'm taking my fifty thousand dollars that I've got saved and I'm going to Tahiti.' "

It would be the first time that the band would encounter an odd peculiarity about its relationship with Phil Walden. Typically, if a band wants a better deal from its record company, it sends its manager to negotiate. But in this case, their manager and the record company were one and the same. They could hardly expect Phil to negotiate with himself — it was a conflict of interest just waiting to happen.

Phil remembered the sequence much differently. He said that he decided the band deserved a new contract and that *he* approached them. "I stepped out of this situation almost entirely from all standpoints other than the fact that I made a suggestion," Phil said. "I did that to avoid confusing the two roles I played there."

An agreement was hammered out and on November 1, 1972, the band took a break from the recording sessions to sign the new contract. The band received a $100,000 advance that Capricorn would recoup from record sales. The contract stipulated the 12 percent rate that Dickey had fought for; financial statements and royalty payments were due quarterly. It was a one-year contract, with Capricorn having up to four annual options, and it called for enough songs to fill up a double album each year of the deal. The band was given unlimited free studio time if it used Capricorn Studios, and Gregg and Dickey agreed to have all their songs published by No Exit Music, the company owned by Phil. Everyone signed the contract, including Jaimoe this time.

There was just one hitch. The band thought the 12 percent rate covered its entire catalog; Phil Walden considered it to cover only the albums released after the new contract was signed. He continued paying the old 5 percent royalty on the four albums the group had released prior to the renegotiation. The disagreement would grow into a bitter dispute that would eventually help topple the musical empire Phil was establishing with Capricorn Records and cost band members millions of dollars.

EVERYONE flew to New York after signing the contract. They had to be at Hofstra University the following morning to tape the band's first national television appearance, the premier of a new late-night show produced by Don Kirshner on ABC-TV called "In Concert." It would also be Chuck's first gig as a member of the Allman Brothers Band. They were the first of several bands to perform that day, scheduled to go on at the ungodly hour, for a musician, of eleven-thirty in the morning. There was a ninety-minute delay before the band finally took the stage about one o'clock and debuted a new song called "Ramblin' Man," a country-flavored tune that Dickey had written. Dickey's eyes darted back and forth as though he was nervous, and Gregg's eyes drooped as if he had just woken up or never went to bed. As Berry played, he moved his legs up and down in time to the beat, like someone walking in a field of tar trying to lift his legs and unable to do it. Berry looked dangerously thin; he had dropped down to 145 pounds.

After the show, the band returned to Macon to continue work on the new album. Nine days later, on a Saturday afternoon, Berry and Kim Payne showed up out at the Idlewild South farm. Chuck was living there with Scott Boyer, the musician who had played with Butch in the 31st of February and was now in a Macon band called Cowboy. "We're going to have a jam tonight, man, and I want you guys to come," Berry said. He was gathering up a bunch of musicians for a show he had dubbed "The Berry Oakley Jive-Ass Revue, featuring the Rowdy Roadies and the Shady Ladies." Berry had reserved the stage at a club called the Ad Lib in downtown Macon. But first, he said, there would be a rehearsal over at the Big House, and Berry told them to come by there at around three o'clock.

After leaving Idlewild South, Berry and Kim rode their motorcycles over to west Macon and hung out a few minutes with Tuffy Phillips, who drove the band's equipment truck. When they left just before two in the afternoon, Berry and Kim headed up Napier Avenue on their way back to the Big House, clowning around and playfully messing with one another on their bikes as they drove. As they reached the intersection of Bartlett Avenue, Kim passed a car on the right side and Berry, driving his dark blue 1967 Triumph, went around it on the left. Kim sprinted ahead of him, then slowed to go through a tricky intersection at Inverness Avenue, where the street goes hard to the right. As Kim went through the sharp curve, a city bus passed by him in the opposite direction.

The bus driver saw the two motorcycles coming toward him and instinctively knew that one of them was going too fast to make the curve. He swerved the bus hard to his right and slammed on his brakes trying to avoid a collision; the skid marks stretched for almost thirty feet. Still, Berry's motorcycle shot across the centerline and slammed into the middle of the bus.

Kim turned around just in time to see the accident. "I knew Berry was probably turning on the gas to catch up with me," Kim said. "I looked back to see how he was doing; I knew he wasn't very good at riding." He saw the Triumph motorcycle bounce off the big bus, then hit it again toward the rear. Berry was thrown from his bike and went skidding across the street. The Triumph went in the same direction and eventually landed on top of him, fifty-eight feet away from the point of impact.

Kim slammed on his brakes to turn around, and a brutal thought flashed through his mind: "Oh, shit, here we go again."

Thirteen

And the Road Goes On Forever

BERRY was knocked out when Kim reached him, but soon came around. "At first I started panicking," Kim said. "Then he got up and walked around like there wasn't nothing wrong. I told Berry to lay there but he got up. Berry talked coherent and seemed all right." Berry was bleeding from the nose and the mouth, but it soon stopped and he walked over to his motorcycle and examined the damage; the front fender, headlight, and left foot peg were damaged, and the motor was dented on the left side.

The police and an ambulance were there quickly. Berry was oddly silent, walking around without saying a word to anyone other than Kim. And all he told Kim was that he was all right and wanted to go home. Patrolman Wayne Bennett was friendly with Berry from working security at a couple of the band's concerts, and he knew that a nosebleed could be a sign of head injuries. "I kept telling him to go to the hospital but he wouldn't," Bennett said.

Berry caught a ride home from someone passing by. A few minutes later, Chuck Leavell pulled up at the Big House. "As I was walking in, some of the guys in the road crew were carrying Berry down the stairs and he was delirious, man," Chuck said. "I said, 'What in the world is going on?' Of course, he'd had his motorcycle accident. He'd gotten up and went back home and then he got delirious and out of his head. He didn't want to go to the hospital but they physically carried him. I had just pulled up in my station wagon. So we all got in my car and drove him over to the emergency room."

Berry was unconscious when he arrived at the Medical Center at 2:55 in the afternoon. "The doctors told me later they didn't think they could have saved him even if he had gone straight from the accident," Wayne Bennett said. "He fractured his skull and was hemorrhaging." At 3:40 in the afternoon of November 11, 1972, Raymond Berry Oakley III was pronounced dead. He was twenty-four years old.

THE funeral was much like Duane's had been. There was a service in a Catholic church and then a private memorial at Hart's Mortuary, across the street from where Duane's funeral was held. Again the band played, with Johnny Sandlin sitting in on bass. ABC broadcast the premier episode of the "In Concert" series just thirteen days after the crash and everyone sat in front of the television as if seeing a ghost. "It was his last gig because he had died the following week," Candace Oakley said. "They aired it and dedicated it to Berry. We sat there and stared at it in a stupor. By that point, you do denial — no, it can't happen; I just won't accept it, anything but that."

In some ways, Berry's accident was even more crushing than Duane's death had been. Their world had already been kicked out from under them once, and they had spent the past year trying to build it back up only to see it crumble yet again. "When Berry was killed, that one kind of floored me," Dickey said. "It hit like [punching his open hand with a fist] . . . Boom! It was hard to deal with. Berry was . . . well, we were all living pretty reckless and we'd been told that if you guys don't slow down a little, this is gonna happen again."

The similarities in the deaths of Duane Allman and Berry Oakley are striking. Both crashed motorcycles. The accidents happened within a thousand yards of each other on two streets that run parallel. Duane had just crossed Inverness Avenue when he collided with a truck at the intersection of Bartlett Avenue; Berry had just crossed Bartlett Avenue when he collided with a bus at the intersection of Inverness Avenue. Both were twenty-four when they died. The drivers of the truck and bus were also each twenty-four.

Had they been tempting fate during those late night jams at Rose Hill Cemetery, conjuring up something out of the legend of Robert Johnson? It was a question that raised fears in the minds of many in the brotherhood. "I caught myself thinking that it's narrowing down, that maybe I'm next," Gregg said.

Butch has always been haunted by the eerie scene in Nashville when Duane OD'ed and Berry prayed to the heavens for just one more year of life for him. "That's when Duane died, it was a year to the day when he got in the wreck," Butch said. "I mean, it was *to the day* a year. And a year and two weeks after that was when Oakley got into his wreck. I don't know what that means, circumstance, I don't know. I'm not really religious, don't really believe in anything. But I figure if there's a God, then he's got a helluva sense of humor. It was like, what have we done to deserve this?"

Candace Oakley is convinced there was some kind of fate at play. In the final year of Duane's life, something changed in the music they played onstage. The band had been good before, even great, but this was something different — music that was almost unnerving in its stark emotion. "It was like their souls knew what their destiny was going to be," she said. "The music was like a soul crying."

Duane's body had yet to be buried; it had been kept in cold storage and Donna Allman had arrived in Macon only days before Berry's death to make arrangements for Duane to be laid to rest. When Berry died, the decision was quickly reached to bury them together at Rose Hill. It seemed only fitting.

Donna and Linda and Candace selected the plots. Duane and Berry each had special grave markers, with etchings designed by Linda. Mushrooms are carved into the sides of both headstones. Put in place at the base of the graves were two small statues of Galadriel and Brittany, in the form of two tiny angels kneeling in prayer. On Duane's stone, the dates of his birth and death are circled by the music to "Little Martha"; a winged scarab, an ancient symbol held sacred by the Egyptians, is engraved above his name. Duane's grave-stone has a Les Paul guitar carved in rich detail, and there is an in-scription that comes from a quotation Duane had written in his diary: "I love being alive and I will be the best man I possibly can. I will take love wherever I find and offer it to everyone who will take it . . . seek knowledge from those wiser . . . and teach those who wish to learn from me."

The inscription on Berry's headstone reads: "Our Brother B. O. . . . Raymond Berry Oakley III . . . And The Road Goes On Forever . . . Born In Chicago Apr. 4, 1948 . . . Set Free Nov. 11, 1972." Above the name is a ram's head, symbolizing his astrological sign. A Fender bass is carved into the gravestone, along with an inscription that everyone thought best summed up Berry's philosophy of life: "Help thy brother's boat across and, lo! thine own has reached the shore!"

NO charges were filed in Berry's fatal accident. A blood test showed he had a .24 blood alcohol count, more than two times the legal limit. But the consensus was the wreck happened because he was a terrible driver — it's easy to misjudge a curve on a bike and that was what had happened to Berry. The Allman Brothers Band took off a few weeks and canceled two shows scheduled in Houston in mid-November with the Grateful Dead. But there was never doubt about carrying on. A statement was released just before Thanksgiving that the Allman Brothers would look for a new bass player and auditions were quickly under way. "Everybody pulled together," Chuck recalled. "They said, 'Look, we're in the middle of a project and we're not going to stop now. Berry wouldn't want us to stop, so let's keep on making music.' We auditioned some guys and Lamar Williams came into the band."

Lamar was Jaimoe's childhood friend from Gulfport. Born on January 14, 1949, to Lemon and Betty Jean Williams, Lamar was the oldest of nine children in a family immersed in music. His father, a professional gospel singer, and mother noticed Lamar's interest early on. "When he was small, we used to buy him little toy guitars and drums, and he'd bang on those like little children will," Betty Williams said. "When he was older and listening to music, he would lie down on the floor and put his head up against the speaker. He said he wanted to hear everything."

Lamar had an uncle living in Michigan who fueled his interest. "He was a jazz head and used to listen to just about everything," Lamar said. "He had a little plastic flute and I picked it up one day and tried to play along with some records. After a while I got to where I was doing it and liking it." Lamar found himself naturally drawn to the bass; he would walk around humming bass lines. "Eventually, I got inspired enough to actually try and play a bass guitar."

His first bass was a Kingston and he was soon proficient enough to join his father's gospel group. Between gigs, he used to walk a few blocks over to his best friend's house, a kid named Johnny Lee Johnson who would later be known as Jaimoe, and they would play for hours in the wash shed behind Johnny's house. In 1964 they formed the rhythm section of a band called George Woods and the Sounds of

Soul and played clubs along the Gulf Coast. Lamar was drafted in 1968 and began playing in a Special Services band. "We would put together shows for guys in basic training, for NCO [noncommissioned officers] clubs and we'd do things around town too," Lamar said.

Eventually, Lamar was shipped out to Vietnam to fight a war that he morally opposed; he couldn't bear the thought of pulling a firearm on somebody else. Lamar told people he arrived at an airfield in Vietnam, then promptly ran between two barracks and into the jungle. He spent the next few months AWOL from his unit. He would wander around the countryside, joining up with an outfit for a few weeks before moving on. His ready excuse was that he had gotten separated from his unit; technically, it was even true. Lamar said that he came down with hepatitis from shooting up dope with bamboo shoots. He came out of the jungle for medical attention and was placed under arrest, handcuffed to his bed. He managed to break free and went AWOL again. A group of military police assigned to track down soldiers missing from their units contained several black members, and they tipped off Lamar whenever they were coming his way. He was honorably discharged in 1970, picked up eleven months' worth of paychecks that had piled up in his absence, and wound up in Charlotte, North Carolina, playing in a group called the Fungus Blues Band.

When the Allman Brothers Band set up auditions for a new bassist, Jaimoe called Lamar and told him that he should come to Macon and try out. Lamar showed up injured; the night before, he had been repairing a strap for his bass and nearly sliced off a finger on his right hand with a knife. Even so, the band liked what it heard. "Our main consideration at the time was finishing the album," Willie Perkins said. "I don't even remember how many people auditioned but a lot of people wanted that job. Lamar was about the last person. The band decided on Lamar, a lot because he was close to Jaimoe."

Johnny Sandlin said Lamar impressed everyone. "He came in and everybody took to him. He was an excellent bass player." Neither Chuck nor Lamar was made a full member of the band. Instead, they were essentially hired hands to the original four, on salary at $400 a week. They also earned union-scale wages as the band went back into the studio to finish *Brothers and Sisters*.

WITHIN days of Berry Oakley's death, Capricorn released *Duane Allman: An Anthology*, a two-record set that details the metamorphosis of Duane's guitar playing from Hour Glass to the days at Muscle Shoals and through the Allman Brothers Band. It was beautifully packaged and one of the earliest rock albums to include a booklet — it has scores of photographs and a wonderful essay by Tony Glover that gives a concise and informative overview of Duane's career. The album kicks off with the unreleased medley of blues songs that Hour Glass had recorded in Muscle Shoals to get away from the stifling hand of Liberty Records. Titled "B. B. King Medley," the cut contains Duane's first great solo on tape. Then comes the "Hey Jude" performance with Wilson Pickett that had propelled Duane's career. There's a version of Champion Jack Dupree's "Goin' Down Slow," an unreleased cut from the short-lived Duane Allman Band. It is the first time Duane's singing voice has ever appeared on a record and is enough to cause chills — the song is the reflections of someone who is dying young, and Duane sings it like a man staring his fate in the eye. The record also includes Duane's guitar work on songs like Clarence Carter's "The Road of Love," and Aretha Franklin's "The Weight" and King Curtis's version of "Games People Play." There is "Shake for Me," from the John Hammond, Jr., sessions, and a great acoustic version of Johnny Jenkins singing the old Muddy Waters song "Rollin' Stone." *An Anthology* also includes one of Duane's greatest performances, "Loan Me a Dime," that is unfortunately marred by a botched mix — the organ intro is barely audible and there are places on the long vamp where Duane's guitar solo is virtually lost.

There are several uninspired selections on the second half of the two-album set, but it includes a gem of an outtake from the *Layla* sessions, "Mean Old World." It features both Eric Clapton and Duane on bottleneck; Duane is mixed to the left playing an acoustic guitar and Eric is on the right playing a Dobro. Then comes "Layla," probably the pinnacle for both Eric Clapton and Duane Allman, two men with careers full of the highest peaks.

The *Anthology* set documents the incredible transformation of Duane's style from what it was at Muscle Shoals to what it evolved into with the Allman Brothers Band. The change was due partly to his growth as a musician and partly to his shifting tastes in equipment. When it came to guitars, Duane had been strictly a Fender man in his early years. He had played a Telecaster with the Stratocaster neck for most of the Hour Glass period, and he plugged into a Vox Super Beatles amplifier. By the time he got to Muscle Shoals, Duane was using a sunburst Stratocaster with a maple neck and playing through a Fender Twin Reverb amp. Duane got a classic slinky Fender sound, aggressive and full of treble. He also used a gadget called a "Fuzz

Face" that distorted his guitar and added sustain. The device used a nine-volt battery and Duane insisted on using batteries that were almost worn out; he said that was the only way he got the sound he wanted out of it.

Duane gave up the Fender sound after he formed the Allman Brothers Band, and the final side of the *Anthology* set gives perspective to the change it caused in his style and tone. In the early days of the band, Duane sometimes played a Gibson semi-hollowbody ES-345 and an ES-335 modified with humbucker pickups. But he eventually settled on a setup of Les Paul guitars and Marshall amplifiers, which naturally gave him the sound that he had been trying to coax out of his Strat with the fuzz box. For Duane, the Les Paul guitar was like finding the perfect woman — the instrument's rich and warm sustain was an ideal marriage for Duane's style of playing and it is no coincidence that his talents came into sharp focus as soon as he began playing one.

When he switched to Les Pauls, Duane played a vintage Standard gold-top before settling on a beautiful 1958 Standard with a tobacco sunburst top and distinctive striping, the guitar he used on the *Fillmore* and *Layla* albums. The Allmans had toured with ZZ Top in the early years of both groups and Billy Gibbons found the guitar for Duane; it had once belonged to Christopher Cross, who went on to win four Grammy awards in 1980. For the most part, Duane used only one guitar onstage and had to quickly retune from standard to open D whenever he played bottleneck. But when Dickey began playing a 1957 Les Paul gold-top, he gave his Gibson SG to Duane, who tuned it to open D and used it exclusively for slide. With its long neck and snarling tone, the SG was ideal for bottleneck guitar.

The *Anthology* album works as an overview of Duane's recording career, especially with the inclusion of the Muscle Shoals songs that were virtually unavailable anywhere else, and it gives a good picture of the breadth of his talent without being redundant. In his review for *Rolling Stone*, critic Lester Bangs complained that the record was uneven, too safe. It was a fair statement, although he used poor examples; instead of "Layla," Bangs suggested using a less obvious classic from *Layla* such as "Bell Bottom Blues" or "I Looked Away." It was a good idea with just one catch: Duane had not played on either cut, another example of the mystery of who played what on that landmark album. Bangs concluded by calling the *Anthology* set a great tribute to one of the true innovators of the electric guitar, someone arguably on a par with Jimi Hendrix. "Duane Allman could take you straight from lava torrents to the cool, cool shade," Bangs wrote. "He had so much to give that all the clichés lose their banality — his passing was a loss to American music in a way that more 'chic' deaths never can be."

THE Allman Brothers Band went back on the road not long after Lamar joined up, playing New Year's Eve at the Warehouse in New Orleans. The club was one of the band's favorite haunts, and the concert was broadcast live over forty radio stations across the South. The gig was the band's way of showing its appreciation to the Warehouse, one of the places that had booked the Brothers from the earliest days. By then the Allman Brothers Band had far outgrown club dates and had evolved into one of the most popular rock groups in the country. *Eat a Peach* was named as one of the albums of the year by *Rolling Stone*, and the band was now one of a handful capable of selling out hockey and basketball arenas. The Allman Brothers would soon become one of the first groups in the post-Beatles era to graduate to outdoor stadiums.

It was the dawning of the Age of Big Business in rock 'n' roll, of incredible money and lavish extravagance by bands that could barely afford to eat a few years earlier. The Allman Brothers were grossing anywhere from $50,000 to $100,000 per gig — a far cry from what they were earning only two years earlier. The tremendous groundswell of popularity around the Brothers was an incredible phenomenon, occurring without the benefit of a hit single and based almost exclusively on word of mouth and reviews that made their music seem so uniquely special that music lovers couldn't afford to miss out on something that cool, that *hip*.

For the recently converted, Capricorn released a double-album set called *Beginnings*, a reissue of the first two studio records. "The album captures the essence of the Allman Brothers during their formative and middle periods," Capricorn said in an ad. "If you've only recently become aware of the Allman Brothers, *Beginnings* will provide new insights into their collective nature as a group."

Things had gotten so big that the band members incorporated in February of 1973 using the name Brothers Properties, Inc. The stated purpose of the new corporation was to "provide entertainment by making personal appearances, singing and playing and recording musical compositions; to acquire real estate, rental property, apartment buildings and hotels; to provide trusts for employees; to provide trusts for retirement income." Each of the four original members owned a 25 percent cut, and Gregg was made president.

The band opened a business office at 721 Riverside Drive in Macon. Willie Perkins was put in charge and it became the financial hub. Willie sorted through the royalty statements, kept track of each band member's income, and even monitored personal finances; Dickey had money mailed weekly to his mother in Florida, and Willie was expected to take care of his alimony and child support payments as well. Brothers Properties purchased the White Oaks Apartments in Macon as a tax shelter for $447,552. There was a small down payment and a bank loan paid for the bulk of it; Phil Walden owned 30 percent, the Brothers had 60 percent, and Willie Perkins and Capricorn treasurer Ted Senters shared the remaining interest. Next, they purchased a shopping center anchored by a Grant's department store in Perry, about twenty miles south of Macon.

Butch didn't know the band was in the real estate business until after they actually owned the properties. "I walked into the office one day and Willie Perkins says we made some investments," he said. "Even at first glance, I wondered why we would put up the money and Phil would have thirty percent interest. That bothered me." But no one really paid attention to the business side. "We didn't even stop to think about it," Butch said. "I mean, we were playing our music. I was making a grand a week and I survived pretty damned good on a grand a week. Willie would say, 'Hey, come in and look at the corporation.' He tried that for a while. I would just get my check and go home."

The band came off the road to work on its new album, and the spring of 1973 was filled with music and weddings. Gregg remarried on February 23, taking twenty-two-year-old Janice Blair Mulkey as his bride. The daughter of a furniture store owner in Macon, Jan had met Gregg the previous October.

Not long after that, on April 14, Dickey and Sandy Bluesky married on the farm in Juliette in a traditional Native American ceremony the *Macon News* called "the most unusual wedding in Middle Georgia." Sandy wore a wedding gown made by hand in 1926, and Chief Stanley Smith, a Creek medicine man, was flown to Macon from Oklahoma to conduct the ceremony. When he arrived, the chief sent Dickey out to find a duck and kill it because the heart had to be sacrificed during the wedding to ensure health and life. Dressed in Indian leathers with feathers dangling from his hair, Dickey headed to the woods while the guests waited. Several shots rang out before Dickey emerged an hour or so later with a dead duck in hand.

The ceremony proceeded with sacrifices of earth, corn, and the duck heart. Sandy agreed to "accept this man as the head of the household and obey him no matter what he does," everyone performed a wedding dance around the fire four times, and then they were pronounced man and wife. Dickey was twenty-nine, Sandy twenty-one. The couple had been living with their daughter on Corbin Avenue in Macon, although Dickey spent much of his time at the farm and the family would soon move there. Dickey was building a large log cabin, had felled the trees himself, and was making most of the furniture.

In June, Chuck Leavell married Rose Lane White, a twenty-four-year-old native of Dry Branch, Georgia, who was Capricorn vice-president Frank Fenter's secretary. Chuck and Rose Lane were married in a duplex on Rogers Avenue, about fifty yards away from the Big House. Leading the ceremony was the Reverend Gerald "Buffalo" Evans, the First Bishop of the Church of Research. Evans had also married Gregg and Jan; however, for their wedding he was a minister with the Brotherhood of New Truth Church.

Evans was born in Oklahoma and gained his nickname because, in profile, he resembled a buffalo. He had worked as a roadie for Hour Glass and when he came to Macon for Duane's funeral, Gregg insisted he stay. Aside from his part-time job as a minister, Evans also worked as a roadie for the Allman Brothers Band. "There was some resentment to his presence at first," Kim Payne said. "People referred to him as a professional friend." But Kim liked Buffalo; he'd known him out in Los Angeles, and he was a kind of spiritual guru for the band.

With success came a changing of the guard on the road crew. Joe Dan Petty left to play bass in a Macon band called Grinderswitch. And the two original members, Kim Payne and Mike Callahan, were fired along with Tuffy Phillips, following a two-day stand with the Grateful Dead at RFK Stadium in Washington, D.C., on June 9 and 10, 1973. Kim threw a Capricorn executive off the stage — Butch said it was Frank Fenter, but Kim said no, it was somebody he didn't recognize.

"I'd had this wreck on my motorcycle and fucked up my right foot, had an ulcer in it. I was on dope to the max," Kim said. "Got up there and I had this attitude problem. There was about three or four hundred people up on this stage and that son of a bitch was about to weave and bounce. I told Tuffy not to let nobody else up on stage. A while later, he came over and said, 'This guy over here is so and so,' and I said, 'I don't give a fuck who it is, tell him to leave. He can't come up.' "

The man asked to see Kim. Already in a surly mood, Kim walked over and immediately slugged the guy. "It was one of those executive types, wearing a suit. The Hell's Angels were doing security there and when they see this guy come tumbling they figure he's a bad guy cause I'd knocked him down the stairs. So they stomped the shit out of him." One of those at the bottom of the steps was Tuffy Phillips, who had been dosed with LSD by the Grateful Dead road crew, and he belted the executive in the face with a beer bottle during the melee.

Butch recalled the incident with a sense of pride — the roadies were just protecting their band's turf. "I'll tell you one thing, nobody got around that equipment," he said. "They'd set it up and then if you got to within five feet of it, you'd go flying. They threw Frank Fenter off the stage one night. And then Phil Walden calls a band meeting, him and Frank, and informs us that we're going to fire Kim Payne, who had thrown Frank off the stage. And we say, 'No we're not, he was just doing his job. Frank messed up. They told him to stay away from there.' We didn't fire him for that but he finally left about a year later."

Kim said he was fired almost immediately. "That night they held a meeting," Kim said. "Phil got mad at the band and told them they were going to have to fire some people." Gregg came by his room later that night and knocked on the door. "Hey, man, got any dope?" Gregg asked; it was his usual greeting. "Man, I just wanted to tell you they had a meeting tonight," Gregg said a little later. "They all voted to fire you and I saved your job for you."

Then Dickey came up to Kim's room and told him he was fired and the vote had been unanimous. "They got rid of me and Callahan, and turned around and got about six guys to take our place," Kim said. "They told us the reason they were firing us — it's kind of funny now — was because of alcohol and drug abuse. Sure, we stayed fucked up all the time. But they did too. Never once did a gig not come through because we didn't have the shit there and have it working and on time. That ain't bad. It required a lot of drugs to get that done to start with. I always thought it was political. Two of the guys they hired were some of Dickey's friends from around Bradenton, Sid and Buddy Yokum, two big bad-ass bikers."

*　　*　　*

AFTER having survived the days of the Hippie Crash Pad and the Econoline van with the cranky heater, it seemed cruelly ironic that neither Kim Payne nor Mike Callahan would be on hand a month later for one of the crowning moments of the Allman Brothers Band — the Summer Jam at Watkins Glen on July 28, 1973. The little hamlet of 3,000 in upstate New York was used to crowds of 100,000 and more descending on the area for the annual United States Grand Prix Formula One race. But the Summer Jam became something else altogether. Just three groups were scheduled to perform: the Allman Brothers Band, the Grateful Dead, and the Band. By Thursday night, a full two days before the concert, a crowd of about 80,000 was camped outside the gates. By Friday, people traveling to Watkins Glen were affecting traffic a hundred miles away in New York City and about 150,000 people, the total number of people that promoters had expected to attend, were already on the grounds.

Fortunately, Bill Graham had been hired to oversee the concert. The sound checks were scheduled for Friday and, to avoid trouble, Graham opened the gates that morning and coaxed the bands into doing the checks in front of the crowd. "The Dead played two hours, it drove the kids crazy," Graham said. "The Band came on and did an hour. The Allmans did two hours. By Friday night, a hundred and fifty thousand people had gotten a five-hour show."

Graham's improvisations worked, as did his preconcert preparations. There were a thousand Port-O-Sans, five helicopters to shuffle musicians to the backstage area, eleven wells for water, a medical tent, and a 50,000-watt sound system. His foresight was fortunate; by the time the Grateful Dead hit the stage that Saturday to open the show, more than 600,000 people had jammed into the raceway.

"We knew there was going to be a lot of people but we'd played in front of a lot of people before," Jaimoe said. "We had to fly in there in these helicopters. As you went in, you started seeing people. Then you start seeing more and more people. That concert, man, it was quite an experience. When you're looking in all kinds of directions and you can't see anything but people, man, it's something."

The Summer Jam at Watkins Glen — bigger than Woodstock, bigger than the Atlanta Pop Festival, bigger than anything rock had ever seen before — was certified as the largest concert in rock history by the *Guinness Book of World Records*. When the Allmans went on that night, everyone had a big case of nerves. "Six hundred thousand in person is a lot of folks," Dickey said. "I mean, when you're on television you're playing for twenty times that many people but you don't realize it. We played in front of a hundred thousand people a lot of times. Playing in front of six hundred thousand people, it's scary. But once you get the first song going, it might as well be ten thousand."

The Grateful Dead kicked off the concert at noon and played a five-hour set. The Band played from six to nine; then the Allman Brothers played a three-hour set that lasted until two in the morning. For an encore, members of all three bands came onstage for a jam that went on another ninety minutes and finished with Chuck Berry's "Johnny B. Goode." It wasn't a musically stellar day, and the crowd was soaked in rain and mud by the time it was over, but it was an event that had its own energy. In the end, Watkins Glen was not only the biggest concert ever but also one of the most well organized. Problems that plagued other festivals were nonexistent; there was no gate-crashing en masse, no epidemic of drug overdoses (the times were changing, most people were drinking alcohol), and violence was minimal.

"You ought to get out and see six hundred thousand people sometime, and all of them looking at you," said Butch. "It was awesome, it really was. And smooth. I mean, nothing happened that day. One kid cut his foot and one guy killed himself parachuting. This idiot, this fool, he jumped out of the plane and he was going to get everyone's attention with a stick of dynamite. So he lit the dynamite and jumped out and threw it. He didn't realize the dynamite's falling at the same rate of speed he was. And just about the time he pulled his rip cord, it blew. Blew him up. He had some flares on his feet and the flares caught his jumpsuit on fire. So by the time he hit the ground, he was blown up and burnt to a crisp. Floated right down into that crowd. God almighty."

Fourteen

Brothers and Sisters

BROTHERS and Sisters was released on August 1, 1973, just four days after Watkins Glen. There had been tremendous pressure going into the studio — it was the first album without Duane and without Berry, expectations were high, and the public was clamoring for new music from the Allman Brothers Band. "It had been a while since the Brothers had had an album out," said Johnny Sandlin. "They were late in getting *Brothers and Sisters* finished, everybody was in a state of shock after Berry died. The release date kept getting pushed back and there was all this pressure from Warners. In fact, there was an ad released early that said the record was available about two or three weeks before it was actually out there, and it just caused major havoc."

The new album was a significant stylistic departure. The music was moving in a different direction, away from the sound that had defined the band when Duane and Berry had been alive. Duane had liked a strong bass and Berry had always been very prominent in the mixes; now, the volume of the bass was lowered until it was barely distinguishable and the band relied more on the piano as the dominant rhythm instrument. "When Berry was killed, it wasn't a matter of some guys in the group moving forward to cover that," Dickey said. "We had to bring in outside influences. We were very lucky to have Chuck Leavell on hand. I think if we'd made any other move besides Chuck at that point, it would have ended just like that. Because he was so powerful that a lot of people accepted that change. That was when it changed. Definitely. There was a different sound. And it would become more different. *Brothers and Sisters*, it was still kind of hanging in there but you could hear it changing. It was a great band but it wasn't the same."

More than anything else, the album marked Dickey's transformation into the band's reluctant guiding force. His country background was pushed to the forefront, and he wrote four of the seven songs and sang on two cuts. Most of all, Dickey's Les Paul was under the spotlight, and *Brothers and Sisters* was his vehicle for stepping out of Duane's shadow and blossoming into a major guitar talent.

The album kicks off with the strutting backbeat of Gregg's "Wasted Words." Dickey plays bottleneck guitar, and his abilities had grown considerably from months of playing slide every night on the road. He takes up Duane's old role, using brief flurries to accent Gregg's sneering vocals. Then he trades riffs with Chuck in an exquisite call-and-answer on the song's fade-out. Dickey's style on the slide is fully realized on "Wasted Words"; it isn't too far removed from Duane but is still uniquely his own. Yet for all his talent on the electric bottleneck, Dickey played it as seldom as possible. "I went through that real tough experience of having to play slide to some of those old tunes," he said. "It was for the audience, because if you're going to play 'Statesboro Blues,' you have to have slide. I would do it and I didn't like to do it at all. And I could play slide, that was the silly thing. But I didn't want to because Duane was famous for it."

"Ramblin' Man" was a song that Dickey had written in the kitchen of the Big House at about four in the morning and his initial inspiration came from the 1951 Hank Williams song of the same title. He originally didn't think it fit the Allman Brothers — it was just too country — and he practically apologized when he first played it for the others. They listened and then looked at him as if he were crazy; it was a *great* song and if the Allman Brothers Band couldn't do it, then nobody could.

The band's performance of "Ramblin' Man" is nothing short of magnificent. Dickey's voice is earnest and sincere, and the song is full of ingenious guitar lines. As it settles into a vamp after the second verse, Berry is underneath the melody and pushing the song with darting bass runs. Studio guitarist Les Dudek plays twin harmony lines with Dickey, and "Ramblin' Man" takes on "Layla"-like dimensions with its array of overdubbed guitar parts. "We really got into utilizing the studio on that song," Dickey said. "The two of us put on about eight guitar parts." The song soars on until Dickey picks up his bottleneck and plays a couple of ghostly sounding riffs, like a final sad farewell to Duane and Berry. "Ramblin' Man" was the last song Berry recorded before his death. A third performance from the *Brothers and Sisters* sessions, an instrumental called "Berry's Jam," was finished but eventually left off the album.

The songs on *Brothers and Sisters* are in chronological order as they were recorded, and Lamar Williams makes his debut on "Come and Go Blues." Lamar shows no reticence to jump into the mix; his bass rumbles up and down the scales just as Berry's had once done. "Lamar had his own way of doing it," Johnny said. "He was an excellent player, a very quick study. It was just like with Duane, nobody could ever take Berry's place. When I listen to stuff now, Berry's even better than I thought he was then. He wasn't just playing the chord changes, he was very much a part of the whole melodic structure of the song and he would play around with the melody. Lamar had a similar style but a little funkier, a little more rhythmic and a little less melodic. He really fit into the songs."

A slow blues called "Jelly Jelly" follows. The song was originally going to be a cover of "Outskirts of Town," a blues standard recorded by Ray Charles. Gregg decided to write new lyrics and make it into an original tune called "Early Morning Blues." "It really got confusing," Johnny said. "They carried it to such an original arrangement that it really had very little do with 'Outskirts of Town.' So Gregg didn't want to do that song. He'd written some new words and never finished them and he wound up doing 'Jelly Jelly.' "

The second side is a brilliant showcase for the band's versatility, as the music shifts effortlessly from a fast shuffle to western swing to country-styled blues. "Southbound," written by Dickey and sung by Gregg, begins on a fevered pitch and never lets up. It is a song of swaggering lust, about a man headed home after a road trip and anticipating a heated reunion with his woman. The song has a furious and inventive buildup underneath the chorus and Chuck's rhythm parts are full of wonderful surprises. The solos on "Southbound" are like the two sides of passion: Chuck's piano is melodic and gentle, as it shifts between styles with graceful flair; Dickey takes no fewer than three guitar breaks, each bristling with a hot-blooded erotic undertone.

"Jessica" is one of Dickey's masterworks — pure, unbounded joy leaping out of the speakers. The instrumental takes elements from several inspirations. Dickey drew from a longtime friend from Florida named Dave Lyle, who played in Wanda Jackson's rockabilly band and taught Dickey western swing licks. Dickey was also inspired by Django Reinhardt, the legendary Gypsy jazz guitarist from the thirties who lost the use of two fingers on his left hand in a fire. "I was thinking about Django Reinhardt when I was writing that song and a lot of it is written so that you can play it with two fingers," Dickey said. "I knew what I wanted to do, but I couldn't quite find it. Then my little daughter crawled into the room and I started playing to her, trying to capture that feeling of her crawling and smiling. That's why I called it 'Jessica.' "

The song opens with Les Dudek playing an acoustic guitar; then the others come in and the music takes off with a rejoiceful opening movement that ends on a climbing riff very similar to the dramatic closing of "Whipping Post." But instead of the impending doom of "Whipping Post," the notes spring up with giddy happiness. The song soon falls into an interlude that is like a tender lullaby — Dudek is strumming the acoustic, Dickey plays a quiet guitar riff, and Butch keeps the beat with a tambourine. Then Jaimoe comes in on congas and Chuck follows on the piano as the song begins to build. Lamar's bass comes in underneath the melody and Butch lifts it up with a drumroll that leads into one of the great piano solos in rock history.

Chuck begins with beautifully chorded runs, and his fingers seem to dance down the keys in a style inspired by Vincent Guaraldi's famous piano theme for the old "Peanuts" television shows. Chuck is very careful not to overplay, leaving breathtaking pauses between his musical phrases, and he closes with an exhilarating series of licks that are full of celebration. The song builds into Dickey's first lead note and, already, he's up high on the fret board as the band churns underneath him. He creates a dramatic tension when he dips down to play bass runs, as though he is locked in a struggle with himself that has to be resolved before he can accept the freedom of the song's unbridled bliss. Then Dickey takes the song back up again and locks in on a series of fleeting notes, played as high on the neck of his Les Paul as one can go. It is one of Dickey's defining moments, a solo full of amazing texture.

"Pony Boy" sustains the good-time feeling and is a fitting finale for *Brothers and Sisters*. The song kicks off with Dickey playing wonderful bottleneck on an earthy-sounding 1936 metal-bodied National Resophonic guitar. The band — only Butch, Lamar on upright bass, Chuck, and Tommy Talton of Cowboy sitting in on acoustic guitar — comes in behind him in a toe-tapping tempo that falls somewhere between country and blues. As the National guitar guides the song to its conclusion, the instruments fall out on the final note, and Dickey and Butch close "Pony Boy" with a brief display of country hambone before they break into laughter.

Brothers and Sisters was a runaway hit, exceeding even the wildest expectations. The album debuted at number thirteen on the *Billboard* charts, hit number one by the first of September, and stayed perched at the top for six weeks. And "Ramblin' Man" became the most unlikely of all possibilities, a hit single by the Allman Brothers Band. It rose to number two on the *Billboard* singles charts, kept out of the top spot by Cher's "Half Breed." The band already had a substantial core audience in place and with the success of "Ramblin' Man" and *Brothers and Sisters*, The Allman Brothers Band suddenly found itself the most popular group in America. The band went on the road for a record-breaking tour. The Allman Brothers played the five-thousand-seat Winterland in San Francisco out of respect for Bill Graham, but a more typical gig was at Three Rivers Stadium in Pittsburgh or Tampa Stadium in Florida. "We played a lot of big gigs, stadiums," said Chuck. "We did one of the first stadium tours of the rock era. It just amazed me that it was that big."

THE album jacket for *Brothers and Sisters* was an effectively simple portrayal of the love and togetherness of the brotherhood. On the cover is a photo of Vaylor Russell Trucks, Butch's little boy, and on the back is a photo of Berry and Linda's daughter, Brittany. Inside is a foldout photo of the band and much of its extended family sitting on the back porch of the band's cabin on the farm in Juliette.

It was a showing of togetherness that no longer really existed — even as the shot was being set up, Dickey and Sandy Bluesky were fighting and he exiled her to town, forbidding her to be in the picture. More than anything else, it was the wives and the girlfriends who were holding together the brotherhood, planning picnics and dinners to keep up the communal feelings. Otherwise, everyone in the band was content to go his own way and they were all pursuing interests that led them away from the Allman Brothers.

Dickey's fascination with Native Americans became a passion after his marriage to Sandy Bluesky. He became so engrossed that he set up the North American Indian Foundation, a nonprofit organization to promote the renewal of Indian culture, and the band performed two benefit concerts that raised $100,000 for the cause.

Butch was content to party every night. He would go barhopping around Macon and inevitably got into trouble. One time, Butch found himself in an all-night joint surrounded by ten good old boys. "I was going, 'Come on, motherfuckers, I'll take you all on,' and they were ready to get me," Butch said. "Dickey came walking straight through the middle of them and grabbed me around the neck and said, 'Come on, let's get out of here.' He got me out in the alley. He was calming me down when this big ol' stocky dude come walking by with his girlfriend and I reached out and grabbed her by the ass and yanked her about three feet. He squared off. Dickey was in between us, trying to stop us." Dickey pulled Butch out of danger and took him down to the studio to pass out. Butch's wildness was costing him his marriage; shortly after *Brothers and Sisters* was released, he and Linda split up after she'd had enough of his wild lifestyle and his flings on the road.

Chuck and Lamar were the new kids in the band and still feeling their way around. "I wasn't a real outgoing guy," Chuck said. "I wasn't the star like Gregg was. Gregg is a star, he was born to be a star, I think. He just fits that image. He's good at that. I was just a guy in the band who was in awe of this whole situation."

Lamar had a natural ally in Jaimoe, his friend from childhood, and Chuck banded with them. Jaimoe was the band's jazz emissary and he soon had Chuck listening to a steady diet. "Jaimoe took me under his wing and there's not another man as well meaning as that one on the Earth, as far as I'm concerned," Chuck said. "He's just a good-hearted human being. Me and Jaimoe and Lamar, we'd get off and we'd rent a ballroom in the hotel we were staying at and just throw some equipment in there and go play. We'd go to the gig early and play during the sound check. We were the only guys that did a sound check; nobody else came. We'd always go and we'd just play and play and play."

Chuck's initial reception from Dickey was less hospitable. They'd sit next to each other on an airplane and not a word would pass between them. "I'd say, 'Good morning,' and that's about as far as it went," Chuck said. "For a long time between Dickey and me, it was 'Hello — good-bye' and get up there and play. It took a while to get to know the cat."

The leadership mantle seemed to fall into Dickey's hands even if he lacked the temperament to take charge. Dickey had a mercurial personality; one day he could be utterly charming and friendly to a fault, then the next day he would fall into one of his black moods and be uncommunicative. Dickey was haunted by his insecurities. He didn't like playing bottleneck because of Duane's reputation. He didn't enjoy singing, preferring to stay in the background and play his guitar. Twice, he changed his name. First, he wanted to be known as Dick Betts; then he adopted the moniker Richard Betts. But there was really no one else to assume the leadership role. Jaimoe had a passive personality and relied on others to take charge so that he could concentrate on his music. Butch was a good old boy who liked to party. And Gregg was just out of it, completely self-absorbed.

"This would have been a golden opportunity for Gregg to come into his own and take command, take control," Kim Payne said. "But he wouldn't have been Gregg if he'd did that. It just wasn't in the cards; if a frog had wings, he wouldn't be bumping his ass all the time. When Berry went down, it was like the last straw to a structure that was already pretty shaky. Dickey was kind of a loose cannon, just bristling with talent and piss and vinegar. He was pretty agitated by the unrest and the lack of direction. There was a lot of dissension going on. And lack of direction."

Gregg was relying more and more on drugs. Just before Watkins Glen, he spent four weeks in Buffalo, New York, trying to kick heroin. But he had absolutely no willpower and a pattern was beginning: one minute Gregg would be swearing that he had finally whipped his drug habit, and the next he would be out trying to score some dope. He was shooting up some of the most powerful drugs imaginable, heroin and pharmaceutical cocaine, and heavy painkillers like Leritine and Dilaudid and Demerol.

Gregg's drug use was a chief cause of turmoil in his home. Janice Allman was no prude but she drew the line at needles. Gregg promised to stop; instead he tried to hide it from her. Gregg once showed up at Kim Payne's place at two o'clock in the morning, and Kim saw several track marks from recent injections on Gregg's arm.

"I betcha she ain't gonna put up with this shit," Kim warned him.

"She ain't gonna know," Gregg responded.

"What are you going to do?" Kim asked. "Turn the fucking lights off every time you have sex?"

Janice and Gregg had a huge fight on Thanksgiving night in 1973. The band played a show in Atlanta, and she found a used needle and bottle in the pocket of his suit. She was furious and it caused even more strife in an already troubled marriage.

Meanwhile, Shelley Allman had filed papers in court asking for more child-support money. "Defendant is now an international celebrity whose band, the Allman Brothers Band, earns millions of dollars each year," her complaint read. Gregg, who had seen his son only once, initially balked, saying there had been no real change in his income. Although he had made over $200,000 during the past two years, Gregg claimed he was virtually penniless. He said his personal checking account was overdrawn and that he owed over $100,000 in loans. Eventually, Gregg gave in and agreed to increase his child support for Devon from $150 a month to $400.

Even with all the backstage discord, the Allman Brothers Band was still capable of getting up before an audience and spinning some magic. The group came off the road at the end of 1973 with a New Year's Eve concert at the Cow Palace in San Francisco. It was broadcast live and drew the largest radio audience since President Roosevelt's fireside chats. *Billboard* magazine gave the Allman Brothers its 1973 Trendsetter Award for focusing attention on Southern rock music, and the band made the cover of *Rolling Stone*. A few weeks after the cover story, the Allman Brothers was named *Rolling Stone*'s Band of the Year. "The Allman Brothers Band have emerged as the band that consistently does more things better than any other group," the magazine wrote. "In particular, 1973 saw the emergence of Richard Betts as guitarist extraordinaire and the mastermind behind their well-deserved first hit single, 'Ramblin' Man.' Between the continued growth of their music on *Brothers and Sisters* and their concerts and tours, they have become the yardstick by which others are measured."

Fifteen

Diamond Dust

THE Allman Brothers Band was on the road in the fall of 1973 when Capricorn released *Laid Back*, Gregg's solo record. The album was dark and contemplative with no screaming Les Pauls, just lots of quiet acoustic guitars and melodic piano parts. It was a melancholy side of Gregg Allman no one had ever heard before. "It does have a mood on it and I was real happy that came across," said Johnny Sandlin, who produced the record and called it his favorite. "The record was kind of dark in places and there was a lot of darkness about, with all these people dying."

The sessions had begun at the same time as *Brothers and Sisters* in late 1972 and continued even as the Allman Brothers hit the road the following spring and summer. The studio band would often cut the instrumental tracks without Gregg's presence, and he would come into the studio to add vocals to an otherwise finished recording. Even when Gregg was at the studio, the album had to compete with the drugs for his attention. "A lot of times it was hard to get Gregg to stay on something long enough to get it done," Johnny said. "He'd drink too much, or whatever, and not be in a condition where you could get what you'd consider the best stuff out of him. Or he'd say, 'I'll be back in a minute' and you'd hear from him two weeks later, wherever he was."

Laid Back is probably the finest record Capricorn released in the post–Duane Allman era, and Gregg had certainly never been cast in a more sympathetic setting. The album begins with a reworked version of "Midnight Rider" that has a feel so ominous it could have been recorded out at Rose Hill in the darkest hours after midnight. The haunting guitar riff that opens the song was actually a mistake. Gregg first used a similar guitar part on a song he wrote called "Southbound" that he had recorded in Los Angeles. He ditched the song, but resurrected the arrangement for this version of "Midnight Rider" and taught the guitar lick to Scott Boyer. Gregg wasn't in the studio when the track was recorded and didn't realize until later that Scott had learned it slightly wrong.

But it is that beautiful error that sets the mood, and then every instrument that follows adds to the song's foreboding, swampy sound — the restraint of Tommy Talton's bottleneck licks, the odd phrasings in Bill Stewart's drums and Jaimoe's congas, and the subtle inventiveness of Chuck Leavell's Fender Rhodes piano. Above all, there is Gregg's voice. Never before had it sounded so rich, so full of depth. If Gregg sounded desperate on the *Idlewild South* version, here he sings as if he is running from the hellhound and about to be caught. On the final verse, his voice is like a man crying for mercy and the fade-out, where he moans "No, no, no, no" over and over in a chilling chant, makes it sound as though his plea has been denied.

"Queen of Hearts" is Gregg's love song to Janice and one of his greatest compositions — Van Morrison meets the southern blues. The timbre of Gregg's voice is warm and sensuous, as soothing as a sweet dream. After two verses, there is a stunning shift from languid ballad to swinging jazz with a wonderful saxophone solo by David "Fathead" Newman, the longtime sax player for Ray Charles. The song shifts back into a ballad before again leaping into the swinging beat as Chuck plays a striding solo on the electric piano.

"Please Call Home" is yet another reworking of an old Allman Brothers song. With the Allmans, "Please Call Home" had been stark. On *Laid Back*, it is given a wall of sound that recalls Phil Spector. The song begins simply with Chuck's sorrowful piano and soon builds into a huge production with a heavenly sounding choir, horns, and pulsating strings.

An old r&b song recorded by Rufus Thomas, "Don't Mess Up a Good Thing," is the album's break from the ballads. It is a jumping tune full of keyboards with Chuck on acoustic piano, Gregg on the organ, and Paul Hornsby on the clavinet. The song is an ideal vehicle for Gregg's voice; he sounds wounded on one line and cocky on the next. Fathead Newman adds a sassy solo and then Chuck comes in for what may be his best solo on an album full of memorable ones. He begins with a run up the scales that is pure artistry, and on the conclusion, his right hand brings the melody down while his left walks up on the bass keys. It is very intricate playing, and very few pianists could pull it off.

Gregg's version of Jackson Browne's "These Days" was as confessional as anything he had recorded. Gregg turns it into a dirge, a prayer to his brother. Browne had concluded the song on an optimistic note, singing that he knows he must not give up his faith that things will someday improve. But Gregg ignores that final line, and it gives his version a completely different tenor. The protagonist never resolves his sadness and he's still trapped by it at the end of the song. Gregg closes with a voice of complete surrender: "Please don't confront me with my failures / I'm aware of them." It is as close to the bone as Gregg Allman would ever get in a song.

"Multicolored Lady" fades in with the sounds of ringing acoustic guitars playing one of Gregg's most gorgeous melodies and underscored by Chuck's graceful piano. Gregg's voice is tender, and the lyrics are particularly effective, especially the way he uses colors to paint the image as he tells the story of a woman crying on a bus and a stranger trying to comfort her.

The album is closed by "Will the Circle Be Unbroken?" — the old Carter Family standard that had reached mythological proportions among the brotherhood in Macon. Duane had played the song at the end of "Mountain Jam" on *Eat a Peach,* and then the band had performed it at his funeral. "That song was a highly cherished anthem," Kim Payne said. "My favorite times in regards to music would be Gregg, very informally, playing the guitar and singing 'Will the Circle Be Unbroken?' Gregg used to sing that song all the time and it would put chills on me."

The version on *Laid Back* sounds like it was recorded on a Sunday morning in a black Baptist church. Gregg's husky voice sings over a quiet piano, organ, and angelic female choir. The song builds to a rousing finale that repeats the chorus over and over, as if it is a chant of affirmation that the brotherhood will continue on without its leaders. Johnny knew it would be perfect for the album's finale: "It had a direct meaning to the situation, in that everyone was trying to pull together and keep what we had going together — what the band had going, what the record label and the whole music scene in Macon had going. It had a lot of meaning to us."

Laid Back is a remarkable album, a southern classic. Never had

Gregg's voice been captured with such clarity and depth. The music is luscious, with a mood that is set in the first seconds and sustained until the end. The ambience of the instruments is masterful, clear and warm. *Brothers and Sisters* had been recorded almost simultaneously with *Laid Back,* yet the difference in the clarity of sound between the two albums is striking. In comparison, *Brothers and Sisters* sounds as though it was recorded through mud. Butch Trucks said he cringes every time he hears "Ramblin' Man" on the radio. "I get embarrassed," he said. "That thing is just tinny and mid-rangy. The recording was terrible."

Johnny Sandlin said it was the band's own fault, another sign of the lack of discipline after Duane was no longer there. "With *Laid Back,* I had a lot of freedom to work with the players and go for the sounds I wanted to go for," Johnny said. "If the bass drum didn't sound right, we'd work with the bass drum until it did. When you start recording with the Brothers, you don't have that much time to work on things because they're not that patient. When you've got them all there, you get what you can right then because somebody's going to have to leave. They'd be set up to play and if something didn't sound exactly right, you just made the best of it."

With the success of *Laid Back* and Gregg's announcement that he would tour in early 1974 with his own group, rumors began spreading that the Allman Brothers Band was finished. Fuel was added to the fire when the band canceled what would have been its first European tour in the winter of that year and a British pop music paper reported it was because Gregg had left the Allman Brothers.

The rumors of a breakup were hotly denied back in Macon and while the future of the Allman Brothers Band was publicly debated, Gregg drafted most of the studio musicians from *Laid Back* to anchor his band for the solo tour. There were guitarists Tommy Talton and Scott Boyer, the two mainstays of Cowboy. Playing bass was David Brown, who had been in 31st of February with Butch and Scott. Jaimoe was in the band, as was drummer Bill Stewart. Chuck played piano and Randall Bramblett handled the saxophone solos. There also was a four-piece horn section, three female background singers, and a string section.

Before the tour hit the road in March, Gregg stocked up on drugs. He had a vial of pharmaceutical cocaine and a large supply of Leritine — a narcotic analgesic that decodes and relieves pain — to take with him. He also had a new running buddy, a former mechanic named Scooter Herring he had hired as his personal valet. Scooter had a seemingly endless pipeline of drugstore dope, the purest and strongest stuff around. Unbeknownst to Gregg, Scooter also was involved in the Dixie Mafia.

UNLIKE the celebrated Mafia of Al Capone and John Gotti, membership in the Dixie Mafia was not contingent on Italian heritage and the organization did not evolve from the cause of protecting immigrants who were getting pushed around in the United States. The two things the organizations did share were propensities for crime and violence. The southern version was a loosely organized group of good old boys who imported drugs, ran prostitution and gambling rings, hijacked trucks, and did just about anything else that might net them some easy cash. "If it ain't a pretty damn good bit of money, I ain't gonna fuck with it," once boasted John Clayborn "J. C." Hawkins, the boss of the Middle Georgia branch of the Dixie Mafia. He had a deadly reputation — if you valued your life, you didn't cross J. C. Hawkins. Federal authorities had been chasing Hawkins for years and once located a potential star witness against him. The witness had turned up with his face blown off by a shotgun. "These people will kill you," Macon police Detective B. B. McDaniel said. "They just don't care."

The Hawkins Gang controlled much of the drug traffic coming into Macon. They imported high-quality marijuana, sold amphetamines, and fenced pharmaceuticals stolen in drugstore burglaries. The gang also had well-placed connections. When Hawkins needed someone to go to Jamaica to pick up a load of marijuana, he sent the brother of a Macon state representative. The gang's prostitution and numbers operations were protected by a group of corrupt Macon police officers, and the organization's influence also reached into state government; it paid bribes to a nursing-home inspector to overlook health-and-safety violations in three homes that J. C. Hawkins controlled. Just as the nursing homes were used as fronts for criminal activities, a motorcycle shop that Hawkins's brother, Recea, ran called The Cycle was used as a cover for Recea's side job as a drug wholesaler. One of the mechanics at The Cycle was Scooter Herring.

John Charles "Scooter" Herring was thirty-six years old and had been a mechanic for his entire adult life. The extent of his relationship with the Hawkins Gang is cloudy, but he often bought drugs from the two brothers, and Recea liked him enough to put him to work at his repair shop. Scooter met Gregg in the summer of 1973 when the singer brought in one of his bikes to be repaired.

Later, Gregg ran into Scooter at the Sunshine Club, a Macon juke joint and well-known drug den. Sitting with some friends and drinking beer one afternoon, Gregg looked up and saw his motorcycle mechanic reeling around the room, obviously fucked up on something. "I asked him what was wrong, what he had taken," Gregg said. Scooter told him that he had taken some Demerol. Gregg's face brightened and his concern for his buddy vanished. "Hey, man," he asked Scooter. "Can you get me any?"

Scooter was all too eager to help out his new friend, the rock star, and a night or so later he pulled up to Gregg's house with some major-league dope. Gregg had told Scooter he wanted downers, and the mechanic had come through for him. There was a bottle of Leritine, a drug Gregg had never heard of but would soon consume almost daily, a bottle of Demerol, and two bottles of morphine. All were injectable, and Scooter thoughtfully included some disposable syringes in the brown paper sack of goodies. Gregg met Scooter out in his driveway and stashed away the bottles. Later, he went back outside and buried them in the yard — he didn't want Janice to find out.

Scooter didn't tell Gregg, but he had a deal working with a Macon pharmacist who was another associate of the Dixie Mafia and J. C. Hawkins. Joe Fuchs owned half-interest in Harrison's Pharmacy and also sold illegal drugs on the side. When Fuchs decided to add a patio to his house, he didn't hire a contractor; he gave the Hawkins Gang nearly three thousand capsules of pharmaceutical speed and they supplied the labor and materials for the project.

Scooter and Fuchs later went into business together, stealing drugs from the shelves of Harrison's Pharmacy and selling them on the street. To conceal the thefts, the two men staged a burglary of the drugstore. Fuchs told police that he had been cleaned out of pain-killers and pharmaceutical cocaine. In reality, Fuchs had gathered the drugs — bottles of Dilaudid, Demerol, biphetamine, Leritine, morphine, Nembutal, Seconal, Quaalude, Percodan, and others — into a box and stashed them away in his stockroom. When the box ran out, Fuchs simply skimmed the drugs from his shelves. One of Scooter's major buyers was Gregg. Another was Kim Payne, who was selling much of his stash to Gregg.

The biggest treasure that Fuchs provided Scooter was the pharmaceutical cocaine. It was on hand at Harrison's Pharmacy because dentists sometimes used it as a local anesthetic, and when Gregg found out that Scooter had access to that, he was like a kid waiting for Christmas morning. Coke bought on the street was always cut, diluted. The buzz would vanish in about twenty minutes and you'd have to snort some more or else sink into a mood as low as it had seemed high only minutes earlier. Gregg called the pharmaceutical coke "diamond dust." It looked like tiny crystals; a few hits of that stuff and a person could fly for hours.

Just before Gregg's tour started, he and Scooter rendezvoused on a dirt road two blocks from Gregg's house. "Scooter's wife was there," Gregg said. "I got in the car, I was in the backseat on the left-hand side, and we drove around and he told me the bag was down on the floorboard. I picked it up and looked inside. There was a big brown bottle of cocaine, there was about a gram missing from it but it was just about full. There was another bottle of Demerol and about five syringes."

Gregg wrote Scooter a check for the drugs. Scooter and his wife were trying to buy a house, and he had mentioned to Gregg that he couldn't come up with the down payment. While Gregg had his checkbook out, he wrote a second check for the amount Scooter needed to get the house. He told Scooter there was no rush in paying it back; for Gregg, just the look on Scooter's face when he handed him the check was payback enough.

Gregg liked Scooter; he was a fun guy to be around and he was reliable. On Valentine's Day, 1974, Gregg hired the former mechanic to be his personal valet for the upcoming tour. Scooter described his duties as "dope holder and procurer and general valet," and it was a giddy turn of events for someone who had expected to be wiping grease off his hands for the rest of his life. All of a sudden he was going on the road with one of the biggest rock stars in the country and living the kind of opulent life he had only dreamed about. "I had a chance to be somebody," Scooter said. "There was no prestige in being a mechanic. It was a good shot to make something of myself. I just went hog-wild over it."

It wouldn't take Scooter long to figure out what Kim Payne had already learned: Gregg's appetite for drugs was insatiable. The man had no concept of "enough." It would become a full-time job, just trying to save Gregg from himself.

Concentrated in the South, the tour kicked off with a warm-up show in Macon. Gregg had a large string section and everybody got a big kick out of it when the orchestra showed up for that first gig wearing tuxedos. From there, the tour went to Charlotte and Durham in

North Carolina. There were stops in Atlanta, Orlando, St. Petersburg, Miami, Birmingham, New Orleans, and Knoxville. The shows, usually in large theaters, attracted capacity crowds.

In early April, Gregg made a brief swing through the Northeast, playing in Boston and Providence. Johnny Sandlin was on hand to record two shows at Carnegie Hall in New York and another at the Capitol Theatre in Passaic, New Jersey, for a live album. The solo tour closed in Cincinnati on April 25, 1974. Gregg played a two-hour show, then left the stage. The crowd clamored for an encore and got much more than that. "I want to squelch a few rumors right here and now," Gregg said. The crowd erupted as Dickey and Butch and Lamar walked onstage to join Gregg, Jaimoe, and Chuck. The Allman Brothers Band played a ninety-minute encore.

NOT long after his tour ended, Gregg had a wisdom tooth pulled and happened to stop by Harrison's Pharmacy on his way home to get a prescription filled for antibiotics and painkillers. "Just by coincidence, there was Scooter standing, talking to Joe Fuchs," Gregg said. "They were both behind the counter. I thought it was kind of strange. Joe invited me to come back and have a cup of coffee, which I did. But I was very nervous about it. Scooter and I left together and I asked him about being, you know, backstage at this drugstore."

Scooter looked at Gregg as if it were the most inane question he'd ever heard. "Where do you think all this is coming from?"

No one was ever supposed to know the identity of Scooter's supplier — that was part of the deal; there was too much to lose. Fuchs nearly panicked when Gregg had found him out, but Scooter reassured him. "Scooter said Gregg was a very tough guy," Fuchs said. "Nothing would ever be said from Gregg Allman concerning the operation."

After his initial consternation, he began to get off on it. Suddenly, Joe Fuchs was hanging around with Gregg Allman, one of the most famous rock singers in the country. Gregg would even go over to Joe's house sometimes and play piano for his little daughter, disarming her with his lazy smile and quiet voice. Like Scooter, Fuchs was star struck.

Once Gregg discovered the source, it didn't take him long to cut out the middleman. He began calling Fuchs directly when he needed a fix, usually a gram or two of pharmaceutical cocaine or a bottle of Leritine. Gregg sometimes sent a courier to pick up his stash, but often would make the trip himself. The two men soon developed a routine. Gregg and Janice lived just a few blocks away from Harrison's. When Gregg wanted to place an order, he would drive over to a convenience store across the street from the pharmacy and call Fuchs from a pay phone outside. They had a code worked out. If Gregg wanted cocaine, he'd ask Fuchs, "Hey, man, can I get any dust?" If it was Leritine he wanted, Gregg would ask, "Can I get some L?" Fuchs was always willing to drop whatever he was doing to supply Gregg at a moment's notice.

Gregg would leave the pay phone and drive to a prearranged spot two blocks away from the pharmacy. Fuchs would drive up from the opposite direction so that they were facing each other. "He would meet me and throw the bag in the car," Gregg said. "We would both say 'Good afternoon' and split." No money exchanged hands; that was Scooter's job. Gregg would build up tabs of one and two thousand dollars, then Scooter would collect the money and pay Fuchs his cut.

Gregg's biggest problem with the arrangement was keeping Janice off his back. She was not shy about challenging both Gregg and Scooter over her husband's fondness for needles. One day she followed Gregg to a deserted dirt road, where he met Scooter and Joe Fuchs. As they were giving Gregg a bag of dope, Janice came flying over the hill in her car. She pulled up to them, got out, and started screaming at Gregg and Scooter. Janice ordered Scooter to follow her home. When he and Fuchs arrived, she was crying and came down hard on them. "I told them it was really upsetting me," Janice said. "I was afraid Gregg was going to kill himself with the needles. And I knew Scooter had been giving the needles to him. He said he had been doing it because he didn't want Gregg to get ahold of any bad stuff. He promised me no more needles."

Gregg's battles with Janice were turning bitter, and the drugs were robbing their relationship of all vitality. Soon after she followed Gregg to his meeting with Scooter and Joe Fuchs, someone cut the coil wire on her yellow Corvette to keep her from going anywhere. Gregg had it fixed, but then Janice began to notice that she wanted to nod off every time she drove the Corvette. She took the car to a mechanic. "It looked like someone had fiddled with it to make carbon monoxide come out in the car," Janice said. "I was getting sleepy driving, and I was getting sick to death of them taking my car apart."

She said she confronted Gregg. "Scooter did it," he snapped. "And Scooter will be over to fix it."

BY the time the Allman Brothers Band kicked off a summer tour in late May of 1974, Scooter Herring had been promoted to assistant road manager. The second stop was at Atlanta–Fulton County Stadium for a show called the Georgia Jam that also featured Capricorn's Marshall Tucker Band, a hungry young Southern-rock group named Lynyrd Skynyrd, and Joe Dan Petty's band, Grinderswitch. The concert drew 61,232 fans, the largest crowd in the ballpark's history. "No other American band could have drawn so many people to Atlanta Stadium as turned out for the Allmans and there is considerable doubt that any of the legendary British bands — the Rolling Stones or the Who — could have done as well either," wrote *Atlanta Journal and Constitution* critic Scott Cain.

At the concert, someone dosed Gregg, Jaimoe, and Lamar. It was intended for Lamar — a bass player from another band gave the drugs to Gregg to give to Lamar and before passing it along, Gregg sampled it. Lamar gave some to Jaimoe, and all three of them wound up on nasty hallucinogenic trips. "We think it was this cat who was after Lamar's gig," Gregg said. "If we hadn't gotten him to a doctor, Lamar could have died. I sure thought I was dying. I was stringing my guitar. An hour and a half later, I was still on my third string. Only reason I went onstage: I figured if I was going to die, I wanted to do it on my axe."

Gregg sat behind his organ, and the keyboard seemed to be lowering and rising and twisting all around like a rollercoaster. He tried following the keys wherever they went, but wound up having to be led offstage because the hallucinations weren't doing much for his muscianship. The band played two sets. The first was a near-disaster, but by the second some of the haze was wearing off and the band finished strong, closing with "Midnight Rider" and then "Ramblin' Man."

The band had flown to Atlanta from Macon in their new toy, *Starship One*. The biggest rock groups, like the Rolling Stones and Led Zeppelin, were going to their gigs in style, aboard private jets. The Brothers decided to do likewise and leased the same Boeing 720 jet that the Stones and Zeppelin had used. "That wasn't an airplane, that was a flying house," said Randall Savage, a reporter for the *Macon Telegraph and News*. "It had a little fake fireplace and a little area with sofas. It had a bar. There was a back compartment with this bed that Allman slept in. Whenever they went out on that thing, Mama Louise over at the H&H Restaurant used to make great big vats of black-eyed peas and corn bread by the ton; they just loaded that plane down with that stuff."

Starship One was the largest craft ever to land and take off from Macon's tiny airport. "Every time we'd land in Macon, the pilots were white-knuckled," Butch said. "That runway was not built to handle an airplane that size. We paid four hundred thousand dollars for that thing and used it about five times. It just sat out there with our name on the side of it and we'd go out there to party in it."

It was a luxury they thought they could easily afford. The band was so popular that other rock groups would be dismayed to hear cries of "Whipping Post!" coming from the audience during their concerts. The Allman Brothers had been voted the most popular rock band in the annual *Playboy* poll, and this came after Duane had been inducted into the Playboy Jazz and Pop Hall of Fame, joining the likes of Miles Davis, John Coltrane, Duke Ellington, Elvis Presley, and Eric Clapton. They were playing a mix of hockey arenas and outdoor football stadiums. There was a planned joint concert with Crosby, Stills, Nash and Young at the Los Angeles Coliseum that would have netted each band an astronomical fee of $650,000. CSN&Y had just regrouped and was embarking on the first complete stadium tour by a rock band since the Beatles; their drawing power was unquestioned — except by Phil Walden. Rather than cobilling the bands, Phil demanded headline status for the Brothers. When the promoters balked, Phil pulled out. "Look, I know how much my act can draw," he said with characteristic cockiness. "I'm not so sure about an act that's just getting back together."

At a time when the members of the Allman Brothers Band should have been sitting pretty, they were fighting a perpetual battle just to hold everything together. The music could still soar onstage, but there were nights when it just didn't click, nights when Gregg was so out of it that his organ was surreptitiously turned down in the mix so that no one would hear him playing off-key. The others were often nearly as close to the edge. "God, the cocaine was pouring," Butch said. "You would go backstage and there would be a line of thirty dealers waiting outside."

Gregg stayed so doped up that he was an accident waiting to happen, putting himself firmly in line to be the third one to go. It almost happened when the band played a series of shows in the New York area and spent several days headquartered in Manhattan. At the hotel, Gregg overdosed. It was serious, his heart stopped beating, and

Scooter and Willie Perkins frantically pounded on his chest and gave him mouth-to-mouth resuscitation to revive him.

Butch said that both he and Dickey also began losing it. "All the people start showing up, all the glad-handers," Butch said. "You just kind of lose your sense of self-worth. I got to where I'd just drink constantly and wake up in the morning and ask somebody what I'd done the night before. Everybody around you was so afraid they were going to make you mad: 'Aw, man, you were so funny, you pissed in Harold's face and that was so great.' And you start thinking, 'Boy, I'm cool.' No matter what you do, no matter how bad you're messing up, everybody tells you that you're okay. So you believe them. And Dickey was going through a similar thing and always getting in trouble."

Dickey and Sandy Bluesky's marriage was in serious jeopardy. She had filed for divorce in May, alleging cruel treatment. They reconciled a short time later, but the relationship remained volatile. Both possessed explosive tempers that cocaine continuously bubbled just under the surface. "One time, up there at the old farmhouse, I went up there to get with him to go do something," Kim Payne said. "He'd sat down to eat breakfast. He didn't like the food and slammed it on the floor. Then he walked in another room, picked up the pool table and flipped it over too for good measure. Just to let her know he didn't like the way she cooked something."

Chuck was scared out of his wits one night when the band was staying in a hotel in New York City. Chuck and Rose Lane were snuggled in bed, feeling romantic. Dickey and Sandy had the adjacent room, and the mood in Chuck's room was interrupted when he and Rose Lane began hearing angry shouts through the walls. Chuck heard doors slamming and decided he'd better peek outside and investigate. He saw Dickey standing in front of the elevator where Sandy had apparently just escaped. He faced the doors, arms bent at the elbows and hands clenched into fists, snorting like a bull primed to attack. Dickey stood locked in the pose for what seemed the longest time. A bell rang and the doors opened. Inside, an elderly elevator operator looked up. His eyes widened, his mouth dropped open, and he froze at the frightening sight in front of him. The elevator man didn't move a muscle. Neither did Dickey. The doors just opened. And then they shut.

Jaimoe and Candace Oakley were like the two keepers of the flame, huddled in the midst of all the chaos and wondering what had happened to Duane's dream. "Personally, I think I should have left the band after Berry died," Jaimoe said. "But I wanted to be pig-headed. I was the very first member. Duane was gone. Berry was gone. I felt like it was a responsibility for me to sit there and try to hold that mess together. Pardon my French, to hold the music together. It was completely different. I thought the studio side of *Eat a Peach* was fantastic, from the fact that it was the first album we cut without Duane and the flavor was still there. After that, it began to diminish and it really didn't know what direction it was going in."

He had grown closer to Candace in the months after Berry's death and on May 24, 1974, Jaimoe and Candace were married. Buffalo Evans, the roadie and hippie preacher, performed the ceremony. And then Lamar married his longtime girlfriend, Marian Janice Belina, on July 6 in Macon, during the break caused by the cancellation of the Los Angeles gig with Crosby, Stills, Nash and Young. Again, Buffalo Evans did the honors.

Chuck would party with the rest of them, but he knew when to stop. Everybody else would be sitting around drinking, and Chuck would be studying and practicing. He was becoming the glue that held everything together, a virtual lone voice of reason, and it prompted jealousy from some of the others. Butch was asked once if anyone in the band had tried to fill Duane's shoes. "One person tried one time, Chuck Leavell," Butch said. "It didn't work, to say the least. He got thrown up against a bathroom stall."

Jaimoe and Chuck and Lamar continued to band together, as far away from the madness as possible. None of the others were hanging out together anymore, much less communicating. Gregg was looking forward to a fall solo tour, as was Dickey, who had his own album due out in August. They had their own entourages — friends and groupies and others who just wanted to party with an Allman Brother. The band members had once shared a two-room apartment; now, everyone had his own hotel suite and his own limo and about the only time they saw one another was on the plane or onstage. They had become what they once had mocked — immersed in that "fucking star trip."

Butch Trucks would remember it as the beginning of the most miserable eighteen months of his life.

Sixteen

Be Proud You're a Rebel

BY 1974, Phil Walden had gathered all the increments of success and he didn't mind flaunting it. He was thirty-four years old, his net worth was estimated to be $5 million, he had a Picasso hanging in his house, and he tooled around Macon in a white Rolls-Royce. When it came to money, Phil looked for every angle. He owned a travel agency and used it to book travel arrangements for his bands. He bought a house in the resort town of Hilton Head, South Carolina, and paid the mortgage by leasing it to Capricorn Records. Phil owned the building that housed Capricorn Records and No Exit Music, and he had his own companies pay him rent.

For all his trappings of success, Phil remained persona non grata in his hometown. He desperately wanted acceptance from Macon's blue bloods and did everything he could to gain respect. The Allman Brothers Band performed numerous benefit concerts in Macon that raised thousands for projects that included playground equipment and scholarship funds. Still, Macon society wouldn't budge. Rather than embrace the movement that Phil had brought to town, there was mistrust and an instinctive prejudice. The common belief in the deeply conservative city was that Phil was running a modern-day Sodom and Gomorrah up at 535 Cotton Avenue.

Capricorn Records was more important to Macon than most locals were ready to acknowledge. The city was becoming known worldwide through the Capricorn logo and it was one of Macon's biggest industries, earning an extraordinary amount of money for an independently owned label. Phil had developed a roster of highly talented southern bands led by the Marshall Tucker Band, a South Carolina group with an innovative mix of rock and blues put into a country base, and Wet Willie, a band from Alabama that played scorching r&b.

The Allman Brothers Band was the lodestar for all the Capricorn groups, carrying them on its back until they were ready to walk on their own. Phil put both Marshall Tucker and Wet Willie on the road opening for his top attraction. Both bands benefited from the hundreds of thousands of fans drawn to see the Allman Brothers, and sold an incredible number of albums with virtually no airplay on the radio.

After the amazing popularity of the Allmans and Capricorn's other bands, it seemed that every label began signing a southern group. They were selling millions of albums, and in all of them you could hear traces of the Allman Brothers Band. Polydor had the Atlanta Rhythm Section, Epic had the Charlie Daniels Band, London Records signed a trio from Texas named ZZ Top, and MCA had the best of them all, Lynyrd Skynyrd. It was a musical genre that people grew to call "Southern rock," and its anthem was "The South's Gonna Do It Again," a song written by Charlie Daniels that was a roll call of the region's greatest bands. Daniels closed it off with the proud and defiant refrain: "Be proud you're a rebel cause the South's gonna do it again."

It was an attitude as much as it was a sound — the same one that Duane Allman had brought to the Allman Brothers: music played lowdown and dirty and honest that celebrated its American heritage. The Vietnam War was over and rock had grown into a multibillion-dollar industry, full of disposable music that often meant nothing beyond an accountant's bottom line and designed to be bland enough to appeal to all while offending none. For the true believers, southern bands offered one of the last vestiges of the musical freedom that had sparked the sixties.

Instead of trying to conform to a commercial sound, Capricorn's philosophy was to highlight and encourage individuality. Capricorn had an unwavering trust and faith in the creative process in a way most record companies didn't. Phil Walden never called down to the studio and demanded a hit record; he knew that if the music was good, the money would follow. "They didn't look over our shoulder and I have to credit them with that," said Paul Hornsby, who was producing Charlie Daniels and the Marshall Tucker Band.

Johnny Sandlin agreed that the freedom to experiment was one of the keys to the Capricorn sound. "Phil had suggestions but he rarely interfered in recording," Johnny said. "I didn't appreciate it at the time as much as I should have. I realized it when I started working for other record companies. What was so wonderful was I was doing exactly what I wanted to do, with the people I wanted to do it with, and it was selling. We had it made."

It was Capricorn's commitment to individuality that led to *Highway Call*, a wonderful country-flavored album by Dickey Betts. Capricorn vice-president Frank Fenter originally came up with the idea of sending Dickey to Paris to record with jazz violinist Stephane Grappelli, who had made his mark as the partner of guitarist Django Reinhardt. Dickey was enthusiastic at the prospects — Django was one of his heroes — but the plan was abandoned after he met renowned bluegrass fiddler Vassar Clements in Florida. Clements had been a prodigy, performing with Bill Monroe by the time he was fourteen years old. He eventually gained fame when he played on the Nitty Gritty Dirt Band's classic album *Will the Circle Be Unbroken?* in 1972.

"I ran into Vassar over at Kissimmee under an oak tree at some bluegrass festival," Dickey said. "We were jamming with him and some guy says, 'Man, don't you know who that is?' I said no. He said, 'That's Vassar Clements.' So we played and played and I called Frank and said, 'What do you think about me doing more of a country album instead of a jazz thing? I met this fiddle player who's America à la mode.' And Frank said, 'Yeah, that's great.' So we did it with Vassar."

After lining up Vassar, Dickey began assembling the rest of his country band. He drafted Chuck Leavell and then John Hughey, who was Conway Twitty's pedal steel guitar player. The studio band was rounded out by a traditional gospel vocal group called the Rambos and a bluegrass group called the Poindexters. "Man, we had an array," Dickey said. "We had so damned much money right then that you could do an album like that even when everybody knew it wasn't going to sell."

Dickey's *Highway Call* explores a path trailblazed by Gram Parsons, who helped alter the sound of country music by rebelling against syrupy string arrangements and pop sounds that dominated the industry. Dickey took country musicians who were accustomed to the traditional constraints of Nashville and unleashed them, inviting them to jam away as they had seldom been allowed to before. "The thing about that album that I'm more proud of than anything else is that it influenced a lot of country music," Dickey said. "Like John Hughey told me, 'Conway never let me play on the C9 neck and that's where all the hot licks are.' And later on, it wasn't that way. So that album was kind of a step in the door of moving country music."

The album begins with "Long Time Gone," a rollicking tune that might have been a logical follow-up to "Ramblin' Man" had Dickey saved it for the Allman Brothers Band. It is a delightful song that explores one of Dickey's recurring themes, the loner toughing it out on the road and anxiously waiting to get back home to his girl. Dickey's voice is rich and warm, showing a depth of emotion that had been hidden before. He overdubbed Dobro parts using Duane's 1932 National Resophonic, which is pictured on the back cover, and he plays a sweet-toned lead guitar that shines on the long fade-out during an exciting call and answer with John Hughey's pedal steel guitar.

Another up-tempo number, "Rain," follows. It's reflective, a song about sitting in a lonely house on a rainy night, and combines the conviction of Dickey's voice with the down-home harmonies of the Rambos. Next is Dickey's prettiest song, "Highway Call," the album's centerpiece even though his guitar takes a backseat to Chuck's piano. It invokes a bittersweet nostalgia for growing up in the South, and Chuck steps out for the first time on the album to play a memorable solo filled with tender sentimentality.

Another celebration of the South follows, "Let Nature Sing." With its gentle country images, the song is like the evening to the Sunday morning Dickey had described in "Blue Sky." The song closes with a long and lovely fade-out. There is no clear lead voice, only a wall of sound from country instruments — Dobro, banjo, mandolin, fiddle, pedal steel — that ring out bright and relaxed on chorus after chorus over the eight-part harmonies of Dickey singing with the Poindexters and the Rambos.

The second side of *Highway Call* is all instrumental. "Hand Picked" is a churning song, pure western swing, with a delightful and playful melody line. Vassar Clements takes the spotlight for the first time on the record, playing twin lines with Dickey on the opening melody before it segues into a long jam. The album closes with "Kissimmee Kid," an instrumental penned by Vassar.

Like Gregg, Dickey charted out a departure for his solo album. Most stars in Dickey's position would have recorded a guitar showcase, long on jamming and short on real songs. But Dickey took the opposite approach, and his solo album highlights great songs and his expressive voice. The entire record sounds relaxed, as if the musicians were set up on Dickey's porch and playing a backyard barbecue.

Highway Call, credited to Richard Betts, was released in August of 1974, on the same day Capricorn issued a double-record set called *Duane Allman: An Anthology Volume II*. Compared with the first volume, the second *Anthology* seemed haphazardly put together. The album includes a rather pedestrian Ronnie Hawkins cover of Carl Perkins's "Matchbox," while another performance from that album, his bottleneck on Hawkins's version of "Down in the Alley," is among the finest of Duane's career. The Hour Glass song that is included is one of the weakest the band cut during the Muscle Shoals sessions. King Curtis's take of "The Weight" sounds too similar to the backing track on the Aretha Franklin version. The album includes only two unreleased Allman Brothers songs, live cuts of "Midnight Rider" and "Dimples," with Duane on lead vocals.

But *Anthology II* does have its moments. There is Duane's powerful guitar on Aretha's "It Ain't Fair," and his performance on Herbie Mann's "Push Push." There is a jewel from the Boz Scaggs album, the Jimmie Rodgers classic "Waiting for a Train," and two unreleased songs from the aborted Duane Allman solo sessions in Muscle Shoals. The gem of the set is an unreleased acoustic version of Delaney and Bonnie doing Robert Johnson's "Come On in My Kitchen." The song was recorded three months prior to Duane's death at a live radio show from Long Island with Delaney on rhythm guitar and Duane on acoustic slide. It is an incredible performance that works on every level — the beautiful blend of Delaney and Bonnie's voices, the interplay between the two guitars, and, especially, Duane's concise bottleneck runs.

For an ego as fragile as Dickey's, the timing of *Anthology II* couldn't have been worse. *Rolling Stone* reviewed the albums together under a headline that read "Duane & Dick: Dueling Guitars," as though there were some kind of competition between them. Dickey had to fight to establish his own identity in the band — many people never really noticed his presence until after Duane was gone — and gaining respect had become an obsession. According to Gregg, Dickey had once verbally assailed a Capricorn publicist, demanding to know, "Why the fuck ain't I as big as Eric Clapton?" His solo album was supposed to be Dickey's moment in the sun, and here was Duane overshadowing him in death just as he had in life.

BOTH Dickey and Gregg took solo bands out on the road in the last two months of 1974. Dickey's tour kicked off first at the Mosque in Richmond, Virginia, on November 1. Dubbed "An American Music

Show," Dickey's band featured Vassar Clements and Spooner Oldham of Muscle Shoals fame on keyboards, along with a horn section and the Poindexters on backup vocals. Dickey had an interesting premise for the concerts: he wanted to give the audience a history of country music and its role in rock 'n' roll. "We start with bluegrass, which is the music that came over to America from Europe," Dickey told *Rolling Stone*'s Tim Cahill, who had been assigned to write a cover story on both tours. "The concept is that you do songs like 'Joe Clark,' things that go back to the 1800s. Then we do a Jimmie Rodgers tune, which is set in the Thirties, and then a couple of Hank Williams numbers, which are up into the Fifties. Then we ease into the electric set."

Cahill caught Dickey's show at the Fox Theatre in Atlanta. There was a dour mood backstage — Dickey's band had been on the road for two weeks but the music had yet to gel — and Phil Walden immediately confronted the writer. "What I want from you is the slant you're going to take because if you don't, I'll see to it that you get no cooperation whatsoever," a paranoid Phil threatened. He wanted to make sure Cahill wasn't writing an article that concentrated on Duane Allman or on rumors the Allman Brothers Band was in trouble. "I'm so sick and tired of that, everybody saying how they're breaking up," Phil said. "How many times do you have to say something isn't true?" He also was concerned that the article might have a *True Confessions* approach, "dirt about a guy's wife, that kind of thing." Later, Phil began to loosen up. "I don't care what you write," he said. "I just think these guys deserve a little bit of respect."

Everyone shrugged off the rumors of discord within the Allman Brothers. Dickey said he was tired of people "playing up the soap opera thing" about the band. Alex Hodges, the head of Phil's Paragon Booking Agency, said the reason for the solo tours was purely economic, that an Allman Brothers winter tour of hockey arenas would kill some of the demand for a big summer tour of outdoor ballparks. Besides, the tours helped promote the solo records.

Cahill wrote that some of the reports of conflicts within the band had as much to do with musical direction as personalities. "The story goes — and here one protects his sources, since talk of disagreements in the band is likely cause for castration at Capricorn — that it is Betts and Leavell who sometimes don't see eye to eye," Cahill wrote. One night, the band was working up new material and Chuck threw out some ideas that frustrated Dickey. "Goddamn it, Chuck," Dickey is supposed to have yelled, "I'm just a country boy and I ain't gonna play any of these fucking *space chords.*"

As Gregg hit the road, Capricorn released *The Gregg Allman Tour*, a double-album set recorded at Carnegie Hall and the Capitol Theatre during the spring. The album had several live versions of songs from *Laid Back* — "Don't Mess Up a Good Thing," a laconic "Queen of Hearts," a driving "Will the Circle Be Unbroken?" Among the highlights are "Dreams," powered by Chuck's rhythm licks on the piano and a wonderful soprano saxophone solo by Randall Bramblett, and a new song called "Double-Cross." There also is a great cover of the Chuck Willis song "Feel So Bad," which had been a hit for Elvis Presley. Gregg's arrangement was pure honky-tonk, with Stax-like horns and Tommy Talton's bottleneck guitar impressively mimicking Duane's style.

"Are You Lonely for Me Baby?" is another gem. Gregg's voice ranges from a gritty roar to a crying wail to biting sarcasm as he does an extended vamp with the female backup singers. Gregg also revived a song he used to play back in Lee Hazen's kitchen in Daytona Beach, "Turn on Your Love Light."

The Gregg Allman Tour has its moments but could have easily been pared down to a lean one-record set. There are places where Gregg is so full of drugs and alcohol that his voice suffers, high notes he strains to reach when he normally would sing them with ease. The album had a disappointing reception compared to *Laid Back*, selling only 216,000 copies. Still, Gregg would brag that he had two up on Dickey — *Laid Back* would outsell *Highway Call* and his solo gigs drew the bigger crowds. *Laid Back* earned Gregg a gold album and eventually sold 570,286 copies, grossing $3,367,220 in domestic sales. *Highway Call* sold a very respectable 338,865 copies and grossed $920,163 in domestic sales, but Dickey's tour sustained heavy losses that had to be repaid by dipping into his royalties from the Allman Brothers Band.

JANICE ALLMAN — worn down from Gregg's thirst for drugs and his always insatiable appetite for groupies — filed for a divorce in August of 1974. Gregg quickly filed a countersuit, saying he was the victim of mentally cruel treatment and adulterous misconduct by Janice. The divorce lay dormant as the couple reconciled and Janice joined Gregg at St. Simons Island off the coast of Georgia during rehearsals for his second solo tour. While he was there, Gregg made an emergency call to Joe Fuchs. He complained that he and Janice were fighting and that he was out of cocaine. The pharmacist hopped in his plane and flew down to the island with a stash. Gregg sent Janice home with Fuchs and the marriage was in limbo once again.

A few days before leaving for the first show on the tour, Gregg and a friend sneaked over to Janice's house and stole her Corvette. Gregg drove the car to his house and waited. The next morning, Janice showed up to reclaim her car and Gregg charmed her. By the afternoon, the marriage was back on again and Gregg was calling down to the band's office to tell a perturbed Willie Perkins to add Janice to the travel party.

The peace lasted only days. The first concert date was in Oklahoma City. On the night of the show, Janice was tired and stayed in their room. Gregg was pissed off — he thought his old lady should be with him at the gig. After the concert, Gregg went back to the hotel. As he reached his door, he turned to a friend, put his finger against his lips, and told him to be quiet. Janice was asleep inside and Gregg quietly packed up his clothes. He walked over to his wife, pulled three one-hundred-dollar bills out of his pocket, and sat them on the night stand. Then he left and checked out of the hotel, on his way to Texas for the next gig.

It was the final straw. Janice renewed her divorce action, and her lawyer made a not-so-subtle threat in the court papers: "Due to defendant's repeated cruel treatment, which will be outlined in detail if called on to do so, it was impossible to continue the marriage." The complaint said Gregg had left his wife for another woman. Janice and Gregg eventually reached a settlement. Janice kept her much-abused Corvette and accepted $740 a month in alimony for two years — a total of $17,760 — in addition to a $14,000 lump-sum payment.

The agreement was finalized on December 16, just weeks before Gregg would walk into a Los Angeles nightclub and spy the woman of his dreams. Years earlier, during the Hour Glass days, he had seen her one night at the Whiskey A Go Go. She walked in wearing a leather beaded dress, with a short guy smoking a cigar. Gregg pointed her out to Duane: "Isn't she the most beautiful woman you ever saw?" Duane looked over at the tall, sensuous brunette with admiration. "Little Brother," Duane had replied "I hope someday you have what it takes to deserve a woman like that."

Seventeen

Cher

IN January of 1975, the Allman Brothers Band was preparing to go into the studio and cut its first record in nearly two years. Rumors continued to circulate around Macon and in the rock press that band members weren't getting along, and people cited the inactivity as proof that something was wrong. Gregg told a reporter the band simply needed a break. He remembered how Dickey had come up to him with a tired look before a show in 1973. "I feel like we're getting up there pretending to be the Allman Brothers Band," Dickey had told him. Gregg insisted the solo projects had saved the band. "We decided it was either we never see each other again, or take some time off," Gregg said. "We made the right decision to take some time off."

Things got off to an encouraging start when the band went back into the studio at Capricorn. It had been a long time since they had recorded together, yet right away they cut a rousing version of the old Muddy Waters song "Can't Lose What You Never Had." Then everything crumbled. There were hard battles over how the Allman Brothers Band should sound. Chuck didn't think the band was sophisticated enough and wanted to move the music toward commercial jazz. Dickey fought to maintain the band's old sound. Others looked for some kind of middle ground. It grew into a constant tug of war.

"Our music is spontaneous and the spontaneity was gone," Butch said. "We sat down one day and had to start talking about our music and that was the beginning of the end."

Everyone could sense the band was on its last legs unless there was some miracle lurking out there somewhere; between all the solo tours and albums, the Allman Brothers Band had become akin to everyone's part-time job. The leadership void only exacerbated the problems. There was no one to rally around, to pull them all together. "They were held together by baling wire by that time," Phil acknowledged later. They were living lives of little concern — spending money like it was coming out of a faucet that would never be shut off and partying every night until the wee hours, ingesting a prodigious amount of drugs and nearly enough alcohol to collectively keep a bar in business.

One of their favorite hangouts was the Red Lamp Lounge, a little joint in the basement of the Dempsey Hotel in downtown Macon. Butch was inside one night getting trashed. He wound up throwing a chair at somebody, missed, and an unamused bouncer walked over to toss him out. A friend saw what was about to happen and intervened. He escorted Butch out of the bar and took Butch to his Mercedes-Benz. Butch was still pissed off. He climbed into his car and glared out the window. The Mercedes was parked up against the brick wall of an office building. Butch cranked it up, put it in drive, and gunned it. The car shot up against the wall, and Butch kept his foot on the pedal. The tires were squealing, throwing off thick smoke with the ugly smell of burnt rubber.

Dickey happened to come around the corner and walked up with a bemused look. "Damn, man, what's wrong with Butch?" he asked. When Dickey heard the story, he smiled and put his arm around the friend. "Ah, let him go and let's go back in," Dickey said. "He'll be all right." They left Butch in the parking lot, still sitting in his Mercedes, glowering out the window, and trying to run his car through that brick wall.

Butch's carousing was causing him trouble with the law. He was charged with driving under the influence and speeding after he rear-ended a car, but the charges were later dropped. Then he was caught speeding and again charged with driving under the influence; this time he was convicted and put on probation for twelve months. Weeks later, two cops said they spotted Butch one night trying to kick in the door of a building near the Capricorn studio. As they got out to investigate, Butch turned and exposed himself. He paid a

$135 fine after being found guilty of disorderly conduct and drunkenness.

It wasn't only Butch; just about everyone was beset with personal problems that were continual distractions. After a brief reconciliation, Dickey's marriage to Sandy Bluesky was again falling apart. If he was sober, Dickey could exude the warm side of his personality; if he was drinking or doing cocaine, he was a man to be avoided. Dickey showed up one night at the Capricorn Studios and trashed the place — the desk in the front lobby was turned over, all the framed gold albums on the wall were either knocked to the floor or left hanging crooked, and most of the potted plants were kicked over. A few minutes after the outburst, a friend walked over to a downtown club and found Dickey sitting at a table. Nearby, a waitress was bent over the drummer in Dickey's country band; he had just been punched out by Dickey and was lying prone on the floor. Dickey was asked what was going on. He grinned. "Just havin' a little fun," he responded.

Jaimoe ate some magic mushrooms one night just before one of his dogs escaped from a backyard pen. Jaimoe went running through the woods in chase and smacked headfirst into a pine tree. It knocked him silly and he lost one of his front teeth. Then he was in a car wreck and suffered a potentially career-ending back injury; there were times when he couldn't lift his arm above his shoulder. Jaimoe was put on heavy pain-killers that affected both his music and his gentle personality.

Recording a new album seemed the least of anyone's concerns. Whenever there was a session, it seemed that at least one member of the band was always someplace else. "Just getting a quorum there to record was basically impossible," said Johnny Sandlin. "If I could get everybody there, I felt like it was a successful day. The band was fragmenting. They weren't getting along for the most part, and they didn't want to spend any more time than they had to with each other."

And then there was Gregg, who disappeared to California just when the sessions were getting under way, and convinced his old friend and Man Friday Chank to go with him. Nicknamed "Chank" because he looked slightly Asian, Hewell Middleton, Jr., had been a shoeshine boy at the black barbershop in Phil's warehouse and met Duane after one of their earliest rehearsals. He grew to love both brothers, and just before his death, Duane had asked Chank to look after Gregg. It was a request that Chank took to heart, and when Gregg said they were going to Los Angeles, Chank packed up his things. It turned into a two-week trip that changed everything.

The first night in California, Gregg went to the Troubadour nightclub to hear blues great Etta James. He wound up sitting in with her, and the club owner convinced Gregg to come back the following night. The next morning it was all over the radio: Gregg Allman will play with Etta James tonight at the Troubadour. Gregg arrived early at the club that night and when Chank got to the dressing room, Gregg rushed up to him. "Hey, man," Gregg said in an excited voice. "Cher's out there."

Chank walked down the stairs to peek out at the crowd. And there she was, the diva of prime-time television, sitting with her boyfriend David Geffen, the president of Asylum Records. Also at the table were her sister Georgeanne LaPierre and Paulette Ann Eghazarian, Cher's secretary and best friend.

Gregg had finagled an introduction to Cher and asked Chank to take a note out to her. Chank felt shy about walking up to Cher — she was a big star and, besides, she was a total stranger. Gregg persisted. "Come on, man," he said. "I'll buy you anything you want, anything." At times like this, Gregg could be like a little child pleading for a new toy and Chank finally gave in. "You don't have to buy me anything, man," he said. "Just give me the note."

Cher later described it as "one of his Southern flower jobs, like 'You're a beautiful lady and I'd be honored if, blah, blah.' Some real jive stuff." Chank hung around the stairway leading to the dressing rooms in case she had a response. Cher got up, walked past him, and into the bathroom. He waited, but it seemed like she was in there forever. Finally, he gave up and went back upstairs with the bad news: Cher had not sent back an answer.

She stayed for the entire Etta James set, and her entourage left the club just before Gregg walked out. Cher's car was parked in an alley out back, and Cher was about to get inside with David Geffen when Gregg stepped out of the stage door. He was on the opposite side of the alley, about thirty feet away from her car. Cher stood there, frozen and almost gawking as Gregg did his "rock star" walk, his arrogant strut, across the alley. He didn't look up, as if too unimpressed to acknowledge her. After they got into the car, Chank leaned over to Gregg. "Man, her eyes were coming out of her sockets," he said. "She was giving you *the stare*." Gregg just smiled.

He agreed to come back to the Troubadour and sit in with Etta James a third time. Again, the club owner put the word out using radio ads. When they got to the club, Chank looked out at the crowd and saw that Cher had returned. And, this time, she had come alone; only

Paulette was with her. When Chank saw that, he walked back to Gregg. "Man, you got her now," Chank said. He was right. Gregg and Cher left together after the gig and the next time Chank saw him, Gregg was driving up in Cher's red Ferrari with a goofy grin slapped across his face.

CHERILYN SARKASIAN LAPIERRE BONO was one of the hottest things in show business, considered by many the sexiest woman alive. She was sharp-witted and seemed sophisticated, with the unique ability to titillate men while inspiring admiration from women. She'd had a string of hit records, including "Gypsies, Tramps and Thieves" and "Half Breed," and her weekly television series was in the Top 10. And all that was in addition to her first wave of stardom with Sonny and Cher. She had grown up in Los Angeles. Her mother, Georgia Holt, was a sometime model and an actress in commercials who had married eight times. Three of those were to Cher's father, John Sarkasian, a heroin addict and compulsive gambler who didn't meet his daughter until she was eleven. Cher dropped out of high school, moved out on her own, and met a long-haired, wild-dressing record producer named Sonny Bono. They began singing together in clubs and, in 1965, Sonny and Cher recorded "I Got You Babe." It sold four million copies, and they married and became one of pop music's most famous couples. After their singing career hit a downhill slide, Sonny and Cher hosted a summer replacement television show in 1971 that became a hit. The show always opened with a brief song and then the couple would banter, often joined onstage by their daughter, Chastity. Cher dressed in daring, body hugging gowns designed by Bob Mackie and had the most famous and controversial belly button in the world. She had transformed herself into a bonafide sex symbol.

As Cher's fame grew, she rebelled under Sonny's domineering personality. She began seeing David Geffen and he gave her the strength to break from Sonny. It was a bold move: not only was her marriage over, so was the career of Sonny and Cher. Geffen helped her straighten out the legal entanglements that followed her split from Sonny, and he helped her obtain a lucrative recording contract with Warner Brothers.

When she was linked to a drug scandal in September of 1974, the heroin overdose and death of a rock musician, Cher found it embarrassing and even ironic. Like a lot of stars, she publicly professed a strong aversion to drugs — but Cher happened to be one of the few who was sincere. She had grown up seeing the tragedies of heroin firsthand, and her drug experiences were limited to the four Benzedrines she had taken when she was a teenager. "I was up for the entire weekend," Cher said. "Chewed the same piece of gum for three days. When I came down, I was a mess. That was the first and the last time for me."

On the night of the death, Cher had been at the Troubadour to hear the Scottish soul group Average White Band. According to Geffen, Cher was having an affair with Alan Gorrie, who played bass for the group. A self-proclaimed "hippie financier" named Kenneth Moss invited Cher and the band to a party at his Hollywood Hills home. When Cher got there, Moss walked over and asked her if she wanted a hit of cocaine. Cher turned down the offer. Later, she saw Moss passing around a glass vial that he said was filled with pure cocaine. Robbie McIntosh, the band's drummer, took a hit and passed it to Gorrie. It turned out the powder was heroin, not cocaine, and both men began having strong reactions.

Cher took Gorrie outside for fresh air. McIntosh was so out of it that they took him into the bathroom and put him in a tub of cold water to try to revive him. When Cher came back inside and saw McIntosh, she wanted to call an ambulance. "No, no ambulance," Moss told her. "Man, I have been through this a hundred times. It will be cool." Cher wasn't convinced. She decided to try to reach one of her doctors and eventually tracked down her gynecologist. After hearing her description of the two men's conditions, the doctor told her that McIntosh should be taken to the hospital immediately; Gorrie, he said, would be okay if somebody walked him around and kept him from passing out. Cher left the party under the assumption that McIntosh was being taken to the emergency room. She took Gorrie home with her to care for him, and would later be credited with saving his life. McIntosh was never taken for treatment. He lost consciousness and died a few hours later. Moss would eventually plead guilty to involuntary manslaughter and be sentenced to 120 days in jail.

Cher came out of the incident with her reputation intact, even enhanced since she had been the cool head in a bad situation. CBS television signed her up to do her own variety show, and it was an instant hit. By the time they went to the Troubadour to see Etta James in January of 1975, Cher's relationship with David Geffen was cooling; he wanted to get married and Cher hesitated. Geffen reminded her too much of her former husband and she was wary after having spent years under Sonny's thumb. Then the rock star from Georgia with the long blond hair and gentle, playful eyes walked into her life.

"It was a full moon, man, and I always get in trouble with a full moon," Cher said. She knew nothing about the Allman Brothers Band but when Gregg came over to meet her, she found herself drawn to him. She liked the sound of his voice, thought it was low and sexy. The first time Gregg came by her mansion to pick her up, Cher was nervous because it was the only time in her life that she had gone out on a date with a stranger. When Gregg arrived, the normally confident Cher was still trying to figure out what to wear. And Gregg kept looking at a mirror in her parlor, nervously straightening his hair, as he waited. Within the first three minutes of conversation, Gregg invited her to go to Jamaica. Cher was turned off.

"When we first went out, we had the worst time, couldn't think of a goddamn thing to say," Gregg said. "I said something that really pissed her off and I didn't know what it was I said wrong. And that pissed *me* off. Finally she says, 'I gotta go. I'll show myself to the door.' That really pissed me off. So I says, 'Tell your secretary [Paulette] I said hello.' That *really* pissed her off."

Gregg took Cher to a club called Dino's on that first night. They sat in the dark room and he picked up her hand and started sucking her fingers. Later, he told Cher that he wanted to go to his hotel room to change clothes. She went with him, Gregg made a pass at her, and Cher pushed him away. "I just said the dumbest thing: I said, 'I'm not that kind of girl.' I just ran out the door," said Cher. "I told him not to bother to show me the way out. Driving home, I was shaking, really angry. It was my first date and it was a bust. I thought, I don't know how to react in the dating world. I don't like it. I don't want to kiss him. I don't know him. He sucked my fingers. What the hell is going on? It was like being sixteen again." And in love.

After spending years of what had seemed like a boring existence with Sonny, Gregg was the most exotic and exciting man Cher had ever seen, dripping with southern charm. And Gregg wanted Cher as he'd never wanted a woman. Part of it was the adventure and challenge of the conquest, and part of it was the attraction of having the chance to catch *Cher,* one of the most desirable women in the world and the woman he had admired from afar a few years earlier at the Whiskey A Go Go. He called her up the next day and asked her to go out again. Cher was blunt. "I don't like you and you don't like me," she said. "I had a horrible time last night and why are you calling?"

Gregg kept his cool. "Maybe we could have a good time tonight," he said. Cher gave in, but the evening again got off on an awkward note. Then Gregg took her dancing. "Turned out to be the key to that whole shootin' match," Gregg said. "We danced our legs off."

Gregg showed up the next day at the house where Chank was staying, bouncing with excitement. "Come on, man," he told Chank. "I told her all about you. She's dying to meet you." But Chank didn't care anything about meeting Cher; the first Hollywood star he'd met had been a self-absorbed bitch, and he had no desire to meet any others. Chank had his own girlfriend back home in Georgia; he missed her and he was tired of hanging out in Los Angeles. He bought a ticket home and didn't even tell Gregg he was leaving. Gregg showed up in Macon a day or two later and told Chank to pack up for an extended trip back to Los Angeles. Chank refused and, surprisingly, Gregg didn't argue. The next morning, Gregg announced he had to go to the airport: Cher was coming in that night on a 10:30 flight.

Chank lived in Gregg's house on Long Ridge Place and he deliberately stayed away until he figured they had gotten in and gone to bed — he still didn't want to meet Cher. He got up early the next morning so he could get out of the house before they woke up and walked to the kitchen. He turned the corner and there was Cher, wrapped up in an afghan that was tied above her breasts. She was squeezing lemons, making fresh lemonade. The image softened Chank; if a Hollywood star could make her own lemonade, she must have some down-home in her. He introduced himself, and sheepishly explained why he had been avoiding her. They spent an hour talking and by the time noon rolled around, Cher had completely won him over.

It didn't take long for word to get out that the most famous TV star in America was hanging out in Macon, Georgia, with Gregg Allman. The press jumped on the story and demanded to know if there was a romance blooming. "She's visiting Macon for a reason," Frank Fenter coyly responded. "Macon is not exactly the French Riviera. You have to have a reason to come to Macon."

After a few days Gregg began getting antsy — Cher was an exciting woman, but he wanted to score some dope. The next night, at one in the morning, he announced he was going out to get some Krispy Kreme doughnuts. He never came back home, and Cher left town the next day in a huff. Gregg followed her out to LA, and quickly patched things up, totally oblivious of the recording sessions that were supposed to be going on down at Capricorn Studios.

Cher knew Gregg had a drug problem but it took her a while to realize the extent of his addictions. Gregg had grown adept through the years at hiding his habit, and Cher was a neophyte in the ways of the drug culture. "I laid down the law on drugs, and it's been wonderful to see Gregg's eyes clear," Cher said not long after they met. "He's really together now."

Gregg did make a sincere effort to cut back on his usage, but he never completely stopped. Cher always wondered why Gregg would say he was cold at bedtime and pull on a T-shirt; she eventually realized he was hiding his track marks. Gregg had a way of acting like a child in need of comfort and he brought out the maternal instincts in women. That was especially pronounced in a woman whose father had been a heroin addict and was absent for much of her childhood. In many ways, it seemed that Cher hoped to save Gregg Allman the way she had wished as a child she could have saved her own father.

Probably the first hint Cher had of the claw-hold Gregg's addiction had on him came when he stormed out of her fifty-four-room mansion one night and didn't return. A few days later, one of Cher's friends called her and said they had just seen someone who looked a lot like Gregg Allman standing at a phone booth. Chank went out in search of his friend, and found Gregg still in the booth. He had no wallet and no money; he was standing there helpless. Chank took him home and Gregg collapsed on the couch, weeping like a baby. He began treatment in a methadone program a couple of days later.

BACK in Macon, the outdoor stadium tour that had been envisioned for the summer of 1975 was falling apart. Gregg was acting as if he had forgotten the Allman Brothers Band even existed, and since he obviously didn't feel obligated to show up for the recording sessions, neither did anyone else. Johnny Sandlin seemed to be spending more time in the studio waiting than recording. "The songs were either Dickey's or Gregg's and if one of them wasn't there, there wasn't much else the others could do," Johnny said. "Chuck was always there when he was supposed to be. And Lamar. It was frustrating. It was the most difficult album I've ever tried to do. That record was rough. That was really rough."

In early May, the *Telegraph and News* broke the story with a headline "Allman Band Album Grinds to Halt." The paper reported that Gregg had refused to return from Los Angeles to record his vocal tracks. No one at Capricorn denied it, and it appeared the story was planted by the label to embarrass Gregg into returning. If so, it didn't work; Johnny Sandlin finally found himself putting the tapes in a box and flying out to Los Angeles to record Gregg.

Things began to look even less promising for the future of the Allman Brothers Band when the word spread through Macon like wildfire on June 30, 1975: Gregg and Cher had gotten married. "It was an elopement," one Capricorn official said. "They didn't let anyone know. We knew they were very close but they never let on they were going to get married." Cher had proposed to Gregg almost immediately after her divorce from Sonny was finalized. They flew to Las Vegas, went to Caesar's Palace, and the ceremony took place in the suite of Cher's lawyer, Milton Rudin.

Rudin had typed up a prenuptial contract and the couple signed it just before exchanging vows. They each agreed to pay their own expenses during the marriage and that each one's earnings would remain separate rather than becoming communal property. The prenuptial left open the issue of alimony and child support in the case of divorce. Las Vegas District Court Judge James Brennan performed the ceremony; Cher wore a two-piece blue satin gown with a white camisole top and Gregg was dressed in a white suit. Cher was twenty-nine and Gregg two years younger. By the time they were declared husband and wife, the secret was out and they had to walk through a phalanx of photographers as they left Caesar's Palace.

The newlyweds went to Jamaica for their honeymoon. A few days later, Chank's telephone rang. It was Cher, crying and hysterical. Gregg had disappeared. She hadn't heard from him for twenty-four hours. He had gone crazy. He'd been calling women he knew on the island. There had been a vicious argument. Gregg grabbed her arm, twisted it behind her back. He tried to make her call him "Mr. Allman." Then he pulled a knife on her and threatened to kill her. Finally, he had stormed out the door. He'd been seen leaving a bar with two large Jamaicans, and she had heard nothing since. Cher didn't know what to do. Chank's girlfriend got on the phone to give her a female perspective. "If I was you," she told Cher, "I'd get on the next plane home and forget him." And that's just what Cher did.

Scooter Herring was at the band's office when Chank showed up to tell him the news from Jamaica. Scooter started calling people he knew on the island and sent them out in search of Gregg. Chank went back home and waited by his telephone in case Gregg tried to reach him there. About ninety minutes later, his phone rang. The caller identified himself as a pilot in Miami. "I've got a guy here who says he's Gregg Allman, and he wants to fly to Macon," he said. "He's got no ID and no money, and he gave me this number to call. I'll fly him but you'll have to have eight hundred and fifty dollars waiting for me when I get there."

Chank agreed, went down to the band office to collect the money, and then headed off to the airport in a limo. The plane pulled in a couple of hours later. Gregg came bouncing off, walking that arrogant strut. Chank liked Cher and he was pissed off at Gregg. He knew exactly what had happened: Gregg stirred up a fight with Cher so he could get out and score some dope. "Hey, man, where's your wife?" Chank asked. Gregg stopped and looked at him, then kept on walking and climbed into his limo without saying a word.

Part IV

Purgatory

It was like a cat in my body. His air is used up, and his claws are out. And he's running around inside trying to get out. Then, bam, the old spike goes in and you can almost see the cat go to sleep at the bottom of your foot. But you know he'll wake up and try to get out again.

— *Gregg Allman, discussing his*
addiction to heroin

Eighteen

Win, Lose or Draw

JUST nine days after she married him, Cher filed for a divorce from Gregg. The story made headlines but Cher was tight-lipped about what happened to her marriage. "Gregg and I made a mistake," she said in a brief written statement. "I've always believed it best to admit one's mistakes as quickly as possible. I am trying to make my own decisions now after years of having them made for me. I'm bound to make wrong ones from time to time, and this was one of those times." Cher said later that when she telephoned Gregg to inform him of the divorce action, he was too high to understand what she was trying to tell him.

After the honeymoon debacle, Gregg headed straight to Buffalo for help at the detox center he had entered prior to Watkins Glen. He began calling Cher, full of apologies and begging her for another chance. He promised he was clean and, this time, swore he was staying that way. Cher found it difficult to turn Gregg away, but remained noncommittal.

A couple of days after filing for the divorce, Cher walked out from behind the curtain on "The Tonight Show" as Sonny was making a guest appearance. It was a remarkable thing to see after they had just spent the past couple of years fighting in public, and suing and countersuing in court. Her surprise appearance with Sonny sparked speculation that they were getting back together, but it was a strictly professional reunion — the ratings on her television series had been dropping ever since she met Gregg, and she was thinking they should revive "The Sonny and Cher Show." Cher was still blindly in love with Gregg and even asked for Sonny's advice. Sonny told her to go to Buffalo.

Just a week after filing for the divorce, Cher gave in and flew to upstate New York for a reconciliation with her husband. That really threw things into a tizzy. Capricorn publicist Mike Hyland found himself defending Gregg against accusations that the whole thing had been concocted for the headlines. "I doubt it seriously," he wearily responded. "They don't need any more publicity."

Cher withdrew her divorce petition on August 1, three weeks after she had filed it. Then she honored an interview she had scheduled with Eugenie Ross-Leming and David Standish for *Playboy*. She told them that Gregg had two problems she thought had been taken care of before the marriage. "When I found out they weren't solved, I decided on divorce," she said. "When Gregg realized I was serious about divorcing him, he set about to change them. And by getting into Gregg's problems, I found out that in some ways my head is on backwards too. Romance and work are great diversions to keep you from dealing with yourself. So now Gregg and I are exploring things together as friends as well as man and wife."

She wouldn't get specific about what had led to the separation. "It's too dangerous to our relationship," she protested. "One thing I can say is that it's hard to be Mr. Cher. He wasn't used to having 75,000 reporters and cameramen show up everywhere we went. Even when we were having a private talk in Buffalo about reconciliation, the press broke in. It was really a drag." Cher went on to say that she'd had to earn Gregg's respect. "Things started to mellow when he found out that I was a person, that a chick was not just a dummy. For him up till then, they'd had only two uses — make the bed and make it *in* bed."

People magazine sent a reporter to Macon to check on the state of things, then put Gregg and Cher on the cover with the headline: "She helps him stay off heroin — and his band is hot again." Gregg told the writer, Jim Jerome, that he had been a heroin addict for two years but was now clean. Cher was his "beautiful butterfly" and he credited her with saving him. "There is a cure for heroin," he said. "It just takes somebody loving enough. I want nothing to keep me apart from Cher." Not even, it seemed, the Allman Brothers Band.

While the romance was playing itself out in the press, the others in the band were still stewing in Macon, trying to finish up the new album and unable to because of Gregg. "I don't enjoy waiting for him but if an artist is not ready to sing, you can't expect him to sing," Johnny Sandlin told a reporter. "Gregg's life affected the band, but sometimes the whole band's schedule stifles the creativity. Everyone sort of got used to it."

Jaimoe was not as judicious and was openly critical of Gregg's lack of attention to the Allman Brothers. He thought Cher should have been more accommodating to Gregg; it seemed as though her career was going forward while Gregg's had come to a halt. "Things are in the wrong order," Jaimoe said. "A love affair can wait. It shouldn't have stopped what she's doing but there's a difference between someone who is already built and someone who is building. And Gregg's still building; Cher's had gold albums out since I was a kid."

MONEY seemed to slide through Gregg's fingers. For someone who was the lead singer of one of the most popular rock bands in the world, Gregg seemed to have very little to show for it. David Geffen had given Cher a fast and hard course in show business *business,* and she was telling Gregg that he should get someone to look over his financial statements from Capricorn — she was sure he was getting ripped off. Gregg put her off because he trusted Phil, and remembered how the manager had stuck by the band during the hard times. The money seemed to be rolling in and Gregg saw no reason for real concern; there seemed to be enough for everybody. But Cher knew a lawyer in New York and Gregg had met with him during the reconciliation in Buffalo to discuss his financial situation with the Allman Brothers Band.

Cher wasn't alone in her suspicions. When Berry had first broached the subject of conducting a financial audit of Capricorn in 1972, everyone scoffed. But a couple of years later, Dickey had begun making the same arguments. *Brothers and Sisters* had sold well over a million copies and grossed over $8 million, and the band had done a sellout tour of outdoor stadiums. Yet in 1974, each of the four original band members had taken home just $124,000, not including songwriting royalties for Gregg and Dickey; Chuck and Lamar were still on straight salaries, now taking home $1,000 a week.

For all the money the band was generating, Dickey thought they were coming out with a mere pittance. Their manager seemed to be leading a lavish lifestyle, especially compared with the band members. Even if Dickey was wrong, he still *knew* the band was getting ripped off in another way. The 1972 contract called for 12 percent royalties, yet the band was still receiving the old 5 percent rate for the first four albums. That hadn't been the way Dickey had understood the contract.

In addition, Dickey was hit with an audit by the Internal Revenue Service for his 1974 taxes. He was growing concerned by the performance of Willie Perkins at the band's office; it was Willie's job to take care of that kind of stuff. Then, not long after that, Brothers Properties — the band's corporation — was hit with an $85,000 bill for back taxes. Beyond the tax troubles, Dickey also thought Willie was getting too independent. Willie had started a company called Great Southern to sell Allman Brothers T-shirts at concerts. "It developed into quite a money-making organization," Dickey said. "He signed my name and, I think, the rest [of the band members] to a deal where we would get ten percent of the royalties on the T-shirts. I thought that was, you know, stepping out of bounds."

Dickey tried to convince the others that something was wrong but his warnings fell on deaf ears. "Dickey was fed up, he was really thinking we were getting robbed," Butch said. "Dickey felt like the business wasn't being done right, that we were spending too much and no one was in control. I thought Phil was the greatest. I trusted him to take care of us. He had invested money in us back in the early days, so I felt like we owed it to him to stay with him. I felt Dickey was being irrational and causing a lot of unnecessary tension."

WIN, Lose or Draw was finally released in late August of 1975, three months overdue, and it was a mess. The entire Allman Brothers Band appeared on only a few of the tracks, and some of the songs were recorded with whoever happened to be in the studio when Dickey was there and ready to work. There are no pictures of the band on the album jacket and the word around Macon was that Capricorn couldn't get everyone together in one room for a photo session. Instead, Twiggs came up with a concept for the cover. There was a shot of an empty table inside Muhlenbrinks Saloon in Underground Atlanta, with a bottle of whiskey, cards, and poker chips on top; beside it is a small table with two chairs leaning forward and propped up against it, in memory of Duane and Berry. The photo is bordered by psychedelic silhouettes of each band member's face.

The album gets off to a strong start with the rousing version of "Can't Lose What You Never Had." As he had done with "One Way Out," Gregg heavily rewrote the song, rearranging some of the lyrics and then adding his own lines. The Muddy Waters original was slower, with a droning blues backbeat, and the Allman Brothers adaptation is so far removed from Muddy's version that it would have been a completely new tune had Gregg written some new verses. The band digs in behind Dickey's swampy-sounding bottleneck and Gregg's impassioned voice. It is a song about someone who has lost it all and is trying to shrug off his troubles with a stoic determination. The band plays with as much fury as it had for a long time, as though all the anger and frustration from the past eighteen months was being released through the pounding drums and gritty guitars, and they wanted to prove to themselves that they could still cut it loose when they really wanted to.

The quality falls off immediately with "Just Another Love Song," Dickey's lament for Sandy Bluesky. It contains some of his best writing as he tells of a marriage falling apart, leaving the "little child payin' all the dues." The song is heartfelt, but the recording never takes off and sounds more laconic than sad. "That was a great song," Butch said. "It's too bad we demolished it."

"Nevertheless" is one of only two originals by Gregg on the album, and the track is marred by a cold he had when he recorded the vocals in California. Gregg slurs through the song's opening lines and his voice noticeably falters, especially when he sings, "Can't keep myself from lovin' you," at the end of the first verse. As much as "Can't Lose What You Never Had" was the band's primal scream, "Nevertheless" sounds like the Allman Brothers going through the motions.

Gregg's cold also inhibits his performance on "Win, Lose or Draw." It is one of his best songs, with music that is fittingly mournful and lyrics that poignantly tell a story. It starts off well; Chuck plays a gorgeous piano and Dickey's guitar seems to soar above the melody. Gregg's voice is stripped down and conveys a sense of stark terror at being alone in a jail cell. But the performance begins to falter when Gregg strains to hit some of the high notes and the arrangement starts overwhelming the song.

"Louisiana Lou and Three Card Monty John" may well be the worst song in the band's catalog, a collection of clichés with a gambling story line that goes nowhere. Neither Butch nor Jaimoe appear on the track. Instead, Johnny Sandlin and Bill Stewart, who are given discreet credits on the album jacket for "percussion," play the double drums. "Why?" Johnny asked rhetorically. "Because we were there. That's the only reason. Jaimoe wasn't available, Butch had gone fishing. Dickey wanted to cut, and Bill and I were there." It was a matter of Johnny getting on tape what he could, when he could.

The album rebounds with "High Falls," one of Dickey's most arresting instrumentals. The song is named for a state park about forty-five miles north of Macon, and at nearly fifteen minutes it is the longest studio track ever cut by the band. It begins with a more refined version of the dreamy introduction used in "Les Brers in A-Minor," and the bass run that kicks off the main portion of the song also is close to the one that Berry had used on "Les Brers." But the similarities end there, as the instrumental swings toward the jazz plateau favored by Chuck Leavell. Normally, Butch is the drummer who powers the music while Jaimoe adds accents and flavorings. But, here, Butch seems to hand over the reins — this is jazz and jazz is Jaimoe's specialty.

"High Falls" is at its peak when Chuck is playing his gliding notes on the electric piano. When Dickey comes in for his solo, he seems hesitant and unsure, as if the jazz chords are intimidating him. His guitar tone is sweet and countryish when it should be snarling, and he never kicks the song up high enough. "High Falls" screams for a climax that never really comes. It was one of the times that Dickey missed the push to get out and really cut loose that Duane used to give him. "Not only was there nobody pushing him, but he didn't have the experience of playing with all the different varieties of music, the different expressions of music," Jaimoe said. "You need more than one thing to fall back on. Then you entwine these things and you grow. And as you grow, you're picking up everything that you're learning and putting it into your bag of tricks."

Butch considered "High Falls" the best instrumental Dickey ever wrote, but thought the band sucked all the life from it. "We played it and played it," he said. "We had free studio time, so we kept playing that thing until we got it perfect — the best cuts we threw in the garbage because there might be a tiny mistake on it somewhere. By the time we got it perfect, it had no fire to it at all. You play something that much and it gets old and it's stale. I mean, we played that song so damned much that it turned into a nightmare. I was down at Grant's Lounge one night and this guy gives me a bump [of cocaine], and what I thought was a bump turned out to be PCP. I took a big blow of it and about ten minutes later I started going out. I grabbed the guy with me and said, 'You better watch me cause I'm losing it.' He drove me back out to the farm. We got there and all I could do was grab hold of this big oak tree out in my front yard. I just grabbed that tree and stood out there for about five hours with the woods just screaming 'High Falls.' It was in the woods, just everywhere, like a nightmare. Oh, my goodness. All I could do was hold on to that tree and try to fight off 'High Falls.' "

The album closes with "Sweet Mama (Lay Your Burdens Down)," written by Texas songwriter Billy Joe Shaver, one of Dickey's best friends. Other than old blues songs, it was the only outside material the Allman Brothers Band had recorded. Again, Johnny and Bill Stewart are the drummers. The song is marked by Dickey's expressive bottleneck guitar and a strong piano solo by Chuck, but it is a weak performance that is hardly a high point for the album's finale.

Just as "Pony Boy" had symbolized the strong spirit that had made *Brothers and Sisters* a great album, the muted and weighted-down performance on "Sweet Mama" seems to sum up *Win, Lose or Draw*. The band had spent six months working on the album and, in the end, it sounds like they all just wanted to go home. Any resemblance between this band and the one that had ruled the stage at the Fillmore East seemed entirely coincidental. "All that stuff was coming to a head then, the decadence," Johnny Sandlin said. "It was pretty crazy. I knew something had to happen. It wasn't going anywhere. You know, to have a band you've got to get everybody in the same room and play. It didn't look very promising during that album, the future of the band."

A twenty-five-city tour that was expected to gross as much as $18 million was kicking off on August 25, 1975, with the grand opening of the Superdome in New Orleans. There were no real rehearsals since Gregg showed up in Macon only a week before the date. A cast was on his right wrist and Gregg offered at least two versions of what had happened: he told one person he had been working on a motorcycle when it fell over on him, and he told another that he had wrecked his motorcycle driving slowly over a set of railroad tracks.

The same week that Gregg returned to Macon, Dickey was hit with another divorce petition from Sandy Bluesky. Their reconciliation had fallen apart and this time the divorce would go through. Dickey agreed to pay Sandy a total of $56,000. He would make two lump-sum payments and then pay her $1,000 a month until she was paid in full. They shared joint custody of Jessica, although the three-year-old child went to live with Dickey's mother and stepfather.

The divorce was bitter, and Dickey flatly refused to perform "Blue Sky" in concert. A month after Sandy filed her petition, Dickey punched one of her closest friends, Leo Asimacopoulos. Leo was standing outside the Red Lamp Lounge around midnight when Dickey came in with Billy Joe Shaver. Leo said he walked up to say hello and Dickey returned the greeting by rearing back and slugging him in the face. A police officer came to break up the fight. Leo went back into the lounge, and Dickey and Billy Joe left.

About two hours later, they showed up at the lounge again. Dickey started cussing Leo and threatening to beat him up. Dickey and Billy Joe were asked to leave and refused. The police were called to remove them. Dickey was livid, and he began scuffling with the officers. When he realized he was going to be arrested, Dickey slipped a Quaalude from his pocket, dropped it to the floor, and tried to crush it with his boot. The cops saw him and charged him with violation of the Georgia Controlled Substances Act, in addition to drunk-and-disorderly conduct and resisting arrest. Dickey was taken to jail and released on $585 bond. He pleaded guilty to all counts except the drug charge and paid $258 in fines. Leo Asimacopoulos filed a simple battery charge against Dickey and a lawsuit asking for $210,000 in damages. Both would eventually be dismissed, as would the drug charge.

Win, Lose or Draw hit the stores as the tour began and the reviews were mixed. Tony Glover, always a big booster of the Allman Brothers, sounded as though he had to talk himself into liking the album when he reviewed it for *Rolling Stone*. "This is a record that grows on you," Glover wrote. "The more you hear it, the more neat little subtleties you hear — the interplay is still tight as ever. If you're into rumors, you'll believe what you want, but the Brothers have just begun an extensive tour and, on the evidence of this LP, they are *together* and riding high once again."

The magazine took a more critical look at the band in a review of a September 13 show at Roosevelt Stadium in Jersey City, New Jersey, headlined "Jaded and Joyless in Jersey: The Allman Bros. Draw a Blank." The review chided the band for endless and pointless jamming, the antithesis of what had once defined the Allman Brothers, and commented that Dickey's white Rhett Butler suits were flashier than his guitar playing. It also complained that Gregg was all but invisible. "Allman's continually diminishing low profile in the band deprives it of its most charismatic and inspiring member," wrote David McGee. "Chuck Leavell simply dominated the set musically with his succinct, intelligent playing."

The band was not in good shape to go on the road. With Gregg's absences, it had been months since they had played together and the communication so crucial to their entire sound had all but disappeared. The magic was still conjured up every so often, but for the most part, it seemed as though it had been misplaced and no one had a clue where to look to recapture it.

EVEN though he was married, Gregg saw no reason not to avail himself of the dozens of groupies who flung themselves at him and the others on the road. Getting laid had always been ridiculously easy for him. Some of the women had lasted two weeks, others twenty minutes. Even though Gregg was handsome and famous enough to have his pick of women, he was basically insecure. If he liked a woman enough to invite her on the road with him, he wouldn't let her go home and pack. "We'll just pick up some stuff in the next town," Gregg would say. He was afraid they were going to leave and not come back. And Gregg couldn't stand rejection; he always made sure he got tired of them before they got tired of him. When he broke up with someone, he'd often have Chank do the dirty work. Sometimes, Gregg would give a ring to a woman and when he was ready to dump her, he'd send Chank to retrieve it. The woman would go running to Gregg, and he'd deny everything.

Whenever she could, Cher broke away from her television tapings to join Gregg on the road. She was standing onstage behind him when the band played at the Omni in Atlanta on October 6, 1975. The Allman Brothers Band was introduced that night by a new friend, former Georgia governor Jimmy Carter, who had launched a long-shot bid for the Democratic presidential nomination. Phil Walden had signed on early as a key supporter of the Carter campaign and arranged the appearance. Carter walked out to the stage to a mixture of applause and playful boos, and his plug for his campaign was met with only polite applause. Still, no one could remember the last time a governor from Georgia had gone to a rock concert to introduce a band, and his presence sent a clear message for the band's fans that the Allman Brothers Band thought Jimmy Carter was a pretty cool guy.

Carter exited and the music began. Wearing brown boots, brown bloomers, and a waist-snugging corset, Cher stayed on the stage for most of the show, swaying with the backbeat. Afterward, the band went to an Underground Atlanta saloon for a photo session and postconcert party. Gregg and Cher cuddled and smiled throughout the night;

she sat on his lap, called him "sweetheart," and burrowed her face into his neck while Gregg nestled her close. "Neither one of us has ever been happier," she cooed.

Happiness for Gregg and Cher seemed forever fleeting. At night after shows, Gregg would look for ways to go out tomcatting around in search of women and drugs. Gregg, Cher, Chank, and his girlfriend, Carrolle, would wind up at the hotel. They usually had the same setup in every city, a suite with a living room between Gregg's room and Chank's room. Inevitably, Gregg would say, "I'm hungry. Y'all wanna go get something to eat?" Cher and Carrolle would agree. Then Gregg would throw in the kicker. "Yeah, and after we eat, we're gonna go party. We heard about this club we want to check out." The two women would protest that they were tired. Gregg and Chank would try their best to convince Cher and Carrolle to go out with them, but everyone in the room knew they were playing a ritualized game.

Finally, Cher would give in and say, "You go ahead, we're just going to order room service." That was all it took; Gregg and Chank would be out the door, and Cher and Carrolle would be left alone. They knew what was going on, where their men had gone. It stayed an unspoken truth, kept at bay by a lingering shadow of doubt that each of them desperately wanted to believe.

Nineteen

Let Gregg Do His Thing

THE trials and tribulations of Cher and Gregg Allman had turned them into media laughingstocks; fodder for Johnny Carson, the *National Enquirer,* and anyone else who wanted to take a shot. An Atlanta band, Darryl Rhoades and the Hahavishnu Orchestra, began performing a parody of "Whipping Post" called "Whippin' Off," where Duane was resurrected from the dead and fights with Cher for Gregg's soul. "I been OD'ed, I been on speed," Rhoades sang. "I don't know why Cher took all my weed." Rhoades was always a little wary when he performed the song. "I'm told that if Dickey Betts ever heard it, he'd cut off my balls," he said.

Cartoonist Garry Trudeau devoted more than a week's worth of strips in *Doonesbury* to the Gregg and Cher marriage/divorce/reconciliation. In the story line, Duke — the character patterned after gonzo journalist Dr. Hunter S. Thompson — has lost his plush post of governor of Samoa and arrogantly goes back to the *Rolling Stone* offices in search of his old job. The editor decides to humble Duke by naming him the Gregg and Cher Bureau Chief. "I'm in charge of an elite corps of raving idiots," Duke complains to his nephew, Zonker. "And they're *nothing* compared to Mr. and Mrs. Allman themselves." To prove his point, Duke gives Zonker a copy of a recent interview with Cher, where she gushes: "Gregg was so thoughtful at our wedding — he stayed off drugs the *whole* week."

The Gregg and Cher Show haunted the band, and it seemed like every reporter who wrote about the Allman Brothers now had just one thing on their mind: the latest on Gregg and Cher, and how it was affecting the band. "Do you guys see as much of Gregg now, since he got his new old lady?" one television reporter asked them.

Everyone froze while Gregg bristled. "Hey, I don't want to talk about that shit," Gregg said. He snapped at the reporter for referring to Cher as his "old lady" even though it was Gregg's favorite term of endearment for his wife. Chuck Leavell intervened. "Let me put that straight for all time," he said. "Gregg and Cher are just like me and my wife, man. Gregg's in love, and Cher is in love. It's just like Dick and Liz, and John and Yoko; they've gotten lots of publicity. I think it's been good, it's broadened both spectrums. That don't hurt any of us, man." Chuck was wrong; it was diminishing the Allman Brothers Band, turning one of the most vibrant bands in history into the backup group for that doped-up singer who was married to Cher.

It was the cause for no small amount of resentment, especially from Dickey. They could all live with Gregg's marriage to Cher, if they had to, but Gregg was treating the Allman Brothers Band like a stepchild he rarely paid attention to. Dickey, especially, was irritated and didn't hide his loss of respect for Gregg. Their subtle tug-of-war was now often erupting into full-blown battle. Gregg loved the trappings of stardom — the big house, best drugs, comely groupies, around-the-clock limo, personal valet, money rolling off his fingertips. Any perk Gregg gave himself, Dickey made sure he got as well. Once Gregg had Chank on the payroll, Dickey decided he wanted a personal valet as well and promoted Buddy Yokum to the job. Gregg had a limo on twenty-four-hour call and when Dickey used it one night, Gregg raised a stink about it. That really pissed off Dickey; Gregg didn't pay for the damned limo, the Allman Brothers Band did. Dickey finally got his own limo. But he didn't forget.

By the time they got to Phoenix in the fall of 1975, things were teetering on the brink of falling apart. With all the cocaine floating around, it had been four or five days since Gregg had slept. Chank was exhausted. He and Gregg had adjoining rooms, and Chank locked Gregg out so he could get some sleep. He woke up to a commotion in Gregg's room. Chank walked over and put his ear to their common door. He decided that Gregg was alone and just throwing things around; he figured Gregg wouldn't hurt himself and tried to go back to sleep.

A few minutes later, there was a soft knock on Chank's door. "Brother, brother," Gregg called out in a whisper. Chank opened the door, and Gregg came walking in with a frightened look on his face. "Dickey, man, he came down and tried to kick my door down," Gregg said. Chank went outside to investigate and saw that somebody *had* tried to kick it down: there was a big crack in the door, running from the bottom up to the handle. Chank shook his head and went back to his room to try to ease Gregg's mind.

WHEN Cher went out on the road with Gregg, her secretary and best friend often went with her. Cher and Paulette Eghazarian looked and acted like sisters more than boss and employee. Dickey had introduced himself to her at the gig in Jersey City in September and asked her out. "She wouldn't take a ride in the limo with me that night, but we stayed out all the next night," he said. Dickey took her to a concert by jazz bassist Charles Mingus, and they soon became a couple. On the surface it seemed like perfect symmetry: Gregg and Cher, Dickey and Paulette; two brothers, two sisters. But it just added to the negativity flowing between Gregg and Dickey — Paulette didn't like Gregg, Dickey didn't like Cher, and Cher was frightened by Dickey as much as she was confused by Gregg.

On the West Coast leg of the tour, their first stop was the Forum, the home court of the Lakers, which holds just over 18,000 people. In a foreboding sign that had begun showing itself, the band failed to fill the house. The band hit Bakersfield next, only to discover that they were playing in a gymnasium that sat 6,000. Worse, there were lots of empty seats.

The Bakersfield concert never took off. Dickey's guitar work was ragged and Jaimoe's back was torturing him. During the midset intermission, Jaimoe lay down on the tile floor of the bathroom; the muscles in his back were knotted up and cramping. Scooter Herring massaged him and applied ice packs, and Jaimoe somehow got up to play the second set. Later, while the crowd clamored for an encore, Dickey and Gregg were backstage screaming at one another behind a door that quickly slammed.

Instead of returning to Cher's house after the show, Gregg gave his chauffeur directions to a Laurel Canyon house. Gregg's relationship with Cher was faltering yet again, and he had begun an affair. The house belonged to Julia Densmore, the former wife of Doors' drummer John Densmore. Julia had had an affair with Berry Oakley just before his death, and that union produced a child, Berry Oakley, Jr.

Because of Jaimoe's back, the band canceled several dates and took a two-week break — Gregg moved into Julia's place near Laurel Canyon. Dickey also stayed out in Los Angeles to be with Paulette, and it didn't take him long to run afoul of Cher. She had just purchased a brand-new white limo. It was parked in her front yard, and Cher had yet to even ride in the car. When Dickey asked if he could use it to take Paulette on a date, Cher made the mistake of letting them borrow it. The limo came back the next morning with the interior totally demolished. Everything inside that could be destroyed had been. Paulette laughed it off. "They sure know how to have a good time," she said. Dickey promised Cher he would pay to have the damage repaired. Cher responded with a pinched smile, and walked away. She did, however, make sure the repair bill was sent to the Allman Brothers Band.

Destruction was becoming one of Dickey's favorite hobbies. He stayed for a while at the Continental Hyatt House near Cher's mansion, and the manager made a frantic phone call to Gregg one day, asking for his help. He said there had been a huge commotion in Dickey's room and that he was refusing to open the door. Gregg and Chank rushed down there, and the manager led them up to Dickey's room. They convinced Dickey to open the door and stood in amazement at what they saw. None of the furnishings in the room were still standing — the bed, television, and dresser had all been completely trashed. The bathroom had been destroyed. And Dickey was leaning against the mattresses acting as if nothing had happened. "Just havin' a good time," he nonchalantly explained.

Gregg and Dickey returned to Macon in mid-November for the rest of the tour. Once again, the marriage between Gregg and Cher was off, and this time it was Gregg who filed for a divorce. After their last flare-up, he was afraid Cher would file again and he decided to beat her to the punch.

The tour resumed in Indianapolis, and because Jaimoe's back woes continued, the band carried Bill Stewart on the rest of the dates as insurance and always set up a third drum set onstage. "There was real big money involved and we didn't know how Jaimoe was holding up," Chuck Leavell said. Whenever Jaimoe's back started acting up, Stewart would take over on his drum set and sometimes all three drummers would play at once.

Nine days into the second leg of the tour, the band went to

Providence, Rhode Island, to play a benefit concert for Jimmy Carter, the former Georgia governor who was making his long-shot run for president. His campaign was in danger of stalling before it even got started because of financial constraints; very few people thought a governor from the Deep South stood a prayer of a chance of being elected to fill the nation's highest office. Then Phil Walden came to the rescue.

Carter and Walden were among the first to figure out a way around a new post-Watergate campaign law that limited individual campaign contributions to $1,000. The law effectively stopped big-money contributions and made fund-raising tougher. To ease the brunt of it, the federal government now matched individual contributions. The Carter campaign was struggling to establish credibility, a process that took money, yet it was next to impossible to raise money without credibility. Then they hit upon an idea to overcome Carter's catch-22: put Phil's acts on the road to raise money for the campaign.

Carter had already impressed members of the Allman Brothers Band. During his term as governor he had popped up in Macon periodically to talk to Phil, and he was taken down to the Capricorn Studios one afternoon when Dickey was recording *Highway Call.* "He came to Macon to meet the Allman Brothers," Dickey said. "He was very proud that a group of musicians from Georgia were reaching so many people. He was just going to drop by the studio and say hello, and he stayed there for about four hours. He was really intrigued by it. He really is into music."

Carter impressed Dickey as much as he had impressed Phil. "Carter came into office, and all of a sudden everybody started coming together — the blacks and the longhairs and the musicians and the welders and the mechanics," Dickey said. "He made a misdemeanor out of reefer in Georgia before they had it in California. It wasn't that he believed that smoking reefer was out of sight, but he was sick and tired of seeing young kids sixteen and eighteen years old going to jail with hardened criminals."

When Bob Dylan made his comeback tour with the Band in 1974 and swung through Atlanta on January 21, Carter threw a postconcert party at the Governor's Mansion. One of the people Carter invited was Gregg Allman, who didn't arrive until early in the morning long after the party had ended. He walked up to the guard shack. "Well, it looks like the place is cleaned out," Gregg told an officer at the gate. "So I just want you to tell Governor Carter that we did show, and to thank him for the invitation." Gregg was walking back to his limo when the guard yelled out, "Wait a minute!" Gregg had a buzz going and his first thought was he was about to be busted. "The governor wants to see you on the steps of the mansion. Now."

The limo went up the drive and Gregg saw a guy standing on the porch. "He didn't have on his shoes," Gregg said. "And he had no shirt. He had on an old pair of Levis with holes in them. And I was thinking: Who is this bum hanging out here at the Governor's Mansion?"

It was, of course, Jimmy Carter. He introduced Gregg to his wife, Rosalynn, and then she went to bed. Gregg and the governor went into a sitting room and began sipping scotch. "You know, I'm going to be your next president," Carter told him. Gregg politely nodded and said, "Okay." Carter ignored the skepticism — he was getting used to it — and plowed on. "I need a little money to do this," he said. Gregg figured Carter would never be president, but he liked the guy and thought it would be a nice gesture to help him.

The first Carter benefit was at the Providence Civic Center on November 25, 1975. The limo driver sent to the airport to pick up Gregg was given specific instructions: take Gregg directly to the venue from the airport and stop under no circumstances. It was becoming a routine for the band's road crew to try to keep Gregg away from alcohol, and they didn't want him getting out at the first package store he saw. Gregg sat quietly in the back of the limo during the ride, and the driver began to wonder what all the fuss was about. The limo reached the Civic Center, and the crew discovered Gregg had foiled their plans again: the limo had a full bar, and Gregg had availed himself of the stash.

At the time of the benefit, Carter had impressed many party heavyweights, to the point that there was talk about a Hubert Humphrey–Jimmy Carter ticket. But his campaign was on the brink of going belly-up. Even with a snowstorm in progress outside, the concert drew a packed house. The audience was an odd mix; in addition to the rock fans who came solely to hear the band, the crowd included numerous Rhode Island Democratic bigwigs. Few of them were endorsing Carter, but they figured they had better hedge their bets and be there just in case he somehow managed to pull off the impossible.

When the band arrived backstage, Carter was there to greet them. "Goddamn, good to see you, man," Dickey said when Carter walked over to him in the dressing room. Dickey smiled warmly and shook Carter's hand with both of his own, and kidded around with the candidate. "Hey, Jimmy, what do you think about singing a song with us tonight?" Carter flashed his toothy grin, but declined. The concert raised about $40,000 for the campaign and, two days later, Carter sent handwritten thank-you notes to everyone in the band. "The Providence concert was a wonderful boost to my campaign for President," he wrote Butch Trucks. "Your confidence and friendship really means a lot to me."

The Providence show was one of five concerts Phil produced on behalf of Jimmy Carter; the Marshall Tucker Band and the Charlie Daniels Band headlined the others. Capricorn announced that the series of benefit concerts raised over $600,000 for the Carter campaign, but the final figure was actually $151,000. Still, that was a significant amount for a candidate who was having trouble generating a thousand dollars a day in contributions. "There is no question," Carter said, "that the Allmans' benefit concert for me in Providence kept us in the race."

Many cynics later saw Carter's public admiration for Bob Dylan and the Allman Brothers as posturing to win the youth vote. But he genuinely enjoyed the music; embracing the Allman Brothers Band when Gregg's heroin use was making the cover of *People* magazine was not exactly a politically safe move. Someone asked Carter whether his campaign would be hurt by his friendship with a rock band with a reputation that was less than stellar. "Anyone who doesn't want a President who likes this kind of music and who is proud of his friendships with the people who make that music, they can go and vote for somebody else," Carter tersely replied.

EVEN though *Win, Lose or Draw* sold 608,000 copies, enough to qualify for a gold record, and grossed over $2 million, it was a major disappointment considering that *Brothers and Sisters* had hit number one and gone platinum. What with the headlines, drugs, medical problems, internal squabbles, and poor record sales, the tour had been difficult, and it was a weary Allman Brothers Band that limped home a week before Christmas in 1975 to play a benefit concert at the Macon Coliseum. Wet Willie opened the show and smoked the stage; by comparison, the Allman Brothers seemed listless and uninvolved.

Cher's career was in no better shape. Her television show had plummeted in the ratings and was in danger of cancellation. When Gregg had filed for divorce in November, Cher was in the midst of negotiating an agreement with Sonny to revive "The Sonny and Cher Show" on CBS. While Sonny was agreeable to the idea, it took some time to hammer out settlements in the lawsuits they had filed against each other. It was yet another amazing moment in what seemed to be a never-ending soap opera; no sooner had Cher split up with her current husband than she was going back on television to do a series with her former husband. Then came yet another twist: Cher discovered she was pregnant, and she reconciled with Gregg yet again, this time only a month after he had filed for divorce. The tabloids had another field day.

Drugs were still a major issue between Gregg and Cher. Gregg hated getting up early in the morning, and instead of using coffee to begin his day, he used cocaine. Chank would put a bump on the nightstand, another on the bureau, then another in the bathroom; Gregg would wake up and follow the trail to the shower. Cher complained that she had come home one day and found her husband and a group of his friends hunched over a table that had lines of cocaine covering it. She went ballistic. "These *people* were doing lines of coke on my fucking coffee table," said Cher. "I was so pissed off. 'Don't you guys have any respect for anything? Get that fucking stuff off my table and don't do it in my house.' "

Gregg no longer had his pipeline into Joe Fuchs's pharmacy; Fuchs had cut him off earlier in the year after he found himself under the heat of an audit by the state's Pharmacy Board. The agency had noticed Fuchs kept ordering pharmaceutical cocaine, decided to find out why, and discovered there was not a single prescription for cocaine on file at Harrison's Pharmacy even though Fuchs had ordered at least nineteen grams in the past year. Worse, other drugs were unaccounted for. Fuchs tried to stonewall the Pharmacy Board at a formal hearing. He accused a former employee of taking the drugs and even denied any knowledge of a burglary at his store. Fuchs survived with a reprimand, but he informed Scooter that their scam was over.

For Gregg, it didn't really matter. It had been a nice thing, getting drugstore dope, but he had connections all over the country; everybody seemed to want to help a rock star get high. Two people that he cultivated in Macon were Frank Dale McCall and Larry Davis, who had a steady supply of heroin and downers. Gregg would go to McCall's house, where pills of every shape and color and dimension would be spread out on a table. Gregg would bring along his copy of the *Physicians' Desk Reference*, the dictionary of drugs. He'd pick up a pill, study it, and then look it up. He was interested in two things: whether it was a downer, and whether it was habit-forming. If the *PDR* said it was addictive, Gregg would set the pill down and pick up something else. McCall and Davis would each be later indicted by a grand jury on several drug-related charges — including the 1975 burglary of a Macon pharmacy, and selling heroin to Gregg. They would plead guilty to reduced charges in exchange for a six-year state prison sentence.

Another one of Gregg's suppliers lived in a house just behind Harrison's Pharmacy. Gregg liked to call him at three or four o'clock in the morning — he'd always identify himself first thing so he wouldn't get yelled at — and see what he could pick up. As often as not, the dealer was asleep. Gregg would get his answering machine and leave a message. The machine didn't automatically erase messages and when the feds busted the dealer, they found dozens of messages on the tape from Gregg Allman. Their interest, to say the least, was piqued.

Word on the street was that the feds were launching an investigation of drug trafficking in Macon, and they might try to squeeze Gregg because of his notoriety. He even complained about it to one reporter in late 1975, saying all the publicity about his drug use was turning up the heat back home in Georgia. "The *People* cover was bad enough: 'She Keeps Him Off Heroin,' " Gregg said. "Great. Now the FBI are hot after me, thanks to that cover."

But Gregg had troubles he didn't know about, problems that were far more dangerous than he could have ever imagined. By the time the Allman Brothers Band took its Christmas break, a federal grand jury was indeed empaneled in Macon and looking into drug trafficking. The investigation was an offshoot of a federal probe of corruption in the Macon Police Department that had landed five officers — including the captain who investigated the burglary of Harrison's Pharmacy — in federal prison. That investigation had tied the officers to the Hawkins Gang, and as the federal grand jury began hearing evidence on the local drug trade, it soon became evident that the Hawkins Gang controlled a hefty share. The feds were eager to use the investigation to put the local branch of the Dixie Mafia out of business. Two names that kept popping up were those of Joe Fuchs and Scooter Herring.

The grand jury also subpoenaed prescription records from sixty area pharmacies, including Harrison's. Questions quickly arose about the cocaine that Fuchs had been ordering, and the drugs that were

missing from his store. Investigators noted that Gregg and Janice Allman had a lot of prescriptions for painkillers on file at the pharmacy.
Prosecutors decided to squeeze Fuchs and Scooter Herring as hard as
they could in order to try to get to J. C. Hawkins, and Gregg Allman
became the perfect wedge.

Gregg knew none of this. J. C. Hawkins claimed he had been
introduced to the singer one or two times, but Gregg probably had no
idea that Hawkins was the boss of the local Dixie Mafia. Even so,
Gregg was still something of an expert on the local drug trade and it
was an unsettling moment when his lawyer called him in early January
of 1976 to say that the grand jury wanted Gregg to testify. His lawyer
told Gregg that he had flatly refused on his behalf, and that everything
seemed fine. Two days later, he called back. "Gregory," he said.
"They're not buying it."

Everything had changed. When the polite approach didn't work,
the feds went to the hardball version. They now informed Gregg's
lawyer that his client was a target of the grand jury and had drug
charges hanging over his head. "It was terrible," Gregg said. "I was up
against the wall, backed in the corner." He had two alternatives: cooperate with federal investigators or face prison. Gregg's lawyer promised to get him immunity from prosecution before he went before the
grand jury. There was one hitch; Gregg would have to give up everything he knew about his drug sources or risk being charged with
perjury if he was caught lying.

On January 14, 1975, Gregg walked into the federal courthouse
and went upstairs to the grand jury room. He was scared to death:
they kept reminding him that if he committed perjury, it would mean
a three- to five-year prison sentence. The session went on for over six
hours and didn't end until ten-thirty at night. The next day, Gregg
made a second appearance. Grand jury proceedings are secret, but
there was no way to keep his appearance out of the papers; Gregg was
too famous and too many people had seen him enter the courthouse.
The news hit the papers the day after his initial appearance, and the
Macon Telegraph reported that the grand jury was investigating local connections to a multimillion-dollar international drug
operation.

An angry J. C. Hawkins went to see Scooter to find out what
Gregg had told the grand jury. "Why aren't you sitting on Gregg?"
Hawkins demanded. Scooter said he wasn't worried. "What that son of
a bitch said don't convict me," Scooter assured the crime boss. "It's
hearsay."

After testifying, Gregg flew to Kansas City to kick off another leg of the Allman Brothers tour. When the band reached Charlotte four days later, the pressure finally got to him. Gregg refused to perform and wouldn't come out of his hotel room. Scooter and Willie Perkins were panicking; they finally sent Chank to talk to Gregg. He found the singer lying pensively on his bed. "I know what you're going to say," Gregg said. Chank didn't push Gregg, he just sat back and listened while he talked about the demands of stardom and how it had gotten him into this mess that might land him in prison. Gregg was tired of it. Everything. He just wanted to get away. He seemed to feel better as he aired his feelings. After a few minutes, he looked up at Chank and said, "Go down and tell them I'm going to go on."

JOE FUCHS'S name surfaced in news reports as a target of the federal grand jury not long after Gregg testified. The stories were specific: Fuchs was suspected of illegally selling drugs, Gregg Allman was one of his customers, and the investigation of Harrison's Pharmacy launched by the Pharmacy Board could not account for thousands of dollars' worth of controlled drugs. Fuchs's lawyer denied there was a correlation between the federal probe and the pharmacist's problems with the state board; he blamed the shortages on poor bookkeeping.

J. C. Hawkins invited Fuchs out to his house after the article appeared. He offered the pharmacist financial help, and assured Fuchs that if he invoked the Fifth Amendment, the longest he could be held in prison was fourteen months. Fuchs agreed to keep quiet, but it was a smoke screen. Fuchs had already rolled over. The feds had enough evidence against him to put him away for years, and he was cooperating with the federal investigation and had already testified at length in front of the grand jury. When J. C. Hawkins showed up at Harrison's Pharmacy on February 3, 1976, to discuss the investigation further, Fuchs had a government-issue Nagra miniature tape recorder concealed in his pocket. The two men began talking about Scooter Herring, and Fuchs told the crime boss that he was very worried.

"Well, there's no need," Hawkins said. He explained that any case against the pharmacist depended on testimony from Scooter, Gregg Allman, and Paul Crawford, another Hawkins associate who had purchased an ounce of pharmaceutical cocaine from Fuchs and Scooter. Hawkins said that he and his boys had already paid a personal call on Crawford to put things into a proper perspective — he wanted to make sure that Crawford understood that prison was a much more pleasant alternative than having J. C. Hawkins angry at him. "I went over there and told Paul like it is," Hawkins said. "Two or three or four years is better than it is to wind up where you don't want to be."

Hawkins had also leaned on Scooter. "I went and talked to Scooter two or three times," he told Joe Fuchs. Hawkins said the grand jury had threatened Scooter with fourteen counts of selling drugs and the possibility of serving fifteen years on each one. But if he told the truth and cooperated, he could get off with a light sentence. Scooter had assured the crime boss that he would keep his mouth shut. "If you're waiting on Scooter to fuck you up, you'll wait from now on. I guarantee you, Scooter ain't saying anything."

Fuchs tried to draw out Hawkins. "Scooter's got such a mouth though."

"He ain't going to tell nothing on you, as far as getting you in trouble," Hawkins said. "And that fucking Gregg Allman, I ain't never seen the son of a bitch but once or twice in my life, much less done no business with him. I think anything he can tell them on you or me, he's going to tell them. But that don't mean nothing. That's hearsay. If Scooter don't say nothing on you and you don't say nothing on Scooter, let Gregg do his thing. That don't mean nothing, Joe. He's a fucking dope addict."

"You don't think Scooter will say anything about you?" Fuchs asked.

"No, siree," replied Hawkins. "I'm going to deny everything until the day I die even if they indict me and give me forty years. I don't like it, but I'll take it."

Hawkins left and Fuchs gave the tape to a group of delighted federal investigators, who had been hiding across the street from his pharmacy. About three weeks later, Fuchs pleaded guilty in U.S. District Court to a charge of conspiracy to possess cocaine with the intent to distribute. Fuchs, forty-two, faced a maximum of fifteen years in federal prison and a $25,000 fine. "I regret and detest what I've done," Fuchs told U.S. District Judge Wilbur D. Owens, a conservative and no-nonsense judge who had little sympathy. Likening drugs to "a cancer that's on society," the judge showed no mercy. Even though Fuchs was cooperating with federal investigators, he was given a ten-year prison sentence.

Gregg was under siege. All the names that were springing up in the newspapers as targets of the investigation were hitting very close to home; they had even announced they were going after Gregg's dentist for prescriptions he had written to musicians recording for Capricorn. Still, Gregg considered it more a distraction than a direct threat. He felt invincible; they would never nab him and they would never get Scooter. In the wake of the investigation, Gregg became a little more cautious about his drug use. But that was all. And after Joe Fuchs copped a plea, Gregg figured it had all blown over.

It hadn't. Scooter didn't tell Gregg that he had turned down a deal similar to the one accepted by Joe Fuchs. Scooter kept his mouth shut, partly out of fear of J. C. Hawkins and partly out of loyalty to Gregg. The band's last tour date was May 4, 1976, in Roanoke, Virginia, and afterward everyone came back to Macon. About two weeks later, word came down that Scooter was going to be charged with selling drugs to Gregg. A group gathered at the band's office on Riverside Drive — Gregg, Scooter, Chank, Willie Perkins, and a couple of other band employees. They had to get a game plan together. If the truth came out, a lot of people were going to be hurt — Scooter wasn't the only one who had picked up drugs for Gregg, from Joe Fuchs and others. Virtually everyone in the room had skeletons in the closet. Chank volunteered to take the rap. Gregg shook his head. Then Scooter interjected. "I'll take the heat," he said. "I can handle it." Gregg wasn't going to argue.

IT was about that time that the Allman Brothers Band learned it was flat broke; eight months on tour had netted the band all of $100,000. What hadn't gone up their noses had gone for the good life out on the road; there wasn't a frill or a perk that the band members didn't have. "Each of us would have his own limo," Butch said. "We'd always get the best suites in the best hotels in town and half the time not even look at it — go in and fall down in bed and not even look at the other room. As soon as I'd get in a room, I'd order five bottles of Dom Perignon and then leave three or four of them for the maid. It was crazy, but it was fun."

Another problem was the road crew, which had grown to about thirty people; some of the roadies were even hiring roadies themselves to do their work for them. "We finally sat down and looked at our staff," Butch said. "There were four or five on there, none of us could figure out what they did. There was one guy who did nothing but open the door to our limousines. That was just fucking insane, absurd."

The information Willie Perkins had was grim. As of February 29, 1976, the Allman Brothers Band had no money. The band's company, Brothers Properties, Inc., had assets of $605,571, and the same amount of money in liabilities. There was a $27,007 overdraft in operating expenses, and the band owed $266,470 to Capricorn Records for advances.

Dickey and Cher had been voicing suspicions about the band's royalties from Capricorn, but now they all knew something was wrong — there had to be more money than this. Dickey urged them to join in an audit of the record company. He had already found someone to do the job and wanted to make it a united effort; he also wanted the band to pick up the costs. Butch and Jaimoe decided to go along. "I thought it would be a good business move and I wanted to answer the questions," Butch said. "I had been defending Phil for a long time and I was looking for some justification for it."

Gregg was for the move as well. But even as he was telling them that the band had to stick together and move as one, he was also telling them the band should use *his* accountant to do the audit instead of Dickey's. Neither Gregg nor Dickey would budge and, because they couldn't reach a consensus, the audit was not pursued by the band. Instead, Dickey privately had his accountant proceed; at the same time, Gregg also had his perform the exact same task.

No sooner had the news hit of their financial straits than the federal grand jury handed up a five-count criminal indictment against Scooter that went beyond what anyone had expected. The indictment, issued May 28, charged Scooter with conspiracy to possess narcotics with the intent to distribute, a count that encompassed his original arrangement with Joe Fuchs and the drugstore burglary they had engineered to cover up the theft of drugs. Scooter also was hit with two counts of distributing narcotics — cocaine, Demerol, Leritine — to Gregg and then two more counts of selling cocaine to two others, including Paul Crawford. Scooter was looking at the possibility of seventy-five years in prison, effectively a life sentence. He was arrested and hauled off to the Bibb County Jail. Bond was set at $100,000. Willie Perkins resigned that day, citing the turmoil surrounding the band.

Since he was falling on the sword on behalf of Gregg and a good half dozen of Gregg's friends, Scooter had the understanding that he would be taken care of. He expected the band to look after his family and pay his legal fees. And he definitely expected to be bailed out of jail almost as soon as he was booked. It didn't happen. Scooter sat in jail for a week. One week stretched into two. Two weeks stretched into three. Nobody moved to get Scooter released, and his frustration grew.

His wife, Karen Herring, showed up at Gregg's house. "I've been down to see Scooter and he told me that if y'all don't get him out of jail by four-thirty this evening, he's going to call a press conference at five," she threatened. Scooter was out of jail late that afternoon, pissed off at Gregg and trying to shake the sinking feeling that he was about to get screwed. Still, it beat the hell out of the possible alternative — a shotgun blast to the face from the Hawkins Gang.

Twenty

U.S. vs. Scooter Herring

WITH the Scooter Herring trial looming just two weeks in the future, the U.S. Attorney's Office became nervous enough about the chances of Gregg Allman skipping town that it asked Judge Owens to have him arrested as a material witness. Owens signed a warrant on June 9, 1976, at 5:40 in the morning. Gregg was taken into custody nine hours later by FBI special agent Ned Myers, then whisked to an out-of-the-way hearing in Americus, about ninety miles southwest of Macon.

The judge placed Gregg under a $50,000 appearance bond and reminded him that he was under arrest and would forfeit the bond if he failed to show up at Scooter's trial. Gregg was then released and Owens ordered records of the hearing sealed. "There will be no public knowledge of this," Owens told those gathered in the courtroom. "You gentlemen are all aware of the problems associated with this case, better than the court is. But I would just caution you that literally no one who doesn't really need to know of this be informed of it."

The day after Gregg's arrest, a multicount racketeering indictment against J. C. Hawkins, his brother Recea, and four other top-ranking members of his gang was handed up by the federal grand jury. They were charged under the federal Racketeering Influenced and Corrupt Organization (RICO) Act, then a relatively new and untried law aimed at prosecuting organized-crime operations. The indictment charged the Hawkins Gang with a series of offenses: the murder of the star witness scheduled to testify against J. C. Hawkins in an earlier federal trial, fixing a federal trial, drug trafficking, arson of one of his nursing homes, possession of counterfeit automobile titles, and possession of a hijacked truckload of shirts. Thirty-five others were named as unindicted coconspirators, a list that included Joe G. Fuchs and John C. "Scooter" Herring.

Gregg flew out to Los Angeles to be with Cher and away from the madness in Macon. When he returned days before the trial, Gregg was placed under the protection of the U.S. Marshal's Office. There had been threats against him and the U.S. Attorney took them seriously. If J. C. Hawkins wasn't after him, then it might be some friend of Scooter's who wanted to get to Gregg before he testified. Gregg was hidden away in the quarters reserved for visiting generals at Robins Air Force Base in nearby Warner Robins. He could see no one and speak only to his immediate family. Cher couldn't leave Los Angeles because of her television show, and Gregg racked up huge long-distance bills on the federal government's tab for calls out to California to talk to her.

A jury of four men and eight women was impaneled on June 22, 1976, to hear the case of *United States vs. John Charles "Scooter" Herring.* John D. Carey was the federal prosecutor assigned to the case. He had been in charge of the civil division of the U.S. Attorney's Office in Macon before he was shifted to the criminal side in time to guide the grand jury's drug investigation of the Hawkins Gang. Carey was a no-nonsense prosecutor who played things strictly by the book. He had never heard the music of the Allman Brothers Band and had given little thought to the media interest in the Scooter Herring trial; his focus was on building his case, not the problems that Gregg's celebrity might cause. But this was another high-profile chapter in the ongoing Cher-Gregg soap opera and the trial was attracting attention from all over the country.

When Carey walked into the courtroom on the morning of June 23 to give his opening statement, the five rows of spectator benches were filled with reporters and curious lawyers. The only person from the Allman Brothers organization in the gallery was its former figurehead, Willie Perkins. When the jury was seated, Carey rose to outline the government's case against Scooter. The decision had already been made that the trial would have a strict focus: transactions involving Gregg, Joe Fuchs, and Scooter Herring. There would be not one mention of J. C. Hawkins or the Dixie Mafia; the court had decided that such testimony could prejudice the jury and might also affect the prosecution's case when gang members were brought to trial. Scooter's connections to the crime boss went completely unreported in the press.

Carey planted the seed with the jury that Joe Fuchs was a conscientious pharmacist who had been corrupted by Scooter Herring. He explained how Scooter and Fuchs met, and how they eventually reached an agreement to distribute narcotics stolen from the shelves of Harrison's Pharmacy. "Scooter told him that he had a market for selling drugs if Fuchs could give them to him," Carey told the jury. "He assured Fuchs that he would never be exposed. Fuchs would get a percentage of the profits, and Scooter would get a percentage of the profits."

Carey said the pharmacist stashed away an ounce of pharmaceutical cocaine in the fake burglary, about twenty-eight grams, and sold it a week later to Paul Crawford. But most of the drugs made their way to Scooter's new friend — rock star Gregg Allman. "You will see how a man who was painting cars and repairing motorcycles got into Allman's rock music organization, and you will see that his ticket to that employment and his instant rise to success was feeding the drug habit of Gregg Allman," Carey said.

Scooter was represented by Thomas Santa Lucia, a lawyer from Buffalo, New York, and Burl Davis, a lawyer from Macon. Santa Lucia rose to make the opening statement for the defense and from the outset, it was obvious the government had pretty much an open-and-shut case against Scooter. There were five witnesses — including Fuchs, Gregg Allman, and Janice Allman — all testifying that Scooter was the main conduit for drugs. There was little to offer in his defense. Santa Lucia was hamstrung by Scooter's willingness to play the fall guy for Gregg and his refusal to accept a plea agreement that included testifying against J. C. Hawkins. The lawyer knew there was much more to the case than met the eye, but he was helpless to exploit it.

Santa Lucia — the only person in the courtroom who consistently referred to Scooter by his given name — offered no rebuttals to what the prosecutor had said, no grand statements of Scooter's innocence. "Before this trial is over, you are going to learn a few things about John Herring," he told the jury. "You are going to learn that he and his wife lost a five-week-old baby. You will learn that John Herring worked as a mechanic here in Macon. And you will learn he later worked for Gregg Allman, of great fame, of great fortune, who I submit to you will be shown in this case is also famous for other reasons. But for now, let's postpone this and hear from Mr. Joe Fuchs, Gregg Allman, John Herring, and let's keep an open mind, and let's hear all the testimony. After you have heard it all, let's decide this case justly."

Joe Fuchs was the first witness. He had been brought to Macon from the Atlanta Federal Penitentiary, where he was serving his ten-year sentence and had been held in solitary confinement, presumably for his protection. Fuchs said he had met Scooter at a car repair shop, and that the two became friends. Soon they began discussing the possibilities of selling drugs. They reached an agreement; Fuchs would get two-thirds of the proceeds as the supplier, and Scooter would take the rest as the distributor.

Fuchs recounted the bogus burglary of his pharmacy. It had happened on a Sunday evening, June 3, 1973 — Scooter jimmied the door to the pharmacy late that night to make it look like someone had broken in. Business had been slow that afternoon and Fuchs had time to stash away a box filled with drugs ranging from cocaine to downers like Leritine, Demerol, Dilaudid, and morphine. Most of the contents of the box would eventually go to Gregg Allman.

With the prosecutor guiding him, Fuchs detailed his introduction to Gregg, how Gregg had eventually circumvented Scooter's role as the middleman. He recalled the telephone calls from Gregg and the hurried drug drops. Scooter eventually insisted that Gregg stop going directly to Fuchs so that he could monitor and control Gregg's intake. "Essentially, we were afraid that Gregg would use too many drugs," Fuchs said. "There was too much a possibility of an overdose."

Fuchs said he charged Gregg $100 a gram for the pharmaceutical cocaine. Leritine was $125 a bottle, and Demerol was $100. Gregg's tab often reached $1,000, but Fuchs didn't worry because Scooter always collected it. According to Fuchs, Scooter was double-dipping. Though he was paid a weekly salary by Gregg, Scooter never stopped taking his one-third cut from Fuchs. The pharmacist remembered an afternoon when, on his way out of town to a pharmaceutical convention, he stopped by the band's office on Riverside Drive to drop off a package of cocaine to Gregg. "At this time, Scooter was the road manager," Fuchs said. "Gregg was there. He called me into the bathroom. I went in, and he gave me ten one-hundred-dollar bills and told me to have a good vacation. We came out and I went back to Scooter's office. Gregg was standing in the doorway. I offered Scooter three or four one-hundred-dollar bills. He hesitated to take them. When Gregg walked off, he took the money. You would have to draw the conclusion I did, that Gregg didn't know about the agreement between Scooter and myself."

In his cross-examination, Santa Lucia tried to counter the image of Fuchs as the benign-pharmacist-turned-drug-dealer. Fuchs testified that on graduating from college he almost immediately purchased a 45 percent share of Harrison's Pharmacy. He said the owner needed money for heavy debts and gave him a good deal. Fuchs then took over full control of the drugstore three years later. By the time of his conviction, Fuchs had owned a fleet of automobiles — two Corvettes, a Lincoln Continental Mark IV, a 1965 Buick, a 1970 Volkswagen — and half-interest in an airplane.

At that point in the testimony, Carey objected to the line of questioning. "I want to show that he made money by smuggling before he got into the pharmacy business," Santa Lucia responded. With the Hawkins Gang off limits, the lawyer had to admit he had no evidence to back up the allegation. Judge Owens sustained the objection and told Scooter's lawyer to move on to something else.

Santa Lucia hammered away at Fuchs, trying to find any weakness to exploit, to the point that Judge Owens interrupted. "If there is some reason to go over something three times, the court will permit it," Owens said. "But just to do the same thing over and over and over again, there's no reason for that, that I can see." From the defense table, Scooter blurted out, "The reason is, he's lying."

Fuchs's testimony was marked by several contradictions. At one point he said he sold drugs to Gregg twelve to fifteen times; minutes later, he estimated it was twenty-five or thirty times. The pharmacist said he insisted on absolute anonymity, that none of Scooter's customers would ever see him. Yet, a week after the faked burglary, Fuchs went with Scooter to sell the ounce of pharmaceutical cocaine to Paul Crawford, another Hawkins Gang associate and unindicted coconspirator in the federal racketeering case.

The sale to Crawford accounted for all of the cocaine that Fuchs had claimed was taken in the burglary of his drugstore. Fuchs said he covered the later cocaine thefts by skimming from his prescriptions; instead of mixing a 10 percent solution, he would make it 7 percent and keep the rest. That didn't jibe with the testimony of an investigator from the Pharmacy Board, who said that Harrison's Pharmacy did not have a single prescription for cocaine on file.

Ultimately, it was impossible to know just how much cocaine Fuchs stashed away from his pharmacy shelves in the faked burglary: the police never took an inventory of what was stolen. Julian Seymour, the police captain who had investigated the burglary, was on the Dixie Mafia's payroll. The only listing of the stolen drugs was a rough estimate Fuchs provided to Seymour when he went to the pharmacy the night of the faked burglary. There was never any follow-up to determine precisely what had been taken. The investigation was lackadaisical at best.

The coincidence of a corrupt cop on the take from the Hawkins Gang investigating the bogus burglary of a pharmacy owned by another Hawkins associate did not escape the notice of Santa Lucia. He got Fuchs to admit that he was acquainted with Seymour prior to the burglary. "Where is he now?" Santa Lucia asked, knowing that the former detective was serving a federal prison sentence.

"I would have to ask Judge Owens," Fuchs discreetly replied. "I'm a little behind on the news."

Owens interrupted. "That's got nothing to do with this case."

Santa Lucia plowed on. "Did you and Seymour plan this burglary?"

"No, sir."

"Did Seymour cover up this burglary for you?"

"No," Fuchs responded.

After reaching that dead end, Santa Lucia turned his attention to Gregg's drug use. Fuchs testified that Gregg's most requested drug was cocaine, followed closely by Leritine and Demerol. He also sold him Percodan, another downer with a heavyweight punch. The lawyer asked Fuchs if Gregg was getting all his drugs from Harrison's Pharmacy; Fuchs replied that he didn't know. "Were you giving him enough drugs to cause him a drug problem?" the lawyer asked.

"He had a drug problem when I met him," Fuchs said.

"He had a drug problem when you met him, and you're giving him a quantity of drugs that were just a little addition to the problem?"

"I am doing ten years for it," Fuchs replied.

Santa Lucia guided the testimony to the day that Janice Allman had followed Gregg to his rendezvous with Fuchs and Scooter and began screaming at them about her husband's drug use. "What was she upset about?" the lawyer asked.

"Gregg had been given some drugs, injection-type drugs. She became very furious about that," Fuchs said.

"About him using needles?"

"Yes."

"What did Scooter tell her?"

"That it would not re-occur."
"Did it?"
"Yes."
"Often?"
"Yes."

WEARING white bell-bottom pants, a tan sweater, and a rawhide jacket, Gregg Allman took the stand shortly before three in the afternoon on the first day of testimony. Security was unusually tight at the federal courthouse. U.S. marshals frisked spectators for weapons as they entered the courtroom and the nearby corridors were patrolled by officers. In a voice so soft that it often could barely be heard, Gregg began the testimony that would help send his friend to prison. Prodded by the prosecutor, he matter-of-factly recounted seeing Scooter stumbling around on a Demerol high at the Sunshine Club and asking the mechanic if any more was available. Gregg described holding clandestine meetings with Scooter and receiving paper bags full of pharmaceutical cocaine, downers, and disposable syringes.

Carey asked Gregg how he knew the cocaine was truly pharmaceutical. "I had had it before," Gregg said. "I knew that, unlike organic cocaine, it is made in a chemical way through a bunch of different washes. Therefore, it comes out very sparkly. It doesn't look like a powder. Actually, it looks like diamond dust. That, in fact, is what we called it. It said, 'Merck, Sharp and Dohme' on the bottle. It smelled like it, it tasted like it. It gets you very high."

Eventually, Gregg learned the identity of the supplier and began dealing with Fuchs directly. "The only drugs that I acquired from Scooter after I started dealing with Fuchs was a gift," Gregg testified. "After he started working for me, Scooter took no money for it." John Carey asked how he knew Scooter had stopped taking money. "That's what he told me," Gregg responded. It wasn't exactly a big boost for Scooter's credibility.

Carey finished his questioning in an hour, and Santa Lucia began his cross-examination by attacking Gregg about the veracity of his testimony before the grand jury. The lawyer noted that Gregg had said he had purchased an ounce of pharmaceutical cocaine from Joe Fuchs prior to hitting the road on his solo tour in 1974; he now remembered purchasing it from Scooter. Why, the lawyer wanted to know, had Gregg changed his testimony? Gregg said he wasn't trying to lie, that he had been nervous before the grand jury. Santa Lucia hammered at Gregg on the point until Judge Owens admonished him to lower his voice.

Santa Lucia shifted the topic to Gregg's drug habit, and Gregg made it clear that he was not going to give up any more than he absolutely had to. He testified that he had not used cocaine in months. He estimated that his old habit had included about a half gram of cocaine and three tablets of Leritine a day. When Santa Lucia asked Gregg about heroin, Carey objected that it was outside the scope of the trial and Owens agreed. Santa Lucia then turned to the drug use that was within the scope of the trial, often with questions dripping with sarcasm.

"What kind of feeling do you get when you shoot Leritine, Mr. Allman?"

"Depending on how much you shoot. It's a painkiller."

"Were you in pain when you shot it up?"

"Yes, sir."

"Where was the pain?"

"All over."

"All over," Santa Lucia said. "Were you in an automobile accident?"

"No, sir."

Judge Owens halted the line of questioning. Santa Lucia asked Gregg to explain the difference between Demerol and Leritine. "They are both painkillers but they have different effects, different feelings," Gregg said. "They are both opiates. Demerol is more physical. You get more of a physical effect than from Leritine." Santa Lucia asked him if he had ever injected cocaine. Gregg answered in the affirmative. "Are you a mainliner, Mr. Allman?"

Carey objected again and the jury was dismissed for the day while the two lawyers argued about how far into Gregg's drug history Santa Lucia could probe. The defense lawyer said it was an important point because the government's case was built solely on the testimony of junkies. "Leritine, as I understand it, is often used as a substitute or a supplement to heroin," Santa Lucia said. "If he's a mainliner and has shot heroin, then he could inject horsehair and wouldn't know what in heaven's name he was talking about."

Owens disagreed. "We are not here to explore every witness's entire life, be it Gregg Allman or any other human being." He told Santa Lucia to back off, and recessed the hearing until the following morning.

Santa Lucia's strategy was to portray Gregg Allman as a hopeless

junkie, Joe Fuchs as a conniving drug pusher, and Scooter as the innocent who got caught up in the middle and had only tried to protect his
rock star friend. But the rulings from the bench that kept the trial on a
narrow path made it a difficult, if not impossible, strategy for Santa
Lucia to pursue. When the testimony resumed the following morning,
Santa Lucia again tried to show that drugs had clouded Gregg's memory to the point it was impossible to believe anything he said. His
handle on the argument was weak — Gregg's recollection that his solo
tour had begun in April of 1974 when it had actually kicked off in
March. Santa Lucia held up a copy of Gregg's tour dates. One by one,
he read off a city and a date, then asked Gregg if he remembered
being there. Santa Lucia was trying to make the witness look like a
fool, rattle him. Gregg kept his cool.

"Do you recall being in Charlotte, North Carolina, on March 16,
1974?"

"No, I don't," Gregg responded. "I'm sure if the itinerary says
we were there, we were there. I just fall out of the plane and play."

When Santa Lucia exhausted that approach, he began to pursue
his other angle, Scooter as Gregg's protector. "Do you recall overdosing on June 10, 1973, in New York City requiring hospitalization?" the
lawyer asked. The Allman Brothers Band was actually in Washington,
D.C. on that date, playing the joint concert with the Grateful Dead.

"I don't recall the date," Gregg responded.

"Do you recall the overdosing resulting in the firing of Kim
Payne?"

"No, sir."

"Does Kim Payne still work for you?"

"No, sir," said Gregg. "If you are suggesting that that was the
reason he was fired, you are terribly wrong."

"After you OD'd, did you have someone to care for you? Bobby
Ellerby?"

"He worked with us," Gregg said.

Santa Lucia asked Gregg about Chank, who became Gregg's
man Friday on the second solo tour in late 1974 as Scooter was promoted to road manager. "He was also my friend," Gregg said. "He was
a man who I tried my best to help to get a job. He did very, very little,
but he did it well. He was my valet."

At that point, Judge Owens interrupted and asked Santa Lucia if
there was a point to his line of questioning. "Bobby Ellerby didn't
work out, Kim Payne didn't work out and Scooter Herring didn't work
out," Santa Lucia said. He told the judge he was trying to show that

no one could protect Gregg from himself, that Scooter and all the others were pawns to Gregg's drug habit. Owens suggested the lawyer move on to something else.

Santa Lucia did coax one concession from Gregg; he said that Scooter had encouraged him to give up hard drugs. "He wanted me to stop using needles, and that happened," Gregg said. "For quite a period of time, I shot up and he would tell me it was costing me a lot of money."

"He was concerned you were spending too much money on drugs?" Santa Lucia asked.

"Right."

"And as far as your health was concerned, you were dissipating yourself. Is that right?"

"That's right," Gregg said, clearly uncomfortable with these questions about his drug use.

"Do you recall overdosing in New York City in June of 1974 when Mr. Herring helped save your life?"

"I remember him helping save my life."

"You overdosed, and were revived and taken to the hospital by Mr. Herring and Mr. Perkins."

"I remember waking up in an ambulance."

"Do you know how you were revived?"

"No," Gregg said.

"You don't recall your heart being pounded on, or being given mouth-to-mouth resuscitation?"

"No."

Santa Lucia closed his questioning by asking, "As you look at Mr. Herring today, he's your friend?"

"Yes," Gregg responded.

John Carey stood up to ask Gregg a couple of questions on redirect. "You testified Mr. Herring is your friend," Carey said.

"That's right," Gregg said.

"And he's still your friend?"

"Yes, sir."

"Why are you testifying, Mr. Allman?"

Judge Owens was growing impatient. "He's here because the government brought him here," Owens snapped. "You don't have to answer that question." With that, Gregg Allman stepped down.

Like her former husband, Janice Blair Allman testified under immunity from prosecution. She said that Gregg sometimes sent her to pick up his cocaine and recalled one night in particular in September of 1974. "We were laying on the bed watching TV," Jan said. "Gregg told me to go and to meet Scooter, that he had some toot, some co-caine, and to bring it back to him. He told me to go and to drive around Rogers or Corbin, and if I didn't see him on one street, I would see him on the next one. I drove to Rogers Avenue, and Scooter was coming the other way. I stopped and rolled down the window, and he tossed me a little medicine bottle and I took it home."

After she outlined her battles with Scooter about Gregg's use of needles, Carey handed her over to Santa Lucia for cross-examination. Janice told him that Gregg was using drugs when they met in October of 1972. When the lawyer asked if Gregg was using heroin, Carey objected and Judge Owens disallowed the question. Santa Lucia then asked if Gregg was shooting up during their marriage. Janice re-sponded in the affirmative.

"Did you have occasion to see him inject drugs?"

"Did I see it? No, sir."

"Would he always sort of go off by himself to do that?"

"Yes, I saw the needles."

"Is it fair to say that your marriage was kind of rocky?"

"Yes."

Santa Lucia tried to discredit her testimony by showing Janice didn't like Scooter. He asked her if she'd had any problems with her car, fishing for the story she had told the grand jury about Scooter rigging her Corvette so that carbon monoxide would pour into the cab. When Janice didn't volunteer it, Santa Lucia began reading her grand jury testimony to her and coaxed the story out. "Did that cause you to have a bad feeling about Mr. Herring?"

"Yes, of course it did," Janice replied.

John Carey asked her on redirect if she had any other reasons for her animosity towards Scooter. "I didn't like him bringing needles and making drugs so available," Janice responded. "It wrecked my marriage."

IT took the prosecution less than two days to present its case. When John Carey rose late in the afternoon to announce the government was resting its case, Santa Lucia asked for a recess for the rest of the day so that he could confer with Scooter and decide whether his client would testify. Judge Owens gave him ten minutes. "Anybody with common sense who has sat in the courtroom and listened to the evidence knows what the state of affairs is," the judge said. "I suggest to you, sir, that you are in as good a position now as you will be in tomorrow morning to talk with that client of yours and decide whether he wants to take the stand."

Following the break, Santa Lucia announced the defense would rest without presenting evidence. The lawyers went on to discuss other matters. At four o'clock, Santa Lucia said that Scooter was reconsidering and might want to testify the following morning. He said Scooter didn't feel fit enough to take the stand that late in the afternoon. Owens smelled a reversible error if he denied Scooter the chance to testify; he decided to recess for the day, saying the defense had the option of reopening its case and presenting Scooter as a witness.

The next morning, Santa Lucia began the proceedings by holding up a copy of the *Macon Telegraph* with a banner headline that said "Allman Under Heavy Guard," and then, in smaller type, "Death Threats Reported." The story, written by Randall Savage, reported that threats had been made against Gregg's life and that U.S. marshals were giving him twenty-four-hour protection. It even included quotes from Owens, who said the federal bodyguards had been ordered "out of an overabundance of precaution." Santa Lucia said the story may have tainted the jury and that he might ask for a mistrial. But, first, he wanted the jurors polled to determine whether they had seen the morning paper. Carey made a very nominal rebuttal, saying the headline was not sufficient cause for a mistrial. But he didn't object to the polling of jurors. Why risk having an appeals court overturn a strong conviction on a technicality when the story probably had no impact at all?

But Owens refused. "It was obvious from the beginning that if there was any case that would draw publicity, it was this case," he said. "After all, can you imagine a rock star who currently is among the more popular in these United States in any courtroom in a drug case, and his testimony not being fully reported? I don't believe the presence of an article in the morning newspaper just by itself is sufficient to cause the court to cross-examine the jury."

Santa Lucia called his client to the stand, and it soon became apparent Scooter would have been smarter to have sat silent. His testimony was brief. He outlined his educational background for the jury, then talked about working for the Allman Brothers. "My job was looking after Gregg," Scooter said. "It was primarily my responsibility to see that he was up and where he should be and performing at the time he should perform." Scooter said Gregg was using drugs, but denied knowing where he got them. He denied selling cocaine to Paul Crawford.

Scooter's testimony was so shallow that John Carey seemed to lack the heart to go for the jugular on cross-examination. He lobbed a couple of soft questions at Scooter, then asked if he had ever purchased cocaine. "I am, respectfully, going to have to assume my rights and privileges under the First, Fourth, Fifth, and Sixth and Ninth Amendments to the question." Carey lobbed Scooter a few more innocuous questions, then said he had nothing further. The prosecutor knew he had the case won: when a defendant takes the stand, then invokes the Fifth Amendment and refuses to answer questions, juries tend to take it as an admission of guilt.

In his closing argument, Carey told the jury that Scooter and Joe Fuchs had reached an agreement to sell drugs illegally. "Then, boom, here comes the bonanza. Gregg Allman. He had a need for drugs. They nickeled and dimed him — one, two, three grams — to feed the habit, to feed his use of cocaine." He said the government targeted suppliers, not users. That was why Gregg had immunity, when Scooter and Joe Fuchs were facing time in prison. "Gregg was a user," Carey said. "His wife was a user." Carey pointed to Scooter. "That's the supplier. That's why he is on trial and Allman is not."

Thomas Santa Lucia had only four long-shot hopes in his closing argument: discredit the witnesses against Scooter, shift all the blame to Joe Fuchs, invoke sympathy for Scooter, and fuzz up the evidence enough to raise questions of reasonable doubt. He began by noting that the prosecution had produced no actual drugs, a fact Carey had explained earlier by saying all the evidence had been ingested. "It just seems impossible to me that the United States of America would even indict a man, let alone convict a man, without drugs in evidence," Santa Lucia argued.

He scoffed at the testimony about Scooter's involvement in the faked burglary of Harrison's Pharmacy. "I can't buy it," Santa Lucia said. "There is no logic to it. It doesn't make sense that anybody had to be involved except Joe Fuchs himself. He did it all. Is there any proof of Herring entering the drugstore? Did anybody see him?"

Santa Lucia then launched into a full-blown attack on the credibility of the pharmacist. "Joe Fuchs had found a pigeon, Gregg Allman, and was sucking him dry," the lawyer said. "Fuchs, who bought half a pharmacy upon graduation, who bought the whole pharmacy within two years after becoming a pharmacist, who owned a silver Corvette and a Mark IV car and a Buick automobile and an airplane.

Fuchs was a drug pusher. Joe Fuchs is still wheeling and dealing. Joe Fuchs was a dead pigeon who had to plead guilty because Gregg Allman's testimony could put him behind bars for a hundred years. So don't feel sorry, please, for Joe Fuchs, poor guy doing his time. He isn't worthy of belief."

The defense lawyer next turned his attention to Gregg. "Allman and Fuchs became very, very close. Joe Fuchs is a money guy. Gregg Allman is a money guy. They make deals and talk together. What need is there for John Herring?" Santa Lucia paused, then shifted topics and tried to draw sympathy for Scooter. "Nothing can happen to Gregg Allman. He keeps his fame. He keeps his fortune. He keeps his publicity. He keeps his music. And he keeps his freedom." He asked the jury to find his client not guilty.

John Carey rose to give the second half of his closing argument, and try to take away any doubts Santa Lucia might have planted. First, he addressed Santa Lucia's contention that Fuchs faked the burglary by himself. "Why didn't Fuchs do the burglary himself?" Carey asked. "I suggest to you that Fuchs wanted an alibi when his store was broken into." He then moved to the subject of Gregg Allman. "Now you heard Allman talk about his use of drugs. It's not easy for anybody to say that. That's harder on him because of who he is. But he told you the truth. The government is not after the user. It's after the supplier and the evidence shows beyond a reasonable doubt that there sits the supplier, the parasite that came to the drug habit of an individual and fed that drug habit and, like a leech, got fat off his drug habit."

The jury was sent out to deliberate just before noon. They took a lunch break, reconvened just before two o'clock, and, an hour later, returned with a guilty verdict on all five counts. That night, someone took a can of spray paint and, near the Capricorn offices, wrote on a wall: "Gregg Allman has murdered the Brothers and rock 'n' roll."

JOHN C. "SCOOTER" HERRING faced certain jail time when he stood before Judge Owens on July 19, 1976, to be sentenced. Joe Fuchs had received ten years, and that was after a plea agreement; Scooter had just forced them to go through a trial. He also continued to refuse to testify against J. C. Hawkins. When the judge asked if he had anything to say, Scooter begged for mercy. "I have given an awful lot of thought to an awful lot of things in the past few weeks, and I genuinely want you to know that for the bigger part of my life there's nothing to be proud of," Scooter said. "But for the last two and a half years, I felt like I was accomplishing something. It's something I had never known before in my life. To be blunt about it, there hasn't been much to me. But for the last two or three years, I have gained some pride in myself. I feel like I have tried with everything inside of me to do the best I could by everybody I could. You just can't imagine how many times that I have sat up with Gregg Allman at night when he'd had too much dope. Not only him, but other people."

Scooter told the judge that he was destitute. He asked to be spared a prison sentence and instead be given long-term probation so that he could work and support his family. He offered to spend weekends in jail. Scooter also said he wanted to work in drug prevention programs. "I know I'm a useful person," he said. "I've laid awake hours and thought about what I would say if there was a possibility for me to go to high schools where the problems exist, and let them know what having contact with drugs and dope and all that has done to me, what I've seen it do to the people that they hold up and idolize. Your honor, I'm begging. But I've got a lot to offer."

Judge Owens, who had been stung by public criticism that Scooter was the fall guy when Gregg Allman should be the one going to prison, listened to Scooter and then began a long soliloquy on the process of justice. He said that granting immunity is a necessary tool to convict criminals. "This court didn't decide to give Gregg Allman or any other human being immunity. Somebody did have to decide it and let's be realistic: if somebody had not been given immunity, you would not have been prosecuted. A whole lot of other people would not have been prosecuted. I say that because the public tells me that Mr. Herring is nothing but a scapegoat. They say the person that ought to be prosecuted is Mr. Allman. Now we are not here trying Gregg Allman. It's unfortunate that somebody who is successful in the entertainment world had to be a witness in this case. You don't create special rules for the entertainment world. The court doesn't look on you as a scapegoat. You are not being treated unfairly. You just got caught."

The judge then turned his attention to the matter at hand. "Your case has troubled me ever since it began," Owens said. "It troubled me that you chose to take that witness stand before twelve people to tell the truth, and you took the Fifth Amendment. I saw you sitting back at that table contending verbally that a witness was lying up there, when you yourself said, 'Judge, if I answer that question, I will incriminate myself.' Well, you couldn't incriminate yourself unless what those people were saying was at least partially true."

Owens chastised Scooter for not giving the grand jury information about the Hawkins Gang. "It would be a better world for you and your wife and your child to live in if you had had guts enough to tell what's going on," the judge said. "Until people come forward, all the grand jury can do is plod along and work, get witnesses back there and sweat them out, give some of them immunity and do the best they can with the limited tools they've got. Without going into specifics, your case involves other cases. You know that, your lawyer knows it and the court knows it. I'm not going to prejudice anybody's rights by speculating on what other cases there may be. I suspect that this is part of a larger puzzle."

With that, Owens announced the sentence. It was the absolute maximum: fifteen years on each count, a total of seventy-five years. But Owens put in an escape hatch. He said Scooter would be studied by the federal Bureau of Prisons and a report would be sent back to the court in three months. "In everyday language, that means that you will be brought back into court and there will be another hearing and the court will determine how much of the maximum sentence you will serve," Owens said. "You could serve all of it. It could be reduced. It simply leaves the door wide open for that to take place."

The implication was clear: Scooter was being offered one last chance to help them nab the Dixie Mafia. If not, he might well spend the rest of his life in prison.

Twenty-one

Soap Opera

THE brotherhood had been betrayed, and Gregg was everyone's convenient Judas. He was shunned by his friends and faced open hostility in every direction. "Allman is finished," one member of the brotherhood was heard to say. "You mean with music?" he was asked. "No," he responded. "With breathing." There was a band meeting to try to save things, but it was useless. Dickey wouldn't even speak to Gregg. No one said it outright, but they all knew: it was over. Gregg fled Macon and went back to the sanctuary of Los Angeles to be with Cher. She gave birth to their son, Elijah Blue Allman, on July 10, 1976, and at least one friend remained loyal: Jimmy Carter, now the Democratic nominee for president, called with his congratulations.

It had been a difficult pregnancy for Cher. She had a history of miscarriages, and when she began having problems during a vacation in Hawaii back in the spring, she had called Gregg in a panic. He flew out to be with her, and Cher would remember the time they spent together in Hawaii as the most idyllic days of the marriage. It was the first time Gregg had hung around in a relationship long enough to see one of his children born, and he was awestruck by his new son. "Cher was walking around for months with this lump, and you know a baby is in there, but you really don't," he said. "Watching him being born was incredible. I'm crazy about him."

Even though he was on the other side of the continent from Macon, Gregg still hadn't given up on the Allman Brothers Band. After months of neglecting the band, as soon as Gregg saw that it was slipping away he began to realize how important the Allman Brothers was to him. He tried calling Georgia to set up band meetings, but no one would take his calls. Gregg finally got through to Chuck Leavell and was told that Butch was saying he'd never perform with him again. The formal announcement of the breakup came in mid-August in, of all things, a letter to the editor that Jaimoe sent to the *Macon News* after a reporter from the *Washington Post* called to ask him about the future of the band.

"There is no more Allman Brothers Band," Jaimoe wrote. "So far as Gregg Allman is concerned, the so-called driving force behind the band, he was no more than any of the original band. He wrote a lot of great songs and we played some great music. I love Gregg Allman, but for eight years I have seen him hurt the people who loved him. . . . he wasted himself on the ones that did not give a damn more than what they could get out of him. They are the vampires, leeches, etc. He overstepped his boundaries when he got a man who saved his life more than once a seventy-five-year jail sentence. Gregg Allman could be a star like Elvis, Sinatra or Elton John. I am sure they all have hang-ups too. I certainly have many hang-ups. For a man that has so much going for him, Gregg is a very insecure person. For these reasons, I can no longer work with or for Gregg Allman, but I still pray for God to help him and all of us. For he is a human being and I love him still."

After Jaimoe's pronouncement, the others soon followed. "There's no way we can work with Gregg again. Ever," Dickey told *Rolling Stone.* "When a man who's worked with you for two years and saved your life twice is sitting there with his life on the line, and you walk into court and tap on the mike and say, 'Testing, one, two, three'; which is a fact, it's what Gregg did. And Scooter's sitting there with his fucking life on the line."

Butch laughed sardonically when he was told that Gregg had decided to put together a solo band and continue playing music. "Who'd want to see him perform?" Butch said. "I tell you, he must be ready to duck bricks. I wouldn't get on stage with him, even if I didn't know him, for fear of my own life."

A few weeks after his conviction, Scooter became eligible for bail after his lawyers filed an appeal. The band received a $125,000 royalty check from Warner Brothers and, without Gregg's knowledge, placed

$100,000 into a certificate-of-deposit account at a local bank as security to get Scooter out of jail. "The band was incorporated so that if the majority rules, we act," Dickey explained. "The majority ruled that we bail Scooter out. One vote abstained." He was asked about the abstaining member. "We don't have his phone number," Dickey curtly responded.

Gregg was hurt by the backlash; he'd never expected the brotherhood to turn on him. He thought they would understand that he didn't have any choice, that it was either testify or go to prison. "Not one of the Allman Brothers Band, not one of the men in the band, was at that trial," Gregg complained. "Therefore, I can only believe that they made up their minds on hearsay alone. I figured when the chips were down, if they were brothers, they wouldn't have turned me out like they did."

No one in the Allman Brothers Band comprehended the workings of the judicial system, nor the weight of Gregg's dilemma. They naively thought that if Gregg had told the jury that Scooter had been hired to help him cope with his drug problem, it somehow would have made the charges disappear. No one knew about the depth of Scooter's involvement, that he had brought on his own fate by his stubborn refusal to testify against the Dixie Mafia.

As the breakup played itself out in the media, J. C. Hawkins and five others went on trial in federal court. With Joe Fuchs as one of the key prosecution witnesses, a jury found them guilty of racketeering charges that included conspiracy to commit murder, arson, and interstate theft. Hawkins was given the maximum sentence, eighty years in prison, and his brother Recea was sentenced to fifty years.

To anyone who would listen, Gregg maintained that he and Scooter were still the best of friends and that if Scooter didn't hold it against him, then why should anyone else? But Scooter was helping to poison the air. "If he's a friend of mine, tell him to come down and split the seventy-five years with me," he told Butch.

Dickey was especially angry. "I'll tell you what makes me so goddamn mad is Gregg is going around telling people that him and Scooter are the best of friends today, and that the [conviction] had nothing to do with the breakup of the Allman Brothers Band," he said. "That's a bunch of bullshit. Scooter feels that Gregg railroaded him. He feels that Gregg could have helped him by telling the truth. He was hired to watch Gregg. When Gregg got in trouble, Scooter saved his life. I've watched Scooter give Gregg artificial respiration while we were waiting on the doctor. He threw Scooter away just because he didn't need him anymore, and there's not one person in this band who won't tell you anything different. That's why there's no Allman Brothers Band."

Despite his proclamations of friendship with Scooter, Gregg was actually scared of his old friend; when he returned to Macon for a visit after Scooter got out of jail on bond, Gregg tried to avoid him. Finally, Chank went to Scooter. He had been in the room when Scooter volunteered to take the rap, and it pained him now to see Scooter going around bad-mouthing Gregg. "Why are you doing this?" he asked Scooter. "*I* know how much he cares about you, and *you* know how much he cares about you." Scooter agreed to get together with Gregg, and they met for about fifteen or twenty minutes. They tried to act friendly but it was awkward; Chank could feel the tension in the room.

After the others had blasted him publicly, Gregg fought back. He downplayed the role of the Scooter Herring trial in the fall of the Allman Brothers, and he wasn't beyond spinning some revisionist history. "The spirit on the last tour was incredibly good," Gregg said. "That's another reason I'm so confused now. I'd never worked harder or sung better. I thought I was starting to get the band's respect back. I was really optimistic. The trouble didn't start until we got off the road."

He placed much of the blame for the discord on Dickey's shoulders. "Since Duane had passed away, he got compared to Duane in so many articles and everything," Gregg said. "A lot of people didn't even notice him until long after Duane had been gone. They'd say, who's the new guitar player in the Allman Brothers? It used to just really kill him. He got really crazy about it. All these rumors I've heard about me doing strange things out on the road and being fucked up, you never heard about the thousands and thousands of dollars that the Allman Brothers had to put out because of motel rooms Dickey and Butch had torn up because of women and drinking."

In late September, Gregg used a forum the others couldn't: *People* magazine. On the cover was a family portrait of Gregg, Cher, Chastity, and Elijah Blue; inside, Gregg told a story of betrayal with himself as the victim. "I've been the fall guy for this whole thing," he said. "The band was gone long before this whole trial thing hit. Nobody knew where the money was [going], and after [my] audit is over, we're really going to find out what broke up the Allman Brothers Band."

Cher complained that she ought to write a soap opera. "Our whole world was shot to ratshit," she said. "Gregory makes a great villain because he's taken drugs." Either Gregg had been less than candid in the version of the Scooter Herring story that he had told Cher, or else she was blindly covering for her man. "They acted as if he had turned his road manager into a drug dealer when it was the other way around," Cher, with a straight face, told *People*.

She again proclaimed Gregg to be drug- and alcohol-free — he had ballooned up to a portly two hundred pounds during the effort — and the couple gave the impression that they had at last found domestic bliss with the birth of their child. "I've always loved Gregory, but until now I never felt it was going to last," Cher said. "For the first time, I feel like married people." Gregg and Cher even announced they were going into the studio together to record an album.

"We had some heavy settling-in pains," Gregg said. "But I'm sure there have been stranger relationships."

IT was Johnny Sandlin who fired the first legal missile at Capricorn Records. Like Gregg and Dickey, Johnny had also hired an accountant to look into his own situation with the record label. It was determined that he was owed $832,591 in back royalties, and Johnny sued. The record company countered that it owed Johnny nothing; it had searched its records and discovered that he owed Capricorn $130,078 for unreimbursed advances. Capricorn scoffed at the audit. "Patently incomplete, inexact, inaccurate, misleading, argumentative and exaggerated" were among the adjectives used to describe it.

There wasn't much room for compromise. Johnny was fired as the court battle wound its way through the legal system, and he retreated to his house out in the country. "The Scooter thing, the drug problems, saying they were never going to play with Gregg again, all that was rough," Johnny said. "It was a terribly uncomfortable feeling and it was frightening, too. Everybody in that whole organization had been involved in drugs to some extent, and you just didn't know what was coming down."

The concern was realistic. *New Times* magazine published a story on Capricorn Records, and on the cover was a drawing of Phil Walden. His right arm was draped around the shoulder of Jimmy Carter and his left was around Gregg, who had a spoon of cocaine raised to his nose. Rumors around town had the federal grand jury now targeting Phil's connections to drugs and to the Dixie Mafia; they were false but people whispered them anyway. "I'm afraid to get a parking ticket," Phil said. "They'll put me away for four thousand years."

The Jones County Sheriff's Department raided the band's farm in Juliette and found a greenhouse garden of forty marijuana plants, along with a stash of magic mushrooms. The caretaker, Andrew J. "Hondo" Ritchie, was arrested but the charges were later thrown out of court after a judge decided there had been no probable cause for the raid and ruled that the search warrant was invalid.

And in September of 1976 Dickey was arrested. Someone had complained about a late-night prowler on Ridge Avenue and two Macon cops, G. L. Dean and T. L. Sanders, were dispatched to investigate. When they arrived, they heard banging noises and someone loudly cursing. They got out of their car, walked around the corner, and saw a man kicking and punching two garbage cans; he was bleeding badly from both hands. When the officers tried to arrest him, he protested: "Hey, I'm Dickey Betts."

They weren't impressed, and as they tried to put handcuffs on him, Dickey pulled back and swung at both of them. He missed, and they wrestled him to the ground. On the ride to the city jail, Dickey didn't let up. He sat in the backseat of the patrol car, screaming and cussing and kicking at the back of the driver's seat. When they reached the jail, he spit on Officer Dean. After he was locked in a cell, Dickey reached through the bars, grabbed several booking sheets, and tore them up. Then he kicked Dean in the chest. Later that night, Dickey destroyed a mattress and the sheets in his cell.

He was convicted in Municipal Court and fined $500 for resisting arrest, destroying city property, and two counts of disorderly conduct. Dickey also was charged with simple battery for kicking the police officer; he pleaded guilty in State Court, and was fined $150 and given a twelve-month suspended sentence.

Ten days after his arrest, a lawsuit seeking to free Dickey from his contract with Capricorn Records was filed in New York City. He also severed his management ties with Phil Walden. When Phil's contract with the band had expired back in 1974, they had all continued on a gentlemen's agreement. By the time Phil got around to formalizing a new deal, Dickey refused to sign it. He had met a young lawyer named Steven J. Massarsky and asked him to manage him and try to straighten out his finances. Massarsky and Phil Walden had once been friends; Capricorn had even paid his tuition for three semesters at Mercer University's law school. Now, Massarsky thought Phil was ripping off Dickey, and Phil thought Massarsky was some "stage-door Johnny" who was throwing unnecessary friction into a successful business relationship.

The lawsuit claimed that Dickey's contract with Capricorn was void because he had been underpaid in royalties by at least $200,000. It also attacked a clause that no one had really noticed when they signed it back in 1972 — anyone leaving the Allman Brothers Band to pursue a solo career would still have to record for Capricorn. Without that provision, a solo album by an ex–Allman Brother might entice bidding wars between rival companies; the kicker in the Capricorn contract was that no one who left the band would get any money up front for a solo album. Instead, they would receive only a union-scale salary during the recording sessions, and then whatever royalties the record might generate. Dickey's lawyer called the terms "unconscionable." They charged that Phil had fraudulently induced Dickey and the others into signing, without legal representation, a contract that "contained provisions to the detriment of Betts and to the exclusive benefit of Walden's recording and publishing companies."

Phil filed a countersuit and, six months later, a settlement was hammered out. Capricorn released Dickey from the contract, which freed him to sign a deal with Arista Records, and Capricorn received a $300,000 payment from Arista for the gesture. Johnny Sandlin had recorded several concerts from Dickey's 1974 solo tour, and Arista paid $25,000 for the privilege of listening to them. If Arista decided to release them, Capricorn would receive another $50,000; if not, the tapes remained Capricorn's property.

The agreement allowed Dickey to use members of the Allman Brothers Band on his solo albums with Arista. But there were several stipulations: they could receive no more than union-scale wages and no royalties; they could receive no featured credits and could not be pictured on the album cover; no more than one former member could be used per song; and the phrase "Allman Brothers Band" could not be used in describing the recordings. Whether it was in existence or not, Phil had the Allman Brothers signed to Capricorn Records and he wasn't going to have the band sneaking over to Arista to record.

Finally, the agreement addressed the audit that Dickey had commissioned to look into his financial situation with Capricorn. Both Dickey and Phil agreed that if no settlement could be reached after it was completed, they would submit the issue to binding arbitration.

GREGG missed the music; he missed performing live. It was his safety net, his way of escaping. Music soothed him like nothing else did, and Gregg felt like a caged animal in California. He liked to go out and jam with other musicians, but there were no clubs nearby. Without the Allman Brothers Band, or even a solo band, Gregg felt like he was a prisoner in Cher's house.

It was tough for Gregg to adjust to her lifestyle, her celebrity. Just the simple act of going out to eat was a major production. Gregg and Cher would get to a restaurant, and someone would invariably spot them and tip off the press. Then when they opened the door to leave, they would be blinded by the light of flashbulbs. One time, the couple went shopping at a mall outside New York City. They were walking around unnoticed until a woman spotted them and began following. Then came another and another. The parade finally reached about twenty people. One of them overcame the group's collective shyness and began walking toward Gregg and Cher to ask for an autograph. As soon as she made her move, all of them came racing behind her. Gregg and Cher turned and fled.

Gregg continued to profess his love for Cher, and he made a legitimate effort to get off drugs and to turn his head from groupies. He had kicked heroin, but was now hooked on methadone and went back for a brief visit to the detox clinic in Buffalo. "I never wanted to be on drugs," he told a reporter. "But I got into them and was too weak to get out. There's only one cure, and that's love. That's what I found in Cher. And I'll be forever grateful we met, 'cause there's no telling where I'd be now."

While Dickey fought hard to get out of his contract with Phil, Gregg remained with Capricorn and started work in late 1976 in Los Angeles on a solo album. Gregg's six-piece band featured guitarist Ricky Hirsch from Wet Willie, drummer Bill Stewart from the *Laid Back* band, bassist Willie Weeks, and keyboardist Neil Larson. While he was recording the album, Gregg again lost control of his drug addiction. He went back to Buffalo and sequestered himself in the house of the physician in charge of the clinic. This time, a prolonged snowstorm trapped Gregg and left him at their complete mercy. They gave him decreasing amounts of methadone for eighteen days, and then Gregg went cold turkey. "I stayed in that house for forty-nine days," Gregg said. "After I had been there a little over a week, the snows hit. I couldn't get out. Man, I begged them to kill me. You talk about torment. For a period of a good two weeks, I never slept more than twenty minutes at a time."

Gregg walked out of the house totally clean, for the first time in years.

*   *   *

WHILE Gregg put together one band and Dickey put together his own solo group, Jaimoe and Chuck and Lamar banded together to form the third offshoot of the Allman Brothers Band. It seemed like a natural progression; the three of them had formed a close bond and often played around Macon under the name We Three. Chuck brought in a guitar player named Jimmy Nalls, who had played with him in Alex Taylor's band. The group was called Sea Level, a play on Chuck's name, and it too signed a recording contract with Capricorn.

While the others continued to play music, Butch decided to get the hell out of Macon. He returned to Tallahassee, enrolled at Florida State University, and cleaned up his life. He had just married Melinda Wadley Edwards, and they already had a child, a son named Seth. Melinda was an artist from Gatlinburg, Tennessee, who held a master's degree from FSU in painting, and Butch considered her the best thing ever to happen to him.

"She was the first one to have the guts to get up and tell me what an asshole I was," Butch said. "I used to wake up in the morning with her and say, 'What'd I do last night?' She'd say, 'You were an ass just like you usually are.' I'd say, 'What? The kid not cool?' Then, after a while, I started realizing she was right. The band split up and I couldn't get out of Macon quick enough. I went back to school. I quit drinking. That's what I needed."

Despite the loss of his flagship band, Phil Walden exuded public confidence that Capricorn Records would continue to flourish. Elvin Bishop had a huge hit with a song called "Fooled Around and Fell in Love," and the Marshall Tucker Band had hit the top of the charts with "Heard It in a Love Song." Phil's star seemed on the rise; he had been named to the Inaugural Committee when Jimmy Carter was elected president in 1976.

But bit by bit, Phil's golden touch was beginning to rust. He was increasingly distracted from his true genius, discovering musical talent and then giving it direction. There were failed real estate ventures, one resulting in a civil grand jury investigation, the political aspirations, and a string of assault charges. By 1975, Phil liked to begin business meetings with a few shots of J&B scotch. Cocaine was becoming a major presence. Capricorn had finished the 1974 fiscal year with a net operating loss, the first in a series of growing deficits, and the Allman Brothers Band had contributed about 25 percent of Capricorn's total income. It had been a long time since the label had signed any bands capable of breaking out — most of the new southern groups were signing with other companies for bigger money.

Yet Capricorn kept spending as if nothing was wrong. By early 1977, the company was coming up short on cash. Phil had to borrow $1.5 million from Warner Brothers. Then he launched his own audit, to check the Warner Brothers books. Not long after that, Capricorn took out a $485,000 loan from a local bank using the label's private airplane as security. Capricorn's financial fortunes were beginning to plummet. "Gregg will get a new band together," Phil bravely predicted. "One good record will turn this whole thing around."

That record certainly wasn't *Wipe the Windows, Check the Oil, Dollar Gas*, a double-album set of Allman Brothers Band live performances from the post-Duane era. Most of the tracks had been recorded by Johnny Sandlin, but he wasn't there to put the album together. "They had fired me for suing them," Johnny said. "They asked me about finishing up that album, and we never could come to terms. I guess that record was a 'milk everything' kind of thing; obviously, there wasn't going to be another studio album anytime soon."

Everything about the record appeared thrown together with little care or concern, from the nonsensical title to the inside photo caption that identifies Chuck Leavell as Twiggs Lyndon. Three of the songs came from the tortured Bakersfield concert, where Jaimoe's back went out and Dickey and Gregg ended the show by screaming at each other backstage. And the mixes robbed the music of its power; the drums are so soft they are indistinguishable. *Rolling Stone* blasted the record, the first time that had ever happened with an Allman Brothers album.

The first of the three post–Allman Brothers albums, *Dickey Betts and Great Southern*, would stand as the one that remained truest to the traditional Allman style. Dickey had put together a band with two drummers and, for the first time since Duane's death, he was playing with another guitarist: "Dangerous" Dan Toler, who played in a Capricorn band called Melting Pot that had opened concerts for the Allman Brothers during the early years. The band may have had the same instrumental lineup as the Allman Brothers, but it had none of the chemistry. The two drummers had nothing of the interplay that defined Butch and Jaimoe. The two guitars had a similar problem — Dan Toler played in a style that was largely a poor man's imitation of Dickey Betts.

Dickey Betts and Great Southern is a mixed package. Three terribly weak and clichéd songs kick off the album but, past that, it begins to pick up some momentum. The record really kicks up on the second side with "Nothin' You Can Do," a fast shuffle driven by Dickey's churning rhythm guitar. It is followed by "California Blues," which Dickey wrote at Cher's mansion in Beverly Hills. While it is a strong song, "California Blues" is also symptomatic of what is wrong with the album. Dickey uses the exact same bottleneck lick to kick off the song that he uses on the first side during the introduction to "Out to Get Me," and his solos on both songs begin and end with the exact same riffs.

A lovely song called "Bougainvillea" is the album's centerpiece. It was another song Dickey started in Los Angeles. "Paulette and I were staying in this little hotel and we were going out to dinner one night, and bougainvilleas were blooming all over the place," Dickey said. "She picked one and put it in her hair. I had that song in five minutes walking down the sidewalk."

Dickey brought in a new friend to help him finish the song, a struggling actor named Don Johnson. The two had met when Johnson was in Juliette filming a movie called *Return to Macon County Line*. One afternoon, Johnson was shooting a scene on a highway out in the country in front of someone's driveway. "After a while, this crazy son of a bitch in a four-wheel drive pulled out of the driveway," Johnson recalled. "He started honking his horn and eventually drove right through the scene. Somebody said, 'Yeah, that was Dickey Betts.' And I went, 'What? No shit?' Later that week, I was at Le Bistro in Macon, Dickey was there, and I bought him a beer." Johnson had always liked to sing, and he dabbled in songwriting; he and Dickey became running buddies, getting together to party and to write songs.

"Bougainvillea" is a great song on an album too content to be mediocre. Aside from Dickey, no one else on the album plays as though he has anything at stake. The album's redemption is the sheer power of Dickey's performances — the vocals are the best of his career, and his guitar snarls through the lead breaks.

Some of the same problems plagued Gregg's first post-ABB album, *Playin' Up a Storm*, which was recorded in Los Angeles. The first few moments invoke the spirit of *Laid Back*, but the mood quickly slips away. The LA production techniques valued perfection over passion. "We may be trying to be a little more precise than Gregg is used to," said coproducer Lenny Waronker. "We're trying to make these tracks almost perfect, and that takes time." The intentions were noble enough, but it stripped the life from the album.

Playin' Up a Storm is full of bad ideas. For anyone who had heard

Gregg perform the songs alone on acoustic guitar, the versions of "Come and Go Blues" and "One More Try" on the album left them feeling robbed. "Brightest Smile in Town," an obscure Ray Charles song, has all the earmarks of a definitive Gregg Allman recording. Dr. John kicks it off with some bluesy piano playing that underscores Gregg's voice. But the piano soon fades in the mix, replaced by strings and horns that are just this side of Muzak. The best track on the album is the cover of Clarence Carter's "That Old Time Feeling," which Gregg renamed "Sweet Feeling." His voice is stunning and, for the first time, the arrangement — the blaring horns, Stax-sounding rhythm guitar, and hot sax solo — fits the song.

For most, *Playin' Up a Storm* was a major disappointment. *Rolling Stone* dismissed the album. "The first thing you have got to do with this record is to forget the Allman Brothers Band ever existed and at one time was the best that America had to offer," wrote Chet Flippo.

It is possible that the best of the three new records — for its pure musicianship, as much as anything else — was the album by Jaimoe, Chuck, and Lamar, *Sea Level*. Everyone in the band plays with determination and conviction, and they take the music toward the jazz direction that they had always wanted to explore. Sea Level had the core members of the Allman Brothers rhythm section, and the album has a cohesive feel that is lacking in the two solo records.

The album reveals two flaws: Chuck's voice wasn't capable of fronting a major band, and his songwriting was still at a formative stage even though the band was dependent on him for its original material. Still, the instrumentals are compelling, and on songs like "Grand Larceny" and "Rain in Spain" Sea Level comes alive and locks into some great grooves. The highlight is the brilliant interpretation of Simon and Garfunkel's "Scarborough Fair," with its moody intro and Chuck's gorgeous acoustic piano.

While each of the records had their strengths, they also all contained significant weaknesses. It was like splitting up the Allman Brothers Band into three pieces and placing them into three different settings. Dickey and Gregg hadn't found musicians who measured up to them, and Sea Level needed songwriters and singers. It quickly became quite obvious that the individual parts could never match the whole.

Twenty-two

Homesick

THE Allman Brothers Band's indifference to the business end had proved so catastrophic that now they were beginning to pay it near fanatical attention. It had taken less than a year for most everyone to wind up broke. The four original members had each earned $51,583 in 1976, just a third of what they had made the year before. After that, there was nothing. Not a single member received a penny in royalties in 1977, and they were each borrowing heavily from their corporation, Brothers Properties. Together they owed over $270,000 in loans and advances.

Everything was in a mess. Band members began getting hit with legal actions for unpaid bills, child support, and alimony. In late 1977, Janice Allman complained in court papers that Gregg owed her $3,750 in delinquent alimony payments dating back to June. He was ordered to pay, didn't, and was hit with another court order when the debt reached $6,000. Gregg came up with the money only after he was found in contempt of court and threatened with jail.

Shelley Allman also was having problems getting her alimony and child support payments. Shelley saw pictures of Gregg living the good life inside Cher's mansion, while she and Gregg's own son were struggling. It made her so angry that she went to the *National Enquirer*. What especially frustrated Shelley was Gregg's remoteness from his son; Gregg had never sent Devon a birthday card or a birthday

The Allman Brothers Band at Rose Hill Cemetery. (*Stephen Paley, Capricorn Publicity Photo / Courtesy Macon Telegraph and News*)

Duane, left, and Gregg, circa 1960.
(*Courtesy Macon Telegraph and News*)

The Escorts clowning around before the Beach Boys concert on Easter weekend 1965 in Daytona Beach. From bottom left: Van Harrison, Tommy Ruger of the Night-crawlers, Gregg, Duane, and Maynard Portwood. (*Lee Hazen*)

Gregg (third row, far left) holds a saxophone in the Seabreeze freshman band. (*The Sandcrab*)

The Escorts onstage for the first big show. From left to right: Gregg, Van, and Duane. (*Lee Hazen*)

Exploring the British blues as the Allman Joys in one of the earliest publicity photos. From left to right: Gregg, Bob Keller, Duane, and Maynard Portwood. (*Courtesy Macon Telegraph and News*)

One of the first publicity photos, by Stephen Paley, at Rose Hill. Even in the early photos, the band projected a spooky quality. From left to right: Dickey, Duane, Gregg, Butch, Berry, and Jaimoe, sitting in the middle. (*Courtesy Macon Telegraph and News*)

The band at one of its favorite stops, the soul food heaven of the H & H Restaurant in Macon. (*Courtesy Macon Telegraph and News*)

Duane took the bottle-neck guitar to places it had never been before. (*Bob Johnson*)

Capricorn worked hard to forge a positive image for band members in Macon, such as with this fashion shoot for the local newspaper. From left to right: Linda Oakley, Donna Allman, and Carol Morgan. (*Courtesy Macon Telegraph and News*)

This eerie photo of
Duane hung on the wall
at the Big House. Not
long after Duane died,
Gregg walked into the
dark house one night
and was spooked
because his brother's
eyes seemed to follow
him through the room.
(*Author's private collection*)

The fatal accident:
Duane's Harley landed
on top of him, then
skidded into the curb.
(*Macon Police photo*)

Berry's Triumph after the crash. (*Macon Police photo*)

The new Allman Brothers Band in 1973 on the back porch of the farm in Juliette. From left to right: Chuck Leavell, Jaimoe, Butch, Gregg, Lamar Williams, and Dickey. (*Courtesy Macon Telegraph and News*)

Gregg and Janice on the farm. (*James Higgins / Courtesy Macon Telegraph and News*)

present. It was as if his son didn't exist. It would break her heart when Devon would come up to her and ask, "How come my daddy doesn't ever send me presents?" or "If Daddy's a star, he can afford to at least send me a card. How come he doesn't do that?"

"It was really sad," Shelley said. "Here's this little guy who looked exactly like his dad, and wanted him so badly but didn't have him around." Shelley finally filed a complaint in court against Gregg, saying he was past due in alimony and child support by $3,150. He settled with her four days after making good with Janice.

And it wasn't just Gregg. Sandy Bluesky filed court papers complaining that Dickey had fallen behind in his alimony by $6,000. Dickey was so broke that he had to borrow $100,000 from Arista Records, using future income from his songwriting catalog as security. And the entire band — which had purchased Berry's share of the farm in Juliette — fell behind in its payments to Linda Oakley. She was owed $24,706 and was forced to initiate a foreclosure sale on the property before the band came through with the money and paid her in full. The band finally sold the farm in 1979 for $300,900.

No one knew why, but Capricorn had stopped sending the band its royalty checks. Butch called up Ted Senters, Capricorn's treasurer, who told him that he would send out the money if Butch would tell him how to divide it up. Butch discussed the situation with Jaimoe, then sent Senters a letter telling him that everyone in the band should get a one-sixth share. Chuck and Lamar had always been on straight salary, and Dickey was not amused when he discovered that Butch had arranged to decrease his split from one-fourth to one-sixth.

"I had the concept this was an agreement that would expedite matters for Capricorn," Butch said. "I was flat broke and we were having a hard time getting royalty checks. My opinion is [Senters] didn't want to send them out. He either didn't have them, or just didn't want to send them out. We hadn't received a royalty statement or check since 1976. I put together my own band, and spent a year working clubs and trying to survive."

Butch's instincts about Capricorn's financial problems were truer than he could have imagined. The Allman Brothers had broken up at the worst possible time for the label, right before the recording industry was hit by a recession, and Capricorn was struggling just to stay afloat. Phil Walden ended the label's relationship with Warner Brothers at the end of 1977 and signed a distribution deal with Poly-Gram that gave Capricorn a much-needed injection of cash. Capricorn got a $1.5 million advance. PolyGram then loaned the label another

$2 million and, as security, Phil put up everything Capricorn owned — all of its recordings, its catalog of albums, its recording contracts, and its studio.

It didn't take Phil very long to begin questioning his judgment on the whole deal. "PolyGram was a bunch of slick-talking northern businessmen with thick suits and even thicker accents," Phil said. "I'd go to meetings, and all they'd ever talk about was billing and payments and five-year plans. I never went to a single meeting where they talked about music."

THE relationship between Gregg and Cher never seemed to find a base, a center. For two and a half years, Cher had given Gregg her unconditional love. She swallowed her pride as he slept with other women and did all she could to nurse him through his addictions. Gregg had managed to stay off heroin, but he did it by trading one vice for another; he now began most of his days by downing a quart bottle of vodka. Some mornings, he was shaking so badly that he had to use a straw.

Gregg and Cher recorded an album together called *Two the Hard Way* that was credited to "Allman and Woman." Johnny Sandlin was brought in to produce, and it turned into an experience every bit as trying as the *Win, Lose or Draw* sessions. "That was another one where you never knew who was going to show up, if the mood was going to be good or bad, if they were going to be in love or fighting," Johnny said. The album was not as bad as it could have been, but it was obvious the record company was interested in the commercial potential more than the artistic merits.

When Gregg traveled to Japan for a brief tour in August of 1977 with his solo band, one of the shows was videotaped for Japanese television, and he looked and sang as though he was at the end of a very long day of sipping vodka. His eyes were drooping and when he very uncharacteristically stood up to dance during "Let This Be a Lesson to Ya," he moved like something out of a zombie movie. Halfway through the show, Gregg walked to the microphone and said, "I'd like y'all to meet a good, good, good friend of mine; she's also my wife, Ms. Cher Allman." She came out to sing "Move Me," a song from *Two the Hard Way*, with her husband. Cher kept glancing at Gregg with a look of pure, unabashed love; he was oblivious, his glassy eyes unable to focus on the adoring woman at his side.

The final straw for Cher came when Gregg nodded out at an

awards banquet in Los Angeles and went face-first into a plate of spaghetti. They separated again on December 1, 1977, and she filed for divorce a short time later. This time, Cher meant it. Gregg did the only thing he knew how to do — he went back to Georgia, determined to put the Allman Brothers Band back together.

"I came back from California after realizing I couldn't live out there, I could merely exist," Gregg said. "The three years I lived out there, I didn't play much at all. So when the breakup came down with me and Cher, I came back east with one thing on my mind, which was to get the Brothers back together. I figured there was still some more in us, more to do. I missed everybody real bad. I mean, they were my best friends, you know? I was homesick. I missed my buddies."

Once he reached Macon, Gregg met with Phil and then they flew to Florida to meet with Dickey. Gregg knew if they could convince him, then the others would follow. It had taken Dickey about a year to soften his attitude toward Gregg. He got a transcript of Scooter's trial, read Gregg's testimony, and told himself, "Goddamn, this guy had his ass between a rock and a hard place." Dickey decided that the whole thing must have been set up by Republicans to discredit Jimmy Carter, and he went as far as to telephone his old partner and reestablish lines of communication. "Gregg made a mistake and how many of us make mistakes?" Dickey told a reporter. "Gregg, he should have been hurt. He deserved it. I think it's about time he was let off the fucking hook, you know? It's been a year, and Gregg's been paying for it and I think he's paid enough."

When Gregg and Phil reached Florida, Dickey didn't say yes, but he didn't say no either. He was in the middle of recording his second album with Great Southern and he told them he might join in a reunion if he could also keep his solo band going.

Butch and Jaimoe, however, turned Gregg down flat. Jaimoe said he didn't want to have anything to do with it. Butch remained opposed until Dickey showed up one night to hear his band in Tampa and sat in with them. For Butch, it was a revelation. "My God, *that's* what's been missing," he told himself. After the gig, Butch and Dickey stayed up all night talking. "He played some new tunes for me, including 'Crazy Love,' " Butch said. "And I started getting excited. I saw how together Dickey was, and he said Gregg seemed to be in excellent shape. So we started talking seriously about putting it back together."

After talking to Dickey, Butch also began reassessing the Scooter Herring trial. "See, we didn't know the full story," he said. "We thought he'd just copped a plea. We just weren't talking to each other, so we made our decision based on newspaper headlines. Dickey and I, we felt like we'd given Gregg a raw deal."

As an Allman Brothers Band reunion inched forward, Dickey's second album with Great Southern, *Atlanta's Burning Down*, was released and it was a near-disaster. "I liked the music we made in Great Southern, especially that first album which I produced and had total control over," Dickey said. "The second, I wasn't as happy with. They brought a producer in. He more or less controlled it, and played down the instrumental parts in favor of the vocals. I didn't especially care for that."

By now, Dickey had added two new members to his band — bassist David "Rook" Goldflies, whom Dickey plopped out of a disco band in Ohio, and drummer David "Frankie" Toler, Dan's younger brother. But the infusion of new blood didn't change much; there was still precious little vitality in the performance of the backup band, and this time Dickey himself sounded mostly disinterested. The album was released and disappeared. Dickey found himself reduced to performing in five-hundred-seat beer joints, a far cry from the tours of hockey arenas and stadiums. "It was really a blast on my ego," he said.

By the time of the release, Dickey and Paulette had married in Las Vegas, left Macon with five-year-old Jessica, and moved to a forty-acre spread Dickey owned on the Manatee River near Sarasota, Florida. "Paulette has been great for me and Jesse," Dickey told *People*. "There's a big difference between a woman who just wants to party with you and one who wants to bring a semblance of order to your life."

Still, the relationship was combustible. Paulette was as antidrug as Cher, and she bristled whenever Dickey drank or got high. Dickey had documented one of their fights on his last album in "Leavin' Me Again," which opens with the line, "She's getting tired of me getting wild all the time." When Dickey introduced the song onstage, it sounded as though he was referring to the night he was punching trash cans and kicking cops: "This is a song about gettin' drunk and takin' a lot of dope, gettin' put in jail, havin' your lady leave you, and writin' a song about it." When Paulette became pregnant, she finally convinced Dickey to join Alcoholics Anonymous. "Right about that time is when I began to realize that I was having a lot of difficulty dealing with it," Dickey said.

Gregg was faring no better. In March of 1978, he checked into Brawner Hospital, a private drug and alcohol treatment center in suburban Atlanta. When the press caught wind of it, Phil dismissed it as part of a yearly checkup.

As time passed, Gregg grew impatient waiting for the Allman Brothers Band to get together. "It looked like it would be forever, and I got frustrated," Gregg said. He checked out of the hospital and decided to spend his summer fishing. Gregg went home to Daytona Beach and was going to hire on as the first mate on a shrimp boat for twenty-five dollars a day. Then the captain told him, "The beard goes and the long hair goes." Gregg changed his mind.

Gregg began sitting in with a blues band called the Nighthawks, sparking rumors that he was going to join the group. There was also talk about Gregg hooking up with the surviving members of Lynyrd Skynyrd, the band from Jacksonville, Florida, that had taken up the mantle after the Allmans disbanded. Lynyrd Skynyrd had grown into one of the great rock groups when it was decimated by a plane crash that killed three members.

But those were just flirtations, ways to pass the time. Gregg's focus remained on getting the Allman Brothers back together. A reporter tracked him down to ask about rumors the band was reuniting. "That's no rumor, man, that's the truth," Gregg said. He predicted the band would have an album out and be back on the road by the end of the year.

IF anything cleared the way for an Allman Brothers Band reunion, it was the Fifth Circuit U.S. Court of Appeals. On March 1, 1978, the court overturned Scooter Herring's conviction because of the *Macon Telegraph* article that had revealed the death threats made against Gregg. It was the paper's lead story on the final day of the trial, and it featured a picture of Gregg being guarded by U.S. marshals, along with a banner headline.

"Although the content of the article was straightforwardly factual, it would be folly to overlook the gargantuan possibilities for juror prejudice that could flow from this publicity," the appeals court ruled. "At the time the article appeared, the jury had just heard Gregg Allman testify in a manner that was extremely damaging to the defense. Thus, reports of threats on Allman's life would be likely to lead any reasonable mind at least to consider the inference that the threats were in some fashion attributable to the defendant or someone acting in concert with him. Since the jury was not sequestered, it would defy common sense to suppose that not a single member had at least glanced at the headline and the photograph."

The appeals court said that Judge Wilbur Owens should have

used more caution to ensure that Scooter had a fair trial. "The appellant was at one time a road manager for Gregg Allman, a prominent musician of the rock persuasion who seems to have a penchant for attracting substantial national publicity," the court opinion noted. "Allman is married to television personality Cher Bono Allman, a figure of some prominence in her own right. This fact may have tended to enhance the volume of public scrutiny accorded Allman. By the time the trial began, the public eye, particularly in the Macon area, was sharply focused on the case."

Scooter, who was out on appeals bond and had gone to work as the road manager for Sea Level, was in Albany, New York, when a *Telegraph* reporter tracked him down and broke the news. "Woo! I'm sitting down now," he said after letting out a loud whoop. "You can't imagine how I feel."

His celebration was premature. The final lines of the Court of Appeals decision left the case in a nebulous position: "The judgment of the District Court is reversed and this case is remanded for further proceedings." Because it didn't come right out and say that Scooter's conviction was overturned, Judge Owens took it to mean that the conviction would stand if none of the jurors had been influenced by the story. He set a hearing to call the jury back to court to determine whether the article had affected the verdict.

A few weeks later, Owens called the jurors into his office and questioned them one by one. They all said they hadn't seen the article until after the trial. One juror said she had heard about the death threats in the hallway of the courthouse, but that it hadn't affected her decision. Owens reinstated the guilty verdict, and the seventy-five-year prison sentence.

Scooter's lawyers were furious and filed an immediate appeal. The case dragged on for months, until the Court of Appeals again overturned Owens and specifically ordered a new trial. Instead, Scooter worked out a plea agreement with the government. With J. C. Hawkins safely in jail, Scooter no longer had to worry about being forced to testify against the crime boss and he agreed to plead guilty to using a telephone to distribute cocaine and possession of a Schedule Two narcotic. This time, Owens was much more lenient and did an about-face. Calling Gregg's influence over Scooter "compelling, powerful and awful," he sentenced Herring to a thirty-month prison term. The judge said he was impressed with Scooter's conduct since his original conviction. "For that reason, you've gotten half the sentence you would have gotten," he said. "If Mr. Allman were standing in front of me, I don't know what I'd do. You were on the bottom of the ladder, but I don't think I'd be living up to my oath if I excused you."

Just before he left for prison, Scooter told a reporter that he had forgiven Gregg. "I don't hate him, there are no hard feelings," Scooter said. "Gregg can't be held accountable for his actions because he was a junkie. The most important thing in Gregg's life was to get a fix. He would have said anything, done anything, testified to anything, to get away and get a fix. Unless you've been around a junkie, you won't understand."

THERE were about five thousand people gathered at the Wollman Skating Rink in New York City's Central Park to hear Dickey Betts and Great Southern on August 16, 1978, unaware that they were about to witness the first performance of the Allman Brothers Band in over two years. Negotiations to get the band back together had continued and, as Dickey prepared to go to New York, Phil Walden decided to give things a push. "What do you think about Gregg and Butch and Jaimoe showing up at your concert in Central Park?" he asked Dickey.

"Shit, that'd be a gas," Dickey responded. All he asked was that it be a surprise; that there be no public announcements beforehand.

Dickey played a set with Great Southern, then called "some friends" to the stage. Butch and Jaimoe stepped out, followed by Gregg. The crowd went crazy as they launched into "One Way Out," then followed it with "You Don't Love Me, "Stormy Monday," "Statesboro Blues," and "Blue Sky." Dickey hugged Gregg during the set and kissed him on the cheek.

"They had a little wooden fence about ten feet tall around the place," Dickey said. "We started playing and everybody off the streets of New York City that could hear it and was familiar with it started heading that way. We had about fifteen thousand people there. They crashed the walls down. It was a real riot."

Eight days later, the band gathered again — this time with Chuck and Lamar joining in — to perform at Capricorn's annual picnic in Macon. The picnic at Lakeside Park was a tradition that Phil started back in 1971 and they had attracted guests that ranged from Jimmy Carter to pop artist Andy Warhol. The guests basked in the sunshine, many openly smoking joints, and listened to music by the Capricorn bands.

When Gregg walked onstage with the rest of the Allman Brothers in front of the hometown crowd, there were tears in his eyes.

The band was given a standing ovation, and then launched into a set of classic material. Afterward, Phil announced the band would be getting together and going into the studio in the fall. There was just one hitch: Sea Level was picking up momentum, and neither Chuck nor Lamar viewed a reunion with much enthusiasm. By then, Sea Level had added Randall Bramblett and Davis Causey, and the band's second album had been even stronger than the first. "Randall is such a great writer, great singer, and great player," Chuck said. "We thought, hey, we've got the ideal band here. Sea Level was an attempt to have a band in the South that didn't necessarily fit the mold."

Jaimoe had already left Sea Level — his back problems had flared up again — and when the Allman Brothers began talking about a reunion, he was in. Like everyone else, he needed the money, and, more, he missed the music. "I was sick of playing loud music, and man, I still don't like to play loud music," he said. "But I sure like playing with these guys."

Chuck and Lamar weren't as willing to leave Sea Level behind unless the reunion could be worked around Sea Level's schedule. "That picnic was a little weird because they knew Lamar and I weren't going to do it," Chuck said. "Before the picnic we had some meetings. They asked us to do it, but we were right in the middle of our third Sea Level album. Plus, at least in our opinion, the guys owed us some money in royalties. We broached on the subject of me and Lamar getting paid for what we were owed on the last few records, and they sort of balked at that."

With Chuck and Lamar dropping out, the band decided to bring in Dan Toler and David Goldflies from Great Southern to round out the group and restore the Allman Brothers to a two-guitar lineup. "Chuck is a great musician but he just didn't take this thing that seriously," Dickey said. "We could see that he wasn't that excited and we didn't want to have to work at his convenience. I'd been working with Danny with Great Southern. And with the Allman Brothers Band, it worked out good because enough time had went by so that it was like we were recreating that sound, but it wasn't like we were trying to take Duane Allman's place; enough time had gone by so that nobody said that."

The Allman Brothers Band was still signed to Capricorn Records, and even though Dickey was headed for an arbitration showdown with the company, the band stayed with the label. This time, however, they had a battery of managers and lawyers advising them. "When the band re-formed, I had no involvement from the standpoint of management," Phil said. "I functioned strictly as the president of Capricorn Records. I think they had four or five managers, and at least five or six lawyers. I know they had a whole roomful of people. Couldn't get a decision out of any of them."

Everyone agreed to the new contract on December 1, 1978. The band's original recording contract with Capricorn was all of eight pages long; this one stretched on for forty-eight and covered just about every conceivable contingency — one entire paragraph was devoted solely to defining a record album. Each member signed the agreement under his corporate entity: Gregg was Lighthouse, Inc.; Dickey was Forrest R. B. Enterprises, Inc.; Butch was Trucks Entertainment, Inc.; and Jaimoe was Frown Productions, Inc. The contract called for five albums, and an advance of $450,000 that would be recoupable from royalties, along with a $150,000 recording budget. The band would receive a royalty rate of 16.5 percent (the rate on the band's back catalog was in arbitration). Each of the four original members was to receive separate royalty statements semiannually, and payments had to be made in four equal shares by four separate checks. Finally, at the end of the contract, the band had to continue recording for Capricorn Records or else wait five years before it could sign a contract with another company.

However, it was becoming doubtful that the label would be around long enough to see the contract through to completion. The top brass at Capricorn had just received the company's annual internal audit, and it revealed that Capricorn was on the brink of insolvency. The label had a gross profit of $6 million during its fiscal year, from June 1, 1977, through May 31, 1978, but that money didn't come close to matching Capricorn's expenses and operating costs.

The audit determined that Capricorn had incurred a net operating loss of nearly $1 million — and that was on top of a $1.3 million deficit the label was carrying from previous years. Moreover, and also distressing, Capricorn was in debt for more money than it had on hand in assets. The label owed PolyGram $3.8 million, Warner Brothers over $1 million, and a local bank $400,000. The auditors cautioned that Capricorn's future rested on its ability to come up with additional financing and on how well it did in the very near future.

Already heavily in debt to PolyGram, Capricorn fell into a disturbing habit of constantly borrowing even more. Over a period of seven months there were ten loans totaling nearly $4 million. Some months, Capricorn was borrowing more money from PolyGram than it was earning in record sales. Even when sales were brisk, the profit went back to PolyGram to repay the loans; in November of 1978, Capricorn grossed $2.1 million, and all but $190,411 of that went to PolyGram. By the time the Allman Brothers Band sat down at the table to sign the new recording contract, Capricorn had borrowed a total of $8.8 million from PolyGram, and still owed the bulk of it.

It was no secret that PolyGram wanted to purchase Capricorn, but Phil resisted the move; he coveted his independence. Still the debts to PolyGram kept mounting. The loans were payable on demand, and if Phil couldn't repay them, virtually everything Capricorn owned would become PolyGram's property. It was as if PolyGram was reeling Phil in, feeding him money month after month with the goal of taking over Capricorn whether he agreed or not. As the loans piled up, PolyGram forced Phil to trim $500,000 from his payroll and operating budget. Capricorn also had to provide monthly statements of income and expenses to PolyGram. It was a pointless gesture. By then, Phil Walden had already dug a hole so deep that Capricorn would never climb out.

Twenty-three

A Real Expensive Lesson

THE Allman Brothers Band settled in Sarasota for six weeks at the end of 1978, getting reacquainted and rehearsing new material. After that, everyone took a couple of weeks off, then headed down to Miami to record the comeback album at Criteria Studios with Tom Dowd at the helm. Like the old days at the Hippie Crash Pad, they all lived under one roof in Miami — but this time it was a swanky mansion complete with maid service and overlooking Biscayne Bay. Dickey had a slew of new songs and the spirit was high; suddenly, they were all in love again. "We feel like it's the first time together," Gregg told *Rolling Stone*. "We're fresh. We've all come through a lot and learned a lot from it. We're older and wiser and better."

Dickey likened the breakup to a family spat. "It's like if you're in a fight with your brother and you fall out, you're almost looking for a chance to patch it up," he said.

Butch had gone to the sessions with no small degree of trepidation; he left believing again. "I came here a little leery because when the thing broke up we were cooked, just burned out," he said. "But the first time I heard the new album I went ape-shit. It's got that energy to it, that feeling and intensity that we have to have. And we're just getting warmed up."

Only Jaimoe seemed reserved. He said he was participating in the reunion primarily because he wanted to study music at Mercer

University in Macon. "I saw this as a way to finance it," Jaimoe said. "I really didn't have no choice."

They called the new album *Enlightened Rogues*, the nickname Duane had given the band back in the early days. And from the opening moments of the first song, "Crazy Love," it was apparent there was indeed a vitality that had been sorely lacking going back as far as 1974. After the *Win, Lose or Draw* debacle and the indifferent solo albums, the new record was a heartening return. The music is full of a sense of pure joy that they are together again, and it is that energy which is at the heart of every performance. Gregg sings with purpose and direction, Dickey plays and sings as well as he ever has, and there is a renewed determination in the interplay between Butch and Jaimoe, whose back pains had been eased with the help of a chiropractor.

"Crazy Love" uses the heavy boogie style that Dickey had utilized extensively on the two Great Southern albums, and everything that was missing in those performances springs to life with the Allman Brothers Band. It is a song of heated lust: "Somewhere down on a back street / Way down deep in the back seat / Is where I first learned how to moan your name." Bonnie Bramlett adds a scorching backup vocal, and Dickey's bottleneck guitar underscores the torrid emotions.

"Pegasus" is a highly charged instrumental that would garner a Grammy nomination for best instrumental performance. An excellent version of Little Willie John's "Need Your Love So Bad" comes next, and it redeems the band for the last slow blues it had tried, the somnolent "Jelly Jelly" from *Brothers and Sisters*. The arrangement is low-key, yet it swings with a natural grace and features a nice performance by harmonica player Jim Essery.

Most of the album's greatest moments come on the second side. "Blind Love," written by Dickey and Don Johnson, is as forceful as any studio cut since *Eat a Peach*. Gregg sings in a snarling voice that comes alive with unbounded cockiness — it could be a sad song except he's not begging his lady to come back, he's daring her *not* to. The song has a half dozen little guitar runs, Butch and Jaimoe drive the song, and Dickey plays the second lead break with a searing guitar that rises out of a dynamic climb-up. This third incarnation of the Allman Brothers Band would never sound better.

"Try It One More Time," written by Dickey and bassist David Goldflies, is a song full of intricate rhythms and is the metaphor for the band's reunion. It becomes a musical conversation between Dickey and Gregg as they alternate singing the verses. "After all this time we've been together, it just ain't right to throw it all away,"

Dickey sings. "Yes, I guess that I been wrong again," Gregg answers. "But, oh, . . . don't you think we oughta try it one more time?"

"Just Ain't Easy," Gregg's best song since "Multicolored Lady," is full of poignant imagery that chronicles the despair he felt living in California. "Your head's severely pounding from the night before / But, baby, you just keep on goin' back, goin' back for more / 'Cause midnight's callin' . . . well, well." Gregg's performance is beautiful; his voice seems to cry with a heartfelt melancholy and Dickey backs him up with a brilliant, lonesome-sounding guitar. For many, it was the highlight of the album.

Enlightened Rogues closes with another marvelous ballad, Dickey's "Sail Away." It too is full of imagery, a lament for a true love lost because of circumstance, not change of heart. The setting is Dickey sitting by the bay in Bradenton, watching a sailboat drift toward the sunset. "Skipping stones across the water / Wonder why I ever thought you'd stay," he sings in a voice of tender regret.

Released in March of 1979, *Enlightened Rogues* jumped into the Top 10 and quickly earned a platinum record with sales going over the one million mark. It set off a new round of Allman Brothers fever; when tickets went on sale for two New York City concerts, the announcement was made on just one radio station, yet both sold out within ninety minutes. "Gregg Allman may not look like Lazarus, but he sure acts like him," wrote *Rolling Stone*'s John Swenson. "Allman's astonishing resurrection here seems less an act of heroism on his part than a miracle on someone else's. After all, in the space of a few years, this artist went from being an exceptional white blues singer and leader of one of the best American rock bands to being a laughingstock, a pathetic churl apparently unaware of the humiliation he suffered at the hands of Hollywood and the glitzy Cher. The proposed Allman Brothers Band reunion promised to be a ghoulish joke, the musical equivalent of *Night of the Living Dead*. Yet *Enlightened Rogues*, the product of that reunion, takes its place not beside the empty, last-gasp *Win, Lose or Draw*, but ranks with the group's greatest albums."

Enlightened Rogues was one of the band's biggest triumphs. And, already, the bottom was beginning to drop out from underneath everything.

THE band kicked off a tour in Jacksonville on April 8, 1979, and then went to Atlanta two days later to perform at the Fox Theatre. It was a sensational show; the band opened with an instrumental version of

"Will the Circle Be Unbroken?" and then went into "Crazy Love," with Bonnie Bramlett sharing the vocal work. Don Johnson joined the band onstage to sing, as did gospel singer Mylon LeFevre and honky-tonk star Gary Stewart. The two-and-a-half-hour show closed with "Jessica," and the band was called back for four encores. The concert finished as it had begun, with "Will the Circle Be Unbroken?" which featured a shimmering three-minute solo by Dickey. After the show, Capricorn threw a celebration party at the Colony Square Hotel.

Backstage at the Fox, the band was hit by a bushel of bad news. Dickey was served with papers from his second wife, Dale Betts. Their original divorce agreement called for $20 a week in child support for Elena Christine, who was now eleven years old, and Dale wanted the amount increased. And band members also learned that Chuck Leavell had just filed a lawsuit against them in Macon, asking for $55,675 in back royalties. Chuck based the suit on Butch's instructions to Capricorn to split the royalties six ways. He complained that after the breakup he stopped receiving any money and when he had asked for an accounting of the band's finances, he had been turned down. A few weeks later, Chuck's lawyer amended the lawsuit and asked for $118,000.

The band responded that the six-way split of royalties wasn't legally binding, that Chuck had been paid in full for his work through his weekly salary. He was hit with a countersuit, saying he was using equipment — including a Fender Rhodes piano, a clavinet, and various amplifiers — that belonged to the Allman Brothers Band. They even got a temporary restraining order that prevented Chuck from taking the equipment out of Macon.

As the case played itself out, Chuck's lawyer argued that even before Butch offered the six-way split, Chuck and Lamar had reached an agreement with Willie Perkins to split 1 percent of the royalties in addition to their weekly salary of $1,000. "Hundreds of thousands of dollars has been paid to Brothers Properties, but no portion was paid to [Chuck]," Donald Weissman, Chuck's lawyer, argued in one legal brief. "Instead the money was 'loaned' or 'advanced' to the individual defendants and used to pay their personal debts, to purchase autos and other assets. Money was also squandered, and finally dissipated while the corporation was under the control of the defendants. None of the loans or advances have ever been repaid, and Brothers Properties is insolvent." The only corporate asset the band still held was the $100,000 certificate of deposit that had been purchased as security for Scooter Herring's bail, and Chuck argued that he should have an equal share of it. The CD matured as the suit dragged on, and the bank gave two-thirds of it, $79,002, to the original four members, then held the balance in escrow pending the outcome of Chuck's legal action.

The case dragged on for months, and eventually a jury was selected for trial. Then came a last-minute settlement, and Chuck received the rest of the money from the CD, a total of $39,501. Days later, Lamar petitioned the court that the money should rightfully be evenly split between him and Chuck. But it was too late — the court said Lamar should have interceded before the suit was settled — and Chuck retained all the money, with much of it going to his legal fees. Lamar later left Sea Level, so impoverished that his children would soon be on public assistance.

AS the Allman Brothers Band hit the road for the first time in three years, Gregg assured a reporter that all the band's financial woes had been solved and that everyone had settled their differences with Phil Walden. "We'd rather go on handshakes and trust, and money up front," he said. "All of which we got."

But in New York City, Dickey Betts and Phil Walden were locked in a legal showdown before a three-member arbitration board. At issue was Dickey's contention that Phil had underpaid him in royalties; Dickey's auditors put the exact figure at $1.9 million. But Capricorn argued that Dickey had been overpaid and was actually in debt to the record label. In addition to Dickey's arbitration, Butch and Jaimoe and Donna Allman, on behalf of Galadriel, had filed suit in New York against Capricorn asking for back royalties. However, Steve Massarsky advised them to put the suit on hold and use Dickey's arbitration as the test case.

The series of sporadic hearings on Dickey's case began just as the band was reuniting, and continued through the spring of 1979. Jerry Shustek, his auditor, told the arbitration panel that it was virtually impossible to determine exactly how much Dickey was owed because of the disarray of the financial documents. "There are no records from the band," he said. "The band's office was closed. We can't locate any of the payments or expenses that were paid on their behalf. I can show you three sheets of paper sent up to me by Butch Trucks which said, 'Royalties: $100,000; $200,000; $300,000.' That is it. No controls, no debits, no contracts, no balances. Nothing. It was absolutely useless."

Dickey's case was based on two main contentions. His first

argument went back to whether albums recorded prior to the 1972 contract should retain the old 5 percent royalty rate or be covered under the new 12 percent rate. Dickey claimed Phil had a distinct conflict of interest between his role as the band's manager and his role as the president of Capricorn Records. Had it been any other record label, Phil would have been beating the doors down to get the 12 percent rate for his band. But because Phil was also the president of Capricorn, it was to his benefit to keep the lower rate.

Dickey's second contention was that Capricorn had charged the band excessive packaging costs. Shustek said the industry standard was twenty cents per album to manufacture the cardboard container and cover; Capricorn had charged the band varying amounts, but it was never under seventy cents per album. Capricorn also charged the band $2.22 per tape, which was nearly a third of the retail price.

Those weren't the only discrepancies uncovered by Shustek. Under Dickey's first songwriting contract, he split royalties 50-50 with Phil's No Exit Music publishing company. In 1972, Dickey's take was supposed to be increased to 60 percent, but he never actually received a 60 percent share. "They were always paid on a fifty-fifty basis, except for the last two periods of the contract when Capricorn overpaid, and paid seventy-five/twenty-five," Shustek said. Capricorn argued that it had merely been deducting a 10 percent administrative fee.

The arbitration board looked at Phil Walden's relationship with the Allman Brothers Band with a critical eye, and they were wary of the many hats he was wearing. "We have a situation where he was the personal manager, he owned the publishing company and he owned the recording company," said Jacob Imbeman, the chairman of the panel. "That is a pretty close relationship. We want him to explain it." Phil offered no apologies, saying he stepped back whenever there was a potential conflict and let Willie Perkins and Frank Fenter handle matters between the band and the record company.

The final decision came down on May 24, 1979. Dickey was awarded a whopping $873,000, the highest such arbitration award ever returned, and Capricorn immediately appealed the judgment to the New York Supreme Court. It was a huge blow to the label, one it was going to have a hard time absorbing.

The arbitration award killed the band's relations with Capricorn. Before, they had only thought they were being ripped off; now, they knew they had been. On July 11, 1979, Steve Massarsky sent a letter to Capricorn that accused the label of breaching the contract. Over six months had passed since the band had signed its new agreement with

Capricorn; royalties and royalty statements were due on a semiannual basis, and the band had received neither.

If the Allman Brothers Band had given some hard shots to Capricorn's stability, the death blow was delivered on July 19, 1979, when PolyGram sent a letter to Macon demanding payment in full on all its loans. Capricorn's outstanding debt was a staggering $5.5 million. Phil stalled for time, frantically trying to figure a way out, but he was under attack on all sides. The New York Supreme Court confirmed Dickey's arbitration award in early August. On August 9, the label's telephones were disconnected; Capricorn had a phone bill of $129,199. On August 16, the Allman Brothers Band sent Capricorn a letter to terminate its contract formally. Phil was incensed, still fighting to keep Capricorn on its feet. "We haven't violated the contract," he declared. "If there has been any violation, it has been by the so-called representative of the Allman Brothers. They are not free. They cannot record for anybody else."

Eight days after that, PolyGram filed a federal lawsuit seeking to take over Capricorn's assets; under the loan agreements, everything that Phil owned — recording contracts, every Capricorn recording, even the studio — had been put up as security for the money. If Phil couldn't pay, PolyGram took over. PolyGram knew it was the end of Capricorn Records. "We took a long time thinking about this, and we had to do a lot of soul searching," PolyGram spokesman Stuart Segal told reporters. "But we felt we needed to do this to protect our shareholders. I can assure you all other remedies were exhausted. We did everything short of this we could."

Phil didn't buy it. "We had five albums on the charts when PolyGram pulled the plug," he said. "It's something I look back on with bitterness. A lot of our spending was based on their advice and encouragement, and it was really contrary to the way Capricorn had operated in the past. They reneged on their end, and there are a number of reasons for that other than financial."

Capricorn next came under attack from its own bands. On August 31, the same day that Scooter Herring reported to the federal prison camp at Eglin Air Force Base to begin serving his prison sentence, Sea Level filed suit against Capricorn to stop the release of its new album, *Long Walk on a Short Pier.* Phil responded by saying Sea Level was in debt to Capricorn to the tune of $321,247.

The Marshall Tucker Band also filed suit to stop the release of a live album called *Stomping Room Only.* Then, on September 25, the Allman Brothers Band filed suit to halt a "greatest hits" album called

Decade that Capricorn had decided to release. Capricorn had already put out a "best of" double album called *And the Road Goes On Forever* during the band's breakup, and there was no reason for the new album other than a last-ditch effort to generate money. "It's just a compilation of the old stuff all over," Steve Massarsky complained. "The songs have been out so many times — you could have bought any of the songs at least two other times."

Phil lashed back. "I know of no 'greatest hits' album that isn't a compilation," he said. "I find it extraordinarily ironic that the greatest single recordings that the band has put out in the last ten years could be labeled 'poor quality' by somebody who is supposed to be representing the band."

Phil waited nearly two months before he could no longer avoid the inevitable; on October 21, 1979, a lawyer representing Capricorn Records and No Exit Music walked into the federal courthouse in Macon and filed bankruptcy papers, seeking Chapter 11 protection from creditors. At the time of the filing, Capricorn claimed tangible assets of $6.3 million and debts of more than $9.1 million; the figure owed to PolyGram alone was $5.4 million. The list of unpaid bills stretched on for a full thirty-two pages, and it included a claim from the Internal Revenue Service for $921,981 that Capricorn owed in back taxes and interest.

The bankruptcy papers also revealed how Phil was using his corporate entities to help finance his own lavish lifestyle. He had drawn an annual salary of $133,761 and owed Capricorn $183,524 in advances, including a $71,000 loan he had taken out just eight months before the bankruptcy. In addition to his salary, he was charging No Exit Music $1,740 in monthly rent for the use of Capricorn Studios. He was charging Capricorn a monthly rent of $200 for the use of his office on Cotton Avenue. There was the second home in Hilton Head that he leased back to Capricorn to cover the mortgage. Phil was a forgiving landlord; he claimed his companies owed him $63,976 in back rent.

Virtually all the musicians signed to Capricorn were owed money. The Allman Brothers Band filed a claim for $3.9 million. Paul Hornsby filed a claim for $395,000; Johnny Sandlin's $832,000 lawsuit was sent to Bankruptcy Court. Many of them knew they had lost money, but they were musicians, not lawyers, and often had no idea about how to go about trying to recover it.

IT hadn't taken long for Gregg's drinking to reach the uncontrollable stage again, and in November of 1979 he checked into a rehab center called the Palm Beach Institute. With him was his new wife, a stunning Russian-born model named Julie Bindas. She was twenty, nearly twelve years younger than Gregg, and they had met in Daytona. "Julie was kinda walking down the beach and I just kinda began talking to her," Gregg said. "I finally got her to agree she'd go out with me. And then I started to fall in love with Julie, deeply in love, and I had to have her respect. I realized then I didn't have a lot of respect for myself. You see, I was getting tired of having to get drunk to get an act together."

Julie didn't drink, but she joined Gregg at the center in a show of support. It wasn't enough. Halfway through the six-week program, Gregg walked out and headed straight for a West Palm Beach bar. He spent the afternoon drinking with a friend, who decided Gregg needed help and pulled him into his car for a trip to the emergency room. Gregg protested loudly, and he grew animated as they arrived outside the hospital. The argument caught the eye of a police officer, who stepped in to investigate and soon found himself in a scuffle with Gregg. The cop finally placed him into custody and handcuffed him. A red-faced Gregg sat in the backseat of the patrol car screaming at the cop, and he was taken to the Community Mental Health Center and admitted overnight for evaluation.

He had to be detoxed at another institution for two weeks before he was allowed to return to the Palm Beach Institute. "Gregg is certainly not the first patient here to do a little road-testing," Darryl Kosloska, the facility's executive director told reporters. "Many patients have a hard time realizing that their addiction is chronic, progressive, and incurable. A road test can show them. There's been a big difference since he was readmitted."

Between Gregg's problems and the Capricorn bankruptcy, the Allman Brothers was pushed into a kind of limbo. The band went back on the road after Gregg's stay at the rehab center and played dates through the beginning of 1980. But it was difficult — there was no new album to promote, and the band didn't even know what record company would release the next one once they went back into the studio. Even though Capricorn had ceased to function as a record company, Phil argued that the Allman Brothers was still contractually bound to his label. The band members thought that was absurd — even if they recorded a new album, Capricorn was in no position to release it. Besides, they had yet to see any royalties from *Enlightened Rogues*. Finally, the band filed papers in Bankruptcy Court to be released from its contract with Capricorn. The motion argued that Capricorn's shaky status made it next to impossible for the Allman

Brothers to earn a livelihood. "Although [the band] has negotiated with several record companies, they have been unable to [sign] a contract because of the uncertainty which exists as to the validity of the contract with Capricorn," the motion said. "The [band] has scheduled a tour of cities to begin within the next week in an effort to survive financially." The judge freed them.

Even before a new recording contract was hammered out, the band went into a little studio called Pyramid Eye on Lookout Mountain, in Georgia, to record and then spent the rest of the summer on the road as the Capricorn bankruptcy headed for a resolution. The amount of the claims against the label had grown to $20 million, and it turned out that Capricorn's assets were worth only about $2 million, less than a third of Phil's original estimate.

The court eventually approved a plan of reorganization submitted by Phil's lawyers, and the big winners seemed to be Phil Walden and PolyGram. For most of the creditors, Phil promised to set up a $500,000 fund to pay them off on a prorated basis over the next seven years. For some, it amounted to maybe two cents on the dollar, if that much. All the bands under contract to Capricorn were released to sign with other labels. PolyGram, meanwhile, took over Capricorn's library of master recordings — a cache that would reap millions of dollars ten years later in the era of compact discs and boxed sets. Because the studio and the offices on Cotton Avenue were owned by Phil and rented to Capricorn, he was allowed to keep them. He also took over sole ownership of the record company.

While Phil Walden survived the fall of Capricorn with his estimated personal fortune of $7 million untouched, each of the original four members of the Allman Brothers Band lost about $1 million. "Phil did kind of beat me out of it," Dickey said. "I just felt like, here we were supposed to be buddies all this time and here I am getting screwed out of a million dollars that I had earned. It ain't like you won it in a card game. It was money that was there, and should have been paid to start with. And had I not uncovered it, there would have been no questions. I guess you just mark it down as a real expensive lesson."

Twenty-four

I'm Leavin'

LISTENING to *Reach for the Sky*, the first album on Arista Records, it was difficult to imagine that this was once the band that Duane Allman and Berry Oakley had guided to such dazzling and inventive musical frontiers. The songs were as clichéd as their titles: "Hell and High Water," "Mystery Woman," "Famous Last Words," "Keep On Keepin' On." Only on Dickey's instrumental "From the Madness of the West" did the band show any signs of life, and that was largely due to the dynamic drum work that included guest percussionist Mark Morris.

Musical trends were shifting and Southern rock was being left behind. The disco era had been ushered in by the movie *Saturday Night Fever,* and in England, a group called the Sex Pistols had released a single called "Anarchy in the U.K." and launched punk rock. In truth, Southern rock had died the night Lynyrd Skynyrd's airplane crashed into a Mississippi swamp. Other southern groups like Molly Hatchet that came along in the late seventies still depended on long, guitar-based jams but did so with little of the inspiration that had defined the greatness of the original Allman Brothers or Lynyrd Skynyrd. The new groups seemed to think that putting together a band with two or three lead guitars and a double-drummer format was all it took to replicate the magic; instead, they only showed how boring the form could be in unskilled hands.

Almost overnight, Southern rock had become tacky. It meant endless boogie jams that went nowhere and seemed to take forever getting there. And the band that had started it all was being told by its new record company to no longer use the term "Southern rock," and that it might be a good idea not to wear cowboy hats and boots onstage because it looked embarrassing. It was depressingly obvious that just as Liberty Records had done with Hour Glass, Arista hoped to transform the Allman Brothers Band into a factory for hit singles. The label wanted breezy-sounding songs, something on the scale of the Doobie Brothers, and for the first time, the word *synthesizer* appeared on the credits of an Allman Brothers album.

It didn't come close to working. "Practically all the cuts trade shamelessly on an image the Allmans stopped living out years ago," Tom Carson wrote in *Rolling Stone.* "Right now, all that the Allman Brothers Band can do is give people the lingering suspicion that they stole their name."

NOW it was Jaimoe who was growing concerned about the finances. The band had lost money on both a European and West Coast tour, and when Jaimoe asked his wife and manager, Candace Oakley Johnson, to look into the situation, the band's management bristled. Candace had a hard time getting her hands on financial records. "For some reason, there was always too much paperwork," Jaimoe said. "I got this report and it had this figure for miscellaneous monies spent that was in the thousands of dollars. Now, I'm gonna take that to my tax man, and he's gonna say, 'What is this? What is this $45,000 miscellaneous? What is this $60,000? What is this $125,000 miscellaneous?' You don't play with figures like that. I want to know everything on there."

The band's expenses seemed to be eating into all the profits, and no one could come up with explanations. "The corporate papers specifically said there will be an outside audit done yearly," Candace said. "Then when I tried to have one done, all hell broke loose." When Jaimoe and Candace didn't back off, Jaimoe was summarily fired. "Dickey was behind it," Candace said. "The pie was getting smaller and Dickey didn't want to share it." The band had a gig in New Orleans and when Jaimoe showed up, Frankie Toler's drum kit was set up onstage in place of his. Jaimoe was hurt, stunned. He stayed for a while, then left and went back home to Macon.

"We were supposed to be partners," Jaimoe said. "They use the word 'brothers.' Well, that's a farce. People might read this and say I sound bitter. I'm cautious. I learned a lesson. I'm not bitter about anything. I'm very glad for the education I have because I don't have to go through it anymore. I'm just sorry it took outside people influencing guys who were supposed to be your partners. When you've been together for twelve years, you're going to take the word of somebody who has been associating in this business of ours for a year? No, I'm going to sit down and listen to what my partner has to say."

Firing Jaimoe only served to further dilute the music of the Allman Brothers Band, and Butch almost immediately regretted agreeing to the move. "It was a lot different with Frankie Toler," he said. "Me and Jaimoe, we had something special going. And the problem with Toler was he played too much like I did. We'd get in each other's way a lot. I'd start playing something, and he's already doing it. And Jaimoe and I never did that."

The band trudged on and went back into the studio in March of 1981 to record a second album for Arista, *Brothers of the Road.* Released in August, it was even worse than its predecessor. Longtime fans found it painful to listen to, and almost no one else took the trouble. The album did have a minor hit, "Straight from the Heart," that came across as a great Doobie Brothers imitation, and the credits revealed another first: the band that had once refused to pose for Annie Leibovitz because they weren't "on no fuckin' star trip," was now acknowledging a hair stylist on the back cover.

In a thoughtful, and quite generous, review in *Rolling Stone*, Robert Palmer said the album sounded as if the band was just marking time. Palmer noted that the band's trademark interplay between the two guitars had been reduced to "terse filler," and that Jaimoe's presence was sorely missed. "Dashed expectations have been an Allman Brothers constant, from the deaths of guitarist Duane Allman and bassist Berry Oakley, to the band's acrimonious breakup to more recent label and management hassles," Palmer wrote. "One is confronted with how drastically the present has failed to live up to the promise of the past."

It was becoming obvious to everyone, even to band members, that things were deteriorating quickly. "The last couple of albums we did, we were trying to break new ground and it just wasn't us," Butch said. "It was getting very contrived. It was the record company, but we caved in."

Dickey was even more succinct. "That album could have been a lot better," he said. "There wasn't a lot of interest put in it from the record company or from the band either. By the time we got around to *Brothers of the Road*, you could tell that whatever it was we had was over."

Onstage, things were slipping just as badly. The music called for brilliant improvisation, and the Allman Brothers was no longer up for the challenge. The crowds at concerts were thinning. The Allman Brothers and the Grateful Dead had once drawn 600,000 to a concert; when the two groups announced a joint Thanksgiving concert at the Tangerine Bowl in Orlando, Florida, it had to be canceled because only 10,000 of the 60,000 tickets were sold.

Increasingly, when the band did play concerts, it was panned in reviews. "Betts seemed to be going through the motions as Toler tried to put some life into the song by turning up his amp rather than playing an interesting solo," wrote the *Atlanta Constitution*'s Andrew Slater after a concert at the Fox Theatre in late 1981. "To call this group the Allman Brothers Band is like calling Paul McCartney and Wings, 'The Beatles.'"

Another review in the *Tallahassee Democrat* was savage: "If the Toler brothers and Goldflies aren't Duane Allman and Berry Oakley, at least they aren't dead." That one prompted an angry letter to the paper from Butch. "I have lived in Tallahassee for some time now, and have read critic Chris Farrell's narrow-minded, inane and ignorant reviews long enough," Butch wrote. "I don't ask for reverence from the likes of Farrell, but I demand respect."

The Allman Brothers Band hadn't been getting very much of either of late.

GREGG dedicated a tender love song on *Brothers of the Road* called "Never Knew How Much (I Needed You)" to Julie. But shortly after the album was released, the relationship broke apart. Like all of Gregg's marriages, it had been turbulent from the first day, and Gregg filed for a divorce in December of 1981. The couple had a child, Delilah Island, who was born on November 5, 1980, and Gregg claimed in court that Julie was an unfit mother; he asked that either he or Mama A be given custody of Island. Julie countered that Gregg had physically abused her when she was pregnant to the point that she had almost lost the baby and had to be treated at a hospital.

Julie claimed that Gregg had cleaned out her bank account and had not told her before their marriage that he was virtually destitute. Gregg's financial situation was indeed dire. The couple's telephone had been shut off and, at one point, they couldn't afford a car. Many of Gregg's belongings had been stored in a California warehouse and were auctioned off when he couldn't pay the storage bill. Gregg had bought a $150,000 house in Bradenton, Florida, then lost it when he couldn't keep up his mortgage payments.

The divorce was in the court system for nearly three years before it was resolved. During that time, Julie was supposed to receive temporary child support of $200 a week, and at one point she had to file a contempt motion against Gregg because he wasn't paying it. In the final decree, she was given custody of Island and awarded $533 a month in child support, along with a 1979 Pontiac and a $2,000 lump-sum payment. Again, Gregg failed to keep up his payments and, this time, he was found in contempt of court and ordered to pay up or go to jail for sixty days. He paid a few weeks later.

While Gregg was in the middle of his divorce from Julie, he was hit with a paternity suit from a Sarasota waitress named Elaina Abdul, who said she had gone to New Orleans with Gregg one weekend and they had conceived a child. Gregg contested the claim, but a blood test led to the conclusion that he was the father. His son, Jonathan Christian Abdul Allman, was born on July 4, 1982, in Sarasota. Gregg was ordered to pay the medical bills for the birth and $75 a week in child support.

While Gregg struggled to sort out his personal life, the Allman Brothers Band was sputtering to a halt. Arista's tight reins had sapped the band of life, and the original members all found it difficult to care anymore. "More than anything else, the record company just broke our spirits," Gregg said.

Butch, for one, was also tired of Gregg's laissez-faire attitude and unreliability. He decided he had gotten too old to be going down to Sarasota for rehearsals and then waiting around a month for everybody to show up. "It just enraged me to be sitting down there wasting my time," Butch said. "In your early twenties, there's no such thing as wasting your time; you'd be out partying and fishing and if we didn't practice, it was okay. The reunion was fun for a while. But, you know, you can't go back. I guess we just grew up too much."

On January 23, 1982, they performed a song called "Leavin'" on *Saturday Night Live*. "Gonna take my guitar / I don't care if I'm a big star / I'm leavin'," Dickey sang. It would be the last performance of the Allman Brothers Band for four years.

Part V

Resurrection

The descent into hell is easy. The gates stand open
day and night. But to reclimb the slope and escape
to the upper air: this is labor.

— *Virgil*

Twenty-five

Seven Turns

AFTER the breakup, everyone went his separate way. Dickey and Butch played together for a while in a band with Chuck Leavell that made the rounds of the nightclub circuit. Except for those three, the band members were estranged from one another. Aside from Chuck, Jaimoe didn't speak with any of the others. Butch was openly disdainful of Gregg. Dickey and Gregg lived within five miles of one another in Florida but they went a couple of years without communication. The brotherhood seemed like a distant, bittersweet memory.

Tragedy was still a familiar companion. Twiggs Lyndon had become the road manager for another old Capricorn group, a jazz-fusion band called the Dixie Dregs. A tour had taken them to upstate New York in late 1979, and on November 16, Twiggs went to a little airport to go parachuting. It was one of his favorite things to do, and he was a veteran of three hundred jumps. He stepped out of an airplane at 8,500 feet, his chute never opened, and Twiggs was killed on impact. He was thirty-seven. Although it was impossible to know, a lot of people in Macon suspected suicide. They said Twiggs had never been the same after Duane and Berry died, and the irony was inescapable — the airport was in a little town named Duanesburg.

Then, Lamar Williams fell ill with lung cancer and doctors theorized that it was caused from exposure to Agent Orange, the defoliant widely used by the U.S. army during the war in Vietnam. Lamar underwent an operation on October 29, 1981, ten years to the day from when Duane died. The surgeons removed a third of his lung and two of his ribs; they thought they had caught it in time. But the cancer soon returned and Lamar was readmitted to the Veterans Administration Hospital in Los Angeles. He died there on January 21, 1983, just one week after his thirty-fourth birthday.

AS the decade passed, Butch cut off his long hair, and his drums sat unplayed for months at a time while he put on a business suit and built a $1.5 million recording studio in Tallahassee. "I don't want to be fifty years old and living in Holiday Inns," Butch said, vowing that Tallahassee would become a music capital like Macon or Muscle Shoals. Jaimoe and Candace Oakley divorced and Jaimoe lived on the verge of poverty in Macon, playing in local bands and struggling to get by financially. "I think about all the mess that happened and, sure, it pisses me off," he said. "Like Marvin Gaye said, I know how bad I've been screwed. That's why I can laugh about it. I learned to be cautious. Whenever somebody wants you to hurry up and do something, you better slow down."

Dickey put together several different bands and played the small club circuit before he finally got a record contract with Epic in 1988. He released an album called *Pattern Disruptive* that was good but barely made a dent in the charts. He went through a bitter divorce from Paulette — the marriage ended when she left him and he flew into a blind rage, chopping up the furniture and cabinets in their house with an axe and destroying toilets and sinks with a sledgehammer. Finally, he grabbed an armful of Paulette's wardrobe out of a closet and piled it on the floor. Then he went outside to the swimming pool, grabbed a container of muriatic acid, and poured it on her clothing. Paulette and Dickey never lived together again and Dickey went into drug rehab.

Gregg remained the road warrior, putting together a band featuring the Toler brothers and playing a steady grind of nightclubs. No major label would touch him, wary of his notorious history and confident there was no longer any market for his music. Gregg surprised a lot of them when he signed with Epic Records in 1987 and released *I'm No Angel,* which spawned a minor hit by the same name and gave Gregg's career a much-needed boost.

Alcohol and cocaine remained an ever-present concern, and

just being on the road offered him constant temptation. "Treatment costs money and the only way Gregg can pay is to work; yet often the only way he can work is to get treatment," Gregg's manager said. Weeks before *I'm No Angel* was released, Gregg had been in jail in Ocala, Florida, serving a three-day sentence for drunk driving. And that summer, Gregg overdosed on cocaine after a gig in New York City; he was given CPR and rushed by ambulance to Roosevelt Hospital. His personal life was in shambles — he was $250,000 in debt — and his music was his anchor. "Performing is my whole life," Gregg said. "It's my peace of mind. On any given night, you can just get up and pour it out. It's that release. When all else fails, no matter what's happened — your old lady and your friends could have all shit on you in the same day — it's the best medicine anybody's ever made."

The Allman Brothers Band, including Chuck Leavell and Dan Toler, performed at the Volunteer Jam in Nashville in 1986 and then again three months later at an anti-crack benefit staged by Bill Graham at Madison Square Garden. Then Dickey and Gregg went on the road together — a set by Dickey's band, a set by Gregg's band, and then a jam session with both groups. When the tour reached Macon, Butch and Jaimoe and Chuck Leavell climbed onstage and the Allman Brothers Band played a 90-minute set. They were all constantly quizzed about a reunion but remained cool about the idea as Dickey and Gregg pursued their solo careers.

By the late eighties, the climate in the music business was shifting again. New life was being given to old bands as fans began replacing old albums with compact discs and "classic rock" radio introduced a whole new generation to the sounds of the sixties and seventies. Once again, the blues made a comeback in the mainstream with the success of Robert Cray and Stevie Ray Vaughan and the Fabulous Thunderbirds. PolyGram dug through its vaults and released a boxed set in 1988 tracing the career of Eric Clapton. The release was a surprise hit, and the label decided to follow it up with a boxed set covering the career of the Allman Brothers Band.

In early 1989, Jaimoe telephoned a friend and offered a mysterious greeting. "Man, I was afraid I'd waited too long," he said. Jaimoe chuckled when he was asked to explain himself. "They say good things come to those who wait. I was beginning to worry that I'd waited too long."

He was calling to say the Allman Brothers Band was going to try it one more time.

*   *   *

THE years had not been kind to the Allman Brothers Band's place in rock history. The original group had largely been forgotten, over-shadowed by what had come after the deaths of Duane Allman and Berry Oakley. Instead of being famed for its extraordinary music, the Allman Brothers was infamous for the tabloid headlines generated by the Gregg and Cher circus. Then the final lineup had turned the band into a feeble caricature of itself and, for most music fans, the Allman Brothers seemed like a very easy band to dismiss. When *Rolling Stone* had celebrated its tenth anniversary in 1977 with a group of critics listing their favorite ten releases during the maga-zine's history, the Allman Brothers had been represented on half the ballots, in the form of the *Fillmore East* album or through Duane's work on *Layla* or "Loan Me a Dime." Yet ten years later, when the magazine celebrated its twentieth anniversary with a list of the best hundred albums since 1967, the *Fillmore East* wasn't even mentioned.

There was initial reluctance from the surviving band members when Epic Records took the initiative to offer a record contract to a reunited Allman Brothers Band in 1989. They were acutely aware that putting together a new group ran the risk of putting the final nail in the band's legacy. But the solo careers of Gregg and Dickey had stalled. Tallahassee wasn't becoming the musical center Butch had envisioned. And Jaimoe seemed lost without the Allman Brothers. Besides, the band members had never really wanted to stop making music with one another. With the PolyGram project under way and with Epic's encouragement, the original four members met in Sara-sota and began serious discussions. "The one thing I wanted to avoid at all cost was any further compromise," Butch told a reporter. "I wanted to be sure we were serious about this, that everybody was committed and willing to bare their guts once more. In the early eighties, it had gotten to the point where we were playing it safe. We were just making the money and going home."

No one wanted a repeat of the Arista debacle, and they agreed first thing that a reunion had to mean a return to the traditional Allman Brothers sound. They insisted on complete artistic control from Epic, and, to its credit, the label agreed. "We told Epic that if we were going to make a record, we were going to do it on our terms," Butch said. "We wanted the freedom to do things the way we wanted to do them, or else we weren't interested. We wanted to go back to our original philosophy and play the kind of music we wanted to play, with no thought to commercial success."

Chuck Leavell was contacted about participating, and he was agreeable with just one catch: it had to be the old band, without the Toler brothers. It didn't take Chuck very long to develop misgivings. He was left out of the loop during the weeks it took to hammer out the details of the reunion, and he no longer had any desire to be treated as a sideman in the Allman Brothers Band. While Chuck waited, the Rolling Stones called. He had been a de facto member of the band since 1982, when the Stones were looking for a keyboard player and Bill Graham recommended Chuck. The Stones were coming out of semi-retirement in 1989, and with the death of their long-time pianist, Ian Stewart, Chuck was offered a much larger role in the group. He had tired of the indecision surrounding the Allman Brothers reunion, and opted to rejoin the Stones instead.

In time, the lineup of the new Allman Brothers Band began coming together. "It was a lot of careful decisions just to make sure we had the right people," Dickey told *Rolling Stone*. "It would be pitiful to have put this band back together just to be an embarrassment. I don't think we could have dealt with that." The first move was obvious — the last version of the Allman Brothers Band had been a mistake that no one wanted to repeat, and the Toler brothers were out. Dickey lobbied for Warren Haynes, a spectacular guitarist and bottleneck player who played in Dickey's solo band, to join the mix, and the others went along.

Warren had grown up in Asheville, North Carolina, and had a strong blues and jazz background. In 1980, he had joined up with honky-tonk singer David Allan Coe and stayed with his band through eight albums. He first met Dickey in 1981 when Coe opened for the Allman Brothers at the Fox Theatre in Atlanta, and later he sat in with Dickey's solo band from time to time. The two guitarists felt a natural musical affinity, and when Dickey had signed his solo Epic contract, he called Warren to invite him to join his band. For the first time in years, Dickey found himself playing with a guitarist who possessed the chops to challenge him. Warren was set to begin recording his own album when Dickey called with the invitation, but there was no way he could turn Dickey down — it was a once-in-a-lifetime opportunity. With Chuck out of the picture, Gregg lobbied for Johnny Neel, the pianist from Dickey's solo band. That left one spot open: bass player.

There were almost thirty auditions before they settled on Allen

Woody, a guitar salesman by trade whose closest claim to fame had been playing in a band led by ex–Lynyrd Skynyrd drummer Artimus Pyle. Allen had met Butch when that band had traveled to Pegasus Studios to record an album. Impressed by what he heard, Butch asked Allen to try out. Allen went to his audition with sure confidence he was going to get the job; he believed it was his fate. He was thirty-four years old and he had grown up listening to the Allman Brothers Band. He was even born in Nashville at the same hospital where Duane and Gregg had been born. And he immediately won over Dickey and the others, just as he had Butch. "He came in there and kicked ass," Dickey said.

The band balked when Epic wanted them to go immediately into the studio; they wanted to hit the road first. This was essentially a new band, and they needed to make sure things still felt right onstage. The four surviving members had to learn how to incorporate the styles of the three new members into the music. They also had to find out if Gregg could be trusted on the road. The record label executives gulped. "Epic was convinced that, within two weeks on the road, we'd split up," Butch said.

The band prevailed again, and a tour was set up in the summer of 1989 in conjunction with PolyGram's release of *Dreams*, the five-record boxed set. The compilation's music began with the Allman Joys and carried through Dickey's last solo album. There were rarities like "Spoonful" and "Crossroads" from Duane and Gregg's sessions at Bradley's Barn in Nashville in 1966, two songs by Second Coming, and unreleased studio versions of "Statesboro Blues" and "Dreams." Two of the most pleasant surprises were a live version of "You Don't Love Me" recorded in New York shortly after the death of King Curtis that sweetly segued into "Soul Serenade," and a searing version of "Drunken Hearted Boy," recorded at the Fillmore East with Elvin Bishop and his piano player, Steve Miller, sitting in.

Most of all, *Dreams* put the Allman Brothers Band back on the map and went a long way toward reminding people just how good the original group had been. The release of *Dreams* prompted the *New York Times* to print a long review on the cover of its Sunday leisure section that pondered the question of why the Allman Brothers had been given such short shrift in rock history. Particularly perplexing to writer Robert Palmer was how Duane Allman's impact had faded; he was now usually pigeonholed as a bottleneck player who had played on "Layla" and was seldom placed alongside the greats of the guitar. "Why is Duane Allman's name seldom mentioned in the same breath as Jimi Hendrix, Eric Clapton, Jimmy Page, Jeff Beck and other sixties guitar heroes — the company in which Mr. Allman so evidently belongs?" Palmer wrote. "*Dreams* provides ample evidence that a critical reevaluation of these musicians' twenty-year career is long overdue."

The summer of 1989 was a time when several legendary bands resurfaced for tours — the Rolling Stones, the Who, Jefferson Airplane, the Doobie Brothers — and the results were mixed. Some of the bands seemed mainly interested in fattening bank accounts. But the Allman Brothers Band served notice that it was taking its reunion very seriously and was looking to recapture the spirit of the old brotherhood. It seemed symbolic that two members of the old road crew, Red Dog and Joe Dan Petty, signed back up for the tour. Onstage, the long jams were back with a purpose and soaring determination. Jaimoe and Butch were playing together as well as they ever had. Dickey already was one of rock's best guitarists, and Warren Haynes's muscular playing was the stimulus Dickey needed to play at his absolute best.

Gregg was sober and in great voice; he had gone back into a rehab center before the tour and was making yet another effort at sobriety, using the alias of "Will Power" when he registered into hotels. Gregg's biggest vice seemed to be a ritualistic preconcert joint he shared backstage with Warren, Allen, and Johnny Neel. Dickey was drinking less. Jaimoe had completely kicked his drug habit and was eating only health foods. When an old friend started to light up a joint one night in his hotel room, Jaimoe told him to go outside to his car.

Warren was turning into a major find who made a significant impact on the music. He smartly invoked Duane Allman when he played songs like "Statesboro Blues" and "Dreams" by playing some of the licks Duane had made famous; yet he also was good enough to add his own personality to the classic material and could skillfully improvise on the long jams like "Elizabeth Reed."

Each night, the band looked out to sellout audiences that were an equal joining of younger fans, who heard the Allman Brothers on the radio and knew little about the band other than that Gregg was once married to Cher, and the older ones, who could say they were there when Duane Allman was sliding his Coricidin bottle up and down the neck of his Gibson.

As the reunion tour expanded to include a fall tour of theaters, a tall blond kid could be seen hanging out backstage at many of the gigs. It was Devon Lane (a combination of "Lenoir" and "Duane") Allman, now seventeen years old and an aspiring singer who at last was becoming a part of his father's life. Gregg's relationships with his children had been virtually nonexistent — Cher complained long and often in interviews that Elijah Blue could count on one hand the times he'd seen Gregg.

Part of the problem was that Gregg had grown up without his father, and was untutored in the responsibilities of fatherhood. Though he had five kids, Gregg had never hung around long enough to get on-the-job training, and his lone role had largely consisted of sending support checks. That began to change only as his children hit their late teens and became musicians. Gregg could relate to them as "one of the guys," a role he was far more comfortable playing, and it helped him to begin to forge bonds with his older kids.

Devon was truly his father's son, almost a spitting image of Gregg and born with a love of music. He was already performing for his family at the age of three or four. Devon listened closely to the radio and would often quiz his mother about the bands. One afternoon, when he was five or six, he heard "Midnight Rider" on the radio. "I really like this song," he told his mother. "Who is that?" There was a sort of awkward silence. "That's your daddy," Shelley Allman finally responded.

Devon was fifteen when he decided it was time to give things a little push. Without telling his mother, he sent a letter to his father in care of Mama A in Daytona Beach. The message was simple: here I am; I'm alive; here's my number and my address; get ahold of me if you want to. Days later, he walked into the living room and nonchalantly announced to a startled Shelley that his dad had just called.

After years of silence, Gregg had telephoned as soon as he received the letter. As difficult as it was, he was eager to use the opening and contact his son. Their conversation stretched out over three hours and by the end, Gregg was teaching guitar chords to his son over the phone. He invited Devon to come to Florida and spend some time with him. Shelley was pleased, but she also had some strong advice for Devon. "Let me explain something to you," she told him. "If you're going to know this man and you're going to form a relationship with him, you've got to realize he's not a responsible person." She proved prophetic. The trip to Daytona was aborted, as was another one that was scheduled after it. Shelley tried to explain to Devon that she didn't think Gregg had ever set out to hurt anyone intentionally, that he just lived for whatever came up at the moment. It didn't help; Devon took the cancellations very personally.

Father and son finally met about a year later. Devon's family had moved to Missouri and when Gregg's solo band scheduled a concert in St. Louis in August of 1988, Devon called his father and told him he'd be waiting at the stage door. "He was really uncomfortable, which I don't blame him," Devon said. "We hit it off. I noticed that we were a lot alike. We have a lot of the same mannerisms and stuff. Then he went out and jammed and just kicked ass, and I was blown away. He was going to be in town for a couple of days, and I went back and hung out with him. We just did a lot of talking and stuff, got acquainted because we didn't know each other. He came back a few months later during my spring break. . . . Trying to catch up on sixteen years, it's tough."

Devon's gutsy determination to get to know his father seemed to spark Gregg to try to mend fences with all his children. His second solo album with Epic had included a very personal song called "Island" that was Gregg's way of reaching out to his young daughter. And for the first time on any album, Gregg had included a thanks on the record jacket to four of his children: Devon, Elijah Blue, Island, and Michael, who had been conceived in 1965 back in Daytona Beach.

When the Allman Brothers kicked off the second leg of the *Dreams* tour, Gregg invited Devon to travel with him. In Boston, at a three-night stand at the Orpheum Theatre, Devon met sixteen-year-old Berry Oakley, Jr., who, like Devon, looked amazingly like a younger version of his father. Halfway through the show, Dickey called for Berry Jr., who walked out onstage lugging his father's bass and plugged in to play "Southbound." Also sitting in on the song was renowned Boston blues guitarist Ronnie Earl. It was an incredible moment: the younger Berry playing the bass like the reincarnation of his father, and Ronnie Earl trading licks with Dickey and Warren for three scorching choruses.

Late that night, Gregg and Devon went down to a little piano bar in the Howard Johnson's hotel. The place was packed, and people began applauding when they walked in. Gregg agreed to play a couple of songs, and sat down behind the piano with Devon at his side. Gregg did two numbers, then began "Fear of Falling," a song from his last solo album. When he forgot the words to the second verse, Devon impulsively reached for a microphone that was lying nearby. He hesitated for a minute, fearing his father might consider it an intrusion, then closed his eyes and began belting out the song. When he finished, he looked up; Gregg was beaming and the audience was loudly applauding. "There was one guy who stood up," Devon said. "It was Dickey. He had never been a dick to me but you know how Dickey is, you've almost got to prove yourself to the guy. And he came up to me and extended his hand for the first time. And he said, 'Man, I didn't know you had it in you.' That was great. And my dad was just grinning, he was really proud."

THE tour closed down at the end of October in Miami, where Gregg invited Devon to come out and sing "Midnight Rider." After that, the band took some time off. Gregg married for a fifth time, this time to Danielle Galiana, a woman he met in Los Angeles who seemed intent on helping him stay straight. And Dickey also remarried, exchanging vows with Donna Marie Barry, who had been a schoolteacher in Rhode Island and, like Sandy Bluesky and Paulette, was a dark-eyed brunette beauty.

Everyone began gearing up for the first Allman Brothers Band studio album in nearly ten years. Warren and Johnny Neel went to Florida and stayed with Dickey at his house on the Manatee River to write, then everyone met in Nashville for six weeks of rehearsals. Tom Dowd was back in the studio to guide them, a message that they understood what was at stake with the new album — it had to be very good in order for the band to build credibility.

Recorded at Criteria Studios in Miami and released in 1990, *Seven Turns* did much more. It was an amazing comeback album for a band that was supposed to have been washed up long ago. The first song, "Good Clean Fun," jumped off the disc like no opening number since "Don't Want You No More" from the debut album twenty-one years earlier. It was a sound that was instantly familiar, yet fresh and alive. Everything was there, all the separate elements put back into their proper context — Gregg's growling vocals, Dickey's screaming Les Paul, and the dynamics between the duel drums of Butch and Jaimoe. In just the first four minutes, *Seven Turns* showed more surprises and inventiveness than the previous two Allman Brothers albums combined. "Good Clean Fun" was selected for a video and included rehearsal footage interspersed with shots of two comely women in pressed-on jeans prowling backstage for rock stars.

"Low Down, Dirty Mean" was another great arrangement, a worthy contender for the best blues the band had ever recorded. It starts off like a Sunday-afternoon front-porch jam with Warren playing the bottleneck on a Stratocaster, Dickey playing along on his 1936 steel-body National, and Johnny Neel adding short bursts on the harmonica. Then the whole band comes in and the song kicks into a strutting backbeat as Gregg sings in a low, menacing growl.

The title track was probably Dickey's greatest song since "Ramblin' Man." He wrote "Seven Turns" during the recording sessions after Tom Dowd asked him if he had a melodic song in the vein of "Blue Sky" to give a different coloring for the record. "I didn't really have anything concrete but I'd been thinking about this one song a lot," Dickey told a reporter. "That's the way I work — I'll think about a tune for six months before I sit down and do it. 'Seven Turns' refers to an old Navajo legend about how there's seven times in your life when you have to make a great decision, and if you make the wrong turn you end up at a dead end. And you either have to stay there, or back your way up and find where you went wrong."

The song begins with the melancholy of unanswered questions and ends with the strength of recaptured faith. The performance is magnificent, from the richness of Dickey's acoustic guitar and Warren's hesitant bottleneck in the opening, to Dickey's warm, questing voice. At the close of the second verse there is a wonderful moment when Warren and Johnny sing harmony with Dickey, as Gregg wails behind them echoing the lines. Then Warren falls in on slide guitar, his coming of age with the Allman Brothers much as "Jessica" had been Chuck Leavell's proving ground.

The second strong blues on the album is "Gambler's Roll," a song written by Warren and Johnny Neel as a showcase for Gregg. His voice is full of gritty drama and nuance, with lines that often fade into lonesome whispers. Warren plays the first solo with a gentle melancholy until the song builds up and Dickey comes in for scorching riffs that roar with abandon. It is great playing, Dickey's best recorded blues solo since "Stormy Monday."

"True Gravity," an instrumental written by Dickey and Warren, was inspired by Dickey's love for the music of saxophonist Ornette Coleman and stands as a showcase for the band's versatility. Dickey began writing the song when he came up with a chugging bass line on one of Berry's old Fenders; then he put a melody on top of it when Warren came to Florida for a writing session. "We worked on that song for two weeks," Dickey said. "I just played bass while Warren played guitar. We stopped one day and made a pot of coffee. I started singing this melody and said, 'Warren, that's it.' We ran back in the room, picked up the guitars, and started playing it."

The song would later be a Grammy finalist for best rock instrumental performance, and the band would perform it with Doc Severinson's band on "The Tonight Show" with Johnny Carson. The horn section made the song sound something like Benny Goodman and His Orchestra on psychedelics, and the jam was a thrill for the Allman Brothers. "That's like an institution, like playing Carnegie Hall," Dickey said. "And it was the first time they'd ever played that way with a rock 'n' roll band. It was really cool." Carson, a jazz fanatic and accomplished amateur drummer, yelled out "Wow!" at the song's conclusion. His enthusiasm for the performance was sincere; the Allman Brothers would be invited back to play with the Tonight Show band again.

Seven Turns more than redeemed the comeback: it was the most exciting Allman Brothers album since *Enlightened Rogues*. It proved the group was a living and breathing *band* again — not the four Allman Brothers and a couple of sidemen — and that made all the difference. "It feels like the Allman Brothers again," Butch said. "It hasn't felt that way in a long, long time."

Twenty-six

Tales of Ordinary Madness

THE cover of *Seven Turns* pictures the band members standing at a rain-soaked crossroads in the early morning, as if they had been there all night commiserating with the ghost of Robert Johnson or some otherworldly spirit they knew from the past. Dickey stands firmly in the center of the photo, underneath the Allman Brothers Band logo, as though he is carrying its weight on his shoulders. It was apropos of Dickey's role in the band; since the reunion he had been firmly in charge of the musical direction and most of the others took their cues from him. He had fueled *Seven Turns*, writing or cowriting seven of the nine tracks and building on the sound he had developed on *Pattern Disruptive*. But as much as somebody had to stand up and take on the leadership post, it was a role that still made Dickey uncomfortable. He was always the happiest when he could stand back and simply play his guitar.

Yet whenever Gregg tried to assert himself, it usually set up little power struggles with Dickey, and Gregg lost most of the time. The feeling that the others ignored him never failed to irritate Gregg. He also resented being treated like a kid; Gregg faced strict regulation from the band's management and they went to great lengths to keep him away from drugs. Old friends were often pulled aside when they showed up backstage and warned not to give Gregg cocaine. While the others considered the measures necessary to keep Gregg reasonably straight and in shape to perform, Gregg considered them oppressive. The irony was that once he was away from the Allman Brothers and left alone, he sometimes stayed sober or drank only in moderation. Then, when he was back with the band, he rebelled under the short leash he was placed under. It became a test of wills: anything they told him *not* to do, Gregg was quite likely *to* do out of spite. The tug-of-war was a constant source of irritation and frustration for everyone involved.

The *Seven Turns* tour kept the Allman Brothers out on the road from July through the end of 1990. This time out, they had new songs to play and the audiences were responding with much the same adulation that greeted the old material. Although *Seven Turns* didn't sell well enough to qualify for a gold record, it provided just what the band members wanted — a firm foundation that kept old fans interested and helped attract new ones. They were making music only to please themselves, the way it had been in the early days, and they had little ambition beyond that. They had tasted superstardom and it was bitter. All they wanted now was something financially and artistically rewarding, but manageable. Very manageable.

The band received considerable media coverage during the comeback. There was a long feature in *Rolling Stone*, a cable television special on VH-1, and laudatory reviews in nearly every city. The Allman Brothers also became a sidebar in a drama unfolding in the Persian Gulf. The world tensed after Iraq invaded Kuwait and then took 156 Americans as hostages to use as human shields at Iraqi military installations. The crisis went on for four months before the prisoners were released on December 10, 1990, just before the Gulf War broke out. One group of hostages reported that their captors had given them a cassette/radio player with tapes of Beethoven, Zamfir, and "old, old Allman Brothers" to keep them entertained during their captivity.

In late 1990, the band traveled to New York City to tape a broadcast on MTV's "Unplugged," the innovative show that put rock groups in an acoustic concert setting. It was a return to the roots of the Allman Brothers Band, like eavesdropping on the old late-night jams at Rose Hill. The crowd was wildly enthusiastic and the band closed with the old Robert Johnson song "Come On in My Kitchen," using an arrangement that Dickey had been performing in his living room for fifteen years. Everyone had so much fun with the "Unplugged" show that an acoustic set became a routine in their concerts.

While the Allman Brothers had again evolved into a tight, cohesive unit onstage, the odd man out seemed to be Johnny Neel. He fit in very well on the new material, but seemed unable to integrate himself into the old songs the way Warren was able to do. Warren and Allen and Johnny had all signed two-year contracts with the band, and at the end of 1990, Johnny's option was not picked up. Gregg wanted to add another keyboard player but the other three members vetoed the idea, preferring to carry on with a six-man lineup that matched the original band.

The Allman Brothers stayed on the road through February of 1991, then began rehearsing and recording the next album under Tom Dowd's stewardship at Ardent Studios in Memphis. They took time off in the spring and Gregg went to Hollywood to appear in a motion picture called *Rush,* the story of two undercover drug cops who eventually become addicts themselves. Gregg convincingly played their target, a mysterious nightclub owner named Will Gaines. The brooding character had very few lines and was far removed from Gregg's own personality, but he was convincing in the role and received good reviews for his acting when the film was released a year later.

Jaimoe used the break to remarry. His new wife was an attractive dancer named Catherine Fellows; they were wed in Old Saybrook, Connecticut, on May 31, 1991, and began living in Hartford. Three weeks after the wedding, the Allman Brothers performed a warm-up show for an upcoming European tour at the Citi Club in Boston. Eric Clapton, Prince, and Van Morrison had all recently played the 1,500-seat room and it had become an "in" spot for popular bands who wanted to perform in intimate surroundings. Tickets for the show had been a hot commodity in Boston, and the room was packed tight when the Allman Brothers took the stage.

It was the first concert in weeks. The band was rusty in spots but seemed fueled by rapt adoration from the crowd; at one point, Jaimoe was even dancing onstage. Everything seemed fine until they kicked into the closing number, "Whipping Post." Dickey appeared visibly irritated at something near the end of the song. Then he inexplicably stopped playing altogether just before the conclusion, holding his guitar and waiting for the song to end. It was reminiscent of a show in Boston in 1989 when Dickey became angry onstage and didn't play a solo during the entire second set.

As the music died down, Dickey walked off the Citi Club stage, went backstage, found Donna, and told her, "Come on, babe, we're getting out of here." While the crowd was clamoring loudly for an encore, Dickey and his wife were exiting through a back door and heading back to the hotel.

The rest of the band members returned to the stage and played without him for thirty minutes. There was an edge to the performance that hadn't been there before, as if they'd stepped up the intensity, firmly determined not to let Dickey's absence make them lose balance. The encore included "Stormy Monday," "Hoochie-Coochie Man" with Warren on vocals, and a stunning version of "Dreams" marked by Gregg's melancholy singing and Warren's bottleneck solo. After the show the band members milled around backstage, acting nonplussed about what had happened. Someone said later that Dickey left because he had a stomach virus.

While offstage struggles had again become a part of the scenery, they did nothing to slow the band's momentum. The new album, *Shades of Two Worlds*, was released while the band was in Europe, and it was a marvelous step up from the reunion album that had preceded it. There was a maturity in the lyrics that had never been shown before, lines that questioned the mysteries of life and looked back with a reflective introspection. The tone was set with the opening number, "End of the Line," a song that Warren and Allen Woody wrote with touch-up work from Gregg. It kicks off with a chugging guitar riff, then the band gently falls out leaving Gregg, sounding alone and vulnerable, as he sings the opening lines that talk of struggling to come to grips with addiction. Then the tempo takes a sudden shift for a chorus that is the chilling tale of a survivor who seems almost surprised that he has lived to tell his story. Dickey plays the first lead as though he's wrestling with a bitter memory, and then Warren follows him with a tender-sounding slide that rises to a dramatic resolution. At the end of the song Dickey comes back in on lead guitar; then he and Warren furiously trade licks as the music fades out.

The album's centerpiece is "Nobody Knows," a magnificent song written by Dickey with Warren's uncredited help on the arrangement. It begins on a riff that recalls "Hot 'lanta" before Gregg comes in to sing words that poignantly capture a man confronting his own mortality, burdened by a desire to find himself and understand his place in the world. It serves as a logical followup thematically to "Seven Turns," and Gregg brings the lyrics to life with a yearning voice floating just on the edge of despair. The song is marked by a long instrumental section that is full of defining moments. Dickey's solo highlights everything great about his guitar playing — his lyrical feel for melody, his ability to improvise unexpected combinations of notes, and, especially, the emotional content that comes across in his music. It is a tremendous performance, maybe the best studio track the All-man Brothers Band had ever recorded.

"Kind of Bird" is one of the band's most ambitious songs; rock bands are simply not supposed to be able to play jazz with a feeling this nimble and full of swing. It was written by Dickey and Warren following an afternoon of listening to Charlie Parker albums. When they picked up their guitars that evening, they began playing bebop notes that quickly turned into an instrumental of sophisticated, inter-locking melodies. The song earned the band its third Grammy nomi-nation for best rock instrumental performance.

The album closes with a masterful reading of "Come On in My Kitchen." Dickey kicks it off with a lonesome-sounding acoustic bot-tleneck; then Gregg comes in moaning a sad melody while Warren adds succinct licks on a National steel-body. Gregg's voice has never been more convincing, more warm and inviting. Dickey's bottleneck gives the song a spooky undertone until the tempo slips into a joyful, foot-tapping shuffle reminiscent of "Pony Boy."

It was a perfect way to close what may be the band's most satisfy-ing studio album, a record with music that effortlessly ranges from rock to hard blues to bebop to country blues. What distinguishes *Shades of Two Worlds* are the adult themes drawn from their own expe-riences; for once, the lyrics are consistently strong enough to match the power of the music.

Rolling Stone took note, saying *Shades of Two Worlds* reached an improvisational level that the band had not approached since the death of Duane Allman. "Creative high points are the product of nei-ther luck nor design," wrote John Swenson. "They occur when artists open the window to their heart and soul. The Allman Brothers Band, two albums into its new identity and fired by the achievement of *Shades of Two Worlds*, should finally be ready to pick up where it left off after *Live at Fillmore East*."

THAT was exactly the intention. Just as the old band had done twenty years earlier, the new version of the Allman Brothers decided to follow its second studio recording with a live album. The original idea was to record it in Macon — a return to the band's beginnings. Four concerts at the City Auditorium at the end of 1991 sold out in minutes. But once the band hit town it seemed as if everything that could go wrong did. The City Auditorium was no place to make a live album; the music seemed to bounce off the walls and the recording engineers couldn't get a good sound on tape. And Gregg was drinking again, seen in a local pharmacy purchasing a quart bottle of generic cough syrup and guzzling it outside. Then the whole thing turned into a media event — CNN sent a camera crew, *Rolling Stone* showed up, and the band went into a circle-the-wagons mode. "It was a circus by the time we got there, everybody talking about making history, and all this," Butch complained. "By the time we got up there to play, everyone was so tightened up, there was no way to do it."

On top of everything else, Gregg and Dickey were going through another of their periodic cold wars. There was a set routine during each concert in which the two of them alternated introducing the members of the band, ending with Gregg introducing Dickey and then Dickey introducing Gregg. But instead of introducing Gregg, Dickey turned away and counted off the beginning of the next song. Gregg noticed the slight and he was still furious when he got back to the Macon Hilton, where the band was headquartered. To reach his room, Gregg had to walk down a long hallway to a private entryway. Inside were two doors; on the left was the door to Dickey's room and on the right was the entrance to Gregg's room. Gregg slammed the door to the entryway as hard as he could, as if he was trying to catch Dickey's attention. "I ain't scared of you," he snarled in a stage whisper at Dickey's door. "I ain't scared of you." He opened the door to his room, then slammed it shut with all the force he could gather. As a tempestuous rock 'n' couple, Mick Jagger and Keith Richards had nothing on Gregg and Dickey.

The four Macon concerts left no one satisfied, and the band decided to record two shows in Boston in early March of 1992. This time there was no hype or buildup; nobody even talked about taping the concert in fear of jinxing it. The setting was the Orpheum Theatre, one of those old, majestic halls, and this time, everything came together. Gregg was back on the wagon, Dickey and Gregg were friends again, and Jaimoe had just returned from the christening of his new baby daughter, Cajai (a combination of Catherine and Jaimoe) in Old Mystic, Connecticut.

It was a magnificent concert, one of those special nights when the music seems to be flowing out of some divine dimension and all the musicians feel as though they're doing little more than acting as the conduits. After playing three hours, they walked offstage with huge grins and hugs. Then Butch turned to Dickey. "Damn, that was a great night," he deadpanned. "I hope we do that well when the [recording] truck gets here." Dickey fell for it; his mouth dropped open in horror until Butch broke out in laughter.

Following the Orpheum shows, there was a record-breaking, ten-day stand at the Beacon Theatre in New York City, where two more shows were taped to round out the album. As successful as the New York concerts were, by the final two shows the band members were itching to get back on the road. "It's been fun but, damn, sometimes you can stay in one place too long," Butch pleasantly complained. Before the show, Warren caused a minor panic when he found himself trapped for a few minutes in the ancient elevator that took people to the fifth-floor dressing rooms. Upstairs, after he was extricated, someone circulated copies of the photo that had been picked for the album cover, a shot of the band standing in front of the Orpheum under a marquee that reads "An Evening with the Allman Brothers Band." As the photos were being taken, Butch had turned around, looked up, and said, "Hey, there's the name of the album."

The concert that night was reminiscent of that special show at Orpheum two weeks earlier. Afterward, most of the band members and some of the road crew climbed into a cramped van for a ride back to the luxurious Park Central Hotel. By then, Gregg had split up with Danielle Allman and had been in the company of a lovely strawberry blond named Shelby for the past several months; he would soon father her baby, a little girl Gregg named Layla Brooklyn. He slumped into Shelby's arms on the ride back to the hotel, silent and reflective as he watched the neon lights of Manhattan flash by in the darkness.

EVERYWHERE the band turned, it found the upcoming live album being compared to the *Fillmore East*. It was an impossible mission. No live record could rival the *Fillmore East*, although there were moments when the new album came breathtakingly close, sparkles of brilliance that were reminders of the greatness of the Allman Brothers Band when it took to the stage.

The chief problem with *An Evening with the Allman Brothers Band* was its lack of adventure, as though the final lineup of songs was contrived to appease egos. The song selection on the *Fillmore East* album had been daring; instead of live versions of the band's back catalog there were four unrecorded blues, an unrecorded instrumental, and versions of "Whipping Post" and "In Memory of Elizabeth Reed" that bore only scant resemblance to the studio cuts. The new live album played it too safe. There was no logic in kicking it off with a live version of "End of the Line" that differed little from the version that also had led off the previous studio album. The inclusion of "Blue Sky" was a good idea, but aside from Dickey's solo, it was a poor performance. "Get On With Your Life" is too much of a rehash of "Stormy Monday." A more interesting choice for a blues would have been "Low Down, Dirty Mean," one of the best songs of the band's comeback.

From there, the album finally begins to blossom. "Southbound" starts on a funky rhythm lick by Dickey that bears little similarity to the original arrangement from *Brothers and Sisters*. Dickey's lead guitar is snarling and dangerous-sounding, and the song peaks near the end when Dickey and Warren begin trading fast riffs. "Midnight Blues," inspired by an old Blind Willie McTell song, kicks off a two-song acoustic set. The song is a showcase for Dickey, highlighting his mastery of the acoustic bottleneck, and his vocal is filled with richness and pleading emotion. The song includes Thom Douchette, who had played harmonica on the *Fillmore East* album.

An Evening with the Allman Brothers Band begins to find a true aim at the mystical heights of the *Fillmore* album as soon as the band launches into the opening licks of "Nobody Knows." It is a thrilling performance — full of crashing cymbals and screeching guitars and lulls and climaxes that show off this fourth version of the band at its zenith. Dickey and Warren may have never played better together than they do during the song's riveting final minutes, when they join together on a repeating riff and then push the song to a seemingly impossible crescendo, trading licks at the conclusion like two warriors locked in a beautiful duel.

The subtle introduction of "Dreams" is a soothing counter to the emotional fire built up in "Nobody Knows." It is a performance marked by the interplay between Jaimoe and Butch, subdued yet brimming with power. The two drummers are supplemented by percussionist Marc Quinones, who had played with the jazz fusion group Spyro Gyra and had been hired to go on the road after playing on a couple of tracks on the *Shades of Two Worlds* album.

"Revival" is a perfect finale, a song full of classic Allman Brothers guitar riffs that spring up with a boundless energy and words that echo the family warmth the band had projected throughout its history. The song had seemed passé not long after the band first recorded it; the Vietnam War was over and the hippie generation was transforming into yuppies. But here, some twenty years later, the Allman Brothers bring it back to life with a new spirit and a fresh vitality.

As good as its best moments are, *An Evening with the Allman Brothers Band* floundered on the charts and never really caught the public's imagination. Epic seemed content to put it out and let it wither on the vine — there was no video to help promote the album and little radio airplay. The record company had planned on releasing a second album with more live material but decided to postpone it because of the poor sales of the first one.

THEN came a long silence. As the tour wound down in the fall of 1992, the relations between band members grew strained and everyone seemed to need a long break. They were supposed to gather in Florida at the end of the year to begin work on a new studio album, but Gregg had moved to California and refused to come back east to work on the record. He had just come out of another rehab center, where he had been under the guidance of the doctor who had helped another notorious addict, David Crosby. Gregg was clean again and told the others that leaving the direct care of his doctor was like asking for an instant relapse. He wouldn't budge, and the rest of the band balked when he asked them to come to California to record. Instead, the album was postponed and the band announced that it had decided to road-test the new material in the spring and summer before heading into the studio.

The Allman Brothers did go to Washington, D.C., in January to perform at one of the inaugural balls for President Bill Clinton; then they went back into hibernation. Warren spent the break recording a solo album in Atlanta with Chuck Leavell producing and playing keyboards. Released in March of 1993, *Tales of Ordinary Madness* was a promising debut that showed off Warren's vocal talents and guitar playing. The record spread panic through the Allman Brothers camp in much the same way that Gregg's first solo album had so many years earlier — they feared that Warren was going to leave the band, and it seemed a real threat. Playing with the Allman Brothers was a dream come true for Warren. But it also could feel confining for someone who yearned to sing and perform his own songs. It suddenly seemed very telling that Warren had refused to have the trademark mushroom tattooed on his upper calf. To try to keep him happy, he was allowed to open up Allman Brothers concerts with his solo band. But that step raised Dickey's ire, and word circulated that he had given an ultimatum: either Warren goes or I do.

The band hit the road again in the spring of 1993, but appeared to be quietly slipping into the cycle that had first shown up in the wake of Duane's death and then again at the end of the second reunion — a couple of years of great music before the personality clashes began intruding. Jaimoe and Butch were the only ones of the surviving original four who were stable, drug-free, and clearheaded. Gregg's refusal to leave California reeked too much of the *Win, Lose or Draw* fiasco, and he fell off the wagon soon after the tour began. Near the end of the second leg in late June, he spent one afternoon swigging vodka and telling a friend that he was headed for rehab yet again during an upcoming four-week break. "In a few days, I'll be lying in agony and seeing spiders on the wall," Gregg said.

Dickey was in no better shape; he burned with the passions that made his art powerful but clouded his private life. He had become ever the loner in recent months, even during concerts. Every night, just before Butch and Jaimoe performed their long drum solo at the end of "In Memory of Elizabeth Reed," a chair would be placed behind a rack of guitars in an out-of-the-way corner where Dickey's guitar roadie was stationed. It had become a routine — while Butch and Jaimoe played, Dickey would sit quietly in the chair, away from everyone and lost in his own thoughts. It was an unspoken rule, enforced by his body language: Do Not Disturb.

Another routine was played out at the conclusion of the concerts. Dickey's roadie would stand by the stage door as the final song of the encore wound down, holding Dickey's dark, full-length western coat spread out in his hands. Dickey would wave to the crowd, put down his guitar, walk off the stage, and slip on the coat. Already clad in his trademark cowboy hat and now looking as though he should be on the plains and headed for the night watch, Dickey would ride back to the band's hotel while everyone else milled around backstage.

Dickey had been the band's navigator since the reunion, and when he began to unravel in the middle of the 1993 tour, it took the Allman Brothers Band to the brink of breaking up. "I got on about a three-year drunk there," Dickey told one writer. "The first two years were a lot of fun, and the last year got to be a living hell." There had been a couple of incidents in June when Dickey stopped playing during concerts. Disaster struck after the third leg of the tour got under way in Saratoga Springs, New York, on July 30. Dickey stayed out drinking after the show. When he got back to his hotel room, he and his wife began arguing and the dispute grew heated to the point that Donna called the police. Dickey allowed two officers to come inside and agreed to let Donna pack her belongings to move to another room while tempers cooled. He soon had a change of heart and refused to let her leave. Before the confrontation was over, Dickey had shoved one of the cops and found himself in custody. He was charged with resisting arrest and obstructing governmental administration, and he spent the night in jail before posting a $1,000 bond. He went home to Florida, and word spread that Dickey was seething because the band had packed up and left town without bailing him out of jail.

The Allman Brothers performed the following night in Vermont with Jimmy Herring of Col. Bruce Hampton's band sitting in on guitar; then they cryptically announced that Ozzy Osbourne guitarist Zack Wylde would play with the band until "Dickey decides to come back." It took exactly one concert to realize it was a mistake. "Brother Dickey cannot be with us tonight for health reasons," Gregg discreetly announced from the stage when Wylde debuted with the Allman Brothers at the Great Woods amphitheater outside Boston. Wylde soon had longtime fans cringing. He was the personification of everything the band members had disdained through the years. He chugged beer and then spewed it out on the audience. He spent a lot of the concert flinging back his long, blond hair. He humped his guitar as he played heavy-metal licks on songs like "Statesboro Blues" and "Dreams" and "Whipping Post." One fan aimed a pair of binoculars on Allen Woody during one of Wylde's solos and caught him rolling his eyes. The Great Woods show was Wylde's first and last gig with the Allman Brothers. That a heavy-metal guitarist was hired in the first place was a sign of the band's disarray. Wylde was replaced by Texas guitarist David Grissom, who gave the band a more sympathetic mix. Later, when Grissom had to return to his regular gig with John Mellencamp, the Allman Brothers recruited Jack Pearson, an old friend of Warren's, to take the second-guitar seat.

While the Allman Brothers Band stayed on the road, Dickey entered a rehab center for a few weeks and then spent his time playing golf and hunting. Dickey entered a guilty plea in Saratoga Springs on October 5, and paid a $295 fine for disorderly conduct. His status in the band was uncertain for weeks. The Allman Brothers camp complained that it seemed as if he was lost in his own world, oblivious of his band being on the road without him. But Dickey had to have time. He had to reach a peace with himself and bring under control the demons that had led to the ugly incident in Saratoga Springs.

In early November, the remaining three original members scheduled a meeting with Dickey in Florida to cement a formal reconciliation. Gregg didn't show up until a day later, but Butch and Jaimoe welcomed Dickey back with open arms. Five days after the meeting, at an Allman Brothers concert in West Palm Beach, Dickey walked out onstage with the band and returned to his normal spot. They played a beautiful version of "Mountain Jam," the first performance of the extended piece in nearly twenty years. Gregg had been singing one of Dickey's new songs, "Change My Way of Living," throughout the tour, but on that night it was Dickey on the vocals. "My life is in such a mess," he sang like he was saying a penance. "There ain't no one to blame but me."

Epilogue

Gregg walked into the lounge of a Nashville hotel one night in 1991 and sat down at the bar. "Allman," he heard someone call out. "You mean you're still walking around?" Gregg looked up and saw a man with graying hair and a beard sitting a couple of stools down from him. Gregg squinted his eyes as he tried to place the face. "Oh, my God," he said with sudden recognition. "The Nightcrawlers."

Mike Stone smiled warmly. It had been years since the onetime manager of the Nightcrawlers had seen Gregg, and the two of them sat and chatted for a few minutes about the old days back in Daytona Beach. Mike was happy that the Allman Brothers were back together and that Gregg was riding a new crest of popularity. Even more, Gregg made a point of telling him he had finally cleaned up his personal life and dried out. Moments later, someone walked up to Gregg, leaned over, and whispered something in his ear. Gregg turned to Mike and said he'd be back in a few minutes; he didn't return for over a half hour. "He comes back and the fucking shit is caked on his face," Mike said sadly, shaking his head at the memory. "He just never grew up."

Like Mike Stone, virtually everyone who knows Gregg speaks of him with a degree of tenderness. They may have just gone down a long list of anecdotes that are like a Greatest Hits of Gregg's Irresponsibilities, but at the base there is a warmth and sympathy. They see him as a man-child, a lost soul in the decades since his big brother died. "As crazy as he was, Duane was the glue for Gregg that kept Gregg moving," said Sylvan Wells, the old guitarist for the Nightcrawlers.

Wells, now a lawyer in Daytona Beach who makes acoustic guitars by hand in his spare time, last saw Gregg in the mid-eighties. Gregg had come to Orlando for a concert with his solo band and called up Sylvan to invite him to the show. They met at the hotel and rode over together in a limo; then Sylvan listened to about fifteen minutes of music and left. "He couldn't even carry on a lucid conversation," said Sylvan. "I told my wife, 'You know, I've always wondered if we did the right thing [breaking up the Nightcrawlers]; well, I don't wonder anymore.' "

Other old Daytona Beach friends, like Lee Hazen, haven't seen Gregg in years. Hazen left Daytona not long after Duane and Gregg and went on to work at Criteria Studios in Miami. He eventually moved to Nashville and built a studio in the basement of his house; Johnny Cash has recorded there, and England Dan and John Ford Coley recorded some of their hits at Lee's house. Lee is now semi-retired from the music business, but he still has reels of music that Duane and Gregg recorded in his kitchen back in Daytona Beach with their first real band, the Escorts. Van Harrison, the old Escorts bassist, lives in Phoenix and works as an engineer. "Gregg played here a couple of times and I tried to leave him a note or a message," said Van. "But there's so much insulation around him, it's hard to get through. I figured I'd have him over to the house. My kids know who he is, and can't believe their old man played with him."

The original Allman Brothers road crew has scattered. Mike Callahan has fallen out of touch with most from the old brotherhood. Although Joe Dan Petty and Red Dog both hooked back up with the band for the 1989 reunion tour, Joe Dan later left to return to Macon, where he makes custom boots. Red Dog still sometimes works with the band on the road. Tuffy Phillips is still in Macon, working construction jobs.

Scooter Herring also has fallen out of touch with old friends in Macon. The others involved in the infamous drug case have all been paroled from federal prison. J. C. Hawkins is said to be living in Florida. His brother, Recea Hawkins, is still in the Macon area, as is Joe Fuchs, the druggist who supplied Gregg's pharmaceutical cocaine.

Kim Payne long ago gave up drugs and has stayed clean. He lives in Montgomery, Alabama, works in a warehouse, and still rides a Harley. Every time he sees Gregg he is invited to go back on the road. "No fucking way, I don't need that," said Kim. "Gregg's constantly in a struggle to straighten up and clean up, and I definitely don't need to get into that shit. Something happens every time me and him get together: first thing we're gonna do is start looking for some dope. Wouldn't neither one of us last very long."

There are many bad memories, times that Kim felt betrayed by Gregg, but he will always carry a strong love for his friend. "Like

Duane told me one time when I had fucked up and done something wrong, he said: 'Don't worry about it, boy; you my hoss even if you don't ever win a race.' That's kind of the way I look at Gregg. He can fuck up all he wants to, but me and Gregg are still friends."

Like most of the people from the old days, Kim remains haunted by the deaths of Duane and Berry. Even twenty years later, he still finds it impossible to shake the eerie feeling that some kind of strange fate was at work. "If all that hadn't happened, how much longer could that high-intensity shit have gone on?" Kim said. "Even without drugs, and I can't imagine that scene without drugs to start with, I couldn't picture that thing going on longer than it did. That was some high-speed stuff, man. Like the *Fillmore* album. It don't get no better than that. What are you gonna do for an encore?"

AFTER battling cocaine and alcohol, Phil Walden's career began to get back on track in the late eighties, and he has revived Capricorn Records in Nashville. There have been no hits but he has a stable of hot young bands with great potential, and some of the old trademark verve is back. "You know," he told one reporter, "there's a theory that Southern rock 'n' roll never died; we just stopped making it."

Phil remains the target of the stubborn anger of people like Candace Oakley, who continues to hold bitterness over what she considers to be his betrayal of the brotherhood. "Maybe I carry it too far; I carried a big hatred for Phil for a long time," she said. "As I get older I'm getting more mellow. When I was younger, maybe I didn't want to admit that we did any wrong. The blame has to be shared, but these are guys who started out at eighteen or nineteen years old. Phil's initial investment was about $120,000; I think he got a pretty fucking good return on his money."

Candace, who remains in Macon and lives with her and Berry's father, also carries an open scorn for the various incarnations of the group that have come since her brother's death. "When Duane and Berry died, the Allman Brothers Band died as it was known," she said. "Everything went to hell in a hand bucket. The only way they can make money now is to play the old stuff. I think if Duane and Berry were alive, they'd be so embarrassed. I could just hear Duane: 'Don't you think you've worn it out yet?' I could hear him tell Gregg: 'Little brother, can't you come up with some new songs?' He and Duane were so close. Duane was like Gregg's father, and then suddenly he's gone. I've always felt badly for Gregg because of that. With siblings, you're so entwined with them that when they die you bury a part of yourself with them."

But Phil still commands loyalty from many of the old Capricorn people and his new staff is peppered with familiar names like Johnny Sandlin, who is once again producing records for the label and recording them in a little studio in his guest house in Decatur, Alabama. Johnny was one of the people who lost big money in the Capricorn bankruptcy. "That was twenty years ago," Johnny said. "We all screwed up. I just kind of gave it up after a couple of years of feeling bitter." Most of the bands Johnny produces are second-generation Southern rockers and ever-so-often he'll find himself wishing Duane was around to fire up a session. "I don't think I'll ever get over his death," Johnny said. "I'm not sad about it anymore, but I sure do miss him." Paul Hornsby, Capricorn's other star producer, is another who has shrugged off any bitterness. He is one of the few Capricorn veterans remaining in Macon and owns Muscadine Recording Studios, where he also works with young musicians who grew up listening to albums that he performed on and produced. He laughed sardonically when he was asked if he was working with anyone nationally known and replied, "There's nobody in Macon doing anything famous anymore."

Chuck Leavell lives on a large farm a few miles south of Macon, where he raises timber and is good enough at it to have been named Georgia's 1990 Tree Farmer of the Year. But farming is a sideline to his busy music schedule. Chuck spent much of 1991 and 1992 on the road with Eric Clapton, and there was another one of life's ironies for the man who had taken over Duane Allman's chair in the Allman Brothers — Duane had fueled Clapton's greatest album, *Layla*, and Chuck helped fuel Clapton's greatest album since, the marvelous *Unplugged*, which swept the Grammys in 1992. When the Rolling Stones got back together for the *Voodoo Lounge* album and tour in 1994, Chuck rejoined them. Chuck looks back on the Allman Brothers Band with bittersweet memories. "When I think of the Allman Brothers, I think of love," he said. "There was a lot of turmoil too. Sure, every family has its arguments; brothers and sisters fight with each other. But there was some true brotherly love there and I'm proud to say I was a part of it. I love them all now as much as I loved them then. Those were some beautiful times, man."

SHELLEY JEFTS smiled easily when she talked about Gregg, her eyes often sparkling at the good memories. "They say you have one great love in your life," she said. "And he was mine." Shelley now lives in Missouri with Devon and a daughter from her second marriage, and she is the editor of a weekly community newspaper. She hadn't seen Gregg for years when she went to an Allman Brothers concert at the Fox Theatre in St. Louis. When he saw Shelley backstage, Gregg walked over and kissed her on the cheek and said, "I want to thank you for being a good mother."

Nothing pleases her more than Devon's relationship with his father. "That is just a prayer that's been answered," she said. Devon went along as a support person when his father entered the drug rehab program in California with David Crosby's doctor in late 1992. "I hope Gregg is able to find some peace," Shelley said. "What's incredible to me is the potential that's there. If all of this is the product of someone who's been hiding behind drugs for years and years, what's really there? It'll be nice to see. Every time Gregg comes back to St. Louis, I try to go. He's always got some woman with him. Always. I'm amazed that he hadn't died from AIDS, first of all. And I've never been able to figure out why he always has to have someone. There's one thing I remember, something he hurled at me because he was trying to hurt me and it worked: 'The only reason I ever married you was because I was lonely; I don't like to be alone.' As I think back to how he's gone from one woman to another, I really think that's true. I don't think he can stand to be with Gregg. And I think that's part of the reason the drugs have always been there."

FOR Devon's nineteenth birthday, Gregg offered to get his son a recording contract. Devon turned him down. "I could have signed two years ago if I would do Southern rock and blues and done the Devon Allman Band," he said. "But I don't want to carry the weight of that around. I'm very proud of who my dad is but that would be too easy. I want to be me."

Devon met his half-brother, Elijah Blue Allman, on the *Seven Turns* tour in 1990 when Gregg invited both of them to travel with him. "I remember walking into the hotel, they got us a room together and Elijah was already booked in it," Devon said. "All the wives of the band, and the roadies, they were just kind of watching. They wanted to see us meet each other. And I just knocked on the door, he opened it up and the damn kid looked exactly like me. Exactly. I just said, 'Well, damn, what's up?' It was very cool."

Like Devon, Elijah Blue grew up with hardly any contact with his father. But as he became a teenager and took up the guitar, that changed. Elijah Blue has certainly inherited Gregg's mischievous side: he turned Gregg into a fretful parent when he announced that he wanted to get a tattoo of a Tide detergent box to cover his chest. He also has grown into a talented guitarist. Elijah Blue toured as a member of his mother's band in 1988 [Cher had the sense of humor to open her concerts with her own version of "I'm No Angel"], and he also sat in with the Allman Brothers at the Red Rocks amphitheater in Colorado. "He stood up and shook for part of it," Gregg said, laughing at the memory. "The last thing he said before he came onstage was, 'Dad, I've got to use the bathroom.' And I said, 'It's too late now.' He's a great player, a real good player."

Elijah Blue's big brother agreed with that assessment. "He's so talented," Devon said. "He really is. I wouldn't tell *him* that, you know. But he is great. He's got it if he wants to use it."

Devon and Elijah Blue aren't the only children of Allman Brothers members with talent. Michael Allman, Gregg's oldest son, sings and dreams of stardom. Duane Betts, Dickey's son with Paulette, is a talented guitarist, and Berry Oakley, Jr., plays the same kind of fierce, in-your-face bass that distinguished his father in a great new band called Bloodline. Butch's nephew, Derek Trucks, had barely reached puberty when he was out on the road playing bottleneck guitar in his own Southern rock band. He plays as though he was born with everything Duane knew about slide guitar and is already taking it further. It is a decidedly unnerving experience to watch the young boy with an Atlanta Braves baseball cap shyly slung low over his face, standing onstage playing a Gibson SG that seems bigger than he is and coaxing sounds out of it as though he is Duane Allman incarnate.

CONSIDERING everything that happened in 1993, it seemed something of a minor miracle that members of the Allman Brothers Band gathered in Florida in the early weeks of 1994 to begin work on a new album. But Dickey was sober and seemingly at peace with himself again, and Gregg was given an ultimatum: if he wanted the band to go forward, he had to clean up his act. Rather than go into a studio, the band decided to set up shop on a soundstage surrounded by cypress trees on actor Burt Reynolds's ranch in Jupiter. There were a couple of weeks of rehearsals; then a remote recording truck was brought in and set up, and the band cut all the tracks live.

Where It All Begins, released in May of 1994, was probably the most consistent of the studio albums that followed the reunion, and the decision to record live with few overdubs played up the band's improvisational strengths. The music has a strong rhythm base throughout and Warren's bottleneck is prominent on nearly every song. Warren also wrote one of the best songs on the album, the bluesy "Soulshine," and sang another.

But *Where It All Begins* belongs to Gregg and Dickey. Their songs document much of the turmoil that had dogged the band over the past eighteen months, and show a willingness to use the music to dissect deeply personal experiences and place them into perspective through the process of writing about them. Gregg's songs demonstrated that even if he hadn't completely escaped his demons, he was at least beginning to think seriously about them. "All Night Train" is a wonderful song, with Gregg using the train as his metaphor for getting high. The singer is warned by a doctor that he has to get off the "all night train," and the conclusion is sadly revealing — Gregg's confession that he began using drugs to keep from going insane, then found himself spending the rest of his life trying to escape from their stranglehold.

Most of Dickey's songs on the album concentrate on one theme: a man hitting the road in search of himself, trying to exorcise the ghosts that haunt him and find a way to start all over again. "No One to Run With" is a musical powerhouse, the Allman Brothers meet Bo Diddley, with a rollicking chug-a-lug fade-out.

Dickey contributed two other strong songs. "Change My Way of Living" is a mid-tempo shuffle with an irresistible chorus that he sings like a man with everything on the line. It is a plea to himself to gain some control over his life. "Change My Way of Living" was written before the incident in Saratoga Springs, and it becomes particularly poignant in light of what happened, as if Dickey saw it all coming.

"Back Where It All Begins" is the album's musical highlight, a song that features an adventurous instrumental section where Warren and Dickey both play long solos over ever-changing tempos. The song continues the theme of a man trying to escape from some unknown trouble, and the resolution is his decision that he must go back to where he began, to a mythological place where "we'll all be singing and we'll all be friends." For Dickey, for all of them, that place is the Allman Brothers Band.

THE band had been in New York City back in 1969 recording its debut album when the Woodstock Nation took over Max Yasgur's farm in upstate New York. They started to drive up to check it out, but when they saw all the traffic they said, "Fuck it" and turned back. Twenty-five years later, the Allman Brothers finally made it to Woodstock and came out roaring with the good-time groove of "Statesboro Blues." A couple of songs later, a kid with an Atlanta Braves hat pulled on backward walked out with a guitar to sit in with the band in front of the crowd of 300,000. When Duane Betts began an inaudible solo, Dickey's face flashed with paternal concern and he rushed over to fix his son's amplifier. And then Duane cut loose, playing melodic and bending lines that could have been his father on the guitar.

Judging from the audience response, the band was one of the hits of Woodstock '94 — on nearly every newscast at the close, when interviewers asked fans to name their favorite band, the Allman Brothers was invariably named. It was only fitting that the Allman Brothers Band was there to represent rock's "elders" at Woodstock '94. As the group entered its twenty-fifth year, its influence was all over the musical landscape. The band kicked off an entire music movement, and perhaps even more important, proved that a rock group from the South could stay true to its heritage and not have to move to New York or Los Angeles to become popular. By standing its ground, the band personified the resurgence of the New South and opened the door for every southern group that followed in its wake, from Lynyrd Skynyrd to R.E.M. to the Indigo Girls. The induction of the Allman Brothers Band into the Rock 'n' Roll Hall of Fame was a sweet vindication for a group that had been all but written off prior to the 1989 reunion.

The troubles have come and gone, but the one constant has always been the music. That was the gift that Duane Allman and Berry Oakley gave the others and it's the one thing the survivors carry with them — the sense of magic, "the fever" that so long ago caused Duane to bar the door after that first jam and say, "Anybody in this room who's not going to play in my band, you've got to fight your way out."

A couple of years before the 1989 reunion, someone asked Butch what the Allman Brothers Band meant to him. "Everything is wrapped up in that," he said. "Hell, it was a lifestyle, a religion, a family. The memories run the gamut — the pain of Duane and Berry, the fun and the excitement, the accomplishments. It was everything." Butch Trucks held a pensive look for a moment. Then he smiled broadly. "Except sex," he said. "That was on the side."

Acknowledgments

I first heard the music of the Allman Brothers Band growing up in Georgia and the moment of discovery is forever fresh in my mind — sitting in a friend's music room on a hot summer afternoon, with "Jessica" booming out of the speakers, and feeling like my very soul was being caressed. For those who were part of a generation coming of age in the South with a definite inferiority complex about their heritage, the Allman Brothers represented much more than just a great rock band. After a decade of being judged by the outside world through the horrific televised images from Birmingham and Memphis and Mississippi, the Allman Brothers and Jimmy Carter came along just when we needed new heroes. They epitomized what was right about the South and gave us a reason to feel proud again.

When newspapering brought me to Macon in 1983, it seemed only natural to begin writing about the Allman Brothers. It was a thrill to play Dickey's gold-top Les Paul while he patiently showed me the opening lines to "In Memory of Elizabeth Reed." I ate barbecue with Butch, rolling with laughter at his stories, and wound up playing guitar in a band with Jaimoe along with musicians who had backed up James Brown and Otis Redding. I learned that Gregg viewed interviews like many people view root canal surgery, and I once spent a week in Florida trying to get him to sit down and talk. This book has been a labor of love — writing about music that has made a difference in my life and the people who created it. But there is another appeal. For a journalist, the Allman Brothers Band offers one of the most fascinating stories in the history of rock 'n' roll. It has all the elements of great drama — love and death and courage and betrayal and survival.

Although the band members did not cooperate with the book, much of the material comes from extensive interviews that I conducted with them in the mid-1980s for the *Macon Telegraph and News*, and I want to thank them for their hospitality and candor. Through the years, I have talked with dozens of people within the Allman Brothers organization and fans who witnessed portions of the band's history. I want to thank them all for their help, insights, and, often, friendships, particularly Kim Payne, Johnny Sandlin, Paul Hornsby, Chuck Leavell, Candace Oakley, Phil Walden, Jerry Wexler, James Williams, Betty Williams, Warren Haynes, Kirk West, Willie Perkins, Alex Hodges, Melinda Trucks, Catherine Fellows and Cajai, Jeanne Fellows, Paulette Betts, Donna Betts, Toy Caldwell, Jimmy Hall, Dan Toler, Frankie Toler, Joe Dan Petty, Charlie Daniels, John Hammond, Jr., Scoots Lyndon, Joan Wooley Harris, Wayne Bennett, Ronnie Earl, Bob O'Dea, Bill Noonan, Bill Lynch, Buddy Johnstono, Howard Allman, Floyd Miles, Shelley Jefts, Devon Allman, Mary Ann Babic, Michael Babic, Sylvan Wells, Lee Hazen, Mike Stone, Van Harrison, Karl Richardson, Ron Albert, Bill Levenson, Marc Pucci, Roger Cowles, Tony Long, Freddie Horton, John Carey, Elliott Dunwody, Tony Cueto, Larry Checkett, Doug Wallis, Bob Johnson, Elaine Jones and Nora Paul at the clerk's office in U.S. District Court in Macon, the helpful staff at the Federal Records Center in Atlanta, the clerk's office in Los Angeles Superior Court, Norma Weart of the *Buffalo News* library, Peggy Deans Earle at the *Virginian-Pilot* and *Ledger-Star* library in Norfolk, and the late Jim Higgins.

Thanks also to Denney Chasteen, Brian Heatherington, Ron Harrell, Kathy Lyles, Curtis Watson, Sadie Estep, Susan Oxenrider, Dora Byron, Robin Stacy, Allen Gunter, Audrey Post, Jodi White, Fred Keirs, Richard Toomey, Ken "Little Bear" Dyer, Jay Bolotin, Eleanor McCarthy, Hilary Horton, Jeff Hiday, Ken Mingis, Tony DePaul, G. Wayne Miller, Anne and Fred Richards, and William S. Doxey.

Also, thanks to those at the *Telegraph* who encouraged me to follow my muse: Roger Bull, Barbara Stinson, Tethel Brown, Rick Thomas, Ron Woodgeard, Oby Brown, and all my friends there. At the *Providence Journal*, Carol J. Young, James Wyman, and Andy Burkhardt were wonderfully supportive.

For help and support over and beyond the call of duty, special thanks to Hewell Middleton, Carrolle King, Susan Cute, Christopher Cute, Ken Lyon, Alice Lyon, the Tombstone Blues Band, Judge O. Rogeriee Thompson, Bill Malinowski, Mary Murphy, Tim Barmann, Lynn Arditi, Linda Henderson, Peer Ravnan of the Middle Georgia Archives, Marty Willett and Surelle Pinkston and Barron Ruth and the others with the Georgia Allman Brothers Band Association, Maryann Bates, Larry D. Wilder, Susan Parker, Susan Cole, Donna Higgins,

William Berry, Virginia Schenk Berry, Paul Hemphill, Julie Barnes Sanders, Mark Sennott, and Suzanne Espinosa.

Also, my deep appreciation to my agent, Connie Clausen, who made the dream come true, and her assistants, Amy Fastenberg and Genevieve Field. Also to Michael Pietsch, who was a wonderful editor to work with, and his assistants, Laura K. Barnes and Jeremy Fields. And thanks to Michael Brandon and Pamela Marshall for the sharp copyediting, and to Barbara Werden, who designed the book, and Mary Reilly, who designed the insert.

And most of all, thanks to my father, Wilson C. Freeman, for the ideals he helped nurture, and to my family for their love and support.

Macon, Georgia
August 1994

Sources

I FIRST began writing about the Allman Brothers Band in 1983 as a reporter at the *Macon Telegraph and News,* and many of the interviews for this book come from research I did for articles. All four of the surviving original members agreed to extensive interviews in 1984 for the fifteenth anniversary of the Allman Brothers, and it was a perfect time — the band had split up, no one was optimistic that they would ever get back together, and they seemed free to be far more reflective and candid than they might have otherwise been. I have drawn on that wealth of information in addition to new research that I conducted specifically for the book. All told, I have talked to nearly one hundred people, and most of them are listed in the acknowledgments. I have used a minimum of unidentified sources in the book, and only those who have given me consistently reliable information through the years and sought anonymity because of their continuing relationships with band members.

Also important in the research of this book was court records. I reviewed tens of thousands of pages of documents, transcripts, and depositions from courthouses and record centers across the country. There are instances in which scenes and dialogue are re-created. Those come from several sources: I witnessed some myself, some come from court testimony, some were depicted in magazine articles, and others are based upon interviews with at least one person who was either present or, in a few cases, heard about an event firsthand from a participant.

The Middle Georgia Archives of the Washington Memorial Library in Macon has nearly every printed word that has ever been written about the band, and I drew extensively from its collection. The *Macon Telegraph and News* library was a valuable source of information in virtually every chapter of the book. And the news libraries of the

Providence Journal-Bulletin, Norfolk Virginian-Pilot and *Ledger-Star,* and the *Buffalo News* also were invaluable.

ARTICLES

Anson, Robert Sam. "The Capricorn Connection." *New Times,* September 3, 1976.

Bell, Joe. "Warren Haynes Interview." *Hittin' the Note,* Summer 1993.

Booth, Frank. "Devon Lane Allman." *Tattoo,* March 1993.

Cain, Scott. "Allman Concert Breaks Records." *The Atlanta Constitution,* June 9, 1974.

Cahill, Tim. "A Tale of Two Tours." *Rolling Stone,* January 16, 1973.

Crowe, Cameron. "The Allman Brothers Story." *Rolling Stone,* December 6, 1973.

———. "The South Also Rises." *Rolling Stone,* March 14, 1974.

Duncan, Robert. "Rhett Butler After the Fall: Dickey Betts Brushes Himself Off." *Creem,* March 1977.

Dupree, Tom. "Elvin Bishop: Gettin' Loose Down South." *Rolling Stone,* July 4, 1974.

Dzeiggel, Oliver C. "The Layla Sessions." *Guitar Player,* November 1990.

Ector, Bill. "Allen Woody Interview." *Hittin' the Note,* Fall 1993.

Fahey, Jym. "Gregg Allman: A Voice from Our Times." *Relix,* August 1993.

———. "Warren Haynes." *Relix,* April 1992.

Ferris, Timothy. "The Fillmore East Closes. More. More." *Rolling Stone,* July 22, 1971.

Findelle, Stann. "The Strange Saga of Brother Gregg." *New Music Express,* December 6, 1975.

Fish, Scott F., and Bill Grillo. "Madness from the South: An Interview with Butch Trucks and Jaimoe Johnson of the Allman Brothers Band." *Modern Drummer,* May 1981.

Flippo, Chet. "Chet Atkins; The *Rolling Stone* Interview." *Rolling Stone,* February 12, 1976.

———. "Getting By Without the Allmans." *Creem.* November 1974.

———. "Playin' Up a Storm." *Rolling Stone,* July 28, 1977.

Forte, Dan. "The Eric Clapton Story." *Guitar Player,* July 1985.

———. "Pro's Reply; Lamar Williams." *Guitar Player,* July 1977.

Gilmore, Mikal. "The Allman Brothers." *Rolling Stone,* October 18, 1990.

Glover, Tony. "The Allman Brothers Are Back in the Game." *Rolling Stone,* November 6, 1975.

———. "Duane Allman: An Anthology." Capricorn Records, 1972.

Harris, Art. "Singing in the Rain." *Rolling Stone,* July 4, 1974.

———. "Waiting for Gregg: Slow Beat in Macon." *The Atlanta Constitution,* August 6, 1975.

Hedgepath, William. "Phil Walden Reinvents Himself." *Southern,* n.d.

Helland, Dave. "Vassar the Rockojazz Fiddler." *Rolling Stone*, August 14, 1975.

Hilburn, Robert. "Gregg Allman Walked Rocky Road." *Los Angeles Times*, October 2, 1976.

Jarrett, Sandra. "Gregg Allman: Life in the Fast Lane." *Singles Country*, December 1983.

Jerome, Jim. "The Allman Band Is Gone, but for Southern Boogie the Best Betts Is Still Dickey." *People*, May 1977.

———. "The Allman Brothers Finally Buries the Hatchet — And Not in One Another." *People*, February 12, 1979.

———. "Cher & Gregg: She Helps Him Stay Off Heroin and His Band Is Hot Again." *People*, September 8, 1975.

King, Bill. "The Enlightened Rogues Return." *Atlanta Journal and Constitution*, February 24, 1979.

———. "The Return of Butch Trucks." *Atlanta Constitution*, October 7, 1977.

Landau, Jon. "Bandleader Duane Allman Dies in Bike Crash." *Rolling Stone*, November 25, 1971.

Lewis, Grover. "Hittin' the Note." *Rolling Stone*, November 25, 1971.

Mandel, Ellen. "The Georgia Peach." *Guitar World*, November 1991.

McGee, David. "Jaded and Joyless in Jersey: The Allman Bros. Draw a Blank." *Rolling Stone*, October 23, 1975.

Mitchell, Mark. "Dickey Betts." *Prime Cuts*, n.d.

Nolan, Tom. "Playin' Up a Storm: Gregg Allman Reveals High Pressure Zone." *The Waxtower*, May 27, 1977.

Obrecht, Jas. "Dickey Betts 1989." *Guitar Player*, August 1989.

———. "Duane Allman Remembered." *Guitar Player*, October 1981.

———. "Layla." *Guitar Player*, July 1985.

———. "Slide Summit: The Allman Brothers Band and Little Feat." *Guitar Player*, November 1992.

Olsen, Stan. "The Allman Brothers Band." *Spec's Rhythm & Views*, August 1991.

Oney, Steve. "A Sinner's Second Chance." *Esquire*, November 1984.

Palmer, Robert. "The Allman Brothers: A Great Southern Revival." *Rolling Stone*, May 3, 1979.

———. "A Band That Gave an Age of Excess a Good Name." *New York Times*, June 25, 1989.

———. "Clapton, The Man and His Music." *Rolling Stone*, April 29, 1993.

Paul, Alan. "Live & Well." *Guitar World*, July 1994.

———. "Wylde & Free." *Guitar World*, July 1994.

Pollack, Phyllis. "Gregg Allman: Talking with the Midnight Rider." *Rocky Road*, December 15, 1983.

"R&B Sax Master King Curtis Dies." *Rolling Stone*, September 16, 1971.

Rehfeld, Barry. "When the Voices Took Over." *Rolling Stone*, June 6, 1985.

Robicheau, Paul. "Capturing the Allmans Live." *Boston Globe*, April 3, 1992.

Ross-Leming, Eugenie, and David Standish. "Playboy Interview: Cher." *Playboy*, October 1975.

Rutkoski, Rex. "Dickey Betts." *Rag*, n.d.

Sacks, Leo. "I Call (and Call) on the Allman Brothers." *Rolling Stone*, July 18, 1974.

Santelli, Robert. "Butch Trucks & Jaimoe: Brothers Reunited." *Modern Drummer*, March 1991.

Santoro, Gene. "The Layla Sessions." *The Layla Sessions: 20th Anniversary Edition*. Polydor, 1991.

Scheff, David. "Playboy Interview: David Geffen." *Playboy*, September 1994.

Schickel, David, et al. "Glad Rags to Riches." *Time*, March 17, 1975.

Schwartz, Jim. "Sea Level: Rock, Funk, and Blues from the South." *Guitar Player*, January 1980.

Shaw, Russell. "A Conversation with Gregg Allman." *Oui*, August 1979.

Siegel, Joel. "Watkins Glen Jam Tops Woodstock: 600,000 Fans." *Rolling Stone*, August 30, 1975.

Slater, Andrew. "Gregg Allman Boogies Past a Painful Past." *U.S.A. Today*, March 21, 1983.

Snyder, Patrick. "The Sorrowful Confessions of Gregg Allman." *Rolling Stone*, November 4, 1976.

Staff, *Daytona Beach Sunday News Journal*, August 5, 1973.

Steinblatt, Harold. "Dickey Betts' Revival." *Guitar World*, March 1989.

Stix, John. "Blues Brothers." *Guitar*, September 1987.

Swenson, John. "The Allman Brothers' Blazing Comeback." *Rolling Stone*, May 31, 1979.

———. "Dreams." *Dreams*. Polydor, 1989.

Uhelszki, Jaan. "To Beat the Devil: The Allman Brothers Comin' Round Again." *Creem*, December 1975.

Walburn, Steve. "Phil Walden: Flip Side." *Atlanta*, August 1993.

Whitehall, Dave. "The Art of the Jam." *Guitar World*, December 1991.

Wilkins, Barbara. "The Cher and Gregg 'Soap Opera' Finds a New Time Slot: The Family Hour." *People*, September 27, 1976.

BOOKS

The Allman Brothers Band. *The Allman Brothers Band Complete* (music transcriptions). New York: No Exit Music Company/Warner Bros. Publications Inc., 1974.

Bono, Sonny. *And the Beat Goes On*. New York: Pocket Books, 1991.

Booth, Stanley. *Rythm Oil: A Journey Through the Music of the American South*. London: Jonathan Cape, 1991.

———. *The True Adventures of the Rolling Stones*. New York: Vintage Books, 1984.

Branch, Taylor. *Parting the Waters: America in the King Years 1954–63*. New York: Simon & Schuster, 1988.

Charters, Samuel. *Robert Johnson*. New York: Oak Publications, 1973.

Clapton, Eric. *Eric Clapton Deluxe* (music transcriptions). New York: Chappell & Co., 1978.

Coleman, Ray. *Clapton!* New York: Warner Books, 1985.

Davis, Miles, and Quincy Troupe. *Miles*. New York: Touchstone, 1989.

The Editors of Rolling Stone. *Rock Almanac, the Chronicles of Rock & Roll*. New York: Rolling Stone Press/Collier Books, 1983.

Flanagan, Bill. *Written in my Soul*. Chicago: Contemporary Books Inc., 1987.

Graham, Bill, and Robert Greenfield. *Bill Graham Presents: My Life Inside Rock and Out*. New York: Doubleday, 1992.

Guralnick, Peter. *Feel Like Goin' Home*. New York: Harper and Row, 1971.

———. *Lost Highway: Journeys & Arrivals of American Musicians*. Boston: David R. Godine, 1979.

———. *Searching For Robert Johnson*. New York: E. P. Dutton, 1989.

———. *Sweet Soul Music, Rhythm and Blues and the Southern Dream of Freedom*. New York: Harper and Row, 1986.

Hemphill, Paul. *The Good Old Boys*. New York: Simon and Schuster, 1974.

———. *The Nashville Sound: Bright Lights and Country Music*. New York: Simon and Schuster, 1970.

———. *Too Old to Cry*. New York: The Viking Press, 1981.

Lowry, Beverly. *Crossed Over; A Murder, A Memoir*. New York: Alfred A. Knopf, 1992.

Marsh, Dave. *Born to Run: The Bruce Springsteen Story*. New York: Dell Publishing Co., Inc., 1981.

Nolan, Tom. *The Allman Brothers Band: A Biography in Words and Pictures*. New York: Chappell Music Co., 1976.

Palmer, Robert. *Deep Blues*. New York: Viking Press, 1981.

Patoski, Joe Nick, and Bill Crawford. *Stevie Ray Vaughan: Caught in the Crossfire*. New York: Little, Brown & Co., 1993.

Payne, Calder W. *Rose Hill Rambles*. Macon: Middle Georgia Historical Society, Inc., 1985.

Taraborrelli, J. Randy. *Cher, A Biography*. New York: St. Martin's Press, 1986.

Weil, Andrew. *The Natural Mind: An Investigation of Drugs and the Higher Consciousness*. New York: Houghton Mifflin Co., 1986.

Weinberg, Max, and Robert Santelli. *The Big Beat: Conversations with Rock's Great Drummers*. New York: Billboard Books, 1991.

Wheeler, Tom. *American Guitars: An Illustrated History*. New York: Harper and Row, 1982.

Wooten, James. *Dasher: The Roots and Rising of Jimmy Carter.* New York: Warner Books, 1979.

Zalkind, Ronald. *Contemporary Music Almanac 1980/81.* New York: Schirmer Books, 1980.

COURT CASES

U.S. District Court, Macon District

United States vs. Gregg Allman
United States vs. Joe G. Fuchs
United States vs. John C. Herring
United States vs. Julian E. Seymour
United States vs. John Clayborn Hawkins, et al.
Claude H. Trucks vs. Phil Walden
Clarence G. Carter vs. Redwal Music and Phil Walden
Northern Songs, Ltd. vs. Redwal Music and Phil Walden
Camille Hope vs. Phil Walden
Bankruptcy Papers of Capricorn Records

Bibb County (Macon) Superior Court

Donna Allman vs. Duane Allman
Gregg Allman vs. Shelley Allman
Shelley Allman vs. Gregg Allman
Janice B. Allman vs. Gregg Allman
Gregg Allman vs. Cherilyn LaPierre Sarkisian Allman
Brothers Properties Incorporation records
Matthews, Holliday, Couch & Hollis vs. Claude H. Trucks
Johnny Sandlin vs. Capricorn Records
Charles A. Leavell vs. Brothers Properties, d.b.a. the Allman Brothers Band
Sea Level vs. Capricorn Records
C&S Bank vs. Brothers Properties
Candace Oakley Johnson vs. Jaimoe Johnson
Jaimoe Johnson vs. Candace Oakley Johnson
Marian Williams vs. Lamar Williams
Michael S. Odom vs. Lamar Williams
Commerce Union Bank vs. Phil Walden and Peggy Walden
State of Georgia vs. Frank Dale McCall and Larry Davis

Bibb County Probate Court

Estate of Howard Duane Allman
Estate of Raymond Berry Oakley III
Estate of Lamar Williams
Marriage Licenses

Bibb County State Court

Dixie Allman vs. Sam Hall & Sons and Charles Wertz
Galadriel Allman vs. Dixie Allman vs. Sam Hall & Sons and Charles Wertz
Leo Asimacopoulos vs. Richard Betts

Jones County (Georgia) Superior Court

Sandra W. Betts vs. Dickey Betts
Linda Elizabeth Trucks vs. Butch Trucks
The State vs. Andrew J. Ritchie

American Arbitration Association

Forrest Richard Betts vs. Capricorn Records

U.S. Bankruptcy Court, Nashville, Tennessee

Bankruptcy papers of Phil Walden

New York Supreme Court

Forrest R. B. Enterprises vs. Capricorn Records

Sarasota County (Florida) Court

Dale Betts vs. Forrest Betts
Paulette Betts vs. Richard Betts
Forrest Richard Betts, UCC Financing Statement
Sarasota County Public Hospital vs. Gregg and Julie Allman
Sarasota County Public Hospital vs. Gregg Allman
Elaina Louis Abdul vs. Gregg Allman
Gregory Allman vs. Julie Allman
Internal Revenue Service vs. Gregg Allman
Real Estate Records
Marriage Licenses

Bradenton County (Florida) Court

Internal Revenue Service vs. Dickey and Paulette Betts
Real Estate Records
Marriage Licenses
Service Records

Los Angeles County Superior Court

Cher, formerly known as Cher Bono Allman, vs. Gregg Allman

MISCELLANEOUS SOURCES

Resume, Butch Trucks.
Duane Allman Dialogues, Capricorn Records (1972).
Macon Police Department records concerning Duane Allman accident.
Macon Police Department records concerning Berry Oakley accident.
Jim Ladd's "Innerview" radio program with guest Dickey Betts, circa 1977.
"The Inside Track with Graham Nash," USA Network, 1990.

Selected Discography

There are literally dozens of recordings with performances by members of the Allman Brothers Band or other artists and bands from Macon. What follows is a list of records that I would recommend to people interested in the Allman Brothers and the Southern sound in general. Many of the records that influenced the members of the Allman Brothers are included. Some of these albums are no longer in print, although many are being reissued in various forms on compact discs; they can also be found in used-record stores.

EARLY INCARNATIONS
The Allman Joys

Early Allman (Dial, 1973). Duane and Gregg's studio sessions from Bradley's Barn, and their earliest professional recordings. This one's for die-hard fans only, more as a curio than anything else.

Hour Glass

Hour Glass (Liberty, 1968); *Power of Love* (Liberty, 1969). Both these albums have been rereleased on compact disc. The first is a virtual wasteland; the second is more interesting. The CD version has several bonus tracks, which Johnny Sandlin thinks must have come from sessions after the rest of the band left Los Angeles and Gregg stayed behind.

The 31st of February

Duane and Gregg Allman (Bold, 1973). Never intended for release, these sessions mark Duane and Gregg's brief tenure with Butch's band.

THE ALLMAN BROTHERS BAND

Beginnings (Capricorn, 1973). A repackaging of the first two studio albums on one compact disc, this is an essential recording for any Allman Brothers fan. The band had yet to learn how to really cook in the studio, but both albums are filled with definitive moments.

At Fillmore East (Capricorn, 1971). If you buy any Allman Brothers album, this is the one. The band at its full glory with daring improvisation that invokes the spirits of Miles Davis and John Coltrane. A classic, one of the great live albums in modern music history.

Eat a Peach (Mobile Fidelity Sound Lab, 1972). The difference in sonic quality between this version and the Polydor counterpart is well worth the extra money the gold-plated MFSL version costs. *Eat a Peach* is basically the *At Fillmore East, Part 2*, and is an essential companion to the live album. Duane's performance at the end of "Mountain Jam" carries a sad beauty; he may have sounded as good, but never better.

Brothers and Sisters (Capricorn, 1973). The sound quality on the CD leaves much to be desired, but it is still one of the band's great studio records, the first full album in the wake of the accidents of Duane and Berry. Chuck Leavell's performance on "Jessica" is worth the price alone, and it also contains the band's hit single "Ramblin' Man."

Win, Lose or Draw (Capricorn, 1975). The Allman Brothers Band in serious decline.

Wipe the Windows, Check the Oil, Dollar Gas (Capricorn, 1976). The album sounds as though it was released because Capricorn needed a quick infusion of cash, yet it stands up better than anyone could have expected. There are times when the old magic clicks in, like Chuck Leavell's solo on "In Memory of Elizabeth Reed" and Dickey Betts's guitar work and vocals on "Ramblin' Man."

Enlightened Rogues (Capricorn, 1979). A noble comeback album from the first reunion. The quality of the music and the performances doesn't reach the level of *Brothers and Sisters*, but it is the only album worth having from this third version of the Allman Brothers.

Reach for the Sky (Arista, 1980); *Brothers of the Road* (Arista, 1981). You can count the number of good performances from both albums on one hand. For true believers only.

Dreams (Polydor, 1989). The boxed set that helped revive the Allman Brothers Band. Some of the choices are questionable — like the quadrophonic mixes of "Elizabeth Reed" and "Whipping Post" from the Fillmore shows (why not unreleased versions?) — but for the most part there is little to quibble with and much to appreciate. The versions of "You Don't Love Me/Soul Serenade" and "Drunken Hearted Boy" are great finds, as are the unreleased studio versions of "Statesboro Blues" and "Dreams." The booklet is informative and packed with great photos.

Seven Turns (Epic, 1990). A wonderful comeback after a nine-year absence. The addition of Warren Haynes elevated the band, and everyone plays as though he means it for the first time in years. The title track is one of Dickey's great songs.

The Allman Brothers Band at Ludlow Garage 1970 (Polydor, 1990). The sound
   quality leaves much to be desired but this is a crucial missing link in the
   evolution of the Allman Brothers, a concert recorded not long after the first
   album and before the group had really jelled into a definitive live band.
   The version of "Statesboro Blues" is unlike any other that Duane performed and reason enough to justify the album. The band also performed
   an early version of "Elizabeth Reed" at the show, but it was inexplicably
   left off the compact disc.

Shades of Two Worlds (Epic, 1991). Another essential album, it takes the foundation laid by *Seven Turns* and raises the stakes considerably. The band
   doesn't get much better than "End of the Line," "Come On in My
   Kitchen," and, especially, "Nobody Knows."

An Evening with the Allman Brothers Band (Epic, 1992). With a little more care,
   this could have been the album it deserved to be. Instead, it is a mixed
   package. But when it is good, it is very, very good.

The Fillmore Concerts (Polydor, 1992). Despite its good intentions, a set to
   avoid. The mixes are revisionistic — Duane's guitar is lowered to the point
   that he can't be heard in places and Berry's bass is no longer in the forefront driving the band. It's a shame because it's great to have the entire
   Fillmore set on two compact discs, and the drum sound is a vast improvement over the original *Fillmore* album. Not enough care and thought was
   put into the package. For example, what's the most famous concert request
   from the seventies? The call for "Whipping Post" from the *Fillmore* album.
   It's not even on this version.

Where It All Begins (Epic, 1994). The latest studio album. Lacks the peaks of
   Shades of Two Worlds, but it is a consistent record with some solid performances and songwriting.

SOLO ALBUMS
Duane Allman

An Anthology (Capricorn, 1972); *An Anthology Volume II* (Capricorn, 1974). The
   first volume of this set is a must-have, and includes many of the greatest
   performances of Duane's studio days, especially the great take on "Hey
   Jude" with Wilson Pickett and "Goin' Down Slow" from his aborted solo
   album. The second disc is worthwhile as well, if only for Duane's great
   bottleneck on Delaney and Bonnie's acoustic version of "Come On in My
   Kitchen."

Gregg Allman

Laid Back (Capricorn, 1973). Some of Gregg's finest moments, with a sound and
   a mood that still sounds fresh today. Gregg and Johnny Sandlin went into the
   studio with the intention of making a great album and succeeded. Essential.

The Gregg Allman Tour (Capricorn, 1974). A solid live album from Gregg's first solo tour. The covers of "Turn On Your Love Light" and "Feel So Bad" are pleasant surprises.

Playin' Up a Storm (Capricorn, 1977). Gregg's voice is enthralling and the song selection is tasteful. But the backing is so slick that it is a distraction.

I'm No Angel (Epic, 1987); *Just Before the Bullets Fly* (Epic, 1988). For die-hard diehards only.

Dickey Betts

Highway Call (Capricorn, 1974). An underrated album that showcases Dickey's superb country instincts. Essential.

Dickey Betts and Great Southern (Arista, 1977); *Atlanta's Burning Down* (Arista, 1978). Of the two, the first album is the more interesting. But Great Southern was not a band that brought out the best in Dickey Betts.

Pattern Disruptive (Epic, 1988). Better than the two Great Southern albums; well worth having.

Sea Level

Sea Level (Capricorn, 1977). The original quartet and probably the best of the spate of solo albums following the first breakup of the Allman Brothers. Chuck Leavell's piano is a pure joy.

Cats on the Coast (Capricorn, 1977). Randall Bramblett and Davis Causey join the mix, and Jaimoe plays a little percussion before leaving to rejoin the Allman Brothers. Included is the closest thing Sea Level had to a hit single, the quirky and memorable "That's Your Secret."

On the Edge (Capricorn, 1978); *Long Walk on a Short Pier* (Polydor, 1979); *Ball Room* (Arista, 1980). These are all musically sound, but none were the breakthroughs the band had hoped for. Much of the Sea Level catalog is out of print, but Polydor has issued a "Best of" on compact disc.

Warren Haynes

Tales of Ordinary Madness (Megaforce, 1993). Warren had been planning this solo album even before joining the Allman Brothers. A strong debut from a major talent.

NOTABLE APPEARANCES
Derek and the Dominoes

The Layla Sessions: 20th Anniversary Edition (Polydor, 1990). If only all boxed sets were this lovingly put together; the packaging even includes copies of the original mixing board notes of Tom Dowd. But the most important thing is the powerful sound in the remix of the original session tapes. For the first time, the guitars are given clarity and you can clearly pick out which lick is Duane and which is Eric Clapton; the results are often quite surprising. The mix is revisionist but outstanding, with the good taste to boost Duane on nearly every track. Essential. The original compact disc issued by Polydor should be avoided.

Boz Scaggs

Boz Scaggs (Atlantic, 1969). One of Duane's finest session gigs. It includes the best mix of "Loan Me a Dime" — one of the definitive white-blues performances and one of Duane's definitive guitar solos. Essential.

Ronnie Hawkins

Ronnie Hawkins (Cotillion, 1970). Includes a searing version of "Down in the Alley," sparked by one of Duane's best-ever bottleneck rides, and Dylan's "One Too Many Mornings" with some nice Dobro by Duane.

Delaney and Bonnie

To Bonnie from Delaney (Atco, 1970). Duane plays bottleneck on several tracks, including a wonderful medley that includes Robert Johnson's "Come On in My Kitchen" and Woody Guthrie's "Goin' Down the Road Feeling Bad."

Motel Shot (Atco, 1971). Duane plays acoustic bottleneck on full versions of "Come On in My Kitchen" and "Goin' Down the Road Feeling Bad." It also has their fluke hit, "Never Ending Song of Love."

The Best of Delaney and Bonnie (Rhino, 1990). A good compilation, though Duane is on only a few tracks.

Herbie Mann

Push Push (Embryo, 1989). The reissue on compact disc contains an unreleased track. Worth having if you want to hear Duane in a jazz context, but disappointing overall.

John Hammond

I Can Tell (Atlantic, 1992). This CD reissue is primarily made up of tracks cut with Robbie Robertson on the guitar, but includes four cuts from the *Southern Fried* album that was recorded in Muscle Shoals with Duane on lead guitar.

Eric Clapton

Unplugged (Reprise, 1992). Clapton's best work in years, propelled by the beautiful piano of Chuck Leavell. On the video, you can see Clapton responding with awe at the conclusion of Chuck's incredible solo on "Old Love." He helped bring out the best in Clapton on record in a way no fellow musician had since Duane Allman.

Rolling Stones

A Rock and a Hard Place/Fancy Man Blues (Atlantic, 1989). The B-side of this single is Chuck's favorite cut from the *Steel Wheels* sessions, and he was sorely disappointed that it was left off the album. It is a great track, and the Stones let Chuck take center stage. The video of a pay-per-view concert from Atlantic City in 1989 is also worth finding; Chuck's piano is prominent in the mix and his rhythm work is a pleasure throughout the concert. It also features Eric Clapton sitting in on "Little Red Rooster."

Voodoo Lounge (Virgin, 1994). Chuck is buried in most of the mixes, but he plays gorgeous piano on "Out of Tears" and harpsichord on "New Faces."

INFLUENCES

Robert Johnson

The Complete Recordings (Columbia, 1990). A brilliant reissue of every known Robert Johnson recording. For all practical purposes, this is where the modern blues began. The songs are still as powerful and eerie today as they must have been fifty years ago.

Blind Willie McTell

1927–33: The Early Years (Yazoo, 1968). Blind Willie's original version of "Statesboro Blues" and a dozen more classic ragtime blues songs from one of the greats.

Atlanta Twelve String (Atlantic, 1972). Recorded in 1949, this reissue includes the original version of "Blues at Midnight." For a modern interpretation of that song, try *Gamblin' Woman Blues* (Red House, 1993) by Paul Geremia, maybe the best white ragtime-blues player alive.

Tampa Red

The Guitar Wizard: 1935–53 (Blues Classics, 1973). One of the pioneers of the modern bottleneck, a Georgia native who gained his fame in Chicago. A classic record.

T-Bone Walker

Dirty Mistreater (MCA, 1983); *Classics of Modern Blues* (Blue Note, 1975); *T-Bone's Blues* (Atlantic, 1989). It's hard to go wrong with T-Bone. All of these reissues give testament to his greatness. *T-Bone's Blues* includes "Stormy Monday Blues" and *Classics* is a two-record set of songs he cut for Imperial in the fifties.

Sonny Boy Williamson

One Way Out (Carosello, 1980). Classic sides he recorded with Robert Jr. Lockwood (Robert Johnson's stepson and an accomplished player in his own right), Luther Tucker, Otis Spann, and Willie Dixon in the backup band.

Elmore James

King of the Slide Guitar (Capricorn, 1992). One of Capricorn's first releases in its second incarnation, this boxed set chronicles the raucous electric slide player who took Robert Johnson and turned him up to eleven on an amplifier. It includes the essential versions of "The Sky Is Crying," "Dust My Broom," "Done Somebody Wrong," and "It Hurts Me Too."

Bobby "Blue" Bland

Two Steps from the Blues (MCA, 1973). One of Gregg's heroes, and an album chock-full of powerful performances ranging from the title cut to "St. James Infirmary" to "I Pity the Fool."

The Best of Bobby Bland (MCA, 1973). The version of "Stormy Monday" that inspired the arrangement on the *Fillmore East* album, plus the original of "Turn On Your Love Light" that Gregg performed in Lee Hazen's kitchen and later used on his first solo tour. An album that was an inspiration to a whole generation of white kids who turned on to r&b music.

Little Willie John

Grits and Soul (Charley). The original version of "Need Your Love So Bad."

Little Milton

Greatest Hits (Chess, 1972). Another one of Gregg's heroes, and an interesting cross between blues artist and soul crooner.

Clarence Carter

Soul Deep (Edsel, 1984). The best from one of the great soul singers, and another major influence on Gregg. Includes the original versions of "Slip Away" and "That Old Time Feeling," which was somehow renamed "Sweet Feeling" on *Playin' Up a Storm*. A warning: Duane's psychedelic bottleneck solo on "Road of Love" has been edited out of the version included on this album.

Ray Charles

Ingredients in a Recipe for Soul (DCC Compact Classics, 1990). If "In the Evening" doesn't grab your soul, then nothing will. Also includes great versions of "Over the Rainbow," "Ol' Man River," and "Busted." This CD version has the original of "The Brightest Smile in Town" that Gregg recorded with Dr. John on *Playin' Up a Storm*.

Ray Charles Live (Atlantic, 1973). A double-album set of live albums recorded at the Newport Jazz Festival in 1958 and in Atlanta in 1959. "Drown in My Own Tears" is as good as it gets.

Genius + Soul = Jazz (Sandstone Music, 1988). Originally released in 1961, this classic includes the original version of "I'm Gonna Move to the Outskirts of Town." Gregg used to play this album incessantly.

Taj Mahal

Taj Mahal (Columbia, 1967). Includes the version of "Statesboro Blues" with Jesse Ed Davis that Duane used to teach himself to play the bottleneck guitar. The backup band also includes a rhythm guitarist named Ryland P. Cooder, who would go on to build something of a reputation on slide himself.

Miles Davis

Kind of Blue (Columbia, 1959). The remixing for the compact disc isn't the greatest, although the record label is now selling a higher-priced version that supposedly corrects the sonic deficiencies. Still, what rich music, with a chameleonlike sound that seems to correspond to any mood. Many consider this the greatest jazz album in history, and it's hard to argue the point. Also try *Someday My Prince Will Come* (Columbia, 1962), *'58 Sessions* (Columbia, 1991), and *'Round About Midnight* (Columbia, 1956).

John Coltrane

Giant Steps (Atlantic, 1960); *My Favorite Things* (Atlantic, 1961). Outside of his sessions with Miles Davis, this is Coltrane at his most accessible. What imagination, to hear Julie Andrews sing "My Favorite Things" and envision it as a jazz piece; it was one of Duane's favorite Coltrane performances.

King Curtis

Live at Fillmore West (Atco, 1971). This is probably King Curtis's greatest album and virtually impossible to find. A true story: I'm in Paris, on my way to Père-Lachaise Cemetery to see the grave of Jim Morrison when I pass by a little r&b record store called DomiSoul on a side street. I walk inside and, a couple of minutes later, I'm holding this album in my hand. I turn around to the owner and tell him that I've been looking for this record for years. The store is empty, and we begin talking about old r&b music. He abruptly grabs the album out of my hands. I'm momentarily stunned — those rude French, you know — until I see him bop behind the counter and slap the album on a turntable. Then he cranks the volume. Moments later, we are dancing to the heart-throbbing horns on "Memphis Soul Stew." What a backup band: Macon's Jerry Jemmott on bass, Bernard Purdee on drums, Cornell Dupree on guitar, Billy Preston on organ, and the Memphis Horns. Recorded the same night as an Aretha Franklin live album that features a legendary guest appearance by Ray Charles, which has just been reissued on compact disc.

The Best of King Curtis (Capitol, 1989); *Instant Groove* (Edsel, 1990); *Blues at Montreux* (with Champion Jack Dupree; Atlantic, 1973). The first two albums are studio tracks that give a good overview of King's brilliant saxophone sound. The last is a very loose live album that still cooks.

SOUTHERN-FRIED MUSIC
Little Richard

The Specialty Sessions (Specialty, 1990). A wop bop a lubop a lop bam boom!

James Brown

Greatest Hits (Rhino, 1985). The best of the Godfather of Soul, from "Please, Please, Please," the song originally recorded in the studio of Macon radio station WIBB, to "Papa's Got a Brand New Bag" and "I Feel Good."
Live and Lowdown at the Apollo (Solid Smoke, 1980). The record label really says it all. The Godfather at his peak.

Otis Redding

Otis! The Definitive Otis Redding (Rhino/Atlantic and Atco Remasters Series, 1993). A definitive boxed set from the King of Soul. If you haven't discovered the magic of Otis Redding, this is the way to do it.
Otis Blue (Atco, 1965). Perhaps his finest single album, with songs that include "Respect," "I've Been Loving You Too Long," and "Satisfaction." Especially poignant is the tender desperation in his reading of Sam Cooke's "A Change Is Gonna Come."

The Rev. Pearly Brown

It's a Mean Old World to Try to Live In (Rounder, 1975). The famous Macon street singer — pictured on the cover of Wet Willie's *Keep On Smilin'* album — plays blues, traditional slave songs, and gospel.

Johnny Jenkins

Ton-Ton Macoute! (Capricorn, 1974). Duane plays on several tracks, a couple of which were actually left over from the Muscle Shoals sessions for his solo album, with Johnny's vocals just put on top. Duane's performance on "Rollin' Stone" is breathtaking. Polydor is reportedly going to rerelease this album on compact disc.

Delbert McClinton

Live from Austin (Alligator, 1989). Gregg's closest rival as a white blues singer, Delbert has been knocking around for years playing his brand of Texas roadhouse blues and was signed to Capricorn when the label collapsed into bankruptcy. Great music from a woefully underappreciated American original. His recent albums on Curb, especially 1992's *Never Been Rocked Enough*, are consistently excellent, but this live album is *it*.

Elvin Bishop

Raisin' Hell (Capricorn, 1974). The best of Elvin's Capricorn records, with great live versions of "Fooled Around and Fell in Love" and "Travelin' Shoes" and "Struttin' My Stuff."

The Marshall Tucker Band

Searchin' for a Rainbow (Capricorn, 1975). Most of the Marshall Tucker catalog is out on compact disc. This is one of their better albums, with "Can't You See" and "Fire on the Mountain." Dickey sits in on the title track.

Where We All Belong (Capricorn, 1974). A two-record set, half live and half studio, and probably their best overall album. "This Ol' Cowboy" is a great performance, and the versions of "Everyday (I Have the Blues)" and "Ramblin' " are scorching.

Greatest Hits (Capricorn, 1978). A good overview.

Lynyrd Skynyrd

Lynyrd Skynyrd (MCA, 1991). This boxed set is an excellent compilation of the best of the Southern rock bands to follow the trail blazed by the original Allman Brothers Band. Also highly recommended are *Second Helping* (MCA, 1974), *One More from the Road* (MCA, 1976), and *Street Survivors* (MCA, 1977).

Wet Willie

Keep On Smilin' (Capricorn, 1974). The album with the Rev. Pearly Brown photo on the cover and a lot of grease-fried music inside. Probably the band's best studio album, with the hit-single title track, "Country Side of Life," and "Lucy Was in Trouble."

Drippin' Wet (Capricorn, 1973), *Left Coast Live* (Capricorn, 1977). Even on a bad night, Wet Willie could blow most bands off the stage. Both of these live albums, one from early in the band's career and one from near the end, showcase Wet Willie at its very best. Listen to the version of Taj Mahal's "She Caught the Katy" from the first, and the strutting "Grits Ain't Groceries" from the second. Dynamite music from a band that never gained the success or respect it deserved.

Greatest Hits (Capricorn, 1978). A good primer with the best studio cuts, but without the fire of the live albums.

Randall Bramblett

That Other Mile (Polydor, 1975); *Light of the Night* (Polydor, 1976). Two pre–Sea Level albums from one of the South's most gifted writers and musicians. These two recordings have recently been combined into one compact disc. Classic records, they feature musicians like Chuck Leavell, Will Lee, Elliott Randall (who played the famed guitar solo on "Reeling in the Years"), the Brecker Brothers, Paul Hornsby, and members of Cowboy.

Cowboy

A Different Time (Polydor, 1993). Capricorn's in-house studio band, Cowboy's own albums were full of exquisite playing and lackluster songwriting. This is a new compilation. Also, Scott Boyer has released an album called *All My Friends* under the name of the Decoys, with guest appearances by Butch, Chuck Leavell, Randall Bramblett, Johnny Sandlin, and David Brown. It is available by mail from BVK Music, P.O. Box 5155, Decatur, Alabama 35601.

Gary Stewart

Out of Hand (Hightone, 1991); *Gary's Greatest* (Hightone, 1991); *Battleground* (Hightone, 1990). One of the great honky-tonk country singers in history, Stewart gave Dickey the Gibson SG that he uses to play electric slide. The greatest hits package has a version of "Ramblin' Man." *Battleground* includes a slinky-sounding slide by Warren Haynes on a great cover of Robert Cray's "Nothin' but a Woman."

Widespread Panic

Space Wrangler (Capricorn, 1992). This album has it all: great songs, great musicianship, and a tremendous version of Robert Johnson's "Me and the Devil Blues." A second-generation band that understands what made Southern rock great.

Col. Bruce Hampton and the Aquarium Rescue Unit

Col. Bruce Hampton and the Aquarium Rescue Unit (Capricorn, 1992). The music is as different as the title suggests. Flannery O'Connor meets rock 'n' roll.

Floyd Miles

Crazy Man (Wild Dog Series/Ichiban, 1992). Gregg's old friend from Daytona Beach. It is a surprisingly good record that retains an old-time soul feel, featuring a great duet with Gregg and three tracks powered by Dickey's lead guitar. Annoyingly difficult to find, but well worth having.

A Fan's Notes

Two fan organizations are of interest to Allman Brothers followers. The Allman Brothers Band Fan Club is operated by Kirk and Kirsten West, who now own the Big House in Macon and plan to open it to the public as an Allman Brothers museum and a bed and breakfast. They also give tours of the Big House. Kirk, who has spent years collecting memorabilia, became the band's tour manager during the latest comeback. The club publishes a high-quality quarterly newsletter called *Hittin' the Note* that's full of interviews, reviews by fans, and updates on the group. For information write to Kirsten West, 2321 Vineville Avenue, Macon, Georgia 31204.

The Georgia Allman Brothers Band Association (GABBA), founded in 1992, is a nonprofit group that hosts an Allman Brothers and Sisters Family Reunion and International Collectors Revival each fall in Macon. The event has drawn fans from as far away as Belgium, Australia, and England. GABBA is dedicated to preserving and promoting the band's legacy. It has raised money to replace the angelic statues representing Galadriel and Brittany that were long ago stolen from the graves of Duane and Berry at Rose Hill Cemetery. GABBA also has "adopted" Rose Hill and conducts regular cleanups at the cemetery. For information, write to Marty Willett, P.O. Box 6354, Macon, Georgia 31208.

Allman Brothers fans who come to Macon and stop by the Convention and Visitors' Bureau are usually steered to Marty Willett, and he can often be coaxed into giving a brief tour of Rose Hill and directions to other places of interest. There is usually a steady stream of visitors to the graves of Duane and Berry at Rose Hill. Most visitors linger for a few moments, pay their respects, and leave. Candace Oakley has grown intolerant of the others — who often hang out around the graves all day, sit on the tombs, and show little respect for the area — and she has threatened to have the site fenced in.

The Middle Georgia Archives at Washington Memorial Library has an extensive Allman Brothers collection under the loving eye of Peer Ravnan, and fans are welcome to browse through the boxes of newspaper articles and other artifacts the library has collected.

The best record shop in town — and one of the very few that appears to have any appreciation of Macon's musical history — is a tiny, hole-in-the-wall place at the Farmers' Market called Play It Again, Sam's. The store has a good collection of vinyl, including a large cache of used Allman Brothers records and much of the Capricorn catalog.

The H&H Restaurant is still open on Forsyth Street and is a "must visit" for fans. Mama Louise can be found in the kitchen whipping up her soul-food specialties. The walls are lined with photos and paintings of the band, and the jukebox still boasts most of the Capricorn hits.

In addition, a multimillion-dollar Georgia Music Hall of Fame in downtown Macon is scheduled to open by 1996. Already inducted are a wealth of musicians with a Macon background — Otis Redding, James Brown, Little Richard, Blind Willie McTell, Phil Walden, and Duane Allman. GABBA has donated numerous items — albums, framed photos, and memorabilia — to the hall of fame and the library archives.

Index